"In *Unmaking Sex*, Anne E. Linton shines expert light on the enormous commotion – epistemological, medical, legal, narrative – occasioned by ambiguously sexed bodies in nineteenth-century France. Her analysis, at once scholarly and humane, gives a more detailed picture of the lives of intersex people in this period than we have ever had before, and offers a new understanding of the importance of ambiguous sex as a concept in post-revolutionary France – unmaking along the way a number of received scholarly hypotheses about how the nineteenth century understood sex. A must-read for all scholars of French history and culture, as for all historians of gender and sexuality."

Andrew J. Counter, author of *The Amorous Restoration*
(University of Oxford)

"*Unmaking Sex* is an impeccably researched and original study of the intersex phenomenon in medical and literary discourses of nineteenth-century France. Through expert synthesis of archival research into over 200 medical cases, Linton provides a cultural prehistory to today's widely debated topic of gender boundaries. This truly interdisciplinary project succeeds in reconstructing a vast and complex network of myth, medicine, anatomy, and rhetoric in relation to the binary-unsettling realities of inde-terminate sex. It will become a must-read for serious scholars of gender and the nineteenth century."

Andrea Goulet, author of *Optiques*, and *Legacies of the Rue Morgue*
(University of Pennsylvania)

"Linton's truly original achievement is to have repositioned nineteenth-century French culture, in its archival breadth as well as in the depth of its literary close readings, within a new critical space. This space is located in the vital tension between Foucault's history of sexuality and contemporary transgender criticism which underpins questions of identity in our own age."

Nicholas White, author of *The Family in Crisis in Late Nineteenth-Century French Fiction* (University of Cambridge)

"Linton offers massive and largely new archival evidence for the struggles of nineteenth-century doctors to determine 'true sex' in ambiguous cases, which she mobilizes to offer brilliant readings of a wide range of canonical and little-known fiction. This book is a model of historically grounded literary criticism and a major revisionist interpretation of how sex was understood in the nineteenth century. Foucault was not quite right about the famous Herculine Barbin case; and *Making Sex* was not quite what I thought it was."

Thomas W. Laqueur, author of *Making Sex* (Helen Fawcett Distinguished Professor of History, University of California, Berkeley)

UNMAKING SEX

During the nineteenth century, words like "intersex" and "trans" had not yet been invented to describe individuals whose bodies, or senses of self, challenged binary sex. But that does not mean that such people did not exist. In nineteenth-century France, case studies filled medical journals, high-profile trials captured headlines, and doctors staked their reputations on sex determinations only to have them later reversed by colleagues. While medical experts fought over what separated a man from a woman, novelists began to explore debates about binary sex and describe the experiences of gender-ambiguous characters. Anne Linton discusses over 200 newly uncovered case studies while offering fresh readings of literature by several famous writers of the period, as well as long-overlooked popular fiction. This landmark contribution to the history of sexuality is the first book to examine intersex in both medicine and literature, sensitively relating historical "hermaphrodism" to contemporary intersex activism and scholarship.

ANNE E. LINTON is Associate Professor of French at San Francisco State University. Her research interests and publications span a wide range of interdisciplinary topics in nineteenth-century cultural studies, including gender studies, science, and medicine.

UNMAKING SEX

The Gender Outlaws of Nineteenth-Century France

ANNE E. LINTON

San Francisco State University

CAMBRIDGE
UNIVERSITY PRESS

CAMBRIDGE
UNIVERSITY PRESS

University Printing House, Cambridge CB2 8BS, United Kingdom

One Liberty Plaza, 20th Floor, New York, NY 10006, USA

477 Williamstown Road, Port Melbourne, VIC 3207, Australia

314–321, 3rd Floor, Plot 3, Splendor Forum, Jasola District Centre,
New Delhi – 110025, India

103 Penang Road, #05–06/07, Visioncrest Commercial, Singapore 238467

Cambridge University Press is part of the University of Cambridge.

It furthers the University's mission by disseminating knowledge in the pursuit of
education, learning, and research at the highest international levels of excellence.

www.cambridge.org
Information on this title: www.cambridge.org/9781316511824
DOI: 10.1017/9781009053037

First published 2022

Printed in the United Kingdom by TJ Books Limited, Padstow Cornwall

A catalogue record for this publication is available from the British Library.

Library of Congress Cataloging-in-Publication Data
NAMES: Linton, Anne E., 1981– author.
TITLE: Unmaking sex : the gender outlaws of nineteenth-century France / Anne E.
Linton, San Francisco State University.
DESCRIPTION: Cambridge, United Kingdom ; New York, NY : Cambridge
University Press, 2022. | Includes bibliographical references and index.
IDENTIFIERS: LCCN 2021029042 (print) | LCCN 2021029043 (ebook) | ISBN 9781316511824
(hardback) | ISBN 9781009053037 (ebook)
SUBJECTS: LCSH: Intersex people – France – History – 19th century. | Intersexuality –
France – History – 19th century. | Sex determination – France – History – 19th century.
CLASSIFICATION: LCC HQ78.2.F8 L56 2022 (print) | LCC HQ78.2.F8 (ebook) | DDC 306.76/
85094409034–dc23
LC record available at https://lccn.loc.gov/2021029042
LC ebook record available at https://lccn.loc.gov/2021029043

ISBN 978-1-316-51182-4 Hardback

Contents

Figures

Acknowledgments

I am grateful for the support of a number of fellowships in the completion of this project, including generous funding from San Francisco State University, Yale University, and from the Beinecke Rare Book and Manuscript Library. I have been fortunate to work with a talented team of editors at Cambridge University Press from whom I have learned much. Bethany Thomas and Natasha Burton have been enormously helpful and efficient editors. I am grateful to Rose Bell, my copyeditor, for her keen eye and deft touch.

I wish to acknowledge the many friends, colleagues, research librarians, and archivists who assisted, advised, and provided feedback on my research and writing efforts over the years. Especially, I must express my deepest appreciation to Ora Avni, David Bell, Dorian Bell, R. Howard Bloch, Patrick Bray, Peter Brooks, Jonathan Cayer, Edwin Duval, Andrea Goulet, Thomas Kavanagh, Bettina Lerner, Jann Matlock, Rachel Mesch, Kevin Newmark, Sara Pappas, Raisa Rexer, Brian J. Reilly, the late Lawrence Schehr, Nicholas White, and T. Chapman Wing. Most of all, I am indebted to Maurice Samuels, who is as brilliant a mentor as he is a scholar, for adroitly guiding this project from its earliest stages and for his astute readings, sage advice, and generous encouragement along the way.

Deepest gratitude to my family who lived with this book for many years and without whose support it could not have been completed.

.

Note on the Text

Because medical photography of intersex has often caused trauma, I have chosen not to reproduce those images in this book, nor the ubiquitous close-up illustrations of external intersex genitalia. Owing to their volume, and often lengthy, redundant titles in French, primary medical sources are cited in the text using author-date. Full references are provided in Works Cited. French titles are translated only when relevant to the argument at hand.

Gender Revolution Before Intersex or Transgender

In 1867, Dr. Basile Poppesco examined a wealthy 25-year-old complaining of "suffering in the genital parts." A man later revealed to be the patient's lover had arranged the visit for "one of his male friends."[1] Upon arriving, the doctor observed a "magnificently ornamented" apartment scattered with "innumerable perfumes," in which "everything revealed the most effeminate coquetry."[2] Yet, to Poppesco's surprise, the "young man" he had expected arrived "attired as a young girl" whose long, flowing locks framed a "remarkable physiognomy," and who swore Poppesco to secrecy in a "perfectly feminine voice" (38–39). The doctor was at a loss to determine the sex of his intriguing patient: "There was a slight something in the manners and carriage of the person, such as led me to demand unexpectedly if he was a man or a woman" (38). Even a thorough medical examination could not resolve the mystery, revealing only an "excessively developed" "clitoris," of nearly two inches, "quite suggestive of the glans" (38). No gonads – testicles or ovaries – could be found. At home, the patient always dressed as a woman, but chose male garments to wear around town. A bewildered Poppesco further reported: "This person had not the slightest predilection for women" but "retained in his service a *personnel* of male domestics" (39). The good doctor was baffled because his patient challenged everything he believed about the differences between men and women. In the end, he reluctantly determined that his case offered "an instance of hermaphrodism in which it is impossible to define the sex" (39).[3]

Much of the history of sexuality has been marked by the Foucauldian claim that the belief in "true sex" – that each body has only one sex – is one product of the nineteenth-century moment which, in many ways, continues to hold sway even now, and is only just beginning to show signs of change.[4] Until very recently (2015 in the United States and 2013 in France), marriage could only take place between a man and a woman, gender-inclusive bathrooms remain a contentious subject, and countless forms and official documents still require us to identify ourselves as members of either one or the other gender, despite increasing challenges to such rigid binary social organization. This was even truer in nineteenth-century France, and a wealth of historiography testifies to the ways in which medicine worked to reify as "natural" the distinctions between men and women.[5] This book presents archival findings calling for a revision of part of that longstanding narrative. While it may be true that nineteenth-century doctors and laypeople believed in the fundamental differences between the sexes, when they encountered cases of intersex, then known as "hermaphrodism," they were often forced to admit that identifying the nature of those fundamental differences was not nearly so evident. Doctors vehemently disagreed with one another about what characteristics mattered the most, what methods were the most likely to produce guaranteed results, and even to what sex a given individual belonged. Many acknowledged that sex could not be determined during the lives of some people, and that only autopsy might yield definite results. Sometimes, even autopsies failed to solve the riddle.[6] More often than previously thought, doctors like Poppesco were forced to admit that they could not determine the sex of an individual at all.

During the nineteenth century, words like "intersex" and "transgender" had not yet been invented to describe individuals whose bodies or senses of self challenged binary sex. But that does not mean that such people did not exist. "Intersex" is an umbrella term for a range of naturally occurring bodily variations, so intersex people have always existed. In nineteenth-century France, those like Poppesco's anonymous patient – whose biological sex could not easily be determined and who *might* describe themselves today as intersex – were called "hermaphrodites," and for the first time there was such widespread anxiety about what to do with these gender "outlaws" that both doctors and novelists scrambled to write on the subject in skyrocketing numbers.

Hundreds of case studies appeared in wide-ranging medical journals, high-profile trials captured headlines, and doctors staked their reputations on sex determinations only to have them later reversed by colleagues. Some patients sought out doctor after doctor in order to attain the outcomes they desired, while others wanted nothing more than to be left alone. But that is only part of the story: while doctors quarreled about what separated a man from a woman, novelists increasingly began to explore debates about binary sex in their fiction, describing the experiences of gender-ambiguous characters and even writing entire novels in which the mystery of a protagonist's sex became a page-turning motor for plot. Canonical fiction by some of the most important French writers of the nineteenth century – from Honoré de Balzac, architect of *La Comédie humaine* (*The Human Comedy*), to Émile Zola, the figurehead of French naturalism – shifted its focus to the enigma of unknown or unknowable gender, and was joined by now-forgotten popular authors writing marginal novels and medical erotica, sometimes posing as doctors themselves.

Historians and literary scholars have long singled out nineteenth-century France as the high point of representations of "hermaphrodism," but *Unmaking Sex* is the first book to explore why through an investigation of both medicine and literature. It is also the first to reconstruct the role popular fiction played in disseminating cultural beliefs about gender ambiguity across science and high-brow literature. This examination of new sources yields new findings: this book marks a departure from the traditional Foucauldian argument that "true sex" was firmly entrenched by the nineteenth century. Rather, it reveals that in many instances, both literature and medicine use narrative as a means to unmask "true sex" as mere fiction.

Until now, literary androgyny has generally been seen as a reflection of mythology's enduring influence, while historians of intersex have not considered how fictional narratives were informed by and even influenced contemporary medical case studies. This book argues that literary representations of "hermaphrodism" are not just throwbacks to mythology, as critics have long argued, but are, in fact, awash with the same cultural and historical anxieties as medical case studies. Fiction engages with the terms of medical and legal debates surrounding nonbinary sex in previously overlooked ways that can transform our understanding of the French canon. Secondly, based on an analysis of over 200 medical case studies throughout the length of the nineteenth century, it demonstrates that medical representations of intersex, which rarely convey consensus, often reveal similarities between the sexes. These findings nuance the popular claim that throughout the nineteenth century, amid the great cultural shifts that saw women entering the workforce and demanding education, science sought to reinforce the clear, biological differences between men and women that would naturalize male social domination and reify traditional notions of family.

The Power of Naming

Today, "intersex" describes many differences in sex traits or reproductive anatomy, some of which had not yet been identified in the nineteenth century, and even today, exactly what counts as intersex is debated.[7] Partly for this reason, the relative frequency of intersex is also contested, although another important factor is that medicine has systematically underrepresented it since the twentieth century via treatments and surgeries designed to engineer its invisibility. Estimates range from 1 percent of births (the likelihood of being born with red hair) to 1 in every 2,000 births. After an exhaustive review of contemporary medical literature, Anne Fausto-Sterling determined that about 1.7 percent of children are born intersex, which is relatively common, when compared to the 0.3 percent chance of having identical twins.[8] Activists working to raise awareness about intersex argue that the false perception that they represent a minuscule fraction of the population has been used to deny them the recognition and basic human rights that they deserve. The Epilogue explores contemporary intersex and the intersex movement as well as the completely different, but also related trans movement in regard to the nineteenth-century roots of the resistance to "true sex" that this book documents, but the following chapters study historical "hermaphrodism" in nineteenth-century literature and medicine. For this reason, I use the historical terms "hermaphrodite" and "hermaphrodism" when citing nineteenth-century materials. Today, neither word is used in a human context, and because both have been perceived as traumatic and/or offensive to many contemporary intersex people, quotation marks further indicate that I am referring to nineteenth-century usage.[9] For ease of readability, quotation marks are omitted when clearly referencing historical use. Because it is important to recount this story compassionately, and not to perpetuate cycles of violence, I have replaced historical terms with contemporary ones in my own analysis.

Just as "intersex" can signify differently, and will continue to change over time, what counted as "hermaphrodism" was highly contested and in constant flux in the nineteenth century, in spite of persistent efforts to pin it down to a single definition or set of bodily attributes. We shall see that in fin-de-siècle France, "hermaphrodism" became entangled with homosexuality in the nebulous discourse of degeneration theory, whereas it is understood today that intersex has no bearing on sexual orientation. Intersex people have all the same sexual orientations as everyone else. In other words, if it's generally true that in nineteenth-century France "intersex" was called "hermaphrodism," there are also important differences between the meanings of both words, and neither should be thought of as stable or monolithic.

Given the longstanding representation of the rigidly polarized binary in nineteenth-century France, it is perhaps surprising that the most-cited definition of hermaphrodism with the longest staying power throughout the entire period was also its broadest. Isidore Geoffroy Saint-Hilaire defined hermaphrodism in the early 1830s as "the coexistence in the same individual of both sexes or of some of their characteristics," which meant that, like the umbrella term "intersex" today, a range of bodily variations would count.[10] Jack Halberstam, following María Elena Martínez, argues that because contemporary models of sex and gender are incompatible with historical uses, we should not use terms like "gay," "transgender," or "intersex" when referencing figures from other eras. Doing so both aligns itself with a "genealogy of power" that "imposes, distorts, or forecloses certain desires, identifications, and experiences," and also might entail "missing an opportunity to discover in the past human possibilities and imaginings that were suppressed or left unfulfilled but that can provide guidance in the present for creating better worlds in the future."[11] Another important distinction between the historical use of the outdated term "hermaphrodism" and contemporary "intersex" is that by the time "intersex" had replaced "hermaphrodite/ism" in the medical nomenclature in the twentieth century, medical technology had changed to such a point that the "medical management" of intersex involved hormone treatments, surgeries, and a team of specialists including endocrinologists, pediatric surgeons, urologists, and gynecologists, some of whom did not exist before the twentieth century. By contrast, during the period that this book examines, surgery was highly risky, anesthesia was not widespread before the second half of the century, human chromosomes were not mapped out, and hormones had not yet been identified or experimented upon. While one finds occasional surgeries on adults, they are comparatively rare, and there was no formal practice of transforming the bodies of babies or young children to align with cultural beliefs about binary sex. Whereas hermaphrodism was increasingly visible in the nineteenth century for a number of reasons explored in this book, once standard protocol involved changing the body to make its appearance "harmonize" with social standards for binary sex in the twentieth century, it began to methodically conceal intersex. Little was communicated to parents, and children were often subjected to unnecessary and irreversible surgeries that caused lasting trauma. The grassroots intersex movement in the 1990s brought intersex back into the spotlight and galvanized change in medical practice, although much work remains to be done. Finally, during the nineteenth century, the binary was largely unquestioned, so sex also determined gender (which was not yet its own soon-to-be problematized category) and sexuality (heteronormatively).[12] This means that distinctions between inter*sex* (those whose bodies differ from what science deems typically male and female) and trans*gender* (those whose gender identity is different from the sex assigned at birth) had not yet been made or named.

But just because the critical framework for understanding sex and gender was different in the nineteenth century, that does not mean we cannot look to the past. In *Before Trans*, Rachel Mesch explores nineteenth-century precursors of trans identities and acknowledges historical differences while arguing that "certain modern critical frameworks can illuminate what was not fully articulated in the past" by "lessening alterity."[13] Similarly, Jen Manion uses they/them pronouns to describe the historical subjects in *Female Husbands* who had been assigned the female sex at birth, and who later married women.[14] Even when the binary was in many ways unquestioned, it is still imperative to look at it, perhaps even more acutely, because tiny moments of resistance forged in an environment without so much as the vocabulary needed in order to define that resistance are the forebearers of the present.[15]

As someone who believes in the importance of preferred personal pronouns for intersex people, trans people, nonbinary people, and others, I endeavor whenever possible in this book to use the pronouns that were used by the individuals themselves. In nineteenth-century France, gender-neutral pronouns did not exist, but even in the highly gendered French language, authors, doctors, and patients sometimes indicate unstable or contested gender in nuanced and fluid ways in their writing, often by alternating between masculine and feminine gender agreements in French. Whenever possible, I have attempted to render this instability in my translations.[16]

Literary "Hermaphrodites"

This book began, as do many, with a question: why is it, I wondered, that so many nineteenth-century novelists describe their characters as "hermaphrodites"? Charles Baudelaire identifies Samuel Cramer, the androgynous anti-hero of his novella, *La fanfarlo* (1847), as "the god of impotence – a modern and hermaphroditic god" (39). Zola calls Maxime (among the many androgynous characters populating *La curée*) a "strange hermaphrodite."[17] Epicene characters span the century.[18] They appear everywhere in Balzac's fiction. Lucien de Rubempré, hero of *Les illusions perdues* (1837–43), resembles "a disguised young girl" or a "wannabe woman" (femme manquée).[19] Henri de Marsay, the chiseled Adonis of *La fille aux yeux d'or* (1835), has "a young girl's skin" and "his smooth face would not have marred the most beautiful woman's body" (5: 1057, 1058). Auguste de Maulincour in *Ferragus* (1833) has "a half-feminine soul" (5: 803). Neither does nineteenth-century literature want for strong and independent women who look and act "like men," according to nineteenth-century cultural beliefs. Balzac's eponymous Béatrix and Cousine Bette could count among their number, along with a host of Rachilde's characters.[20] Gender-bending forms a central plot element in George Sand's fiction, critics have long observed.[21] Sexual ambiguity and mutability are recurrent themes In Joris-Karl Huysmans's *À rebours* (1884), while androgyny plays such a decisive role in Jules Barbey d'Aurevilly's *Le Chevalier des Touches* (1863) that the gender of nearly every character reads as uncertain in some way.

Among the myriad characters described as "hermaphroditic" or "androgynous," a number of novels rely on unknown or mysterious sex to generate plot. In Henri de Latouche's *Fragoletta* (1829), Balzac's *Sarrasine* (1830) and *Séraphîta* (1834), and Théophile Gautier's *Mademoiselle de Maupin* (1835), the desire to "figure out" the gender of central characters motivates each novel's entire plotline. A year of archival sleuthing in Paris allowed me to identify still more. These were strange, long-forgotten novels melding fiction and medicine, with titles such as *Clémentine orpheline et androgyne* (1820), *L'hermaphrodite* (1885), and *L'hermaphrodite au couvent* (1905). The storyline of such popular novels centers on the life and trials of intersex people and their struggles to integrate into society. Often, they rehearse scenes bearing an uncanny resemblance to established classics. Yet, unlike the androgynous characters in the French canon, these popular characters are described as physiological "hermaphrodites," and doctors or medical sex determinations almost always play a central role in the plot development.

While sifting through archives for lesser-known novels, I was also culling hundreds of case studies of doubtful sex from the medical record, and finding intriguing parallels. Doctors faced with cases of "hermaphrodism" achieved little enduring consensus about how best to determine and assign sex in nineteenth-century France. Their attempts to locate a set of attributes that could identify ambiguous bodies unequivocally as either male or female increasingly unmasked the idea of any indelible, "pre-scribed" bodily truth as cultural fiction. In the absence of compelling scientific findings, they often resorted to imaginative narratives in order to support their arguments. What did it mean that, at precisely the same time that a profusion of androgynous characters debuted in fiction, surgeons, lawyers, clinicians, and scientific popularizers were all clamoring to publish on the identical subject?

This book traces the previously untold medical and literary history of hermaphrodism during the highpoint of its visibility, in nineteenth-century France, when legal cases made splashy headlines, medical publications skyrocketed, and even novelists scrambled to write on the subject. For the first time, it reveals the profound influence that intersex had on contemporary writers and its central place in debates about science, social order, morality, and sexuality that are still with us to this day. In what follows, I argue that novelists explored prescriptive medical debates about sex in their own way by experimenting on them in fiction with gender-nonconforming characters, storylines, and even medically inspired fictional case studies. In these novels, authors harness the power of unknown sex to drive the plot, and, much like their medical counterparts, often reveal blurred gender boundaries even as they claim to endorse heteronormative values.

Literature and Science

In nineteenth-century France, efforts to classify and categorize bodies reached a frenzied pace spurred by the rising power of medicine and the nascent field of the social sciences. Along with the invention of new technologies, the social sciences established and differentiated categories for the purpose of statistics and surveys. Meanwhile, authors such as Balzac and later, Zola, pursued their own investigation of social "types" through fiction. Both Balzac's *La Comèdie humaine* and Zola's *Rougon-Macquart* cycle of novels are deeply invested in the representation of social categories, and both realism and naturalism share origins that can be tied to the scientific discourse of the time.

By the turn of the nineteenth century, naturalists had already confirmed that while no human being could possess complete male and female reproductive systems, individuals did exist who presented with a mix or blend of attributes that were commonly considered to be male and female. Contemporary novelists were certainly aware that such people existed because they wrote about them in their fiction, and not merely the "hermaphrodites" of imaginative myths. A short story falsely attributed to Guy de Maupassant described a "hermaphrodite" so terrified of being outed that s/he preferred to die rather than to submit to medical treatment, lest the secret be revealed.[22] Under the entry for "hermaphrodite" in Gustave Flaubert's satirical *Dictionary of Received Ideas*, one reads: "Piques curiosity. Try to see some."[23] The appearance of "hermaphrodite" in Flaubert's spoof dictionary confirms its cultural cachet and ironically mimics the longstanding scientific tradition of attempting to define and redefine hermaphrodism, while simultaneously evoking the voyeuristic desire latent in many nineteenth-century narratives, raising the specter of the "freak show."[24] Throughout the nineteenth century, some intersex people traveled around Europe displaying themselves at fairs, medical schools, or in private consultation for a fee. Madame Gauthier, a "hermaphrodite" under police surveillance for suspected illegal prostitution, was allegedly slated to appear in the Exposition universelle for all of Paris and the world to behold. Divorce cases claiming hermaphrodism made the front page in French newspapers, and sometimes crossed the Atlantic. Jurists, psychologists, clinicians, surgeons, patients, and even novelists had something to say about "hermaphrodism."

Strong ties bound science and literature in nineteenth-century France and what we think of today as two fundamentally and nearly diametrically opposed fields were not always considered so in the past. In his foreword to *La Comédie humaine*, Balzac cites the influence of several scientists on his goal of studying "social species" through literature. Foremost stands Étienne Geoffroy Saint-Hilaire, a renowned naturalist whose contributions to embryology and anatomy extended to the study of "monstrosity." As we shall see in the first chapter, his son, Isidore Geoffroy Saint-Hilaire, followed in his father's footsteps to become the reigning authority on hermaphrodism in the 1830s with the publication of his multi-volume magnum opus, *L'histoire générale et particulière des anomalies de l'organisation chez l'homme et les animaux* (1832–37). In it, the younger Geoffroy Saint-Hilaire offered the broad definition of hermaphrodism cited above that would exert incredible staying power throughout the century. At that time, positivistic medicine and science were engaged in reclaiming what had once been considered magical or marvelous as merely poorly understood expressions of the natural world. In his 1837 dictionary definition for "hermaphrodite," Dr. Marc takes Geoffroy Saint-Hilaire's new research into account: "we know, from M. Geoffroy Saint-Hilaire's father's beautiful works on monstrosity, works on which his son has followed suit, [. . .] that often monstrosity is merely the persistence of one of the transitional phases of fetal development" (1837, 250). The advent of the field of teratology (the study of congenital variations, labeled "monstrosity" in the nineteenth century), combined with new medical specializations such as gynecology, now sanctioned by the creation of Chairs at the Faculté de médecine, and the ever-increasing array of medical publications, meant that all kinds of bodily variations, rare or not, were becoming increasingly visible in nineteenth-century France.

Hermaphrodite Myths

Given the prevalence of androgynous characters and the importance of "hermaphrodism" as a plot device in so many major novels, the theme could scarcely have been overlooked by recent literary scholars. Indeed, numerous critics have analyzed the role of androgyny in Balzac or Gautier's writing, or in various other authors' work. Comparative and broad survey studies also exist in which scholars trace the theme of androgyny from Romanticism to Decadence. However, these works predominantly discuss hermaphrodism in terms of "myth," and they often differentiate between conflicting representations of this myth in the first and second halves of the nineteenth century. Proponents of the "myth of the androgyne" explain "hermaphrodism" as part of our "universal imagination," claiming that it bears no relationship to living individuals. According to A. J. L. Busst's 1960s study of "hermaphrodism" in literature, for example, the "continuous and widespread interest focused on the hermaphrodite during the nineteenth century owes [...] almost nothing to observation of the natural world."[25] Rather than describing literary representations of "hermaphrodism" in terms of ahistorical myth, this book situates them within a specific, yet ever-evolving historical context. In so doing, it aims to avoid the pitfall of portraying representations of androgyny as either timeless or somehow detached from daily existence.

Through the inclusion of new sources, my approach impacts the accepted timeline of fictional representations of hermaphrodism. Literary critics often theorize a temporal and thematic separation between two different types of representations of androgyny: an idealized "romantic androgyne," and a damned, "decadent hermaphrodite," which allegedly divide the century roughly into halves. These distinctions do not hold up to scrutiny, especially when one considers popular fiction. Jane de La Vaudère's *Les androgynes* (1903), for example, posits two seemingly contradictory views of androgyny within a single work. The "androgyne" artist Jacques Chozelle is depicted as the last debauched expression of a society on the verge of extinction, much in the same way as was Huysmans's Des Esseintes in *À rebours*. Yet, the love between two young characters, André and Fiamette, is also described as a highly idealized "hermaphroditic" union. Joséphin Péladan's decadent work, *L'androgyne* (1891), which imagines an idealized "hermaphrodite" at the fin de siècle, also speaks to this contrast. The mirror image of La Vaudère's highly sexualized androgyne, Péladan conceives of a flawless, asexual creature that hearkens back to Balzac's *Séraphîta*.[26] The third chapter discusses other novels that problematize distinctions between apparently opposing representations of androgyny.

When pressed, even the staunchest proponents of the "myth of the androgyne" admit that not all authors or even all novels permit easy categorization into either the idealized myth of romantic androgyny or the dark myth of decadent hermaphrodism, but individual exceptions are not meant to affect the general rule. This book argues instead that looking beyond "myth" will reveal new explanations. This is not to say that the realm of myth holds no sway in fictional androgyny. Its presence is undeniable in references to Plato and Ovid, and in many characterizations. Rather, these allusions reflect, in part, deep-seated social and cultural anxiety about sex and gender and the role they would play in the ordering of society amid a perpetual flux of regime change, industrial revolution, and shifting notions of family. I base this claim on evidence outlined in the first two chapters, which shows that the sudden outpouring of interest in fictional "hermaphrodism" corresponds to an increasing fixation on intersex in several other domains, including medical and legal discourses and popular culture. I am not arguing that apprehension about social sex underwrites all nineteenth-century representations of androgyny, but I do contend that even works which seem at first utterly removed from worldly desires and corporeality, such as Balzac's *Séraphîta*, nevertheless betray vexed attachments to material sexuality.

The Fiction of "True Sex"

The first half of this book endeavors to recover the stakes behind the meteoric rise of historical intersex in nineteenth-century France. Based on hundreds of case histories, dissertations, treatises, textbooks, dictionaries, and legal documents, my research shows that "hermaphrodism" became the nexus of cultural, social, political, and even professional anxieties, such that although its relative frequency likely remained unchanged, its visibility increased dramatically. Owing to technological and scientific limitations, sex determinations relied heavily on the same narrative devices found in contemporary fiction. By neglecting works of fiction and vulgarized medical texts, past scholarship has overlooked an important facet of the history of sexuality. In order to understand how commonplaces about "hermaphrodism" were disseminated to various publics, eventually to appear in Flaubert's *Dictionary of Received Ideas*, these sources merit closer examination. Like popular fiction that dynamically engages with canonical literature, high- and middle-brow medical texts reference each other in a complex web of resonances.

Part I offers a cultural prehistory of intersex that provides a new framework in which to understand literary representations of androgyny, analyzed in Part II. The first two chapters argue that "true sex" was not an already accepted and easily identifiable truism as conventional historiography contends, but rather was highly contested in cases of hermaphrodism throughout the entire century. Chapter 1 demonstrates that the nineteenth-century medical record undermines the idea that each person could have only one sex. Throughout the period, several doctors made a stand for "true hermaphrodism," many more could not identify the sex of their living patients, and "experts" constantly disagreed not only about their findings, but also about how best to establish sex in unclear cases. Chapter 2 examines the largely overlooked writings of nineteenth-century clinicians, scientists, lawyers, and jurists who actually called for a third sex to be added alongside the ranks of "male" and "female" because, quite plainly, there were individuals for whom no "true sex" could be identified. The inflexibility of the Napoleonic Code, which required that all infants be registered as either male or female at birth, was challenged by doctors and legal forensics experts who believed either that the Code was out of step with scientific progress or that it did not do enough to protect cisgender citizens. In sensationalized court cases that riveted domestic and international audiences – both scientific and lay – doctors and jurists struggled to reconcile cases of "doubtful sex" with scientific evidence, social welfare, and the Code itself.

Precisely because no one method for determining sex proved entirely foolproof, doctors and medical forensics experts often relied on narrative to support their claims – a narrative that closely mirrors the one being developed simultaneously in contemporary fiction, and especially, but not exclusively, by realist fiction.[27] Teratology and realist fiction share a common origin in the burgeoning social and natural sciences in the early part of the nineteenth century. This shared narrative and common birthplace serves as a transition into my examination of literary androgyny in the second half of the book. In the third chapter, I show how long-forgotten popular novels become important intertexts for major works of fiction on hermaphrodism. Whether the influence is intentional and acknowledged, as Balzac admits of Latouche's *Fragoletta*, or perhaps unintentional or repressed, as may have been the case with J.-P.-R. Cuisin's *Clémentine*, these popular novels become a "missing link" between medical discourse and fictional representations of androgyny. In both *Fragoletta* and *Clémentine*, for example, doctors and medical sex determinations play important roles in plot development, allowing us to reconsider the stakes of Mademoiselle de Maupin's transition to a masculine identity, which Gautier describes as a "medical" project. By examining classic fiction by Balzac, Gautier, and Zola through the lens of forgotten popular novels, we can see how works that have been described by literary critics as rehearsing a timeless version of myth are also interrogating the very same social anxiety that one finds in contemporary debates surrounding "hermaphrodism" in medicine and the law. Just like their medical counterparts, novelists experiment with "hermaphrodism" using their own literary techniques, harnessing the power of unknown sex as a means to keep the reader reading. The final chapter reveals how the theory of degenerate heredity transforms narratives of hermaphrodism both in medical case studies and in the fictional context of Zola's *La curée* (1871). The fin-de-siècle natality crisis in France elevates the stakes of hermaphrodism and non-reproductive sexuality, illustrating how social anxiety can fundamentally alter scientific findings, and how science can, in turn, influence lived experience in fundamental ways.

The vertiginous literary rise of hermaphrodism has not been studied in tandem with its simultaneous explosion in medical representations with sustained detail or throughout the entire length of the nineteenth century, and contemporary intersex scholarship has not yet been brought to bear on historical analyses.[28] This should come as a surprise, given that both historians and literary scholars have singled out the nineteenth century as the period during which the presence of "hermaphrodism" reached its zenith. I am not suggesting a causal link between both types of representation, although, as we shall see, the two do often mutually inform one another. Rather, I argue that both literature and medicine share a common ground as part of the cultural production of their time. In their own way, each has employed strategies to regulate and dispel the perceived "threat" of hermaphrodism to the gender/sex binaries structuring society. These differences were constantly being reformed in the crucible of social and economic turmoil of nineteenth-century France. Sometimes, in spite of their authors' intentions, medical and fictional texts subvert the very male/female binary they had set out to bolster. Other times, encounters with patients led doctors to question their beliefs about binary sex.

Though the medical record privileges the doctor's voice, it too provides glimpses of the choices made by those like Poppesco's patient, who lived out their lives as gender outlaws.[29] These choices stand not necessarily in defiance or as a conscious act of rebellion, but rather as private and frequently anonymous efforts to find feasible solutions to life's daily problems. In spite of its incomplete nature, the medical record offers us small windows into the lives of past human beings, allowing their stories to be seen and heard, even if the historical record has left them to us incomplete, and often problematically viewed from the outside. By sharing these stories, this book aims to add the voices of historical individuals to the important work being done by contemporary intersex activists who raise awareness about the many variations of the human body and the people who inhabit them. This is not always a heartwarming history; the subjects examined in this book faced prejudice, medical imperialism, even criminalization, but their courageous resilience gives hope for a better future while pushing back against longstanding beliefs in the history of sexuality.[30]

Patients Who Sex Themselves

By the time Isidore Geoffroy Saint-Hilaire published his treatise offering that broad definition of hermaphrodism in the 1830s, there was already enough written about it in the medical literature that patients could read up on gender variations on their own, and several did. This is exactly what happened before a highly intelligent and educated woman called "Marie B." came to see Dr. Benoît on August 24, 1840.[31] Marie B. kept busy by managing her father's affairs, and Dr. Benoît remarks on her business acumen and perspicacity on several occasions, taking care to detail not just her body, but also the love story that had landed her in his office.

Back in 1834, the first suitor fell for Marie B., asking for her hand in marriage. He would not be the last. Marie B. was aware that her body was different, so she consulted Dr. M.***, who claimed that "a very simple operation" could solve Marie's "problem," and right then and there, in his office, made an incision that was intended, said he, to "artificially reestablish the opening of Marie's vagina" (25). According to Benoît, "Marie did not know the immediate result of this procedure," but when Dr. M*** asked Marie to return the following day to complete the operation, Marie opted against it, "worrying that her mysterious visits would be maliciously interpreted by the public" (25). Whether because she feared that people would discover her difference, or that they would suspect she was pregnant, the operation was never completed, and so Marie continued to "rebuff marriage proposals for specious reasons," while nevertheless researching the matter on her own (25). Benoît explains that Marie

> did not lose all hope of gaining feminine attributes. She wanted to study her anatomy herself, and read with avidity certain books on hermaphrodism. Her tastes and penchants being those of a woman, she persuaded herself that she belonged to this sex, and she lived henceforth in accordance with this belief. (25)

Marie B. had made her own sex determination, and she chose to wear only women's clothing from that point onward.

Soon after, another suitor fell in love with Marie B., and, since the diverse pretexts she invented did not at all deter the young lover, she decided to impart to him the secret of her sexual conformation. It was in vain; probably not imagining the entire truth, her suitor seemed to attach little importance to it and persisted in his plans. The marriage was on the verge of taking place when Marie, wiser and better informed, asked for a delay of a few days in order to reflect on her situation. (26)

It was during this period of reflection in the waning days of summer that Marie B. arrived at Dr. Benoît's surgery along with a list of three pointed questions, undoubtedly informed by her medical readings: "1 What is my sex? 2 Am I able to contract marriage? 3 Is there occasion to perform some type of medical operation upon me?" (26).[32] After a thorough examination (down to the way in which she threw a stone), Benoît determined that "Marie B. is a man in whom the reproductive organs arrested during development" (34). Perhaps because Marie believed herself to be a woman and dressed as one, Benoît's findings do not influence his use of pronouns, for even after he determines that she is a "man," he continues to refer to her as a woman using the French feminine pronoun "*elle*" (35). In response to Marie's incisive questions, Dr. Benoît is emphatic: *she* is a male; unsuited to marriage, and no surgery exists to "remedy" her "condition." No information is provided about how Marie took this news or whether it influenced in any way her decision to live as a woman. Doctor-patient privilege prevented medical men from revealing their findings to the authorities, and there is no reason to believe that she could not have simply found another doctor to provide her with a more satisfactory diagnosis.[33] After all, she had done it once before, and patients were frequently examined by multiple doctors, even the most celebrated of whom, as we shall see, often disagreed vociferously.

Dr. Benoît does not remark on the existence of hermaphrodism in general. He does determine a "true sex" for Marie B., which is predicated on clinical observations and many cultural stereotypes (some of which are still lingering to this day, such as men are intelligent and have good heads for facts and figures; and others whose significance has been lost to the past, like Marie throwing a stone "like a man," whatever that means). But in spite of the "true sex" determined by Dr. Benoît, he continues to address Marie as a woman, which is to say, in agreement with the "true sex" she had identified on her own.

Methods

The hundreds of case studies, treatises, dissertations, forgotten popular novels, newspaper articles, medical forensics documents, and dictionary entries that form the base of my primary research for this book represent considerable archival work. I identified case studies in periodicals by sifting through indexes for nineteenth-century medical journals, and by seeking out sources listed in bibliographies. My findings build on the work of historians Alice Domurat Dreger and Geertje Mak, whose books provide comparative studies between "hermaphrodism" in France and elsewhere in Europe. Dreger's *Hermaphrodites and the Medical Invention of Sex* is a history of the biomedical treatment of hermaphrodism in France and Britain in the late nineteenth and early twentieth centuries (1868–1915), and cites 80 French case studies.[34] Geertje Mak's book, *Doubting Sex: Inscriptions, Bodies and Selves in Nineteenth-Century Hermaphrodite Case Histories*, references under 40 French cases, roughly half of which overlap with Dreger's source material. The following chapters offer analysis of over 100 more cases than have been previously cited. I identified additional French sources by reading American reviews of foreign medical literature and through the United States National Library of Medicine. In the United States, I conducted research at the Yale University Medical Historical Library, and the Beinecke Rare Book and Manuscript Library. In Paris, I located material in archives at the Bibliothèque nationale, the BIU Santé Médecine, the former Musée Dupuytren, and the Préfecture de Police.

Despite the large number of cases I amassed, my approach is more qualitative than quantitative. Owing to internal contradictions, the possibility that an individual discussed anonymously in one case was later examined in another, and the variable number of cases discussed within a single document, nineteenth-century case histories are problematic to analyze quantitatively. Regardless of the number of cases discussed within a single document, I counted each source as only one case, and I recorded the date of publication, author, whether or not the author claimed "hermaphrodism" was possible, and if a gonadal definition was used to determine sex. I examined roughly 300 French documents related to uncertain sex between 1776 and 1960 for comparative purposes, but the window of my in-depth study includes over 200 cases and extends from 1800 to 1920. I selected this window to accommodate important fictional representations of androgyny, and because surgical innovations revolutionize medical responses to intersex by the 1930s, such that later cases no longer address the same concerns as their predecessors. All documents were either published in French or, in extremely rare instances, are summaries of French cases printed in foreign journals.[35] Likely because this book is based on many more nineteenth-century French cases, considers the entire length of the century, and draws from a wider range of sources than existent studies, its historical findings diverge from previous scholarship. I outline the nature of these differences in the first chapter.

Nineteenth-Century Hermaphrodites

Why are there so many "hermaphrodites" in nineteenth-century fiction and medicine? I have gestured in this introduction to a number of explanations that will be fleshed out in the coming chapters. Sex variations became increasingly visible owing to the shift to large hospitals and the growing number of medical publications. The poor filling public hospitals, as well as "King Cholera" and rampant venereal disease, alerted doctors to the potentially widespread incidence of intersex as sex variations were uncovered during autopsy or treatment for unrelated reasons. Determining sex in ambiguous cases became a means for doctors in increasingly specialized medical fields to claim superiority over those in rival specializations. Medical discourse staked its mounting authority on a hyperbolic knowledge of the body – one that often surpassed what was actually technologically or medically knowable. This meant doctors had to rely on narrative in order to palliate a lack of scientific evidence. At the same time, realist fiction took, in some ways, a more "scientific" approach to knowing the world. Even before Zola's experimental method repurposed literature as a new means of conducting "scientific experiments," Balzac was inspired by the burgeoning social sciences to explore social "types" in fiction. "Realism" – the pejorative name Balzac's critics chose for his fiction and literature like it – aimed to represent the world "as it was," rather than as it should be.[36] The landscape of the metropolis of Paris itself was changing, and along with it, so too were the people who called it home. France's urban centers afforded increased anonymity in which individuals outside of the family unit could make their own living and their own lifestyle choices. This shifting sense of family and the advent of new social identities during the course of the nineteenth century, combined with a plummeting birthrate at the fin de siècle, elevated the stakes of doubtful sex – made the uncertainty surrounding "hermaphrodism" more relevant, more poignant, and magnified its resonance to a wider audience.

Taken individually, none of these threads seem particularly revealing, but woven together by narrative, they tell a more compelling story. In nineteenth-century medicine, narrative serves to answer the question of uncertain sex in the absence of scientific proof. It promises legibility of a bodily variation that was otherwise unreadable for many reasons, not the least of which is that the language to describe it satisfactorily was lacking.

Yet, from within the highly gendered limitations of the French language, and the perhaps still more rigid confines of a largely unquestioned binary, we find nineteenth-century doctors and novelists who did not always reveal "true sex."

Almost from the moment of birth, having a gender was a social necessity in nineteenth-century France. French law gave doctors three days to record sex on the birth certificate, and from that moment forward, whether they listed "male" or "female" would determine what kind of education one could receive, what kinds of jobs one could have, how much one would be paid for them, and even whom one could marry. A wealth of historiography attests to the ways in which nineteenth-century medicine labored to naturalize the distinctions between men and women, yet when doctors were confronted with historical cases of intersex, more and more of them began to realize that there were some individuals who could not be classified as one or the other, casting the entire binary into doubt. At the same time, novelists increasingly began to imagine characters who did not fit neatly within the gender binary, sometimes creating entire novels in which the mystery of a character's gender identity actually motivated the plot. Everyone in nineteenth-century France accepted that there were differences between men and women, but for the first time both medical and literary narratives came to the surprisingly similar conclusion that determining the exact nature of those differences was excessively difficult, and even sometimes strictly impossible. Instead, both medicine and literature suggest that some differences between men and women are merely prescribed fictions – products of cultural construct rather than scientific fact.

PART I

A Cultural Prehistory of Intersex
from the Archives

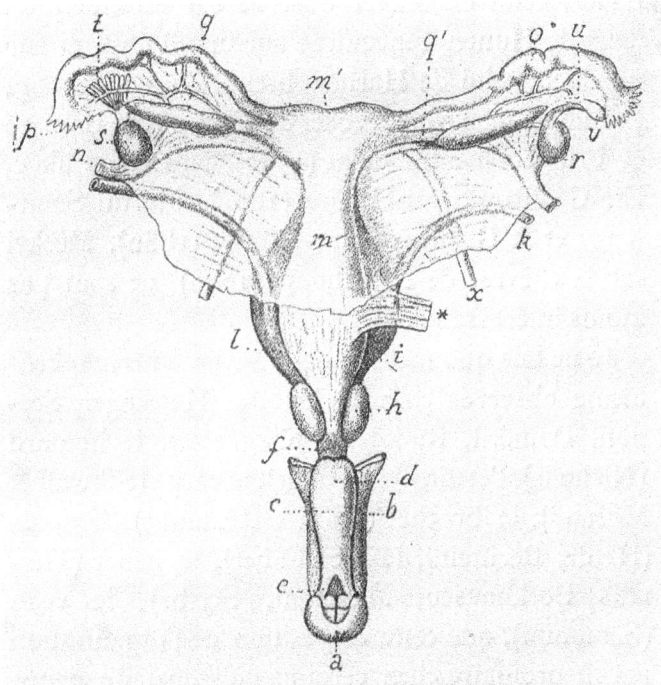

Fig. 19. — Organes génitaux de l'hermaphrodite vrai de Heppner.

a, gland du phallus; — e, orifice uréthral; — b, corps caverneux; — c, urèthre; — d, bulbe de l'urèthre; — f, portion membraneuse de ce canal; — h, prostate; — i, vessie; — l, vagin; m, utérus; — x, ligament rond; — k, uretère; — r, testicule; — U, hydatide; — O, oviducte; — q', ligament utéro-ovarien; — q, ovaire; — t, épididyme; — p, pavillon de la trompe; — s, testicule; — m', fond de l'utérus; — x, ligament utéro-rectal.

Figure 0.1 The Genital Organs of Heppner's "True Hermaphrodite" (1872), from Charles Debierre, *L'hermaphrodisme; structure, fonctions, état psychologique et mental, état civil et mariage, dangers et remèdes* (1891).

CHAPTER I

Prescribed Fictions
Stories of "Hermaphrodism" vs. "True Sex"

Although hundreds of nineteenth-century case studies document medical sex determinations from the doctor's point of view, there is only one known first-person account of what enduring one felt like from the patient's perspective. It was penned by Herculine Barbin, whose memoirs describe the medical encounter with calculated suspense and dramatic prose: "Standing near my bed, the doctor considered me carefully, with great interest, while letting out muffled exclamations such as: 'My God! Could it be possible!'"[1] Visibly confused, he pokes and prods "as if to find the solution to a difficult problem" (126). The doctor's dehumanizing fascination and groping hand compound the already debilitating physical pain and mounting alarm produced by his invasive examination as his fingers explore bare skin: "My disheveled clothes revealed the upper part of my body! The doctor's hand moved over it indecisively, trembling, down to my abdomen [...] I let out a piercing cry while pushing it away vigorously [...] his hand slipped under my sheet [...] it did not stop there!!!" (126). The doctor at last finds what he was looking for with a breathless spasm of realization, but dares not announce his diagnosis: "The poor man was in a state of terrible shock! Sentences escaped from his throat by fits and starts, as if he were afraid to let them out."[2] He had discovered that Barbin, who had spent more than twenty years living as a woman, was not a woman after all.

Laden with sexual tension and peppered with exclamations, euphemisms, and other rhetorical devices, Barbin's melodramatic style deploys the codes of fiction, which fuel its novelistic suspense. If the journal did not figure in Tardieu's 1874 medico-legal treatise, and Michel Foucault had not later unearthed biographical information confirming its authenticity, Barbin's writing might have easily passed for a product of literary imagination. Incredibly, it will become just that with Dr. Caufeynon's 1905 *L'hermaphrodite au couvent* (*The Hermaphrodite in Convent School*) – a novelized, eroticized, and mostly plagiarized rendition of Barbin's memoirs.[3] Meanwhile, the memoirs also deeply impacted medical literature, which often cites Barbin's tragic suicide as a cautionary tale of incorrect sex assignment. Dr. Caufeynon, a penname for the self-proclaimed "Dr. Fauconney" – who also published a pseudo-scientific treatise on hermaphrodism, but who was probably not actually a doctor – offers one example of the complex interplay between literature and medicine in nineteenth-century representations of hermaphrodism.[4]

The intricate layering of Barbin's autobiographical writings is central to the telling of this book and to Barbin's life. This is as much because of the literary influence and style of Barbin's prose as of the material context of its publication. Barbin's memoirs were never published on their own, and the complete manuscript was lost. Instead, only excerpts were compiled by two influential men who sandwiched them between carefully curated historical, literary, and medical documentation, using Barbin's story to buttress their own arguments about "true sex." Both times, first in the last quarter of the nineteenth century, and then roughly a century later in 1978, the memoirs inspired a flurry of scholarly commentary as well as fictional adaptations.

Barbin's historical memoirs were, in some sense, always intertwined with literature; s/he was a highly educated and well-read student of it, and s/he chose as a fictional avatar the gender-neutral name "Camille," which was frequently used in literary accounts of intersex, most famously by Henri de Latouche in his influential novel *Fragoletta*, which would, in turn, inspire Latouche's better-known peers Honoré de Balzac and Théophile Gautier to write their own "hermaphrodite" novels. As we have seen, since the nineteenth century, Barbin's memoirs inspired fictional imitations. Caufeynon is only one example of a writer who attempted to sensationalize them; Foucault published another one in his dossier alongside the memoirs. In our own time, Jeffrey Eugenides claimed that his "frustration" with the way Barbin chose to write them (melodramatically, and evasively when it came to anatomical details) gave him the idea for his controversial, Pulitzer Prize-winning novel, *Middlesex*.[5] Morgan Holmes explains that it is partially the lack of "first-person accounts of living as/with intersex" that "have left Barbin's story vulnerable to those who would make hir life whatever they will."[6] Today, Barbin is arguably the most well-known historical intersex figure, whose birthday on November 8 marks the Intersex Day of Remembrance.

Barbin's memoirs are related to fiction in one other overlooked way: both times they were published, the influential men who did so used them in order to make weighty arguments about the nature of "true sex," but close review of the medical record reveals that the story of nineteenth-century hermaphrodism is not as linear or as monolithic as their writings would have us believe. And just because the memoirs offer the only autobiographical, nineteenth-century account of intersex, that does not mean that they are the only story worth being told about it, or that Barbin was alone in many of his/her experiences.

This chapter analyzes medical representations of historical intersex in France in order to lay bare their literary aspirations and inspirations. Although doctors often reference the purely empirical nature of their methods, it shows how the overlapping spheres of fiction and medicine produce shifting definitions of "hermaphrodism" throughout the century. This analysis problematizes the oft-repeated historical argument that a belief in "true sex" crystallized in the nineteenth century around the intersex body. What has been overlooked is that, in addition to the difficulty of determining gonadal sex in living patients, there were also a number of doctors who argued against the very notion of "true sex," claiming that for some, "true sex" lay out of reach, either because it was impossible to determine, or because it was not binary.

In what follows, we shall see how some doctors made a stand for "true hermaphrodism"; many more could not identify the sex of their living patients, and experts often disagreed not only about sex determinations, but also about how best to make them. Precisely because no one method proved infallible, doctors and medico-legal experts relied on narrative to bolster their claims – a narrative mirroring the one being developed simultaneously in contemporary fiction. The intricate imbrications of science and literature underline the importance of storytelling as a powerful means to explore uncertain sex, and while the case study is a narrative genre by definition, nineteenth-century case studies of hermaphrodism can be especially novelistic when doctors compensate for sparse empirical evidence by marshaling the codes of fiction.[7]

Telling Herculine's Story

One cannot tell the story of nineteenth-century hermaphrodism without first telling that of Herculine Barbin. As the author of the only extant memoir describing, in his/her own words, his/her own experiences as an intersex person in nineteenth-century France, Barbin's writings are, in their own right, perhaps the most important historical document for telling that story. They remind us that behind every medical case study, every court document, every treatise or dissertation, there were historical individuals who experienced triumphs, love, and hardships that the medical record can never reveal. Like contemporary intersex people fighting hard to change medical paradigms, Barbin and the anonymous subjects described fleetingly by doctors had complex and sometimes conflictual relationships with medicine. The profound and long-lasting cultural impact the memoirs exerted cannot be overstated, and the way the manuscript was published has influenced our understanding of the history of sexuality to this day.

But Barbin's memoirs are also at the heart of this story because of what happened *both* times that they became famous. Firstly, this was in the nineteenth century, when Barbin's tragic suicide sparked a burst of publications about the dangers of incorrect sex assignment at birth that arguably shaped the biomedical treatment of intersex for decades; and secondly, when Foucault misleadingly claimed to have rediscovered them in the twentieth.[8] According to his 1978 presentation of Barbin's memoirs, and to his lectures at the Collège de France, Foucault intended to devote one of the volumes of the *History of Sexuality* to the study of "hermaphrodism," but he never did so.[9] His intention nevertheless reveals that he understood the central role played by intersex in the history of sexuality. Ultimately, Foucault wrote very little on the subject, citing only a handful of cases, yet his thesis of "true sex" from his preface to the English edition of Barbin's memoirs remains one of the more enduring tenets of the history of sexuality, to the point that it has achieved the status of conventional wisdom.

Called "Alexina" by friends and family, Adélaïde Herculine Barbin was born on November 8, 1838, in the town of Saint-Jean-d'Angély, and listed as a girl on the birth certificate, consistent with the French law requiring sex to be recorded within three days of birth. Barbin experienced his/her own gender in layered and shifting ways and s/he signaled this in writing by alternating between masculine and feminine gender agreements in French. In the second paragraph, Barbin describes *his* current anguish and solitude (after the legal sex revision we later discover) by repeating the masculine form of the adjective "alone" (*seul*). In the third, s/he uses both the masculine form of the French adjective "worried" (*soucieux*) and the feminine form of the adjective "cold" (*froide*) (64). "Soucieux" could be read to agree with the masculine word for forehead (*le front*), and predominately, the italicized words reflect Barbin's identification with the female gender up until the time of the legal sex change, after which point Barbin transitions to masculine gender agreement in French. According to Tardieu, the intentional emphasis on gendered forms was indicated with underlining in the manuscript, which both he and Foucault render using italics.[10] However, Tardieu only printed the part of Barbin's writing that he found the most "interesting," and because the complete manuscript has been lost, we cannot check whether he was a faithful scribe.[11] The English translation problematically erases nearly all of the gender instability carefully crafted by Barbin, preserving only a few gendered nouns in italics, and none of the italicized gendered adjectives referenced above.

On June 21, 1860, Dr. Chesnet offered decisive testimony that Alexina was, in fact, a man, and Barbin's birth certificate was legally amended to read "male."[12] "Alexina" became "Abel" in the revised record. Abel soon embarked for Paris with its promise of anonymity and a fresh start. Instead, Barbin records an endless struggle to find kinship and work, and an agonizing descent into loneliness and poverty. Soon after, Tardieu loses interest in Barbin's despairing and emotional prose, silencing the author by truncating the memoirs and leaving the incomplete version that remains to this day. Barbin's story picks up again in the worst way possible: in February of 1868, Abel's body was discovered by a police commissioner and a physician from the state registry office. Suspecting that the young man had committed suicide by carbon monoxide poisoning in order to cut short syphilitic suffering, the doctor inspected Abel's genitals, and found astonishing anomalies. When news reached the Faculté de médecine that a "hermaphrodite" had recently passed, Dr. E. Goujon performed an autopsy in order to preserve the case for science, but while researching for his publication, Goujon discovered that Barbin had already debuted in the medical literature eight years prior, when "Abel" had replaced "Alexina" in the eyes of the law.

In an uncanny premonition suggesting that the author intended to be read, Barbin had predicted that "a few doctors will make a small clamor over my remains; they will break all the mechanisms of its extinct motivations, will draw new insights from it, will analyze all the mysterious sufferings that were heaped upon a single human" (164). In point of fact, Barbin created more than a "small clamor," and would become a famous intersex person long before Foucault ever "rediscovered" the memoirs. Foucault incorrectly alleges that "Neither Alexina's case nor her memoirs seem to have aroused much interest at the time."[13] On the contrary, perhaps no other single case is more frequently mentioned by doctors in the second half of the century. Scores of articles, theses, treatises, and textbooks reference Barbin's sad tale.[14] Franz Neugebauer, the most prolific contemporary collector of case studies of hermaphrodism, even justifies his work based, in part, on Barbin's life.[15] What is more, Alexina's story would attract continued medical fascination well into the twentieth century.[16] Nearly every doctor alluding to Barbin evokes the suicide as a worst-case scenario for incorrect sex determination at birth. Tardieu labels Barbin a "poor, unfortunate person," and "the cruelest and saddest example of the fatal consequences brought about by an error committed on the civil registry at birth" (1874, 61). Doctors speculate effusively about what triggered suicide. Dr. Tapie suggests that Alexina's shocking sex determination was to blame, while Dr. Brouardel insinuates that an impossible marriage must have broken Barbin's spirit.[17] Facing destitution, Abel also writes of lost employment and failed interviews since *he* could not cite Alexina's past work experience teaching in convent school to potential employers. Speculation aside, we will never know exactly why Barbin blocked the chimney one winter night. Barbin left a suicide note addressed to his/her mother, purportedly asking for forgiveness, but it, too was lost.[18] There is also no known photographic or visual rendering of Barbin's face, despite recent scholarly speculation about Nadar's famous series of photographs of an intersex person that would have coincided with Barbin's time in Paris.[19] As is often true of nineteenth-century case studies of intersex, the lone surviving depictions of Barbin are of the genitals.[20] Frequently, such drawings, photographs, and even wax molds of genitalia also immortalize the unbearable medical fingers that Barbin had so poignantly described.[21] I have chosen not to reproduce any of these images in this book.

At the heart of both nineteenth-century fictional and medical representations of hermaphrodism, Barbin's story demonstrates the importance of narrative when exploring gender boundaries. Barbin might have structured the memoirs on existing literary models which also dealt with uncertain sex, or telling his/her own story might have helped to take back the control that was displaced by medical and legal intervention. Judith Butler remarks that Barbin read a great deal; that a firm grasp of the classics as well as of French Romanticism formed part of his/her education, and that "h/er own narrative takes place within an established set of literary conventions."[22] Butler detects the influence of romantic and sentimental narratives of impossible loves, Greek mythology, and Christian hagiography, to which I would add Latouche's *Fragoletta*, because, as previously mentioned, Barbin refers to herself/himself as Camille, the name of the feminine manifestation of the intersex protagonist. Authors often chose the epicene name "Camille" for androgynous protagonists since, as the narrator of Gaston d'Hailly's *L'hermaphrodite* (1885) points out, it applies to both men and women in French (58). Latouche's 1834 novel is frequently remembered as the first nineteenth-century novel about a hermaphrodite, but in the third chapter, we will see that this honor belongs to a long-forgotten popular novel by J.-P.-R. Cuisin. The literary influence in Barbin's memoirs has often been observed, but not related to the larger narrative of intersex stories in which it participates, or the future narratives it would inspire, both medical and fictional.

Hybrid Genres

Foucault cites Armand Dubarry's "strange novel" *L'hermaphrodite* (1898) as inspired by Barbin's case, although except for also showcasing an intersex protagonist, they share little else.[23] Surprisingly, Foucault fails to mention Caufeynon's *L'hermaphrodite au couvent*, which transforms Barbin's first-person memoirs into an eroticized novella in the third person. In Caufeynon's forgotten rendition, Alexina becomes "Paule," which converts easily to the masculine "Paul," making it a convenient choice for the legal sex revision to come. Caufeynon picks up where Tardieu left off by further paring down Barbin's memoirs, but this time only to highlight the most sexually charged moments. Plagiarizing entire sections, he never acknowledges the source of his creation. Seen through Caufeynon's distorting lens, Paule becomes a corrupting pursuer whose childhood infatuations amount to illicit sexual contact. While Barbin had described first love in relatively platonic terms, Caufeynon fabricates licentious scenarios in which Paule, overcome by an "irresistible" nocturnal urge to visit her friend, covers her face with kisses while at the same time caressing her "barely formed breasts."[24] The simplified narrative Caufeynon extracts from Barbin's memoirs makes room for more elaborate embellishments on the intimate details of Paule's scandalous relationships with her "innocent" fellow convent-goers and nuns. Terrified by a storm, Barbin had described springing into the arms of a nun instinctively, nightgown and all, and then feeling suddenly ashamed. In addition, Caufeynon has Paule enlace the "Lord's Virgin" with her legs, and then includes a "violent spasm" that rattles her pelvis and leaves her panting for air on the ground (31).

An uneasy juxtaposition of science and fiction characterizes *L'hermaphrodite au couvent*. At times, Caufeynon waxes lyrical on the beauty of virginal female forms, while also including "scientific" explanations for physiological processes.[25] Caufeynon reveals information found only in Barbin's medical case studies to complete his analysis, confirming that he read them, even though they do not figure in his compendium at the end of the novel.[26] At one point, he even describes in great technical detail how an intersex Paule could have nevertheless achieved orgasm with her lover, Sister Marie des Anges. At the end of his eclectic work, Caufeynon tacks on several case studies of hermaphrodism – though significantly, not Barbin's. This will "prove" the "truth" of his story, which he had promised from the outset: "What we can affirm is the absolute veracity of the facts that we relate, which are supported by evidence of irrecusable authenticity offered at the end of this story."[27] Doctors frequently tout the expurgating qualities of "truth" when exploring taboo subjects, so that Caufeynon's remark becomes a trope in the medical record.[28] Perhaps, in Caufeynon's mind, this scientific addendum would counterbalance the sexual and authorial transgressions of his work. Of course, his pledge of authenticity also pays lip service to a longstanding literary tradition with roots in the eighteenth-century libertine novel.

Occasionally, Caufeynon also interrupts his story in the way of a Balzacian narrator in order to signal key moments and clarify unfamiliar situations. After intimating that Paule is the instigator of amorous nocturnal forays, for example, he explains that this will all become clear to readers once they learn that Paule is *really* Paul, and thus, a kind of innate masculine pursuer (58). Tardieu also finds a heteronormative explanation for Barbin's apparent lesbianism irresistibly tempting in his preface, and includes explicative footnotes to that effect. Tardieu destroys the carefully constructed suspense of the memoirs with the addition of a footnote explaining – in dry medical terms – that Alexina is "really" a man, and that it was a constricted testicle rather than menstrual cramps that were causing excruciating pain.[29] Nevertheless, Barbin's narrative proves surprisingly resilient to Tardieu's interjections as narrator. Tardieu had promised that Barbin's first medical visit would prove his diagnosis of "strangulation of the seminal gland," but, as we have seen, the bewildered doctor who administers this exam never announces his findings, choosing instead to issue veiled warnings about working alongside young girls. The nameless doctor's examination, which opened this chapter, belongs to Barbin because it is s/he who tells it, and because s/he does so with the diegetic feel of a novel, the reader can push on in the trance of suspended disbelief that usually only fiction affords. Despite Tardieu's best efforts to clarify and classify, Barbin's story unfolds without him – almost in spite of him – building suspense undaunted by footnotes. Likening the memoirs to fiction is not intended to lessen the trauma that Herculine Barbin experienced, but rather to show how the telling of these experiences participates in a narrative tradition that stretches before them and continues long after them. Barbin's story deeply impacted both fictional and medical narratives to come.

Medical Storytelling

L'hermaphrodite au couvent renders explicit a kind of popular fascination produced by "hermaphrodism" that remains merely latent in most medical case studies, and its conflation of science and fiction further erodes any semblance of empiricism. Yet Caufeynon's hybrid compilation actually resembles many contemporary scientific and medical works on the subject. In his opus on hermaphrodism and sterility, Pierre Garnier bemoans the potential threat of incorrect sex assignment with erotic and fantasied imagination akin to Caufeynon's novel:

> Should one or another of these poorly sexed individuals be called to religion or teaching, morality would be gravely compromised. If it is a man-woman admitted to a seminary, what will happen to the young Levites, as in any other congregation or monastery? It would be even more dangerous if it were a woman-man [. . .] it would set fire to the convent, consuming all of the nuns! It would be still worse if it were at school. What would it be in the barracks, if the pre-recruitment examination did not fortunately prevent this type of mistake! (1883, 496)

Although Garnier does not mention Barbin's case explicitly, his hysterical rendition of worst-case scenarios echoes elements from the memoirs, while his sequence of alternating exclamations and rhetorical questions becomes a kind of fictional strip-tease, inviting the reader to imagine sordid scenes from school and convent.[30] Even racy scenarios in the barracks give the author pause, despite the fact that pre-recruitment physicals allegedly prevented their very existence. This double discourse disguises a provocative evocation of illicit sexuality behind a moralizing tone and euphemistic structure in the same way that Caufeynon passes off pornography as scientific fact.[31] Multiple doctors reference a type of "hermaphrodite" dubbed a "Gavroche," transforming Victor Hugo's romanticized street urchin into a "malformed" adolescent who exploits his "condition" by seeking the financial protection of an older "pederast" partner.[32] Dr. Laupts's 1896 work on perversion further blurs science and fiction. Aside from publishing the autobiographical writings of a nineteenth-century homosexual as the *Roman d'un inverti-né* (*Novel of a Born Invert*) – prefaced by the famous novelist Émile Zola, no less – he signals historical individuals as fictional types. Laupts notes "a certain type of very in-style and perverted flirt who was not invented by a writer, but who exists and is easy to find in reality."[33] Was Laupts imposing a fictional model onto a historical person, or was the literary representation already based on historical example? Cross-fertilization renders causal flow difficult to determine.

With their minute descriptions, imaginative explanations, and paternalistic doctor-as-narrator, case histories of hermaphrodism often resemble their novelistic counterparts. In 1892, Dr. Jules Boeckel published a case of an individual whose outward appearance he describes as entirely masculine, but inside of whom he was astonished to discover a uterus and fallopian tubes. Boeckel's style is acutely novelistic, and he describes dissecting his patient's "mysterious organs" with verve, as if he were a first-person narrator in a mystery novel: "This organ is certainly a Fallopian tube, a cystic Fallopian tube, or I am quite confused indeed, I exclaimed to myself, adding, in a tone that was half joking and half convinced, the tumor that I mistook a moment ago for a herniated caecum must be a uterus!" (1892, 87). The same year, Dr. Guermonprez would publish an equally perplexing and novelistic case. By cultivating description in order to create suspense and exploit the mystery of "doubtful sex," Guermonprez's rendition even shares the "hermeneutic code" that Roland Barthes identified as one trait of realist fiction.[34]

On July 4, 1892, the arrival of an unusual note introduced an even more remarkable patient and piqued Dr. Guermonprez's interest. So much so that the good doctor seized on the occasion to model his case study on a detective mystery highlighting his keen observation and quick wit. The note simply read: "subject interesting from a psychological standpoint," but Dr. Guermonprez already saw much more: "The person in question wears women's clothing in a very strange manner; her features are hard, her bearing awkward, her speech hesitating and laconic, and her look is as enigmatic as the letter of introduction announcing her."[35] Over the next few paragraphs, Guermonprez's case study of Louise-Julia-Anna amasses physical description in the way of the popular physiognomy and realist novel, from the belt around her waist to the ribbons in her hair. In keeping with the great literary masters, the doctor's descriptive analysis abounds with meaning so that each detail represents a clue in the code of the patient's identity:

> Her bearing is one of awkwardness that is poorly disguised by the tilt of her head to the right. Her outfit is poorly adjusted, lacking grace and lightness. All the elements comprising it fit with the styles of the season, but her brooch is placed maladroitly off center, her belt rises more on one side than the other, the ribbons in her hat are arranged without taste, and the entire look shows a type of negligence that is not at all the consequence of ill intent but rather one that manifestly stems from an absence of good taste, of proper order, of care for one's self, of fashionable dressing, that characterize some unskilled women; there is nothing that resembles, even from afar, coquetry. (339)

Like Mme. Vauquer's disintegrating dress in *Le Père Goriot*, the mounting evidence of sartorial codes is adduced to reveal something about the wearer herself. And just like Balzac, Guermonprez interprets as he describes. Under the doctor's intense observation, the patient's ill-adjusted accoutrements reveal that Louise-Julia-Anna is usurping a feminine identity, and is *really* a man. Even though she has carefully assembled all the correct elements to signify femininity (stylish clothes, accessories, hairstyle), it is the way she deploys them that is damning: the broach is off-center, her belt uneven, her hat and ribbons placed haphazardly. Although Guermonprez concedes that "unskilled women" also dress this way, in this instance he determines that Louise-Julia-Anna's vestimentary failure and its implied feminine inability emanate from her deeper, "true" masculine identity. In an effort to prove this point, Guermonprez includes illustrations in which he has placed the patient in "virile" poses, calculated to emphasize her musculature and "masculine" stature. He carefully details how removing Louise-Julia-Anna's earrings and blocking out her feminine hairstyle with his hand permits a glimpse of her disguised masculine self, but this voluntary blindness only highlights the inability of a prescribed masculine sex to account for the gender "transgressions" presented by Louise-Julia-Anna's mixed-sex body.

"True Sex" vs. "True Hermaphrodism"

Like Guermonprez's absolute faith in "true sex," Tardieu's insistence on Alexina's heteronormative "true masculine sex" cannot fully compensate for the life lived as a woman. Perhaps because of this incompatibility, Tardieu must justify Alexina's love for Sara as an expression of Abel's "true" masculine sex, and Abel's suicide, equally inevitably, as a result of his sudden awareness of irreparable "physical infirmity." According to Tardieu's narrative, Abel's incomplete maleness spurs self-loathing that can only end in suicide:

> We shall see the victim of a similar error, after twenty years spent in the clothing of a sex that was not his own, in the throes of a passion that he, himself ignored, finally alerted by an explosion of feelings, and then returned to his true sex at the same time that he became aware of the real feeling of his physical infirmity, disgusted by life, and deciding to end it by suicide. (1874, 61)

It is important to point out that Barbin, unlike Tardieu and even many contemporary readers, does not rationalize his/her attraction to Sara as an expression of some deep, masculine "true sex." As Morgan Holmes has rightly suggested, this essentialist reading of the memoirs is fundamentally a misreading.[36] But Tardieu, a leading forensic medical specialist constrained by the legal code, admits only two sexes, as does the Napoleonic Code. So, while Tardieu considered Alexina a "malformed" male, s/he was nevertheless a man, which meant s/he was *not* a woman. The heteronormative, one-body-one-sex rule is hard at work for Tardieu. In other words, it did not matter that Barbin had a vagina, was raised a girl, or taught in a convent school.[37] It did not matter that some doctors claimed s/he would not have been able to marry a man.[38] What mattered was that s/he had testicles, and by the time Tardieu published Barbin's memoirs in 1874, the gonadal definition of sex reigned supreme. Alice Domurat Dreger has shown that during the time period she memorably calls the "Age of the Gonads," cases of ambiguous sex like Barbin's were predominately decided following a golden rule: men had testicles and women had ovaries. Owing to the gonadal definition of sex, most doctors were emphatic about Barbin's maleness. Basile Poppesco, for example, writes of Barbin: "the autopsy clearly showed that he was a man" (1874, 38).

Dreger's thesis of the increasingly restrictive definition of hermaphrodism fits within the accepted history of sexuality. If "true sex" – the idea that each body has one and only one sex – took root in the nineteenth century, then it makes sense that its culmination would see the disappearance of hermaphrodism, which at its most basic level implied a combination of both male and female attributes. Indeed, Dreger finds that the gonadal definition of sex signals the practical extinction of the "hermaphrodite" – a term increasingly replaced by the word "pseudo-hermaphrodite," whose "true sex" the doctor could nevertheless decipher. Dreger situates the "Age of the Gonads" during the last quarter of the nineteenth century, but according to Foucault, the age of "true sex" dawned much earlier. During the eighteenth century, Foucault argues, doctors were not concerned with "recognizing the presence of two sexes, juxtaposed or intermingled, or with knowing which of the two prevailed over the other," and began "deciphering the true sex that was hidden beneath ambiguous appearances."[39] Foucault describes how with the advent of this paradigm shift, doctors began "to strip the body of its anatomical deceptions and discover the one true sex behind the organs that might have put on the forms of the opposite sex."[40] Dreger's "Age of the Gonads" (1870–1915) seems to crown the imperialism of "true sex" with its doctrine of determining sex by identifying the nature of gonadal tissue.

According to Foucault and conventional historiography, the one-body-one-sex rule inherited from the eighteenth century has followed us, in many ways, into the twenty-first century.[41] But this was not always so. Foucault romanticizes the centuries before the emergence of "true sex" as a period of "free choice" for "hermaphrodites."[42] Following Foucault, Thomas Laqueur has argued that the biological determination of sex separates the nineteenth century from earlier periods defined by a "one-sex model" which held sex as a social and cultural marker more than as an ontological category.[43] Foucault has been criticized for his willingness to conceptualize the time before "true sex" as a period of "free choice" in which intersex people could freely choose their own sex without medical intervention.[44] Even so, his thesis of a medically imposed "true sex" remains an unchallenged, and frequently touted truism of the nineteenth century.

If, as the story goes, the modern age of "true sex" hearkened in the nineteenth century, then the "Age of the Gonads" sounded the death knell of the "hermaphrodite." But Dreger's pioneering study of hermaphrodism in nineteenth-century France and England offers a much more detailed and nuanced account than Foucault's scant remarks on the subject, and although one of her key arguments is the identification of the "Age of the Gonads," her book is often unfairly reduced to that argument alone.[45] The memorable name she chose for it has possibly contributed to this fact. In the documents that Dreger examines, she demonstrates that although there was increasing consensus that the gonads determined "true sex" in France and England between 1870 and 1915, there remained considerable disagreement about which sex to assign on a case-by-case basis, especially in living patients whose gonads were not available for microscopic study. Doctors also sometimes refused to enforce the heteronormative one-body-one-sex rule, and "allowed" or "enabled" homosexual marriage either through surgery or an apparent unwillingness to trouble a happy home by alerting all parties concerned (or the authorities). More recently, Geertje Mak has revealed an increasingly nuanced history of hermaphrodism by turning away from doctors' opinions about "true sex," and toward their practices in determining cases of "doubtful" sex.[46] Inspired by Annemarie Mol's "praxiographic" technique, Mak's approach aims to examine how sex is "enacted" in ambiguous cases in the hope of avoiding the traditional epistemological criticism of medicine which forever depicts a medically defined objective "true sex" as a silencer of a patient's subjective "true sex."[47] Mol warns that such criticisms unintentionally cite scientific findings as if they were consistent and readily identifiable entities, whereas they frequently differed, depending on extra-scientific factors that varied according to local and historical circumstances.[48] Ultimately, Mak's central argument confirms Dreger's claim that the practical determination of "true sex" differed widely from its theorization.

In order to show the previously overlooked intersections between medicine and fiction, I have examined the narrative of uncertain sex in the identical case that both Dreger and Mak have analyzed: that of Louise-Julia-Anna. Because of Guermonprez's unmitigated belief in "true sex," Dreger selects his case study to typify the "Age of the Gonads." Mak, however, has expertly shown that in practice, no one "true sex" emerges from Guermonprez's case since his various techniques for determining the nature of Louise-Julia-Anna's internal organs – feeling, listening, observing – produce "different sexes."[49] No matter how rigid Guermonprez's belief in "true sex," argues Mak, his practice reveals an ambiguity incompatible with his theory. As my close reading illustrated, Louise-Julia-Anna's case subverts "true sex" in a way that undermines the alleged supremacy of the gonadal model and pushes beyond a theoretical vs. practical distinction. Despite his seeming allegiance to the science of "true sex," his narrative calls its overarching authority into question by revealing its insufficiency to account for Louise-Julia-Anna's mixed-sex body and lived experience. Guermonprez's narrative summons common literary tropes – a gesture that reveals that scientific practices and technology were not the only factors in the calculus of sex. If testicles unequivocally signified masculinity during the "Age of the Gonads," why need Guermonprez bother with the overture of a detective novel focusing on external appearance?

I suggest that the gonadal definition standing alone was not sufficient to determine sex even in Guermonprez's moralizing case, and required the buttress of a narrative which could recapture deviant elements of Louise-Julia-Anna's sex and bind them in a convincing explanation. If Louise-Julia-Anna was "really a man," then what were discordant truths to Guermonprez – her attraction to men, her unwavering belief that she was a woman, her feminine attire – needed to be explained away. What may be surprising to modern readers is that in order to accomplish this, Guermonprez resorts to a story heavily invested in the codes of fiction rather than simply accumulating scientific evidence.[50] Faced with a historical case that challenges medical reasoning, the doctor turns first to novelistic narrative in order to glean the necessary authority to pronounce "true sex." This gesture breaks with the typical storyline of domineering nineteenth-century medicine and the well-documented literary adoption of scientific power (in the manner of Zola following Claude Bernard, etc.).[51] Instead of the authoritative doctor confidently categorizing ambiguous bodies based on scientific models, we find Guermonprez marshaling physical description in the way of a realist or detective novelist.

Guermonprez's exploitation of literary forms not only menaces the empirical façade of his scientific work, it also speaks to the insufficiency of these very models.[52] It is clear from the energy he pours into the rhetoric of defending his conclusion of Louise-Julia-Anna's "evident masculinity" that even he is conscious of the limitations of his science. Guermonprez acknowledges, for example, that the techniques for determining the somatic nature of gonads are highly contested. In one unruly footnote, he anticipates that critics might doubt his identification of testicles in Louise-Julia-Anna: "the reader might be tempted to doubt the certainty of my affirmation. He might wonder if the glands observed were not ovaries, instead of being testicles."[53] Guermonprez's response to such a counterexample is a purely rhetorical trump card devoid of scientific merit: "This doubt could visit the mind of a critic *who did not personally see and verify* the characteristics observed in this particular case" (343). The reader might object, he determines, but *only I know*, because *only I was there*. "Take my word for it" hardly epitomizes the scientific method, but it does harmonize nicely with Guermonprez's authorial persona.

Guermonprez's case illustrates that even during the "Age of the Gonads" the mere presence of testicles did not signify masculinity all by itself; essentialist gonadal sex was only one important factor among many. Rather than being cast as a physical reality inscribed on and throughout the body, even in the nineteenth century, "true sex" required decipherment, interpretation, and the construction of a narrative argument that addressed counterexamples. This narrative compensation for bodily reality reveals the contested nature of "true sex" at a time when recent historiography has alleged that this axiom was most firmly entrenched. Laqueur, for instance, has written that "By the nineteenth century, [. . .] Any notion of genuine sexual ambiguity or neutrality is nonsense because sex is absolutely there in and throughout the body."[54] But many nineteenth-century case histories reveal (sometimes in spite of themselves, as it was for Guermonprez, and sometimes more overtly, as it was for Poppesco) that, because multiple sexes can be inscribed on a single body, "genuine sexual ambiguity or neutrality" *always* haunts medical declarations of sex in doubtful cases and threatens to unravel the carefully constructed narrative of "true sex."

Historians have long held "true sex" and the absolute separation between the sexes as motivating factors behind the medicalization of sexuality in nineteenth-century France. "True sex" emerges out of this discourse as a kind of seamless and uncontested narrative, so that even when practice differs from theory, the theory itself is assumed to remain entirely unscathed. In what follows, I will present further evidence showing that "true sex" never enjoyed such unchallenged authority within the nineteenth-century history of hermaphrodism in France. A number of experts actually protested the increasingly restricted definition of hermaphrodism, arguing that "true hermaphrodism" did exist, and that the gonadal definition was a poor indicator of sex, or did not account for the full range of human possibility. A close reading of case histories will reveal that the seeming imperialism and inflexibility of the binary model was at once a reaction to and a testament of widespread efforts to subvert it.

By examining the critics of the gonadal definition of sex, we can begin to understand how rivalries between clinicians and surgeons, emerging specializations vying for a slice of medical authority, and other professional obligations actually influenced the allegedly impervious "one-body-one-sex rule," undermining the very foundations of "true sex." This will demonstrate that the nineteenth century was not a uniform period during which "true sex" always prevailed. My approach does not lead to "truth," but rather shows how many voices produced competing, layered, and even fictional narratives of "hermaphrodism." It will seek to place these narratives back into the historical context of domestic and international concerns in nineteenth-century France. The omnipresent literary obsession with intersex remains closely tied to medical representations and offers further evidence of the contemporary cultural anxiety surrounding cases of ambiguous sex and sexuality.

The Persistent Patient Seeks Second Opinions

Three years after Louise-Julia-Anna was warned by Dr. Guermonprez that her very existence was criminal, she sought a second opinion with Dr. Hallopeau in Paris.[55] Neither Mak nor Dreger discuss Louise-Julia-Anna's follow-up cases, and to my knowledge, they have eluded critical notice. Unlike Dr. Guermonprez, who strove to cast his patient as a man who maliciously deceived himself and others, Dr. Hallopeau does not describe Louise-Julia-Anna as an evident male following the gonadal definition. According to Hallopeau, "the external genital organs of the subject, named Louise-Julia-Anna, unite masculine and feminine characteristics" (410). By virtue of her testicles, Louise-Julia-Anna is "a man," he admits, but this fact does not detract from her self-identification as a woman, which

Dr. Hallopeau honors, although without using the feminine pronoun. Instead, Hallopeau relies on the clinical periphrasis "the subject" (*le sujet*), which is masculine in French, to describe Louise-Julia-Anna, making what he says about her difficult to translate grammatically. In the original, Hallopeau's circuitous diction enables him to avoid committing to either "he" or "she," so his description reads as slightly more gender neutral than any English translation can elegantly render. Hallopeau starts by identifying his patient as "a man," but then enumerates a long list of her feminine qualities that work to unmake that identity:

> Our subject is a man with diverse feminine attributes, they are to such an extent that he [*il, le sujet*] was recorded on the birth registry as a girl, that [the subject] has always considered [the subject's self] to be a woman, that [the subject's] existence is exclusively feminine, that [the subject] is currently residing at Saint-Louis Hospital in our women's ward and we would not know how, without creating real difficulties, to transfer [the subject] into the men's ward. (410)

Louise-Julia-Anna must have ignored Guermonprez's instructions entirely, because according to Hallopeau, she convinced a "very distinguished Belgian surgeon" to remove one of her testicles the very same year she saw Guermonprez, in 1892. Hallopeau explains that Louise-Julia-Anna is now hoping that the other would be removed as well: "currently, the subject is asking to have the other testicle removed because it gets in the way of sexual relations" (411). Unlike Guermonprez, who alleged that his patient was utterly unable to mimic any feminine qualities and made an unconvincing woman, Hallopeau describes an individual who identifies as a woman and lives as one, and one who experiences desires and emotions shared by many other women of the time: "The subject has for several years been a brewery girl, we have witnessed, on several occasions, gestures of modesty, [the subject] has nevertheless had numerous sexual relations, but only with men; the assumption that [the subject] could have other kinds seems to offend [the subject] deeply" (411). Hallopeau describes Louise-Julia-Anna's "feminine looks" (*allures féminines*) and "identity," so perhaps it was because she passed as a woman that he is not visibly bothered by her attraction to men (410). Both for Hallopeau and Guermonprez, part of "acting like a woman" meant being attracted to men, partially because the distinction between sex and gender had not yet been made, and partially because, in heteronormative nineteenth-century France, sex determined sexuality. One wonders then, was Hallopeau less judgmental toward Louise-Julia-Anna because she was raised as a woman and identified as one, and so, her attraction to men was, in that sense, heterosexual? (It was clearly Louise-Julia-Anna's gonadal "homosexuality" that had so incensed Guermonprez.) I want to be careful not to imbue Hallopeau's comments with transhistoric significance, and it is important to point out that the modern concept of "gender identity" is anachronistic in nineteenth-century France, yet part of what Hallopeau's narrative reveals is that he is more attentive to Louise-Julia-Anna's desires and life lived as a woman than is Guermonprez. Hallopeau reluctantly describes his patient as a "a male pseudo-hermaphrodite," but he highlights the insufficiency of this term to describe Louise-Julia-Anna as a mixed-sex individual: "There is no doubt that this is a question of what one would call a male pseudo-hermaphrodite. This denomination leaves something to desire in the sense that it does not sufficiently indicate that the patient is a *mixed being* presenting, at the same time as the male sex, true female attributes" (412). In the end, Hallopeau prefers to call Louise-Julia-Anna an "androgyne," and recommends this term to the larger scientific community (412). Hallopeau recommends retaining the term "hermaphrodite" only for individuals "who really unite the two sexes," while determining that "androgyne" and "gynandre" will better describe mixed-sex subjects like Louise-Julia-Anna than male and female uses of "pseudo-hermaphrodite" (411).

Whereas Guermonprez went out of his way to describe Louise-Julia-Anna as a deceptive person whose true identity only an expert like himself could determine, Hallopeau sees a person who passes as a woman and whose identity is feminine, causing him to call into question the gonadal definition of sex by proposing new terminology. Hallopeau refrains from comment on Louise-Julia-Anna's sexual practices or lifestyle. The stark contrast of his writing against that of Guermonprez demonstrates just how subjective the scientific narrative could be. It also reveals the limitations of medical power, for try as Guermonprez might to scare Louise-Julia-Anna into living his way, she could always seek another medical opinion – and another, and still another – until she found one that would meet her needs.

And, that is *exactly* what Louise-Julia-Anna did. It seems that Louise-Julia-Anna was willing to travel some distance in her surgical quest, because two years after visiting Hallopeau in Paris, the now 28-year-old journeyed further south to consult Dr. Jablonsky, who presented her case in 1897 to the Society of Medical Sciences in Poitiers, some 550 kilometers southwest of Lille where she had first seen Guermonprez.[56] From Jablonsky, we learn that Louise-Julia-Anna was born in Fort-Mardyck (now the commune of Dunkirk), just 16 kilometers from the Belgian boarder. She was registered and raised as a girl. At the age of eight, a hernia had formed in her groin, and as a teenager, she started developing the facial hair that was remarked upon by both earlier doctors.

Unlike Guermonprez, and even Hallopeau, who had identified Louise-Julia-Anna's "testicle," Jablonsky had doubts, and not once did he suggest that Louise-Julia-Anna was a "man." Instead, Jablonsky thought Louise-Julia-Anna was either a "true" or an "apparent hermaphrodite," and he described much of her anatomy as feminine. Jablonsky notes a 3-centimeter "penis, or rather a clitoris," and a hernia that, four years prior, had become strangulated and necessitated surgery in Brussels. For the first time, in Jablonsky's account, the excised organ has metamorphized into an "ovary," which was confirmed as such during the operation, he avers (1898, 125). All three of the doctors who wrote up Louise-Julia-Anna's case reference multiple emergency medical interventions, and excruciating pain caused by recurring strangulations of the gonads that Louise-Julia-Anna had been attempting to have removed for years. Perhaps Louise-Julia-Anna realized that telling doctors about the excised "testicle" wasn't furthering her goal of having the other one removed, and so she told the story differently this time. Or maybe Jablonsky just got it wrong. Either way, for Jablonsky, who titles his presentation "Note on a case of hermaphrodism," the mere fact of possessing one ovary wouldn't necessarily mean that Louise-Julia-Anna was not *really* a "hermaphrodite," because "among certain hermaphrodites, from the category that has been called lateral hermaphrodism, it is possible to have male organs on one side and female on the other side" (125). Ultimately, Jablonsky expresses some doubt about whether the round mass he found in the right side of her "well-conformed labia majora" was truly a testicle. "One could take it at first for a testicle," he writes, but apparently Jablonsky was not sure owing to the "ovary" which had been earlier identified surgically on the opposite side. Dr. Raoul Blondel later uses Louise-Julia-Anna's case as evidence of the difficulty of distinguishing gonadal tissue, critiquing Jablonsky: "even at autopsy, the organs in hand, errors have been made by the best observers. Only microscopic study of the organ is question can reveal its true nature; such was the case for Polaillon, who took an ovary for a testicle, and that of Jablonsky who took a testicle for an ovary" (1899, 77).

Jablonsky does not comment on whether he or another member of the Society of Medical Sciences of Poitiers would perform the desired operation. Castration was a prisonable offense at the time, so if they did intend to operate, not publicizing that information would have been wisest. In three case studies, three different experts determined three divergent sexes for Louise-Julia-Anna, and not one of them lined up with her self-identification as a woman. But that was the one that mattered most.

Louise-Julia-Anna's belief that she was a woman was a source of relentless resilience that led her from doctor to doctor. She refused to take "no" for an answer.

Does "True Hermaphrodism" Exist?

The same year that Jablonsky reversed Guermonprez's diagnosis and claimed Louise-Julia-Anna was a "hermaphrodite," Dr. Guinard rose to make an important declaration to the Society of Medical Sciences in Lyon: "Hermaphrodism exists, I absolutely believe it, not only because of the facts, but also because there is nothing irrational about it" (1898, 180). Guinard was responding to an earlier discussion sparked by a case of "apparent hermaphrodism," in which his colleague, Dr. Louis Dor had announced, equally emphatically: "There is no real case of hermaphrodism in the literature" (ibid., 179). Guinard went on to list fifteen case studies in man and beast confirming his argument, and concluded with a long digression explaining, moreover, how the origins of hermaphrodism could be explained logically given known "facts" of early development in embryology.

Remarkable in several regards, Dr. Guinard's stand on the existence of hermaphrodism bears remembering. First of all, it takes place in 1898, situating it well into the putative "Age of the Gonads" which, according to now conventional wisdom, should have precluded its existence.[57] At a time when other doctors busied themselves by dismissing earlier case studies of hermaphrodism on the basis of insufficient thoroughness or absent histology, we suddenly find Guinard defending the scientific honor of his colleagues and predecessors in no uncertain terms: "It seems quite difficult to believe that all of these authors were wrong and took something for a testicle or an ovary that was not one" (182). Secondly, Guinard's manifesto betrays defensive undertones which at last become comprehensible when he admits having personally discovered cases of hermaphrodism, including one in a goat, that had been published three years prior. Even though Guinard regrets not having preserved his specimen "with jealous care," he asserts: "I am absolutely sure of what I saw" (182). Here again we find Guermonprez's "take my word for it" rhetoric. Does Guinard fear that Dor's claim for the inexistence of hermaphrodism will void his earlier contribution to the field?

Guinard was not the only doctor with a vested interest – however petty – in the definition of hermaphrodism.[58] In 1891, Dr. Jouin made a similar appeal by calling on the Society of Gynecology to dismiss a growing consensus that "true hermaphrodism" existed only in non-human animals, while the term "pseudo-hermaphrodism" more accurately described ambiguous sex in human beings. Like Guinard, Jouin takes it upon himself to defend earlier cases as "facts," "absolutely conclusive, by the way, already recorded in Professor Le Fort's dissertation (Paris 1863), and that seem to me not to afford the room for the slightest doubt" (1891, 259).

The real target of Jouin's attack was Dr. Samuel Pozzi, a rising medical star and playboy of the Third Republic.[59] Pozzi became something of a darling of the Belle Époque, with close ties to key literary figures. He was a personal friend of the Prousts, and Marcel Proust writes adoringly of him.[60] You may recognize Pozzi from his famous 1881 portrait capturing the doctor's charismatic flair for drama, by the American artist John Singer Sargent, or from Julian Barnes's recent biography on the subject.[61] "Dr. Pozzi at Home" depicts the surgeon bedecked in a crimson dressing gown recalling ecclesiastical majesty of yore, as he gazes off into the distance in front of lavish red curtains, one foot pointed in a stylish gold slipper, mustaches bristling. Sarah Bernhardt, one of Pozzi's numerous lovers and a life-long friend, addressed him as "Doctor God." In addition to being a consummate ladies' man (earning him the alternate epitaph of "doctor love"), poet, amateur hypnotist, and numismatist, Pozzi's steely reputation as a surgeon was assured by the likely apocryphal description of his death. After being gunned down in 1918 by a former patient who believed that a surgery Pozzi had performed on him had caused impotence, Pozzi supposedly refused anesthesia and directed most of the vain operation intended to save him.[62] Dr. Jouin claimed that Pozzi had swayed the Society of Surgery to resolve that true hermaphrodism did not exist in humans, on June 8, 1881, the very same year as his portrait by Sargent.[63] Jouin hoped that the Society of Gynecology would overturn this decision: "But this judgment does not seem without appeal, and perhaps it is the Society of Gynecology's responsibility to revise it after having learned the facts" (1891, 259). After listing a number of "irrefutable facts" and explaining the embryological origins of hermaphrodism in the manner of Guinard, Jouin concludes his oration with a call to action:

> We must reject therefore the overly radical parts of the Society of Surgery's theory, and admit that anatomical hermaphrodism truly exists, that male and female pseudo-hermaphrodism are infinitely more common than true hermaphrodism, but that in reality these types of monstrosity cause sterility, if not impotence, and that true hermaphrodites and pseudo-hermaphrodites are, physiologically, almost all neuter beings. (Ibid., 266)

Although both Jouin and Guinard define true hermaphrodism narrowly, as a combination of male and female internal organs (importantly, not just gonads), they believe hermaphrodism is possible, and that its existence displaces the possibility of "true sex" in rare cases.[64] Even though Jouin opens his article with a gonadal definition of hermaphrodism, the body of his article later defines "transverse hermaphrodism" as the possession of internal male reproductive organs and external female genitalia, and vice versa, so that simply having testicles would not eliminate the "true" epithet.[65] Jouin implores "it seems that if we refuse to these unfortunate people the sex which they outwardly resemble, it can only be to classify them as true hermaphrodites."[66] Despite his previous definition then, in the end, Jouin actually advocates counting some individuals as "true hermaphrodites" who, under the gonadal definition, would have been classified as "pseudo-hermaphrodites."

Notwithstanding Jouin's assertion, if one takes a closer look at the infamous 1881 meeting of the Society of Surgery, many doctors do *not* agree with Pozzi about the categorical elimination of "hermaphrodism," and they proffer conflicting ideas about how best to determine sex. Their "theory" is actually the result of heated debate sparked by Dr. Magitot's 1881 presentation of a "hermaphrodite," offering surprisingly little agreement, and certainly not any kind of unanimous position.[67] Before the paper even begins, Magitot's title alerts us to the contested definition of hermaphrodism with the addition of a footnote. Though the title, "A New Case of Hermaphrodism" leads the reader to believe that the patient, Ernestine G..., is "a hermaphrodite," a footnote identifies this term as problematic from the outset. The note reads: "It is only in order to conform to tradition that we designate this new case under the name of hermaphrodism. We shall see, in effect, through the reservations that we formulate that the interpretation of this kind of facts should, according to us, be entirely modified."[68] As if the title/footnote combination were not confusing enough, the paper itself also sends mixed messages. Initially, Magitot defines Ernestine G. as "a true hermaphrodite, following Geoffroy Saint-Hilaire's classification, and falling into the class of *imperfect bisexual hermaphrodites*" (447). However, a few lines later, Magitot reverses his opinion, stating:

> this individual is therefore not likely a hermaphrodite at all, and it is appropriate to add that none of the analogous facts that authors describe justify this title [...] One could thus go further to say that there perhaps does not exist in science a single rigorously verified case of true hermaphrodism in man. (445, 448)

Both this inconsistent reversal and the footnoted title smack of uneasy compromise.

Indeed, Magitot's discussion section reveals that his presentation sparked a lively debate producing little consensus. Pozzi opens by denying the existence of hermaphrodism and declaring the patient a male with hypospadias, identifiable by his "evident testicles": "There cannot be a case of true hermaphrodism in this patient. One recognizes the characteristics of complete hypospadias on his body. [. . .] The subject has two evident testicles, even though they are atrophied" (448).[69] Elsewhere, Pozzi insists on histology in order to prove the presence of testicular tissue, but here demonstrates inexplicable certainty based on oral testimony and a single picture, in the absence of either a firsthand examination or microscopic evidence. Perhaps because of these lacunae, M. Tillaux is unswayed by Pozzi's testimony, and cites the patient's past menstruation as evidence of internal "female" organs such as ovaries and a uterus:

> The sex determination of the patient who was presented to us does not seem as simple as several of our colleagues believe. The menses, appearing three times at puberty, create doubts for me. Are we not in the presence of a true hermaphrodite possessing testicles and perhaps also, at the same time, a uterus and ovaries? Cases of true hermaphrodism exist, after all, such that one cannot deny a priori the bisexual nature of this individual. (450)

Pozzi then retorts that apparent menstruation offers no proof of the existence of ovaries, and casts further doubt on historical case studies of hermaphrodism.[70] Forgetting that a moment earlier he had identified testicles without the aid of a microscope, Pozzi quips: "The sphere of true hermaphrodism becomes smaller and smaller. The old autopsies have lost credibility now that we know that testicles can remain inside the abdomen [. . .]. Moreover, these findings were not corroborated by microscopic examination" (450). Following another heated exchange, Dr. Tillaux persistently refuses to give in to Pozzi's interpretation, after which Dr. See seems to second Dr. Tillaux by offering evidence to suggest that hermaphrodism exists after all.[71] Dr. Farabeuf also endorses Tillaux's dissention with the final word of the article:

> That which determines sex is the organ producing the spermatozoa or ova. In the absence of an autopsy which could alone determine the existence of ovaries, the menses, even if incomplete, have a certain worth, and I do not see why they would not prove that the subject possesses rudimentary female sexual organs, such as an imperfect uterus, or adnexa of these organs, a vagina or a part of a vagina. (452)

In practical terms, Farabeuf denies the possibility of hermaphrodism, since the only true hermaphrodite would be deceased and available for autopsy, but on a theoretical level, he disagrees with Pozzi by admitting its possibility. Amazingly, Farabeuf manages to do all this while both reinforcing and subverting the gonadal definition. Farabeuf defines sex as the existence of testicles or ovaries, but he also weighs the value of "incomplete menstruation" in his calculus. Moreover, he defines sex as emanating from the organs that "produce sperm and eggs," even though microscopic evidence had demonstrated that Ernestine G.'s "testicles" did not produce sperm.

The article itself offers additional resistance to the one-body-one-sex rule. In brazen disregard for the French Civil Code, which mandates that each child be registered as either male or female within three days of birth, M. Lannelongue recounts an anecdote in which he refused to determine the sex of a child for several months, until clearer evidence emerged (449). While most of Ernestine G.'s secondary sexual characteristics are qualified by the author as either "male" or "female," s/he presents a blending of these characteristics so that in the end, the assigned "masculine sex" fails to recover the previously defined "female characteristics." In this way, Ernestine G. resembles Louise-Julia-Anna, who believed herself to be a woman and dressed accordingly. For example: "The general shape of the body, the muscle masses are those of a man. The larynx, however, is not salient and the voice is manifestly feminine" (445). Magitot further qualifies Ernestine's "three menstrual periods, the development of the breasts, and the timbre of the voice" as "feminine attributes," but the existence of other apparently sexless features undermines any one "true sex" (447). Magitot describes Ernestine's face as being entirely androgynous: "the face has no determining sexual characteristics" (440). Ernestine's sexual desires, sometimes considered in the medical calculus of sex (as they were by Hallopeau above), provided no indication of heteronormative "true sex" since they were bisexual (445).

The disagreement surrounding Ernestine G.'s case is important because it shows that even in an instance held as an overwhelming consensus that hermaphrodism did *not* exist, significant resistance to this thesis endured. Members of the Society of Surgery remain stubbornly divided about how best to assign sex, and several overtly challenged the gonadal definition.

Even more shocking is that similar stands for the existence of hermaphrodism are not uncommon in the nineteenth-century case record and often appear in well-cited works, like that of Charles Debierre in 1891. They occur frequently enough in the French medical record that doctors Faucher and Bourdin would write in 1899 that "most authors" believe that hermaphrodism exists.[72] Émile Laurent's treatise from 1894 apparently chooses to disregard the entire debate about true hermaphrodism since, he writes, "There exists in man evident cases of true hermaphrodism; and no one would think now to call this fact into question" (149–50). While Laurent's statement is certainly hyperbolic, no shortage of theses, treatises, case studies, and textbooks fervently maintain the existence of hermaphrodism, and a number of articles even include "true hermaphrodism" in their titles.[73] Léon Le Fort's dissertation of 1863, for example, supports the "true hermaphrodism" thesis. Huzé de l'Aulnoit classifies his patient as a "neuter hermaphrodite" (1861, 181). Gillette's 1874 case does not determine the sex of his patient in any certain terms, describing him/her as a case of "hermaphrodism with a male appearance." In Laugier and Tardieu's definition for "hermaphrodism" in the *Nouveau dictionnaire de médecine et de chirurgie pratiques* (1873), the authors claim that while hermaphrodism exists in the field of physiology, it does not exist in the medico-legal field. On the contrary, Tourdes and Hermann's entries for "hermaphrodism" (in teratology and in legal medicine) in the *Dictionnaire encyclopédique des sciences médicales* allege that "neuter hermaphrodism" exists in teratology, and in the legal field, "true hermaphrodism" also exists (1899, 636). The entry for "hermaphrodism" in the *Dictionnaire usuel des sciences médicales* from 1885 makes no mention of "pseudo-hermaphrodism," for example, but does refer to "true hermaphrodism."[74]

Revising the Timeline of "True Hermaphrodism"

Because existing histories of hermaphrodism in nineteenth-century France do not cover the entire length of the century, the timeline is currently incomplete.[75] We have seen that according to Foucault, already by the turn of the nineteenth century, hermaphrodism was thought to be impossible. Diderot's *Encyclopédie* had emphatically rejected the possibility of true hermaphrodism in the eighteenth century, and although he does not cite them, many cases would support Foucault's claim.[76] For example, J. L. Moreau's article, "Quelques considérations sur l'hermaphrodisme" (1796–97, 243), and Itard de Riez, who wrote: "We are now convinced that all these so-called hermaphrodites are only beings whose sexual organs came out from nature's hands disfigured or incomplete" (1798–99, 298). As the title of Jean Michel Moreau's richly engraved work of 1773, *Boy and Girl Hermaphrodites Seen and Drawn from Life by One of the Most Celebrated Artists and Engravers with Utmost Care for the Usefulness of the Studious*, suggests, careful study had revealed the "true sex" of the famous eighteenth-century hermaphrodites designated as "boy and girl" hermaphrodites. Marie Augé, born in Paris in 1755, was without testicles and so classed as female (see Figure 1.1). Raised as a boy, Louis Hainault, drawn in 1752, was said to have both a complete female and male reproductive

FILLE HERMAPHRODITE,
Vu & dessinée d'après Nature, pour l'utilité des Studieux.

Figure 1.1 Marie Augé, from Jean Moreau, *Garçon et fille hermaphrodites vus et dessinés d'après nature par un des plus célèbres artistes et gravés avec tout le soin possible pour l'utilité des studieux* (1773). Courtesy of the Wellcome Collection.

system, yet is nevertheless identified as a "boy hermaphrodite" in the text (see Figure 1.2). Claude Champeaux's 1765 treatise concludes by suggesting that "no true hermaphrodite ever existed; [. . .] one should only see as a slight of nature the deformities that gave credence to such fables" (55). Similar statements characterize the first decades of the nineteenth century. In 1817, Dr. Balthasar-Anthelme Richerand's popular *Nouveaux éléments de physiologie* declares "hermaphrodism, or the union of both sexes in the same individual is impossible in man and in the great family of red-blooded animals. Publications cite no true case" (395).[77]

Dreger's pathbreaking history of hermaphrodism in France and Great Britain spans from 1868 to 1915, with the "Age of the Gonads" extending roughly from 1870 to 1915.[78] If one examines, however, the entire nineteenth century, there are at least two reasons why the "Age of the Gonads" may be a somewhat misleading moniker, at least in France. Firstly, Dreger posits this period as one in which doctors increasingly agreed that gonads should constitute the sole marker of sex. In addition to both herself and Mak, who have shown that in practice, the gonadal rule often remained unenforced, I have shown that, in France at least, direct efforts to subvert its authority characterized the entire period, and even the consensus to determine sex gonadally was not reached by all groups of doctors, or increasingly agreed upon in a linear, or unilateral way. Secondly, "the Age of the Gonads" implies that there was only one. But, if one attempts to describe the French prehistory of intersex throughout the length of the entire nineteenth century, it becomes immediately evident that there exists no direct progression toward "true gonadal sex." Instead, French case studies seem to reflect more of an uneven, and even cyclical pattern.

Already, in 1815, the influential German anatomist Johann Freidrich Meckel can be credited with what is considered the hallmark of the "Age of the Gonads." That is, Meckel distinguished between "true," glandular hermaphrodism and "pseudo-hermaphrodism," which constituted an apparent disjunction between gonadal sex and other secondary sexual characteristics.[79] Simultaneously, in France, Pierre-Auguste Béclard proposed a similar definition. In his famous 1815 presentation of Marie-Madeleine Lefort, Béclard argued that ovaries and testicles represented the quintessence of femininity and masculinity:

> In the human species, the ovaries, uterus, and vagina essentially characterize the female sex; just as the testicles, the spermatic testicles, and the penis constitute the essential nature of the male. But these sexual organs, all useful for reproduction, do not all have the same importance in the distinction of the sexes. The ovaries and the testes, organs that secrete ova and sperm, occupy the first rank.[80]

GARÇON HERMAPHRODITE .
Vu et Dessinée d'apres Nature pour l'utilité des Studieux.

Figure 1.2 Louis Hainault (1752), from Jean Moreau, *Garçon et fille hermaphrodites* […] (1773). Courtesy of the Wellcome Collection.

Also in 1815, Dr. Worbe stakes the claim of his (deceased) patient's masculinity upon the testicles discovered during his autopsy.[81] In life, legal and medical confrontations had resulted in iterative identity changes for Worbe's patient, known successively as Marie-Jeanne, Marie-Pierrot, and finally Denis-Jacques. Neither is histology an absolutely new innovation linked to the "Age of the Gonads." In his 1939 treatise, *Hermaphrodites and Surgery*, Louis Ombrédanne writes that as early as 1830, histology had become the dominant method for determining "true sex": "It is in 1830 that [Johannes] Müller endeavored to highlight histological findings which, from then on, take the value of an absolute test in the observations of the time" (29).[82] In an 1837 French translation of Burdach's physiology treatise, the German author defines hermaphrodism as the presence of both an ovary and a testicle (272).

But in France, things began to change when Isidore Geoffroy Saint-Hilaire, son of the renowned anatomist, Étienne Geoffroy Saint-Hilaire (to whom Balzac's *Le Père Goriot* is dedicated), defined hermaphrodism broadly as "the coexistence in the same individual of both sexes or of some of their characteristics."[83] Known as the "Father of teratology," the younger Geoffroy Saint-Hilaire coined the term itself in the 1830s.[84] While cases from the late eighteenth and early nineteenth centuries generally suggested that true hermaphrodism did not exist (consistent with Dreger's findings at the fin de siècle), Geoffroy Saint-Hilaire's work marks a major shift in medical consensus, inklings of which can be found in several cases leading up to the publication of his famous multi-volume treatise on teratology. Meckel's anatomy treatise, which had been translated into French in 1825, suggested that just because instances of "absolute" hermaphrodism in humans had not yet been recorded, that was not a reason to discount the theoretical possibility of their existence (684). Then, in 1833, Dr. Bouillaud made a formal stand for the existence of "true hermaphrodism," and, as we shall see, the first call to revise the Civil Code to add a "third sex."[85] Geoffroy Saint-Hilaire's taxonomy was presented to the Académie des sciences the same year as Bouillaud's treatise in 1833, and garnered critical acclaim when it appeared in his influential treatise on monstrosity (1832–37).[86] From that point on to the end of the century, Geoffroy Saint-Hilaire's work would become the most cited taxonomy in France.[87]

Geoffroy Saint-Hilaire's work showed that the human reproductive system developed along natural pathways from organs that started out as intersex. He therefore naturalized hermaphrodism by postulating its origin as various types of "arrested" or "excess" growth in the typical development of the male and female reproductive systems. Geoffroy Saint-Hilaire separated hermaphrodism into two classes and seven orders, which he determined by imagining a grid that cut the body into six segments.[88] At its core, Geoffroy Saint-Hilaire's taxonomy relied less on the presence or absence of a given organ than on the overall tally of "male," "female," and "neuter" parts in each of the six segments. For example, the first two orders of hermaphrodism without excess (the name for the first class) are "masculine hermaphrodism" and "feminine hermaphrodism," which consist of an "essentially" male or female "sexual system" (2: 36). Geoffroy Saint-Hilaire does not equate the concept of "essentially male" or "essentially female" reproductive systems with essential parts or gonadal tissue. His chart even includes a description of "perfect hermaphrodism," which would unite a "complete female and male sexual system," although he admits that this category is an unrealized theoretical placeholder. Geoffroy Saint-Hilaire, does, however, provide for "neuter hermaphrodism" when the reproductive organs appear intermediate between the two sexes, and the individual belongs "really to no sex at all" (ibid.). He also accounts for "mixed hermaphrodism," which is described as "a partly male and partly female reproductive system" (ibid.). Moreover, the term "pseudo-hermaphrodite," introduced in the nineteenth century by Meckel, and again ubiquitous by the time Pozzi began writing on hermaphrodism, does not figure in his taxonomy.[89]

For Geoffroy Saint-Hilaire, it was possible for an individual to exist without a binary sex, or to present with a mixed sex such that it was impossible to ascribe a sex to certain types of "hermaphrodites." Widely influential in its own time, Geoffroy Saint-Hilaire's work is important as a testament to the overlooked fact that the nineteenth century does not form a homogeneous block of time in which "true sex" always won out over doubtful sex. Of "neuter hermaphrodites" Geoffroy Saint-Hilaire wrote:

> The hermaphrodism that following Paré's example I called *neuter* merits [. . .] this name as much legally as from a physiological point of view: how can one relate a male or female-type reproductive system that only has analogous relationships to the still-undecided sexual type of the early embryo? The hermaphrodite mixed by superposition is in the same situation: characterized by the discordant mix in equal number of a certain amount of male and female parts, it is placed precisely in the middle of the interval that separates the two sexes, without one being able to find a single reason to bring it closer to one or the other. (1832–37, 3: 576)[90]

Geoffroy Saint-Hilaire did not take "true sex" as a given in all cases. He did not think all, or even most, hermaphrodites were pseudo-hermaphrodites, and even though he could see that self-impregnation in humans was nonsense, he identified classes such as "bisexual," "mixed," and "neuter" hermaphrodism which precluded the idea of binary sex by their very definitions.

In Dreger's discussion of Geoffroy Saint-Hilaire's classification system, she rightly stresses that he is not preoccupied with "true gonadal sex" and that pseudo-hermaphrodism does not figure in his taxonomy; but because the period covered by her book prevents her from contrasting Geoffroy Saint-Hilaire's taxonomy with that of its predecessors, the reader cannot know that Meckel in Germany and Béclard in France, following on the heels of the Enlightenment philosophers who had revealed true hermaphrodism to be mere myth, had privileged a more rigid, gonadal definition of sex only a few years before (144–45). This is no fault of Dreger's – her book focuses on the period between 1868 and 1915 in both France and England – but because she uses Geoffroy Saint-Hilaire's "early classification system" as a point of contrast to the "Age of the Gonads," some readers have incorrectly imagined that as the nineteenth century progressed, the definition of hermaphrodism, at first broad under Geoffroy Saint-Hilaire, became increasingly restricted until, with the "Age of the Gonads," "hermaphrodites" became ostensibly extinct.[91]

Instead, I believe that the persistent resistance to "true gonadal sex" throughout the century owes its enduring presence, at least in part, to the longstanding influence of Geoffroy Saint-Hilaire's definition and taxonomy of hermaphrodism. In 1875, for example, the *Nouveau dictionnaire de médecine et de chirurgie pratiques* still makes use of his classification system, and so does not differentiate sex based on gonads alone. Rather, the author, Dr. Maurice Laugier, defines hermaphrodism in teratology, following Geoffroy Saint-Hilaire, as "the state of those who, having the appearance of one sex, present some characteristics of the other" (1873, 490). Throughout the nineteenth century and well into the twentieth, fellow scientists and doctors not only hail Geoffroy Saint-Hilaire as "the father of teratology" with steady frequency; they cite his cases, terminology, definitions, and on occasion even his assertions about the relative frequency of hermaphrodism.[92] In 1886, Auguste Lutaud recommends that forensics experts follow Geoffroy Saint-Hilaire's definition and classification system of hermaphrodism (9–10). The very same year that Pozzi would proffer his own taxonomy of hermaphrodism, alleging that true hermaphrodism did not exist, Tuffier and Lapointe published an article deeming Geoffroy Saint-Hilaire's definition "the best" that contemporary science had to offer (1911, 209). Recall also that in the infamous 1881 meeting of the Society of Surgery, the proponents of "true hermaphrodism" arguing *against* Pozzi cited Geoffroy Saint-Hilaire's definition. As late as 1920, Paul Lahaye's thesis still calls Geoffroy Saint-Hilaire's definition of hermaphrodism, now nearly a century old, "the best" science had to offer (12).

The question of "true sex" always seems to circle back to Herculine Barbin. When Laqueur stated that "genuine sexual ambiguity" and "neutrality" was "nonsense" by the nineteenth century, he quoted Tardieu's now familiar treatise on identity (in which he first presented Barbin's memoirs) as evidence. Here, Tardieu writes that the question of sex is biological and a "pure question of fact that can and ought to be resolved by the anatomical and psychological examination of the person in question."[93] But we have seen from the case record that Tardieu was not painting the full picture. Real ambiguity and neutrality did exist in the nineteenth century because bodies that challenged the confines of the two-sex model existed then just as they exist now, and however imaginative and unempirical nineteenth-century medicine (and Tardieu) was, there were still many doctors who realized that assigning sex in doubtful cases was at best an approximation, and at worst, a gross misrepresentation with catastrophic consequences. Frequently, the "true sex" of a patient was not discovered at all, or was reversed by later diagnoses, and a number of authors rejected the gonadal definition of sex in favor of a less rigid definition of hermaphrodism following Geoffroy Saint-Hilaire, which would allow for sex outside of the binary.[94]

A more interesting question asks why Tardieu was bound and determined to make sex a soluble question of fact. I investigate this question in greater detail in Chapter 2, but for now, suffice it to say that Laqueur rightly identified Tardieu as "the leading French forensic physician."[95] As such, Tardieu's professional expertise resided in his ability to make clear, convincing determinations that the courts could use to uphold the Code. And since the Civil Code admitted only two sexes, Tardieu had little incentive to fill his medico-legal opus with a subtler (and more ambiguous) account of determining sex.

My research shows that in cases of "hermaphrodism," rather than sex being "absolutely there in and throughout the body," "true sex" was only imperfectly determined by doctors who often acknowledged, not without frustration, that their techniques for assigning sex failed to capture the complexity of their patients and/or to convince their colleagues that the eventual determination was the correct one. No nineteenth-century method for ascertaining the presence of ovaries or testicles was foolproof. Even Guermonprez's meticulous examination was contested, and, despite Pozzi's faith in histology, it did not always produce consistent results.[96] Even if their articles were initially accepted, the peculiar nineteenth-century habit of resuscitating decades-old cases in order to refute them meant that no publication was ever really safe.[97] In this way, the contested thesis of "gonadal sex" might be read against itself as evidence of a sinking suspicion that "true sex" could not easily be mapped out and pinpointed on a body – that, in fact, it might not exist at all. Maybe, for some, "true sex" was not naturally binary.

With the advent of "new" social identities like "feminist" and "homosexual" in the last decades of the nineteenth century, historians have documented the contemporaneous medical and scientific obsession with creating new natural laws intended to circumscribe the dangers posed by unruly bodies doing unruly things. What if instead of interpreting "gonadal sex" as proof of the medical belief in "true sex," we read it instead as a kind of last-ditch attempt to link sex to some bodily truth – however arbitrary, however illogical? Such efforts might have been orchestrated as part of some larger social or political agenda, but also may have cherished less grandiose intentions. Perhaps some doctors rallied to a definition that, if agreed upon, might finally allow their publications to withstand the test of time. Or perhaps a surgeon like Pozzi simply realized that basing sex assignment on gonadal tissue would give him the professional edge over his clinician colleagues. (Recall that Jouin called on the Society of Gynecology to reject the Society of Surgery's "resolution" against hermaphrodism.[98]) Perhaps the rivalry was also regional.[99] Geoffroy Saint-Hilaire had popularized a broad definition of hermaphrodism, which Dr. Pozzi contested vociferously in the 1880s, marking a Parisian shift. Several of the stands for "true hermaphrodism" came from outside of the capital. Provincial doctors may have been pushing back against Parisian hegemony as flashy doctors like Pozzi dismissed earlier cases outright. Whatever the case, and certainly a combination of factors was at play, there is enough belief in "true hermaphrodism" throughout the century to confidently state that the gonadal definition proved a very poor fail-safe indeed.

Although many nineteenth-century case studies of hermaphrodism are less novelistic than that of Louise-Julia-Anna, the majority nevertheless include external physical or psychological descriptions that often conflict with gonadal sex, while still more cases show that gonadal sex could not even always be determined or agreed upon. Perpetual bickering about which sex to assign in doubtful cases further highlights the instability of medical sex determinations, while doctors who "rewrite" earlier case studies in order to revise diagnoses are reminiscent of authorial figures. If "true sex" rarely materializes uncontested from their cases, what does emerge is a kind of fictional narrative – one that seeks to explain bodily variations with the accumulation of so-called "facts." More often than not, these "facts" have nothing to do with science (like Guermonprez's insistence that *real women* know how to dress). Instead, they merely reflect cultural beliefs about the differences between men and women in an endless loop of circular logic.

As gatekeepers of knowledge, doctors, like novelists, interpret their observations in order to render them intelligible to readers, but these interpretations come to us in the form of stories, stories that are tied to a historical moment whose passage signals their instability, and whose empirical nature is already suspect from their incessant literary borrowings and hybrid genres.

CHAPTER 2

Outlaws from Birth
"Doubtful Sex" and the Civil Code

In 1881, the sensational French court case of a woman wed to an alleged "hermaphrodite" found its way into *The New York Times*. Under the piquant title "Queer French Lawsuits," the article related the woes of Mademoiselle Mercedes Martínez de Campos, a wealthy 22-year-old who had entered into marriage with the slightly younger and considerably less well-off Count San Antonio. "No one can reasonably blame" Mademoiselle de Campos's petition for annulment, the author reasons, since "she believed and hoped to marry a person of a different sex than her own."[1] Yet, the sexual identity of the newlyweds and the exact grounds for annulment remained in doubt for the *Times* author, who nevertheless concluded with excitement: "decidedly we are in the presence of a mystery!"

As the case broke, the French legal periodical *La Gazette des tribunaux* covered every detail and twist of plot in three separate installments between July and December.[2] Here, it became clear that the request for annulment centered on a claim of the husband's "sexual indeterminism."[3] With Balzacian verve, Campos's lawyer cast the young bride as an innocent target of treacherous deceit and a hapless victim of her own extreme wealth. Mademoiselle de Campos represented "one of the oldest Spanish families," and, in addition to being well educated, was also "very pretty, with the piquant of those exotic beauties who evoke hot climates" (Dec. 21, 1251). Moreover, the Spanish beauty boasted a staggering dowry worth 5 million francs, which, her lawyer claimed, incited "much covetousness, even among the ranks of the greatest Spanish nobility" (ibid.). So much so that the duc de la Torre, the bridegroom's father, had allegedly hatched a double marriage plot that would unite his son to Mercedes and his daughter to Mercedes's brother. Even with a title, his young son was not nearly as attractive a potential suitor as Campos. "He, on the other hand," claimed Campos's lawyer, "was still only a schoolboy, not yet eighteen, and whose intelligence was no better developed than his body: a child incapable of becoming a man!" (ibid.). Despite her initial repugnance, Mercedes nevertheless eventually consented to wed the impish Count under pressure from her brother, who was smitten with the Count's sister. (He had been led to believe that his happiness hinged on the success of his sister's marriage.) The lawyer-cum-narrator warned: "Such were the preliminaries of this union whose results you shall see; [. . .] the conspiracy hatched against this young girl deprived of her natural support and who was led to the altar as a victim of greed and ambition" (ibid.). With their marriage hastily executed in Paris, Campos "soon noticed that her husband treated her with a frigidness incompatible with the most natural feelings of the naivest affection" (ibid.). After many tears and laments from his bride, the cornered husband eventually admitted that their union would never be complete. A trial separation and a modest bribe of 5,000 francs per month were intended to muffle the scandal. However, when pleas for a formal separation and more money were ignored, an outraged Campos finally sought legal protection.

"Marriage," her lawyer reminds us, can "only be contracted between people of differing sexes" (ibid., 1252). This was, and remained for well over a century until 2013, a condition for marriage in France. Mademoiselle Campos, however, "affirms that her so-called husband is not a man," and her lawyer further described him as "a person whose gender cannot be precisely determined; an incomplete or complex being who was not anticipated by the Civil Code" (ibid.). Mr. Banaston, standing in for the district attorney, was left with an even greater sense of mystery: "What is the Count de San Antonio? Is he a man, a woman, both at once, like those hybrid beings of which mythology speaks and the Louvre possesses a specimen? We do not know. [. . .] It is therefore a mystery that will have to be illuminated" (ibid.).

In order to penetrate the enigma, Mr. Banaston decided that the court should recruit "experts to examine the pathology of her pseudo-husband" (ibid.). Unable to resist insinuating the Count's impotence, Mr. Banaston argued that only such expertise could determine whether "Misses de San Antonio, I was about to say Mademoiselle de San Antonio," was telling the truth (ibid.). But eight days later, the civil court of the Seine determined that the affair lay outside of its jurisdiction since the young couple was not of French nationality (Dec. 28, 1275). This decision abandoned the journalist to fears of unresolved mystery: "shall the mystery that hovers over this singular case whose legal investigation was postponed be revealed one day? As is often the case in situations like these, one presumes that there will be no conclusion" (ibid.).

Even though the annulment trial never went to court (and relatively few similar cases ever did), nineteenth-century France was obsessed with the legal ramifications of intersex.[4] Both medical and legal experts clamored to write on the subject. Entire treatises were dedicated to the implications of birth, adolescence, marriage, death, conscription, and inheritance for a "hermaphrodite."[5] Nearly every medico-legal reference from the time offers a section on "hermaphrodism" or at least addresses the questions raised by "doubtful sex" in chapters on birth and divorce (or legal separation, when divorce was illegal).[6] Jurisconsults emphatically contradicted one another about rules applying to "hermaphrodites," and the case record was inconsistent. Articles appeared in periodicals ranging from the popular press to specialized medical fields in surgery, psychology, gynecology, and even anthropology. Why is it that an issue that affected a relatively small percentage of the population suddenly became a zone of frenzied publication? Certainly, the enduring thrill of mystery had a role to play. But there was also a deep-seated anxiety about what could and should be done about gender "outlaws."

As illustrated in the previous chapter, "hermaphrodism" was becoming increasingly visible due to a skyrocketing number of medical journals, improving technology in surgery and histology, the shift toward large, modernized hospitals and maternity wards, which increased the visibility of all bodily variations, and the creation of new fields such as teratology and gynecology. Professional disputes between experts representing different specializations (for example, surgeons and clinicians) also came to the fore, as we have seen. Moreover, well-documented social change was wreaking havoc on binary gender throughout the long nineteenth century. The Industrial Revolution ushered women out of the home and into the workplace; massive commercial centers allowed for the accumulation of material wealth in the middle class and placed male workers alongside female ones. Disastrous foreign policy led to wars that decimated the male population, and compounding matters was the fact that newly working, educated women were having fewer and fewer children. Sexuality that challenged heteronormative binary sex, such as "inversion," and other precursors to homosexuality, were also increasingly studied (and therefore increasingly visible) in medical literature. Yet, during the same period that the appearance of hermaphrodism and the blurring of sexual and gender boundaries seemed to reach its apex, the French legal code stubbornly denied its very existence.

Since no legal category existed to describe individuals who were neither clearly female nor clearly male, historical intersex people became "outlaws" in the nineteenth century. The rigorous Napoleonic Code required all infants be sexed "male" or "female" and registered formally on the birth certificate within three days of birth. Marriage sanctioned only binary sex. The entire society had been predicated on a belief, now shaken, that both sexes were entitled to distinct rights and responsibilities. Yet the surprising story of "hermaphrodism" and the law is not that authors constantly acknowledged the inability of legal reality to account for natural reality; it is that they actually proposed that the laws be changed. Of course, their motivations were various. Some doctors called for stricter regulations to safeguard the faltering institution of marriage or to bolster oversight of initial sex declarations at birth in order to minimize later legal sex revisions. But there was also a vocal contingent advocating the creation of a third classification of nonbinary citizens to be added to the Civil Code, while still others claimed that "true sex" might be impossible to determine before death for some.[7] To listen to their fervent prose, it becomes clear that what is at stake in their debates is not merely the future of a tiny fragment of the population, but rather, the entire social structure, and who would have the power to change it.

Outlaws from Birth

"God forbid one accuse us of wanting to push things too far," wrote Dr. Charles Vanswygenhoven in 1844, "but the study of hermaphrodism touches the very foundation upon which society rests" (44). As proof, he cited the process by which every French birth must be recorded. Though lengthy, the unruly passage merits citation for its sheer freneticism, which reveals the anxiety of scientific powerlessness in the face of "doubtful" sex:

> But when in doubt, what to do? Guess, or declare that the newborn is whatever sex is apparent at the moment, [...] and not realize one's error until several days later ...? What is to be done now? Share with the civil registrar that doubt surrounds the child's true sex and ask him to wait several days before recording the newborn on the civil registry? But the delay fixed by law is about it expire, and a decision must be made, the registrar is waiting, and science remains undecided. [...] But science! Has it not come further than this? Has it taken a step forward only to have acted hastily, with carelessness? And if so, is it not partially responsible to its citizen for the error of which it is guilty? Will it compensate him for the embarrassment, the suffering, the thousand and one inconveniences that it will have caused? Imagine the limitless tortures that those like Jean-Pierre, Louis Hainault, [...] and so many others had to endure, who, during the same period when law freed man, saw their legal sex changed and were forced to conform, after those struggles against modesty that one feels but does not describe, to other uses, other beliefs, other customs. The horror of these positions can be measured by all the repulsion that one would feel to find oneself in the same situation. (1844, 52)

Vanswygenhoven's visceral response to "the horror" of hermaphrodism illustrates the shortcomings of methods to determine birth sex, and great concern for the enduring effects of such scientific imprecision.

Even in the early part of the century, forensics treatises, articles, and dictionary entries included precepts dictating how to determine sex in difficult cases.[8] But Isidore Geoffroy Saint-Hilaire's widely read work in the 1830s shook the foundations of these step-by-step guides with the claim that even such "golden rules" could not resolve all doubt. In the third volume of his magnum opus, he wrote that authors of such precepts falsely "lead one to believe that applying the rules that they outline will avoid serious difficulty and produce infallible results" (1832–37, 3: 574). According to Geoffroy Saint-Hilaire "this is doubly misleading; I showed it in my history of hermaphrodism, via a discussion of many of these supposedly infallible rules, and I must say it here again, the sex determination of hermaphrodite is nearly always very difficult, and often, it is even absolutely impossible" (ibid., 3: 574–75). Over the course of the century, many doctors would echo him. In 1880, Trélat warned his readers: "You may be called upon to pronounce judgment for forensic determinations of an individual's sex; the difficulties that you will encounter may be very great; you cannot even rely on authors' scientific authority, for their opinions are divided" (59).

Vanswygenhoven's scandalous scenario may sound improbable, but the medical record is replete with cases in which an infant's sex could not be determined at birth or within the following allotment of three days.[9] Still more cases exist in which a patient's sex was only discovered at adolescence, or during an unrelated medical examination later in life.[10] In 1886 alone, Paul Brouardel conducted six consultations in which he determined that an individual had been sexed incorrectly.[11] Dr. Franz Ludwig Neugebauer's compendium of 1,261 cases of hermaphrodism identified more than 500 instances in which an individual had been ascribed the wrong sex.[12]

Chance played too great a role in discovery, worried Pierre Garnier in 1883: "The majority of these cases were only discovered accidentally after death, moreover by the second chance that there was an autopsy, which is enough to surmise that a much larger number of them pass by undetected" (498). With his typical deprecatory tone, Garnier feared that such cases suggested a dense population of licentious "hermaphrodites" who escaped detection: "It is to be expected that many deformed, incomplete men remain hidden, disguised under women's clothing, fulfilling all of their functions. There are even those who take advantage of their sterility in order to surrender themselves to libertinage, to prostitution, and to the most audacious depravation" (506). Though they did not always share in Garnier's fearmongering, most doctors hypothesized that more cases of hermaphrodism likely existed than had previously been imagined.[13]

In many instances, sex was only possible to determine after death.[14] Marie-Madeleine Lefort, for example, was scrutinized by the most prominent doctors in the capital over the span of a lifetime. First presented to the Faculté de médecine in Paris in 1815 at the age of sixteen, Lefort's gender remained contested until her death in 1865 (see Figure 2.1).[15] In life, the

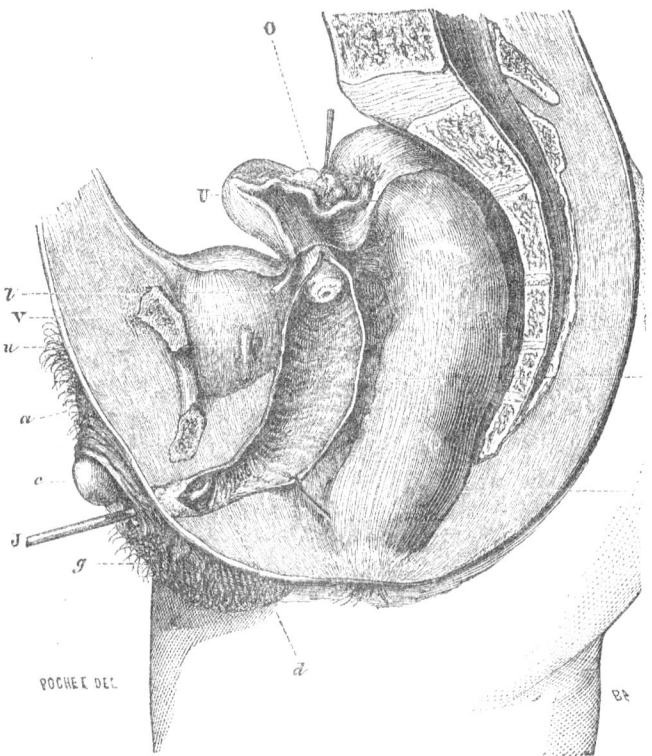

Fig. 15 — Marie-Madeleine Lefort. Coupe sagittale du bassin
pour montrer les organes génitaux.

J, sonde introduite par l'ouverture principale au-dessous du clitoris
M, vagin; O, ovaire; T, trompe de Fallope; U, utérus; l, ligament
rond; V, vessie; u, uretère; d, orifice de l'urèthre; R, rectum, g, grandes
lèvres de la vulve.

Figure 2.1 Abdomen of Marie-Madeleine Lefort at Autopsy, from Debierre,
L'hermaphrodisme [...] (1891).

majority of medical men believed she was a man, with only Béclard arguing from the outset that she was a woman (see Figure 2.2). Lefort's autopsy vindicated Béclard, becoming a famous example in later case studies that outward appearance was no guarantor for the nature of internal organs.[16] Giraud's case of Adélaide Préville proved the converse could also be true.

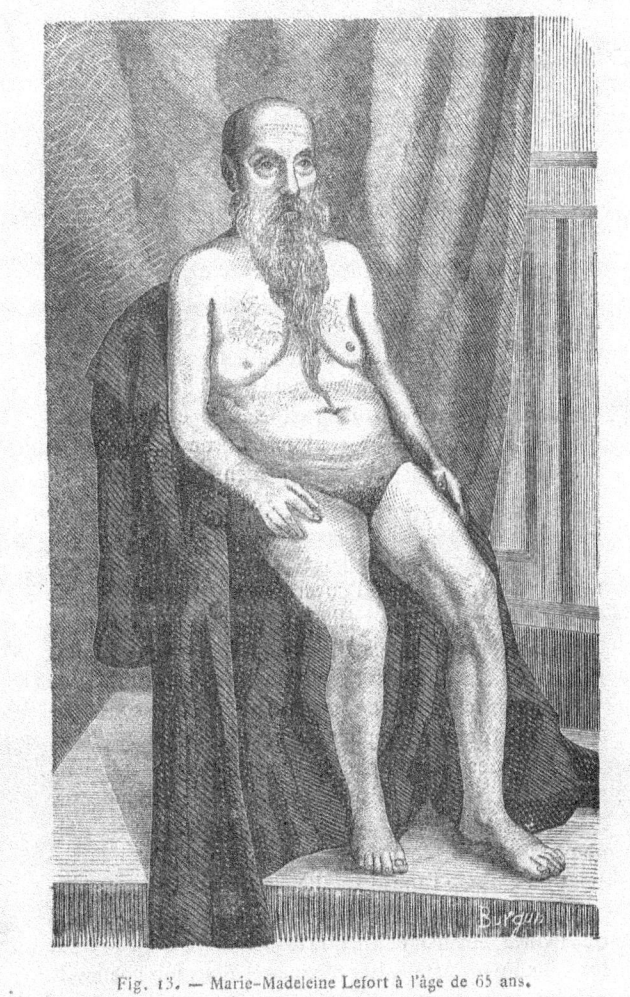

Fig. 13. — Marie–Madeleine Lefort à l'âge de 65 ans.

Figure 2.2 Marie-Madeleine Lefort, Sixty-Five Years Old, from Debierre, *L'hermaphrodisme* [. . .] (1891).

Préville, who lived as a woman, was determined upon death to be male.[17] Drs. Théodore Tuffier and André Lapointe alleged that "the discovery of a testicle in an individual classed as female being operated on for a suspected herniated ovary" was a "nearly banal occurrence" (1911, 253).

Increasingly, doctors began publishing cases of couples who, like Mademoiselle de Campos, had unwittingly married a member of their own sex because of incorrect sex assignment at birth. As we saw in the last chapter, a number of prominent physicians were even claiming that a fraction of the population was simply neither female nor male. "The choice of sex becomes arbitrary in this case," acknowledged Dr. Gabriel Tourdes (1889, 648). Faced with an "arbitrary" choice between equally incorrect sexes, a number of doctors called for a third, nonbinary sex to be added alongside the official ranks of "female" and "male."

Calling for a Third Sex

In a 2006 article, Geertje Mak aimed to set the record straight about "doubtful sex" in the nineteenth century. Contrary to Julia Epstein's claim that the first French call for adding a third category of sex to the civil law sounded in the 1880s, Mak shows that "during the late 1840s [. . .] there had already been suggestions in France to change Article 57 of the *Code Civil* and to introduce the *sexe douteux* (doubtful sex) category for registration at birth."[18] The reference here is to Dr. Joseph-Napoléon Loir, who had advocated sharper supervision of sex determination at birth as early as 1846, and in 1854 presented a paper to the Académie des sciences morales et politiques entitled "The sexes regarding the civil registry. How to prevent errors resulting from their anomalies."[19] Loir proposed a tripartite revision of civil law that would require a physician to be present at birth in order to minimize sexing errors, enable "doubtful sex" to be recorded on birth certificates, and mandate a second physical examination of anyone falling into this category before they would be allowed to marry. In point of fact, however, Loir's oration merely echoed similar proposals spanning the previous two decades. He was not the first in history to seriously consider a third legal category of sex.

Calls for nonbinary sex appeared and reappeared throughout nearly the entire span of the century. Numerous doctors from Jean-Baptiste Bouillaud to Frédéric Dubois, Pierre-Auguste Béclard to Charles Debierre, recommended adding a "neuter sex" or a "doubtful sex" category alongside male and female.[20] While this seems at first surprising, given the longstanding historical representation of the nineteenth century as one in which science and medicine sought an absolute separation of the two sexes, calls for nonbinary sex make sense in light of the failings of the gonadal model and the highly contested definitions of hermaphrodism outlined in the previous chapter. Faced with the daunting task of reconciling individuals whose sex could not be determined to a legal system that denied their existence, medical jurisconsults turned to authoritative prose when evidence was sparse. When it came to the law, resistance to "true sex" was not always intended to protect historical intersex people, but the Code's very silence about "doubtful sex" paradoxically fostered a vociferous debate about it, affording some doctors and patients leeway to practice and live in ways that others wished could be outlawed.

Denying a vanguard role, the inaugural phrase of Loir's discourse credits the names of famous doctors, anatomists, and legal experts who inspired his paper: "The most recommendable authors such as Marc, Orfila, Mr. Isidore Geoffroy Saint-Hilaire, and others, have justly complained in their writings of the insufficiency of provisions of French civil law concerning the distinction and declaration of sex in matters of civil status" (1854, 1).[21] Starting with Charles Chrétien-Henri Marc's earliest articles on hermaphrodism in 1811, these authors had suggested that sex determinations were difficult, and sometimes even impossible.[22] As we saw, Geoffroy Saint-Hilaire advocated for nonbinary sex in the 1830s by writing that "neuter hermaphrodites" "merit [. . .] this name just as much legally as from a physiological point of view" (1832–37, 3: 577).

If Loir was not the first to appeal for a "neuter" sex, neither was he the last. Garnier called for a revision of Article 57 to add "doubtful sex" (sexe douteux) in 1885 (292).[23] In 1899, Xavier Delore reiterated that if uncertainty as to an infant's sex existed at birth, "one should write on the margins of the birth certificate, *doubtful sex*; the municipal officer, warned in this way, will call a meeting when the patient has reached puberty between the concerned party, his/her father, and the doctor."[24] Evidence suggests that this was already happening, despite express legal stipulation to the contrary.[25]

Arguably, pleas to amend binary sex in the Civil Code spanned the entire century because considerable debate raged throughout the same period among French medical experts about what types of hermaphrodism were possible. This debate has been largely overshadowed by a more clear-cut claim that doctors increasingly rallied around a gonadal definition of sex. It has been argued that the strict gonadal definition of sex led to the practical eradication of "hermaphrodism" because of the difficulty of identifying male and female gonads in living patients. As we saw in the previous chapter, however, even the so-called "Age of the Gonads" was not a period of harmonious consensus among experts. And, as long as science continued to allege that cases of hermaphrodism existed, the French legal code that stubbornly required infants to be sexed male or female at birth would appear to fall behind scientific progress.

The most frequently cited proponent of that argument was none other than Isidore Geoffroy Saint-Hilaire, whose multi-volume magnum opus (1832–37) made him the reigning authority on hermaphrodism. Geoffroy Saint-Hilaire's life work made it explicit that legal categories inadequately reflected natural reality:

> I will remark that current legislation, by admitting only two large classes of individuals to whom it imposes responsibilities and accords different rights [. . .] does not truly encompass the totality of cases; because there exist subjects who really have no sex: such are neuter hermaphrodites, and also hermaphrodites mixed by superposition; and, conversely, other individuals, bisexual hermaphrodites who present both sexes to the same degree.[26]

As long as doctors and scientists like Geoffroy Saint-Hilaire were willing to admit that individuals existed who could not be classed as "male" or "female," their bodies would come into conflict with the law. Geoffroy Saint-Hilaire's proposal had more to do with scientific positivism – a belief that science and medicine could enlighten the law – than it did with a critique of social and sexual hierarchy enabled by binary sex. But it also seems reductive to claim that nineteenth-century proposals to add doubtful sex to the civil status "were aimed at better controlling unruly sexes, not to make space for alternative ones."[27] Certainly, such was often the case, but other factors both private and professional were at play as well, and, as we shall see, a number of doctors actually subverted heteronormative, binary sex or considered whether adding a third category might adversely affect those who would fall into it.

It is nevertheless true that, in addition to Geoffroy Saint-Hilaire's belief that the law lagged behind science, a second powerful motivation for revising the Civil Code became safeguarding the general population against the "dangers" of doubtful sex. Nearly two decades before Loir's oration, in 1833, Dr. Bouillaud had already called for a kind of "civil death sentence" for hermaphrodites, callously reasoning that such a measure would be less "barbaric" than ancient law which had condemned them to a physical death.[28] Science shows that "hermaphrodites exist," wrote

Bouillaud, and those who deny it are "superstitious" (498). Bouillaud believed that individuals who "hold a sort of middle ground between man and woman" should not enjoy social privileges (475). They should be denied "a bunch of civil rights" and were "incompatible with certain political rights" (494–95). Nonbinary individuals, whom Bouillaud labeled "neuter," were "beyond the law," and foremost, they should not be allowed to marry: "Would not such a union be an outrage to both morality and physiology, even if our Civil Code has not yet said anything on the subject?" (494–95). Bouillaud viewed historical intersex people as a kind of sexually inferior race or "third sex" – sadly, one of the earliest uses of the term: "Without doubt, nevertheless, they are neither women nor men in all of their purity; they are a composite of man and woman, a sort of *third sex*, of *métis* or of *sexual mule*" (490). Marshaling the racist discourse of colonial France, Bouillaud (like Loir after him), hoped hermaphrodites could be prevented from marrying, but also from holding office or inheriting (494–95). If they had no legal rank, then they should have no civil rank, he maintained. In the next chapter, we shall see how the literary character Mademoiselle de Maupin reclaims the "third sex" as a position of empowerment, two years after Loir's speech, in Théophile Gautier's most famous novel.

Debierre's take on nonbinary sex was of a similar ilk, except that, like Geoffroy Saint-Hilaire before him, he observed that the law failed to reflect the current illumination of scientific knowledge: "I conclude that current legislation is faulty. The Civil Code is wrong in only admitting two categories of individuals, because in society, albeit exceptionally, there exist three categories: men, women, and ... those who are neither one nor the other" (1886, 338). A staunch advocate of his colleague Debierre's proposal, Alexandre Lacassagne, founder of the Lyon school of criminology, leveraged his 1887 medico-legal treatise to argue for the urgency of adopting it:

> Legislation is incomplete, insufficient, or in need of revision when it does not encompass all existent types. There are individuals who come into the world with malformed genital organs. The most likely sex is indicated [. . .] and the individual is recorded on the civil status registry. From this day forward there can be misunderstandings, errors that threaten morality and disturb the harmony of families [. . .]. Sex determination is sometimes very difficult, even for the most competent of men. (79–80)

It was not just the future of "hermaphrodites" that was at stake, according to Lacassagne. Family life and morality needed protection, he claimed. In 1902, Lacassagne doubled down on the existence of human hermaphrodism in the discussion section of a bovine case that was presented by colleagues: "Cases of true hermaphrodism exist in man as in beast; it is regrettable that French law requires newborns to be declared one of only two categories, male or female, not only can it be difficult or even impossible to determine at birth, it is also not that simple."[29] Lacassagne wished France were more like Germany or Austria, which allowed sex to be initially declared as "doubtful," and revisited later on (ibid). Debierre's proposition incited argument even in seemingly unrelated spheres for many years to come.[30] In 1903, Jarricot reasoned that only by continuing to publish cases of "doubtful sex" would lawmakers eventually become convinced that the Civil Code merited revision (7).

Criticism of the call for nonbinary sex ranged from the impracticality of implementing it to concerns that legally ranking some individuals as "neuter" would be damaging. Louis Le Contellec's 1910 thesis summarizes the latter anxieties:

> This proposition gives cause for certain concerns. Firstly, if it were adopted, it would draw attention to hermaphrodites who would more than ever become targets of mockery. Effectively, they would belong to a neuter sex and the public could only ever see them as a subject of curiosity and derision. Secondly, what would the so-called neuter sex include? [...] Moreover, what would be the place of these neuter people in society? We don't believe that the question of pseudo-hermaphrodism can be answered in this way. What is needed is to require medical examinations for sex determinations. That doctors be sufficiently educated about genital malformations so that they pose the least risk of committing an error. Finally, that in uncertain cases, the doctor inform the family, and insist on his doubt. (53)

Tragically, Le Contellec's ultimate recommendation that a doctor warn the family of his uncertainty would become the antithesis of sex recommendations in the twentieth century, when conventional wisdom held that intersex children should be assigned a sex as soon as it was feasible, and that as little doubt (and often, information) as possible should be conveyed to parents.

In 1911, Drs. Tuffier and Lapointe inverted Bouillaud's argument to claim that binary gender was a social necessity for all, in spite of the difficulty of determining it:

> Hermaphrodites must be classed among men and among women; for to condemn them because of the law to live on the margins of the two sexes would be to return in part to the conceptions of antiquity and the Middle Ages. The possession of a sex is a necessity of our social order [...]. The

modification of the Civil Code proposed by Debierre does not therefore seem desirable to us. (256)

Dr. Auguste Lutaud also worried that the proposed revision would effectively "place an individual outside of society from childhood" (1886, 14). Instead, he suggested that revising civil status was a question of personal prerogative:

> We believe that the individual should be declared to belong to the sex that seems the most probable at the moment of birth. He is free later on, if he should decide, to have his civil status modified, a right that cannot be refused to him. But he is also free, if he desires to remain in obscurity and avoid a kind of useless scandal, to keep the civil status that was given to him at birth. (Ibid.)

Unlike Debierre, Lutaud advocated for patients' rights, rather than those of society.

According to Dr. Brouardel's *Cours de la médicine légale* from 1900, however, Debierre and Lacassagne's recommended amendment was rejected on purely financial grounds. The legal revision would have required the creation of "birth inspectors," which, to Brouardel's chagrin, was prohibitively expensive (32). In 1887, Brouardel himself had proposed a different strategy. He hoped that impotence could be formally added to the list of causes for divorce/separation (57). Others suggested that cases of "doubtful sex" be reevaluated at puberty, when physical examination might yield clearer results than an evaluation immediately following birth.[31]

Dr. Debierre, on the contrary, apparently cared little about any adverse consequences of his proposed legislation for historical intersex people. His unwavering intent lay in protecting society against the "dangers" of "hermaphrodism": "As it is, the Civil Code does not offer sufficient protection to families and to society," he pleaded in an 1886 essay titled, "The Hermaphrodite Before the Civil Code" (337). If there were any doubt as to Dr. Debierre's motivations, he would quell them here by calling for the addition of a formal clause that would make hermaphrodism grounds to nullify a marriage. The proposed addendum to Article 180 would read: "congenital malformations in genital organs that render fruitful intercourse absolutely impossible and create an error on the physical person are a formal cause for marriage annulment" (ibid., 342).[32] As we shall see, however, attempts to restrict rights because of impotence or sterility would run into their own set of legal roadblocks.

Screaming Legal Silences

Nineteenth-century authors viewed medieval practices concerning hermaphrodism with a mix of horror and curiosity. They were quick to distance themselves from the superstition that had once equated androgynous bodies with evil omens or satanic manifestations. Yet, as we saw above, even when decrying ancient laws which put hermaphrodites to death, some, like Bouillaud, appealed for a "civil death sentence," which would forfeit an individual's rights as a member of society. Ironically, the brutal clarity of this stance was made possible by the Civil Code's very silence on all matters relating to intersex.

While other European countries often possessed laws or jurisprudence governing intersex bodies, the Napoleonic Code, in place since 1804, both eliminated impotence and other genital variations as grounds for divorce/separation and omitted to acknowledge nonbinary sex. This meant that if someone had unknowingly married a person whose sex was contested or nonbinary – as was alleged in the case of Mademoiselle de Campos – exiting the marriage would prove difficult, if not impossible. In the strictest sense of the law, simply proving the "husband's sexual indeterminism," as her lawyer had hoped, would likely not have been enough. Similarly, his second claim of "the impossibility of a union with an individual of poorly defined gender," likely would have fallen under the legal protection of impotence, which was not seen as grounds for annulment.

But this had not always been true. Under *l'Ancien Droit* (French law before the Revolution), impotence was considered grounds to annul a marriage, explains lawyer and legal historian Marcela Iacub.[33] In order to prove impotence legally during the Middle Ages, an examination of the genital organs was conducted and attempts were made to verify and measure penile erections. Experts used objects to imitate penile penetration in order to attest to vaginal opening, diameter, and depth, but because even this extremely invasive examination could not prove the actual sexual performance of both individuals, the process of "congrès" was ultimately adopted as a method of proof in 1587 (103). Congrès required the couple to perform vaginal coitus before a group of doctors, surgeons, and matrons (ibid.).

Nineteenth-century doctors congratulate themselves on having abandoned this scandalous, ancient practice. In his entry for "impuissance" in the *Nouveau dictionnaire de médecine*, Dr. Siredey avers that the Civil Code remained intentionally silent on the subject of impotence in sections on marriage, divorce, and filiation, "because of the difficulty of the burden of proof for establishing it, and the scandal that this proof would cause."[34] According to Siredey, "Since the Revolution, impotence has no longer been considered a cause to annul a marriage: because the law permits spouses to separate under the pretext of incompatibility of temperament (incompatibilité d'humeur), it became useless to invoke impotence" (469). Since spouses could now cite incompatibility as an irreconcilable differ-ence, Siredey hoped that the "shameful" question of impotence could at last be passed over in silence.

Nineteenth-century French legal treatises often define marriage as "the association of two individuals owing each other mutual fidelity, help, and assistance throughout life."[35] This definition did not necessarily imply any kind of sexual or procreative contract. In Germany, by contrast, explains Brouardel, "marriage is believed to reside in the sexual act itself, complete and incurable impotence sustained during marriage is grounds for divorce" (1887, 58). In England, where impotence laws were still in place until 1934, the spouse of a sterile intersex person could have the marriage annulled.[36] The general consensus in French medical treatises was that impotence was not grounds for divorce, since "nowhere does it say in jurisprudence, in any absolute way, that impotence is a cause that can be raised against a spouse."[37] In spite of this, a number of doctors and lawyers *did* argue that various types of impotence or congenital variations should prevent marriage or enable divorce. In fact, "doubtful sex" was at the center of a legal maelstrom over the basis for both marriage and divorce. The ambiguity resulted from two other facts, as Siredey explains: "Nevertheless, as it is a principle that marriage can only be contracted between two people of differing sexes, and that Article 180 of the Civil Code allows for marriage to be annulled when there is an *error* of the person, the authors who wrote about the Civil Code took this as cause to raise a lively controversy" (469).

Not only regarding marriage, laws surrounding the birth and inherit-ance of "hermaphrodites" were more clearly delineated in both England and Germany. The old Prussian Code specified that if a child should be born whose sex could not be determined, then at eighteen years old, this individual would have the right to choose his/her own sex. In the case of inheritance disputes, though, a brother could challenge his sibling's deci-sion by bringing in an outside "expert."[38] Although a number of doctors applauded the German strategy of waiting until adolescence to declare sex in doubtful cases, the Prussian law also attracted derision for its apparent "generosity," possibly owing to the particularly hostile relationship between France and Germany in the years following the Franco-Prussian

War: "a German person had a more enlightened idea," chided Brouardel, "He would give someone permission to marry as a man or as a woman upon promising to use the genital organs only one way."[39]

According to Theodric Romeyn Beck's *Elements of Medical Jurisprudence* (1838), the German law was nearly identical to the original law used by the French before the advent of the Civil Code.[40] Beck observes: "An old French law allowed [hermaphrodites] great latitude. It enacted that hermaphrodites should choose one sex and keep to it" (129). In his 1872 article, Jalabert concurs:

> the old French jurisprudence had adopted the rule of Roman law. Those who are so conformed [hermaphrodites], says Denisard, are reputed to be of the sex that prevails in them and they are not permitted to prefer the other sex. The most severe penalties were inflicted against those who subverted this last prohibition. (132)

Regarding inheritance, English jurisprudence was clear, describes Beck: "The English common law on this subject [. . .] is thus laid down by Blackstone and Coke. 'A monster having deformity in any part of its body yet if it hath human shape, may inherit'" (1838, 131). Moreover, "every heir is either a male or female, or an hermaphrodite, that is both male and female. And an hermaphrodite [. . .] shall be heir either as a male or female, according to that kind of sex which doth prevail; and accordingly it ought to be baptized" (ibid.). Unlike its neighbors, post-Revolutionary France possessed no laws governing intersex, neither regarding birth, nor inheritance, nor marriage.

"Hermaphrodites" on Trial

The Napoleonic Code contained several articles describing legitimate legal grounds for divorce or separation – neither impotence nor "hermaphrodism" figure among them.[41] However, this did not prevent some doctors and medico-legal experts from arguing that historical intersex people could not legally wed, and if they did, that their marriage could be dissolved in the eyes of the law.[42] And it did not prevent cases from appearing in court. As is evidenced by the sensationalism of Mademoiselle de Campos's case above (which made *The New York Times* even though it was never formally tried), when an alleged hermaphrodite's marriage was to be tested in the courtroom, it was sure to garner considerable attention.

The famous eighteenth-century case of Anne Grandjean was an early testament to this fact. Anne, who had been declared female at birth, began to dress as a man at the age of fourteen on the orders of a confessor, when an adolescent Anne began to "look" and "act" increasingly "masculine." Everyone in his hometown of Grenoble accepted Jean-Baptiste (as he was now known) as a man, and he eventually legally married a woman named Françoise Lambert. Trouble started for him when he moved to Lyon with his new wife, where his ex-girlfriend informed his wife that Jean-Baptiste had been listed as a female at birth. He was then clapped in irons for having "abused the sacrament of marriage," for which he was tried and convicted. On appeal, however, Jean-Baptiste was acquitted on the grounds that he (and everyone else in Grenoble) believed himself to be a man, and so he did not knowingly deceive his wife.[43]

In addition to the formal calls for adding either a "neuter" sex to the Civil Code, or allowing for "sexe douteux" to be indicated on birth certificates, or for officially adding a clause that could allow for impotence or genital variations as grounds for divorce or separation, a vocal contingent of nineteenth-century doctors and jurisconsults attempted to restrict the rights of historical intersex people by interpreting the Code in its broadest sense. Proponents fell into two camps. Either they claimed that an obscure clause in the Civil Code allowed for divorce when an individual presented "an error of the person," or they relied on jurisprudence and broad interpretations of the spirit of the Code to show that certain kinds of impotence (or sometimes sterility) constituted grounds to terminate a - marriage.[44] Whether the "impotent" individual was affected before or after marriage, was or was not aware of the condition, as well as the precise type of impotence, became crucial to these doctors and was discussed ad nauseam in medico-legal treatises. Fierce debate ensued. The case record itself was inconsistent, occasionally indicating impotence as grounds for divorce, but more often rejecting it.[45]

The most well known of these nineteenth-century cases was so because Dr. Ambroise Tardieu, who participated in the trial as an expert, published all the legal proceedings in his 1874 treatise, *Question medico-légale de l'identité*, and because it was extensively covered in the press, both domestic and international.[46] As we saw in Chapter 1, this was the very treatise in which Tardieu published Herculine Barbin's autobiographical writings.

In 1866, Monsieur Antoine-Etienne Darbousse, a 23-year-old landed proprietor, wed 25-year-old Anne-Justine Jumas, and, after living with her for more than two years, appealed to the civil court of Alès to annul their marriage because, he claimed, "she possesses none of the essential organs which are indispensable to characterize the feminine sex, and consequently cannot be recognized as a woman."[47] The strange case of Darbousse and

Jumas was later cited in numerous treatises and articles as appeals and reversals drew in more experts and sent the case to the highest courts in the land.[48]

Jumas's original appeal to have the case thrown out on the grounds that the six-month statute of limitations on annulment had already elapsed was dismissed. Darbousse claimed that his wife "possessed neither breasts, womb, ovary, or vagina; that her pelvis was as small as that of a man, and that although twenty-seven years of age, she had neither menstruated nor perceived any periodical lumbar or abdominal pains."[49] The court of Alès ordered that Jumas be officially examined by the midwife of Montpellier Maternité, who was to confer with Dr. Fabre. Fabre was then to report the midwife's findings to the court – "A rather derogatory procedure on the part of a doctor of medicine in relation to a midwife!" quipped the author for the *Medical Times* (ibid.).[50] Jumas, however, refused to submit to examination, and appealed to the Cour impériale de Nîmes.[51]

By the time the case appeared there, Darbousse had found additional support in Dr. Henri Legrand du Saulle, championed in the *Medical Times* as a "well-known medical jurisconsult, who espoused his cause with almost indignant enthusiasm" (100). Legrand du Saulle claimed that no woman could be without menstruation or breasts or any of the external and internal reproductive organs, but he would need more scientific evidence in order to determine whether she was a man. The most likely scenario, he concluded, was that Jumas had "no sex at all" (1874, 19). Astonishingly, Legrand du Saulle volunteered this assessment without ever examining the patient in question.[52]

Jumas then countered with her own expert. Dr. L. Carcassonne had presumably examined her in the interim, since he provided a document alleging that his patient had some "female" body parts including a pubic bone and urinary meatus that resembled those of a woman, as well as apparent labia and a clitoris. Intercourse would nevertheless remain impossible, continued Dr. Carcassonne, since Jumas's vagina was imperforate. The court of Nîmes was persuaded by this evidence and sided with Jumas, reversing the decision of the court of Alès by ruling that since impotence was not grounds for divorce, the configuration of Jumas's genitalia was irrelevant.[53] Attempts to show that Jumas was not a woman remained unconvincing, they asserted. Quite the opposite, Dr. Carcassonne's statement showed merely that Jumas possessed some kind of "birth defect," but was nevertheless "really a woman."[54]

The saga continued, though when France's Supreme Court, the *Cour de cassation*, annulled the ruling at Nîmes and ordered a new trial before

Montpellier's appellate court. Darbousse brought in two heavy hitters: Dr. Amédée Courty, and the extremely influential Dr. Tardieu.[55] Like Tardieu, Courty wrote up the court details for publication.

Courty promised to forego "personal opinion" in favor of "scientific observation," which, he claims, had rendered the formerly "obscure" mystery of sexual identity "so clear in our times."[56] Despite his goal of clarity and scientific proof, like Legrand du Saulle, Courty will offer his recommendation based solely on court documents and testimony. In fact, none of the medico-legal experts will actually perform any kind of examination on Jumas, which means that their use of narrative must compensate for the absence of scientific findings. Given the frequent and fierce disagreement in interpretations even when doctors thoroughly examined patients (as we saw in Chapter 1), it is difficult to imagine how any expert could presume to determine sex without a physical examination; but presume they did, and the courts were swayed by their authoritative declarations. Experts evaluated the legitimacy of Mr. Darbousse's "so-called marriage" with Anne-Justine Jumas based on the spouses' statements, a midwife's testimony, and the certificate delivered by Dr. Carcassonne (1871, 473). Courty's formal conclusion states that although Jumas possessed some female organs, she was without a vagina and she could not become pregnant (474). Paradoxically, what was missing counted the most: "from all appearances, the most important may be precisely the missing one" (475).

As one might imagine, demonstrating that Jumas possessed no "essential female organs" without ever actually examining her would involve some creative license, as well as a compelling narrative. Initially, Courty distinguishes between "essential" and "accessory" body parts. The former are "ovaries, fallopian tubes and the womb in women; testicles, vas deferens and their reservoirs in man" (476). The latter included secondary characteristics such as breasts, relative hip measurements, and so on. Even if externally Jumas was a "woman," this did not prove she had what it took to be a woman on the inside, he posited (474). Courty goes to great lengths to explain that while internal organs are "fundamentally different in the two sexes," and develop as such, the external ones are "identical" "at their core," which is to say, they develop along the same pathways (476).[57] Courty continued by citing a number of cases of doubtful sex examined throughout his career in which the patient's internal organs had no bearing on the body's external appearance, although he does not expound on how he had identified the nature of the internal organs in those cases, or what facts allowed him to express such certainty (480).[58] Instead, he concludes that Jumas's apparent external female genitalia in no way guaranteed internal female organs. Ultimately, Courty determines that since Jumas had never experienced menstrual symptoms, she must not have internal ovaries (485). Of course, menstruation was certainly not a general requirement of being female, even in the nineteenth century, as both prepubescent and postmenopausal women knew. Nor were functioning gonads at all a factor in determining sex in doubtful cases, according to staunch proponents of gonadal sex, like Dr. Samuel Pozzi. Courty also perfunctorily dismisses the possibility of having an internal combination of a testicle and an ovary, or some gonadal organ uniting characteristics of both glands, despite multiple reports of contemporary cases that showed evidence to the contrary (477). After having dismissed all external appearances as indicative of the nature of internal organs, he nevertheless claims that the narrowness of Jumas's hips precludes the existence of ovaries (483). As we saw in the last chapter, hundreds of cases of individuals whose internal organs did not match their outward appearance or social sex can be found in the medical record – Courty had referenced this fact himself earlier in his document. Forced to acknowledge that Jumas might still have internal female organs, since proving otherwise would be impossible without some kind of examination, he nevertheless goes on to claim that she lacks essential generative organs, by labeling her a kind of sexless being: "the person in question should therefore be categorized among those teratologic subjects who have no sex to speak of, and who consequently cannot be united in marriage to any normally configured individual, regardless of the sex of the latter" (487). In spite of Courty's authoritative claim, there was, in fact, no legal category for "teratologic" humans that excluded them from marriage in France.

Tardieu, heralded as a medical man of the highest caliber, also offered testimony fraught with inconsistencies and contradictions. Rather than first accumulating evidence in order to assess Jumas's sex, Tardieu begins his report with a legal discussion about the most reliable way to annul a marriage. This approach makes it seem as though Tardieu started with a desired outcome and then manipulated his interpretation in order to justify it – the very antithesis of the scientific method. Tardieu opens with the original ruling of the civil court of Alès from April 29, 1869:

> Given that marriage is fundamentally the legitimate union between man and woman; that it can thus only be meaningfully contracted between two people of different sexes; it follows that marriage is necessarily contradicted in its purpose when the apparent spouses are of the same sex, or one of them is absolutely lacking the natural organs constituting sex itself [. . .].[59]

Together, the courts of Alès and Nîmes reiterated this point, so Tardieu deduced that the only sure way to annul a marriage was to prove that both people were of the same sex: "As an absolute necessity, we must arrive at the demonstration and the certainty of identity of sex between the people who believed that they had contracted marriage" (1874, 11). Relying on the court's description, Tardieu then elaborated a definition of sexual identity that weighed even the absence of sex: "The identity of sex in such a case does not necessarily imply an apparent sameness of conformation in the two individuals, but only the absence of constitutive sex organs of a different sex in one of the two, and the existence, apparent or hidden, of essential organs of the same sex" (11). This, he determined, was "a pure question of fact that can and must be resolved via anatomical and physiological examination of the person in question" (11). It is worth remembering, however, that Tardieu will never perform the medical examination required by his method.

A moment after claiming that "I do not admit that there are beings devoid of sex," Tardieu nevertheless concedes: "it is possible that a single individual unites organs belonging to both sexes, but that is such an excessively rare exception that it need not concern us here" (12). Moreover, he proffers the additional rhetorical argument that in the case of "true hermaphrodism," the affected individual would be "incapable of being legally married, because, no matter the sex of the spouse, there would always be an identity of sex, which is to say, marriage nullity, between the two" (12).[60] Since Tardieu disallows the possibility of a person without binary sex, he enumerates only two possibilities: either Jumas is "a malformed woman, impotent, and ill-suited to sexual union," in which case "there are no grounds for nullity in the strictest sense of the law," or she is "a malformed man, offering the deceptive appearances of feminine sex" (12). But alleging that Jumas was a hermaphrodite with whom any union would result in a same-sex marriage would undermine Tardieu's earlier definition of sexual identity. Perhaps to avoid this equivocal stance, he instead argues that Jumas is a man, albeit an "abnormally" conformed one.

In order to do so, he must first deconstruct Carcassonne's certificate which had claimed that Jumas "has all the appearances of a person of the feminine sex" (14). Such a statement is incompatible with the doctor's ensuing description, contends Tardieu. Even though Jumas exhibits some female genitalia, key elements are lacking. He italicizes the crucial parts: "but *there is no vagina*, or, at least, this conduit, *if it exists*, is imperforate. It follows that the act of copulation *is impossible*, and, therefore, *impregnation. The breasts are underdeveloped, the pelvis narrow*, but nothing else recalls the masculine sex in any of its attributes" (4). The court, imperfectly understanding the science of anatomy, was wrongly swayed by Carcassonne's statement, he argued.[61] According to Tardieu, the certificate is silent on the most important details, "the womb and the ovaries," which he identifies as "the constitutive and essential organs of the feminine sex" (15). Tardieu contrasts this "essential" bodily truth to the mere outward "appearance" of femininity in the same way as does Courty. In fact, he claims the physical description of Anne-Justine Jumas actually outwardly coincides with "the cases of congenital malformations of the masculine sex wrongly described under the name of *hermaphrodite*, and in which there is sometimes the nearly complete outward appearance of the female sex, while in reality, on the inside there are distinctive characteristics of virility" (15). To Tardieu, Jumas looks less like a woman than some "hermaphrodites." Such cases are "relatively common," he adds, "and compose the vast majority of those causing sex errors and false inscriptions on the civil status registry" (15).

As promised, and despite the "insufficiency of material proof, and the absence of serious and complete medical legal expertise," Tardieu nevertheless maintains that "it is not impossible to come to a positive opinion and to pronounce certainty with the utmost likelihood" (16). Given Jumas's lack of menstrual symptoms coupled with her narrow hips, Tardieu concludes that "neither womb nor ovaries existed in this person" (17). (In fact, Jumas *had* claimed to experience menstrual symptoms such as lower back pain and cramping, but since no documentation existed to record this claim, the appeals court of Montpellier suggested that it was likely fabricated.[62]) Anticipating counterarguments, Tardieu asserts that Jumas is nothing like those "real women" who also never menstruate because she does not outwardly appear female; she has neither breasts nor womanly hips (17). Tardieu's conclusion reveals an intentionally restrictive view of biological sex: "Because she is not a woman, one must infer, if one willingly complies with the previously outlined considerations, that she is a man, a malformed man, but a man" (18). In the cases in which it is impossible to determine sex, or in which "there is an absolute absence of sex" (those cases over which he had previously suggested we should not linger because of their excessive rarity), Tardieu recommends following Briand and Chaudé's prescription: "In the case of neuter hermaphrodism with an absence of sex, such individuals *should be regarded as being of masculine sex*, because one does not see in them female genital organs, and because the absence of characteristics of virility does not depend therefore on testicular absence or atrophy" (18). Suddenly, and rather inconsistently, given his previous line of argumentation, Tardieu now declares that Jumas falls into this last category. Even though Jumas possessed some external "female" genitals and no one professes to have probed for interior organs – be they ovarian or testicular in nature – Tardieu now declares Jumas a male hermaphrodite by default, while simultaneously eschewing the term "hermaphrodite."

This is very curious given the importance of internal, "essential" organs in Tardieu's view. Why would Tardieu claim that all women needed a womb and ovaries in order to count as "real women," while simultaneously arguing that Jumas was still a man even if she had no testicles at all? One can only conclude that either "essential" organs exist only in "female" individuals or that Tardieu applies his rule inconsistently. The most plausible answer for Tardieu's erratic theorizing is that he is endeavoring to contrive findings that would coincide with the original court of Alès's definition of sexual identity. This tension was already present in the definition he initially elaborated, since it asserted that sexual identity could be founded on either the absence or the presence of sex ("marriage is necessarily contradicted in its purpose when the apparent spouses are of the same sex, or one of them is absolutely lacking the natural organs constituting sex itself [. . .]" (7). The rub for Tardieu is that he has relied on an idea of "essential sex" in order to render his narrative more compelling and scientifically verifiable, but the idea of "essential sex" is fundamentally incompatible with a person who either lacks the organs of binary sex (if "essential organs" do not exist) or whose essential organs cannot actually be examined, but rather only be guessed at following clues provided by "non-essential" organs.

Despite these many inconsistencies, the court was swayed by Courty and Tardieu's analyses, and eventually rejected the defendant's appeal to refuse an expert medical examination. The court instead referred the case back to the original court at Alès where the final ruling was rendered on January 28, 1873. The verdict reflects the influence of jurisconsults, with textual citations of Tardieu and Courty throughout.[63] Here, Tardieu is celebrated as "the most qualified man of science in this field" (27). Jumas's refusal to submit to another physical examination also worked against her. The court argued that it demonstrated a "calculation" on her part "in order to avoid providing new weapons to her adversary" (28). Like Tardieu, the court found that Jumas "really" lacked "the constitutive organs of sex," and even though they did not know whether she belonged "to the masculine sex or to the neuter sex, if it exists," they ruled to annul the marriage, with costs (29). From this case, Tardieu confirmed his initial claim that although impotence would not constitute grounds for divorce, "sexual identity" would (30).

My close reading of court documents from the case of Anne-Justine Jumas reveals several important trends. First, it is clear that the courts relied on forensic jurisconsults in order to render their decisions in cases of doubtful sex. The court of Nîmes was swayed by Dr. Carcassonne's certificate, just as the influence of Drs. Tardieu and Courty's arguments are evident in textual citations in the verdict rendered in Montpellier, even though the last two never actually performed a physical examination of the defendant. Second, although doctors clearly do ascribe more value to certain organs than others in the calculus of sex – Tardieu and Courty reference "constitutive" and "essential" organs – there is no overt consensus that the nature of gonads matters most. A masculine sex is determined without ever finding testicles. Tardieu defines female constitutive organs as a combination of both ovaries and womb, but the explicative nature of breasts, genital hair, testicles, ovaries, fallopian tubes, menstrual cramps, and lower back pain all figure in the debate over Jumas's sex. Ultimately, the Montpellier verdict is rendered without ever verifying the nature of the gonads, and the characteristic that seems ultimately the most compelling to experts is the narrowness of Jumas's hips. Given the difficulties of establishing the nature of internal organs in living patients – even when they submitted to physical examination – proponents of gonadal sex would always fight an uphill battle when attempting to "resolve" cases of doubtful sex. Like Tardieu and Courty, they would likely be forced to undermine their own hierarchy by relying on "non-essential" organs as secondary evidence of "essential" ones, just as Courty and Tardieu claimed Jumas's narrow hips suggested an absence of womb and ovaries. Third, it is clear from inconsistencies in the expert opinions of Legrand Du Saulle, Courty, and Tardieu, that attempts to claim that all individuals were exclusively male or female met with considerable difficulty. Dr. Courty writes off an entire school of thought by summarily dismissing the possibility of a patient combining gonads from both sexes.[64] Because neither he nor Tardieu seriously entertain this possibility, the court would have no way of knowing that contemporary findings had already contradicted their statements. Tardieu equivocates on whether or not nonbinary people could exist at all. He argues both that Jumas is a male and later, that she is a being without sex altogether. Finally, and most importantly, all of this expert testimony illustrates that, far more than scientific evidence, the court was most compelled by the power of narrative and the ability to articulate a rhetorical argument that would hold the case together. The weighty reputation of Tardieu's name, the bravado of his claims to clarity, and his promise to prove his point with pure scientific data seem to count more than the actual evidence itself. The fact that experts drew radically different conclusions highlights this point. Of their testimony, the *Medical Times* would report:

> It is evident that "doctors differ" just as strongly on one side of the Channel as on the other. We have seen one witness declaring the defendant to be possessed of no sex at all, and another that she was a woman, but of faulty construction; and now we have so high an authority as Professor Tardieu stating that the Court was really dealing with a man. (101)

Tardieu was an eminent figure and there can be no doubt that this case contributed to his renown. In a sense, his entire career had been built upon the idea that the body could be confessed by an expert practitioner. This idea was predicated upon a new kind of faith in medical power, and it fits perfectly with Michel Foucault's elaboration of how the confessional model was adopted by medicine. But even within Tardieu's lifetime, the cracks were beginning to show, and by the time of his death in 1879, prominent doctors insisted that some of his theories were plainly false. Tardieu's external "stigmata" of pederasty, including tapering "dog-like" penises, or "funnel-shaped" anuses were openly questioned in 1879 by Brouardel, who argued that the diagnostic value Tardieu attributed to these characteristics "seems very exaggerated," and simply was not present in numerous cases.[65] Just as some of Tardieu's more outrageous claims about the easily identifiable outward physical signs of pederasty eventually drew criticism, his belief in binary sex, too, increasingly came under fire. By 1887, Lacassagne was emphatic. "Neuter" beings exist, he wrote, and Tardieu's claim to the contrary was "indefensible in our times" (88). Like the experts divided on the subject of nonbinary sex, the case record was inconsistent, as Lacassagne observes in the same work:

> The rulings of the court of Trèves (1808), of the court of Alès (1869), [and] those of the court of Montpellier (1872) admit marriage nullity when it is proven that genital organs are opposed to the natural goal of the union of sexes; the jurisprudence of the court of Riom (1828), that of the court of Nîmes (1869), and that of the court of Caen (1882) on the contrary, admit marriage nullity only when sexual identity is proven. (92)

Given the checkered case record surrounding impotence, the practical appeal of proving sexual identity becomes evident. Since none of the formal legal changes proposed by doctors regarding "hermaphrodism" were ever passed into law in the nineteenth century, the only surefire means of dissolving legal matrimony became the demonstration of sexual identity (as Tardieu had predicted). The overwhelming consensus at the time was that the Civil Code disallowed same-sex marriages, and as such, doubtful sex could only occasion divorce when either two men or two women were wed.[66] This fact would become another pragmatic motivation for medico-legal experts to strain to demonstrate that only two sexes existed, just as Tardieu had endeavored to do. If the court could reliably dissolve a marriage only when two people of the same sex were united, then it was in the expert's interest to illustrate sexual identity, and to minimize claims of nonbinary sex to the greatest extent possible. Even though, as I showed in the first chapter, numerous doctors professed the existence of hermaphrodism throughout the century, the pervasive legal denial of its presence helps to illustrate why others (among whom figured a number of medico-legal experts) simultaneously claimed that hermaphrodism did not exist and that the "true sex" of individuals could always be identified through careful scientific study – expertise they alone could provide.[67]

The legal landscape in France would remain unchanged until the April 6, 1903, ruling of the *Cour de cassation*. This case was initially tried in 1901, when an unhappy husband filed to annul his marriage on the grounds that his wife lacked sexual organs differentiating her from a man: "having neither vagina, nor ovaries [. . .] even though she possesses breasts and a clitoris [. . .] in reality [she] is not a woman but rather an incomplete person with whom the law never intended to impose a union with a man."[68] The court's final ruling announced: "Marriage can only be legally contracted between two individuals belonging, one to the female sex, and the other to the masculine sex; therefore its existence is dependent on the double condition that the sex of each spouse be recognizable and that it differ from that of the other (Civil Code, Articles 144 and 180)." For Marcela Iacub, the 1903 ruling inaugurated the reign of "appearance" over "truth" about sex.[69] It was not until the mid-twentieth century, she argues, that the notion of "erreur" was finally interpreted in its broadest sense as a deviation in the individual's anatomy rather than a mistaken civil identity. If the "error" was deemed to be "déterminante," meaning that knowledge of its existence would have prevented the marriage, then it was considered grounds for annulment (115).[70] Almost a century after Debierre and his colleagues urged lawmakers to revise the Civil Code, Article 180 was modified by the law of July 3, 1975, which "ensures that an error in the essential qualities of the person constitutes grounds for nullifying a marriage."[71] Over time, Iacub argues, this evolution of marriage away from a consenting union toward a bodily and sexual contract would spread to other legal realms, making the sexual act the foundation of paternity (122).

While the 1903 ruling had established merely the appearance of sex, later twentieth-century rulings would become more concerned with the "true sex" of individuals. Iacub alleges that these efforts were contrived to address the new medical "problem" of "transsexuality," and to restrict the rights of trans people, who, although they might have the "appearance" of a given sex, the court ruled, were not "really" who they claimed to be (123).

From Medical Fears to Patients' Stories

The need to create laws governing marriage and intersex was made evident by the mounting number of publications that "outed" unintentional same-sex marriages. In 1899, Neugebauer would accumulate a staggering fifty such cases. "And how many roam the streets who don't dare make their presence known?" worried Debierre (1891, 138). Garnier feared that the legal blind spot might mean same-sex marriages among "hermaphrodites" were more prevalent than had been previously imagined: "To cite the rarity of these cases in order to contest the basis and the urgency for this proposition would be another mistake. The exact number is unknown owing to the law's imprudence and its silence" (1885, 292).[72] Otto published a case of a woman who had thrice been married before her last husband attempted to divorce her on the grounds of "genital abnormalities."[73] Delacroix published another case in 1870, seemingly without being able to convince the allegedly same-sex couple to petition to have their marriage dissolved.[74] As we shall see in the final chapter, this trend gathered a frenzied pace during the natality crisis at the fin de siècle. As the birthrate plummeted, preventing sterile marriages became a kind of patriotic duty for some doctors. In 1886, Debierre opined: "What is the purpose of marriage, the supreme goal, if it is not family? This is certainly a primordial law if one ever existed on earth; it goes beyond that, it is a social necessity which, today especially, is essential for all the French" (340). This ancient law should supersede the Code, he claimed: "The union of the sexes, a natural and primordial law, or rather a necessity of nature, came long before all of our legal codes" (340).

However, not all doctors involved in such cases shared Debierre's view that intersex people should not be allowed to wed or that every same-sex marriage should be dissolved. To gesture to the extraordinary diversity of responses to the legal challenges posed by intersex in the historical record, we can look to a few exemplary individual responses made possible largely because of the Civil Code's refusal to acknowledge the science on non-binary sex. We have seen that the Code's silence regarding hermaphrodism prompted some to argue vehemently for new legislation that would safe-guard binary sex, confirming the Foucauldian thesis of "true sex," but it simultaneously enabled others to subvert it. This is important because even though case studies focus on bodies, or more precisely, on doctors' inter-pretations of bodies, clues that illuminate patients' lived experience also filter through discourse and can work to counterbalance medical objectifi-cation, much in the same way that Jumas resisted medical examinations. Each case problematizes the narrative of "true sex," either in theory or in practice, inviting more nuanced histories of sexuality.

In 1899, the same year that Neugebauer published the compilation of same-sex marriages that so terrified his colleagues, Dr. Raoul Blondel described a case quite the opposite. A certain "Madame X" from Angers, forty-five years old, came to Dr. Blondel complaining of "problems" con-cerning "the genital parts" (les parties) (1899, 75). Madame X had not married in her youth (despite multiple proposals) because she had never menstruated, and her parents thought it wrong to allow their apparently sterile daughter to wed. But when she met a sexagenarian who wanted to marry her but did not want children, she at last consented. Although the happy couple had been married for eighteen months at the time of her medical visit, the patient reported that she and her husband were only able to practice imperfect intercourse because of "some insurmountable material obstacle" (75). Complicating matters further, a fall six months earlier had caused a hernia to appear in Madame X's groin. Nevertheless, the newlyweds found even their approximate coitus pleasurable, and Madame X hoped some type of surgery might further facilitate intimacy. After a thorough examination, however, Dr. Blondel identified more enduring obstacles: "in sum, this is a case of an androgyne of the male sex presenting complete hypospadias, with the persistence of a masculine uterus, separated from the vestibule of the pseudo-vulva by a sort of hymen" (76). Madame X was really Monsieur X, thought Blondel. Although Blondel resorts to qualifiers like "pseudo" and "sort of," in order to mitigate the apparent femininity of Madame X's internal organs, it does not influence his use of feminine pronouns when referring to her, and he does not pass moral judgment on her "same-sex" marriage. Blondel's findings may have revealed that Madame X's happy marriage was void in the eyes of the law, but he was not sure that this fact concerned him as her doctor: "a final word. From a social point of view, it is clear that the marriage of this unfortunate woman was null. Were we therefore authorized, in such conditions, to undertake, as she requested, a procedure that would permit more complete relations with her husband [?]" (77). Apparently, Blondel answered in the affirmative, since he set a date for surgery with Madame X, which was intended to facilitate her sexual relations. In the end, though, Madame X failed to appear at the appointed time and the surgery was never performed: "But either she changed her mind or her husband raised some objection, I never heard from her again" (77).[75] Madame X's sudden disappearance highlights another important facet of the medical record: namely, that it is incomplete, often providing us with only glimpses into patients' experiences.

While Blondel offered his scalpel in service, in 1890, Dr. Debout simply fashioned his patient a bandage to alleviate pain from her herniated testicle, without ever suggesting that she revise her civil status or change her lifestyle. Debout did not inform his patient about her testicle either, raising the question of medical paternalism, an anachronistic concept at the time. It was not even uncommon for doctors to remove gonads without explaining the precise nature of these surgeries to their patients.[76] Dr. Jalifier, for example, congratulates himself for having excised testicles from his patient without informing her. Castration was a prisonable offense, so while Jalifier's medical paternalism is not uncommon, his nonchalant tone is unusual:

> Of course, I was careful not to draw the attention of my patient to her defect. I treated her as a woman because such was her conviction, and because an inopportune revelation could have had disastrous effects on her morale. After removing her testicles, she will emerge all the more a woman, in order to peacefully continue her existence. (1910, 868)[77]

The mere possession of testicles had no bearing on whether or not his patient was a woman, according to Jalifier, and removing them would only help her realize "more fully" her feminine identity.

To offset every meddlesome doctor like Guermonprez (discussed in the first chapter) who denied scientific evidence because of a moral agenda, there were many more like Blondel and Jalifier who considered both medical evidence alongside their patients' desires.[78] In 1891, Dr. Pozzi, who generally harbored a rather poor opinion of intersex patients, nevertheless described the marriage between two particular individuals of the same sex in the most ideal of terms:

> the husband adored his wife and she, happy, doted on her husband with the most lively tenderness, she never tired of telling of their joy and happiness together; and in her confidences made to old girlhood friends she let it be known that their conjugal relations were in every way fully satisfying.[79]

Like Blondel, Pozzi sees no need to trouble a happy home (in this instance, at least), and in spite of his determination that the "husband" and "wife" were actually the same sex, he relies on heteronormative grammar and diction in French to depict the harmony between them. Because this couple outwardly conformed to social and cultural gender stereotypes, Pozzi lauds their shared affection.

Occasionally, patients' desires are legible in the medical record itself. In 1876, Dr. Thézet anxiously wrote to his colleagues for advice. The doctor's young patient, who presented with intersex genitalia, had vowed to commit suicide if she was not allowed to marry. At first, Thézet had advised the girl's mother not to let her marry since she could not have children, but now that her life was in danger, he wondered if he could, from an ethical standpoint, enlarge her vagina to make intercourse, and therefore marriage, possible. Thézet's colleagues insisted he must first verify the presence of a uterus, which they atypically describe as the essential organ of female identity:

> Everything that there is or is not to do in this case depends absolutely on the existence or nonexistence of the womb. If the uterus exists, the subject is a woman, and it is appropriate therefore to attempt the suitable means of allowing her to fulfill the functions of her sex. If there is no uterus, prudence and morality prescribe abstaining. (1876, 613)

No follow-up indicates whether Thézet heeded his colleagues, or what became of his patient.

One of Dr. Polaillon's patients took matters into her own hands. When her doctor refused to enlarge her vagina surgically, apparently because he believed her to be a man (despite admitting her extremely "feminine features" and referring to her consistently with the feminine pronoun "elle"), she repeatedly endeavored to have intercourse with men anyway, which ultimately produced the same effect. Polaillon examined his patient three more times after her initial visit in 1887, and each time he observed that her "vaginal opening" (dépression vaginale) had grown in size: "She was able to dissimulate her congenital malformation; and her lovers, in availing themselves to find what did not exist, did as much as surgery could have done" (1891, 559).

Many doctors contented themselves merely to discourage marriage for intersex patients, or even chose to remain silent on the question of marriage, omitting to offer any advice on the topic whatsoever.[80] Dr. Tuffier's patient, a fashion model, threatens that if he will not remove her testicles, she will simply find another doctor who will. (As we saw in the first chapter, this was also Louise-Julia-Anna's response to Guermonprez's threats). Tuffier quotes her as stating:

Why not remove this horrible mass from my left groin that would be in the way if I wanted to pose for painters? Since you can do nothing for me, I'll go find the famous surgeon D. . ., who will know how to make me a woman! If I were like other women, I would have married and I would not need to work for a living. (1911, 218)

Even Tuffier, who advocates discouraging marriages as much as possible in cases of hermaphrodism, suggests that if the marriage has already taken place, it is not for a doctor to become involved after the fact.[81] Other patients recorded desiring to marry but believed that they were either not able or were not allowed to do so.[82]

For the person whose sex was contested, the law bore lasting consequences. We have already seen what a legal sex revision meant for Herculine Barbin, but Barbin's demise is merely the most well-known denouement among myriad others. In 1866, for example, Crecchio published the case of Marie-Joséphine-Marguerite Marzo.[83] Marie was identified as a girl on the birth certificate, but gradually virilized, and Marzo's parents began dressing their child as a boy at the age of four. Joseph, as he was then known, hoped to marry in his teens, but panicked when he remembered his birth certificate, which would need to be produced in order to acquire a marriage license (184). Marzo appeared to be a man both to the woman who eventually married him, and to the doctor who examined him, but his old birth certificate identified him as female, which meant he could not get married without a legal sex revision.[84]

Some doctors aided their patients in legal sex revision. When Marie X, who had been registered as a girl at birth, came to Paris to have his civil status amended in 1886 to read "male," Dr. Alcide Benoist complied, much to the chagrin of some of his colleagues. The doctor ultimately determined that his patient, who believed himself to be a man and could earn a better living as such, was, in fact, more like a man than a woman: "we believe that Joseph-Marie X's birth certificate should be modified, [. . .] it is only fair to attribute to him the sex that prevails in him and that seems the best suited to his tastes and the most apt in order to provide for the material needs of his existence" (1886, 87). Some of Benoist's colleagues implied that he had allowed his science to be overly swayed by his patient's desires. In 1889, Pozzi mentions a patient who has no intention of formally revising her civil status to male, regardless of his findings: "having passed for a woman up until now, changing civil status would be repugnant to her, but she regrets not having been taken for a man at the outset" (606). Dr. Jean Tapie claimed that the reason his patient was morally bereft was his incorrect civil status, and the doctor was persuaded that once it was rectified, his patient, then a petty criminal, would choose a nobler path (1888).

Still others made a life out of crime. Emélie Estelle Gauthier, a "herm-aphrodite" and suspected prostitute, was under police surveillance. Her file at the Préfecture de Police in Paris indicates that Gauthier (or Gautier, as she is sometimes named) "is a female hermaphrodite [une hermaphrodite], and the conformation of her genital organs is so unique that she derives profit from them."[85] According to the eight-page document:

> she only receives the rich, and she is also allegedly in relations with the most famous doctors of the capital. She also apparently gives viewings at the Medical School, and in sum this woman is supposedly an extremely rare subject because she unites the two sexes, without being deformed, which, it seems, is never seen among hermaphrodites. (np)

Similarities in the cases make it likely that Gauthier was the identical patient examined by Dufour at the age of fourteen in 1856.[86] Gauthier's police file indicates she had married in 1864 and was now the widow of a certain Jean Boussaton. Her external appearance was that of a woman: "she easily wears women's clothing, she looks very neat, and nothing on the exterior of her person indicates that she is a female hermaphrodite." The police author identifies her as "a veritable phenomenon" visited by famous and powerful contemporaries. Tucked into the pages of her file is a business card with an address that reads: "Madame Gautier visible Tuesdays, Wednesdays, Thursdays and Fridays, from noon to six o'clock." According to surveillance notes, Gauthier charged, on average, between 20 and 100 francs to display her curious anatomy to visitors. The sliding scale depended on the rank and profession of her viewers. (Surveillance notes between 1876 and 1878 indicate that a count, viscount, and marquis, among others, had intimate relations with her.) She even made house visits. "She allegedly has herculean strength," records the police spy, or "mouchard," who puzzles over the fact that of her eight feeble sisters, Madame Gauthier is the only strapping one: "What is peculiar is that Madame Gauthier's mother married at the age of nineteen and had nine children, eight of whom were girls and who are all of delicate health and constitution, whereas only Mrs. Boussaton, a hermaphrodite, is as robust as an athlete." The file also records that Madame Gauthier was slated to appear during the upcoming *Exposition universelle*.

As the diversity of these examples illustrates, historical intersex people lived as gender outlaws in unique ways. Some used their bodies for financial gain, while others strove merely to lead quiet, unremarkable lives. Medicine both helped and hurt them, as did the law. Some medical men risked reputation and career to provide care that their colleagues deemed socially harmful. Others refused to provide treatment at all. Jurisconsults such as Tardieu made a name for themselves as forensics experts, in part, by arguing the cases of individuals whom they sometimes never even examined. Although the historical record privileges the word of "experts" over the voices of patients, clues to their thoughts and feelings can be gleaned from the actions and reactions that are preserved in medical cases. As we have seen, these clues reveal an expansive array of individual responses to inhabiting bodies that challenged the binary in a historical moment when that binary went largely unquestioned. Their stories offer an important historical addition to the work being done by intersex and trans activists today.

Throughout the nineteenth century, historical intersex people came into conflict with the law from the moment of their birth. They motivated surgeons to test the limits of their talent and some doctors to break their Hippocratic oaths. Jurisconsults enthusiastically contradicted one another about the veracity of sex determinations, while influential men labored to revise laws regarding birth certificates, marriage, and inheritance. Ultimately, the only party remaining silent on "hermaphrodism" was the Civil Code itself. And this silence called out with a deafening roar that carried from the courtroom right onto the front page, ensuring that a legal blind spot only increased the visibility of those it tried not to see.

PART II

Contextualizing High and Low Literary Narratives

Figure 3.1 Clémentine, Sword Raised. Frontispiece of vol. 1 of J.-P.-R. Cuisin, *Clémentine orpheline et androgyne* (1883).

Is She or Isn't He?
Plotting Ambiguous Gender

Je ne suis plus une femme, je ne suis plus un homme, mais un lion.

Figure 3.2 Frontispiece of Cuisin, *Clémentine orpheline et androgyne* (1820).
Courtesy of the Bibliothèque nationale de France.

The swashbuckling, gender-bending protagonist of J.-P.-R. Cuisin's long-forgotten popular novel, *Clémentine, orpheline et androgyne, ou les caprices de la nature et la fortune* (*Clémentine, Orphan and Androgyne, or the Caprices of Nature and Fortune*) (1820), is rendered in the novel's frontispiece wearing a dress (breasts exposed), while brandishing a sword and declaring, triumphantly: "I am no longer a woman or a man, but a lion" (see Figure 3.2). During the scene in question, Clémentine, unjustly attacked, slays would-be assailants with virtuoso swordsmanship while repudiating the labels of *woman* or *man*.[1] It is Clémentine's righteous anger that affords a space of proud gender nonconformity in this scene, but from the outset Clémentine identifies as a gender outsider: "*Man and woman*, destiny said to me; and *neither one nor the other* cried nature in time, humiliated and revolted" (1: 3). At first marginalized on the outskirts of the binary, in the heat of battle Clémentine surpasses male and female identity to embody the heart of a lion.

Merriam-Webster recently chose the singular personal pronoun "they" as the word of the year for 2019, noting its skyrocketing use by one person whose "gender identity is nonbinary."[2] Although gender-neutral pronouns did not yet exist in nineteenth-century France, Rachel Mesch has shown that gender nonconformity certainly did, and "the challenge of finding the right gender pronoun [. . .] has historical precedent."[3] Clémentine would certainly be one literary example of such a precedent. In Part I, we saw how doctors like Bouillaud sometimes resorted to the "hermaphrodism of language" in order to describe patients whose bodies did not conform to binary sex.[4] Others switched between masculine and feminine pronouns, or attempted to side-step the problem entirely by circumlocuting gendered pronouns using periphrasis (such as "the patient," or "the subject"). In this chapter, we will see how novelists deployed many of the same strategies, even creating "hermaphroditic words" (*paroles hermaphrodites*) when faced with the challenge of using gendered pronouns to describe androgynous characters.[5] Writers experimented with more than just pronouns though. Several of the most famous authors of the nineteenth century wrote entire novels in which the gender of the central protagonist remained in doubt, and actually became the mystery pushing the plot onward. *Clémentine, orpheline et androgyne* was merely the first example of a sudden proliferation of literature that used unknown sex or gender as a motor for plot. Although the rise of hermaphrodism in nineteenth-century literature has often been attributed to mythology, this chapter argues that now-forgotten popular novels (such as *Clémentine*) are important intertexts that enable us to see overlooked connections between the ways both doctors and novelists used narrative as a means to dissect social and cultural beliefs about binary gender. Like the doctors in Part I who argued that "true sex" was a fiction for some of their patients, this new literary hermaphrodism was predicated upon calling binary gender into question.

Doubtful Sex Driving the Plot

Early in the nineteenth century, while the lowly novel aspired to the repute of its neighboring genres and its function seemed up for grabs, a cluster of texts, both popular and canonical, realist and romantic, were penned about hermaphrodism. The first, as we have seen, was Cuisin's now-obscure *Clémentine, orpheline et androgyne* (1820). Next appeared Henri de Latouche's immensely influential (although today commonly neglected) *Fragoletta, Naples et Paris en 1799* (1829). *Fragoletta* would, in turn, inform Honoré de Balzac's use of androgyny in both *Séraphîta* (1834) and *La fille aux yeux d'or* (1835), and Théophile Gautier's masterpiece, *Mademoiselle de Maupin* (1835). These novels would be followed by a later spate of works showcasing androgynous characters, such as Émile Zola's *La curée* (1872), Rachilde's *Monsieur Vénus* (1884), and Joris-Karl Huysmans's *À rebours* (1884). In addition to these well-known novels, a number of popular texts also appeared around the fin de siècle with epicene characters and/or intersex protagonists. *Les demi-sexes* (1897) and *Les androgynes* (1903), both by Jane de La Vaudère, investigate blurry boundaries between the sexes and medicine's role in forging these distinctions. In 1885, Gaston d'Hailly published *L'hermaphrodite*, which bears the same title as Armand Dubarry's medico-libertine novel from 1898. Both novels recount the life and trials of an intersex person; however, the former ends on a happy note while the latter culminates with a suicide modeled after Herculine Barbin's own tragic death.

Almost invariably overlooked by critics, popular novels merit closer examination because they enable us to reread canonical texts with a new set of eyes. I will argue that the full stakes of androgyny in works like Balzac's *Séraphîta* and Gautier's *Mademoiselle de Maupin* can only be appreciated in the context of the now largely forgotten novel *Fragoletta* by Latouche. Moreover, popular fiction incites a revision of longstanding temporal and thematic distinctions separating what has come to be known as "the romantic androgyne" and the "decadent hermaphrodite." My rereading of canonical literature in light of popular fiction will invite us to reconsider what scholars have long held as the ahistorical "myth of the androgyne," which alleges that literary androgyny bears no relation to historical intersex. Contrary to this critical viewpoint, I argue that both popular and canonical works share ties to medicine that are anchored to shifting historical forces within nineteenth-century science.

If, as Peter Brooks has argued, narrative is the dominant nineteenth-century mode of representation and explanation, then novels whose plots rely on ambiguous sex in order to keep us reading reflect not only our desire as readers to progress toward meaning, but also our need as members of a community for models to help us work through social constructs of gender and sexuality.[6] Like the plethora of plots relying on mysterious gender, the ubiquitous literary "figure of the hermaphrodite" mirrors increasing historical challenges to the binary, and plays into the sociological aim of nineteenth-century novels to reflect the full spectrum of character types.[7] In this way, gender ambiguity represents a paradigm for the function of the realist text. Regardless of genre, however, the way we read the text is bound up in the way we read gender. This crucial realization enables us to avoid the familiar pitfall of interpreting literary "hermaphrodism" as a constitutive element of any given genre. Because androgyny simultaneously evokes and refutes the binary, it is tempting to see it as a device designed to forge and test the boundaries of genre. And while not without truth, this quality has engendered a number of somewhat circular arguments among critics who study a selection of texts on androgyny within a certain genre and then begin to read androgyny as a reflection of that particular genre.[8] Representations of androgyny exceed the confines of any single genre, but owing to the extremely pervasive nature of the theme, any literary investigation would necessarily be selective. This chapter analyzes only those works in which unknown sex arguably functions as the central motor of plot. I do this in order to illustrate the range of different authors' attempts to use historical intersex as a central structuring force in their works, and to reveal similarities with the medical narratives discussed in Part I. Case studies of hermaphrodism find their literary corollaries in those works in which the central character's gender is unknown, either to the reader, or to other characters.

To varying extents, in well-known novels like *Sarrasine*, *Séraphîta*, and *Mademoiselle de Maupin*, the question of gender or sexual identity motivates the plot and holds the reader in suspense until the denouement. This proves equally true in less well-known novels like *Fragoletta*, and even in forgotten ones such as Cuisin's *Clémentine* and in d'Hailly's *L'hermaphrodite*. This suspense promises a temporary excursion away from sexual difference, captivating the curious reader, but ultimately sublimates such "dangerous" forays, allowing for the reestablishment of heteronormative values which had at first seemed threatened. As Roland Barthes remarked in reference to *Sarrasine*, in these novels, ambiguous sex becomes the most basic textual enigma or "hermeneutic code," which invites the reader to continue reading.[9]

Each novel provides a different strategy for working through situations that challenge a nineteenth-century society built upon the cultural belief in sexual difference. In Balzac's *Séraphîta*, the androgynous creature Séraphitüs/Séraphîta is desired both as a man and a woman by his/her two admirers, Minna and Wilfred. Before any kind of love can be consummated, we discover that the androgyne is not really of this world at all, but rather an angel. Séraphîta seems, at first, to tidily resolve all conflict by dying and allowing Minna and Wilfred to discover love for one another. Balzac treats readers to all sorts of scintillating innuendo but ultimately saves them from a "guilty conscience" through a heteronormative/religious ending. Ascension (*Séraphîta*), death (*Fragoletta*), an apparent revelation of "true sex" (*Sarrasine*), and separation (*Mademoiselle de Maupin*) are all literary strategies used by the novel to sublimate danger to earthly binaries.

Yet, there is also a sense in which all of these novels subvert their own efforts to contain and control as if to unconsciously affirm real-world diversity. In *Sarrasine*, for example, the artist dies (as "punishment" for his homosexual desire?) but androgynous Zambinella lives on. In fact, the castrato becomes a famous courtesan whose prostitution constitutes the ill-gotten source of the Lanty family's mysterious wealth. (And the *raison d'être* for the entire novella since the narrator's explanation of the identity of the gorgeous figure in the painting and of the ghostly old man is the pretext for the telling of the story in the first place.) The inherent tension between a normalizing ending that at first appears to eliminate the "threat" of androgyny, but that upon closer examination actually undermines clear binary distinctions between men and women, can be read as another fictional corollary to the often-unsuccessful efforts to determine "true sex" in the medical field. In this way too, literature engages with the historical debate that we saw raging in the medical and legal fields in the initial two chapters.

Historicizing the "Myth of the Androgyne"

Scholars have relegated the vertiginous rise of hermaphrodism in nine-teenth-century French literature to the realm of myth despite a simultaneous increase of medical and scientific works on the subject. Heavily invested in the mythological origins and symbolic functions of "hermaphrodism," these critics have overlooked the history of medicine in favor of the ahistorical "myth of the hermaphrodite."[10] Influenced by the Jungian "archetype of the collective unconscious," critics Marie Delcourt and Mircea Eliade argue that the "hermaphrodite" is a "myth" forming part of our "universal" imagination, bearing no relation to living intersex people.[11] Echoing Delcourt, A. J. L. Busst suggests that the "myth of the androgyne" holds timeless and universal appeal: "the conception and representation of androgynous men and gods figure prominently in almost every religion and mythology of practically every country and age."[12]

The problem with these studies, as Frédéric Monneyron points out, is that they do little to explain the reemergence of androgyny as a theme in the nineteenth century proper.[13] Monneyron's work investigates the cultural and historical forces affecting the resurgence of hermaphrodism in literature. One of these forces is medicine, but although Monneyron briefly recognizes the simultaneity of medical investigations of hermaphrodism and literary portrayals, he does not scrutinize the medical record. Because this link has not been explored in detail or throughout the entire century, the "myth of the androgyne" is long overdue for critical reevaluation.

According to Busst's analysis, because "true hermaphrodites" "do not exist," they cannot find novelistic expression:

> However, Maupin is not and cannot be perfectly androgynous, for the true hermaphrodite is too far removed from reality to be represented otherwise than imperfectly by a living character in a novel which aspires to any degree of realism. And it is precisely because it does not truly exist in reality that the hermaphrodite [. . .] is so beautiful. (41–42)

Busst's sources led him to this conclusion. Because he considers no popular novels, he assumes that fictional representations of intersex never depict "true hermaphrodites," and because he neglects the medical record, he does not acknowledge that "hermaphrodites" existed in the nineteenth century, just as intersex people exist today. Busst also conceived of this sentence in the 1960s, at the peak of a time during which intersex had become virtually invisible since medical protocol dictated that the bodies of intersex children be shaped to align with binary gender very soon after birth through medical treatment. Following John Money's now-debunked research in the 1950s, doctors recommended that children never be informed about their diagnosis, and the full truth was often withheld from parents as well. The Epilogue to this book explores how the intersex rights movement finally brought about the rejection of Money's theories and gave rise to new medical protocols for intersex patients. In this way, perhaps Busst's own historical moment blinded him to seeing intersex as anything other than an imaginative myth. Whereas Busst claims that fictional representations "owed practically nothing to biological or scientific observations," I will show that medicine and science do play key roles in a number of novels (1). Moreover, Busst's allegation about the unrelated nature of literature and medicine betrays a view of science as an objective reflection of reality, whereas, as illustrated in Chapter 1, nineteenth-century science on hermaphrodism frequently engaged in the same imaginative fantasies as fictional accounts.

A second hallmark of scholarship on the "myth of the androgyne" is a neat temporal and thematic distinction separating what has come to be known as the "romantic androgyne" and the "decadent hermaphrodite." According to Busst, literature represented the "myth of androgyny" differently in each half of the century: the early, idealized androgyne in the first half of the century, which Busst calls "healthy and optimistic," can be contrasted with a decadent, "pessimistic" representation of hermaphrodism in the second half, described as "unhealthy" (10). The two literary representations of androgyny are diametrically opposed for Busst, so that early romantic portrayals symbolizing progress, redemption, unity, solidarity, virginity, and harmony find their "exact antithesis" in later portrayals resonating degeneration, damnation, fragmentation, individualism, promiscuity, and disaccord (11). Similarly, Eliade argues that the symbol of androgyny "degrades" at the fin de siècle, as materialism and eroticism replace spiritualism.[14]

One problem with such polarized extremes is that most authors stubbornly refuse to gravitate to them in a consistent way. Medical efforts to classify ambiguous bodies in the nineteenth century met with a similar fate. As we saw in Part I, try as they might, medical and legal experts were routinely unable to categorize historical intersex people as either male or female without fierce polemics. Even Busst had to admit that not all writers fit easily into each category (Balzac, for example) and that there was a period of overlap during which both types could be found (12).[15] Nevertheless, he situates a shift around 1850 – though the motivations for the selection of this year remain inexplicit (38). In Busst's timeline, as disillusionment gradually replaced early optimism, pervasive dissatisfaction with everyday life led to escapism through literature (40). A clear separation between romantic androgynes and decadent hermaphrodites remains an underlying presupposition in many works, both literary and historical, even though scholars have drawn attention to the misleading nature of such dichotomies. This chapter offers new evidence that popular literature on hermaphrodism further erodes critical distinctions dividing androgyny in the first and second halves of the century.

Clémentine: The First Popular "Hermaphrodite"

If Cuisin's 1820 novel, *Clémentine, orpheline et androgyne*, were the only nineteenth-century work on hermaphrodism, nothing any literary critic has ever said about representations of "hermaphrodism" in literature would be true. Here is a novel composed nearly a decade before *Fragoletta*, the work nearly always cited as the first in a long line of novels about intersex. *Clémentine* also purposefully engages with medical discourse on hermaphrodism half a century before authors like Huysmans and Zola would fashion fiction out of medical representations of sex and sexuality at the fin de siècle. Nor can one describe Clémentine as an idealized androgyne handed down from mythology (as are supposedly prevalent in the early part of the century). Like her decadent counterparts, Clémentine is a "hermaphrodite de nature," quite unlike Gautier's transing Mademoiselle de Maupin, with whom brave Clémentine nevertheless shares an affinity for swordplay, as we have seen (1: 5).[16]

Despite the polemical relationship of Cuisin's novel to longstanding literary criticism, *Clémentine, orpheline et androgyne* already somehow contains nearly every theme and seemingly many of the same scenes that will later come to be exploited in future works on hermaphrodism: cross-dressing, androgyny, incest, mistaken identity, *mise en abyme*, meta-theatre, medical discourse, and performative gender. *Clémentine* also poignantly brings to the fore the typically complex resonances between fiction and historical fact. By raising the thorny question of influence, it also sets the stage nicely for the onslaught of androgynous characters appearing in the 1830s and stretching on to the fin de siècle.

Like the later popular novel, *L'hermaphrodite* (1898), by Armand Dubarry, Cuisin's story is recounted in the first person from an intersex protagonist's point of view, and details the difficulties of a marginalized person endeavoring to integrate into society and to find love. The novel contains the two-volume adventures of the "hermaphrodite" Clémentine, who suffers cruelly until at last finding love and marriage to an open-minded marquis. Claiming to have discovered the "real memoirs" of a historical intersex person, Cuisin rehearses the familiar eighteenth-century convention of fiction passing itself off as fact. (This is the same strategy that Gautier will later adopt for his epistolary novel about the cross-dressing Mademoiselle de Maupin, and the one employed by Gaston d'Hailly in his 1885 novel, *L'hermaphrodite*.) Like Pierre de Marivaux's Marianne, Clémentine is a humble orphan, raised first by a benevolent parish priest, whose quest to uncover the secret of her birth becomes a central, if often interrupted, aim of the novel. Also called Clémentina by others, Clémentine is predominately feminine-gendered in the French text. Like

Marianne, Clémentine feels herself to be noble, and just like Marivaux's heroine, her elevated sentiments inspire the selfsame belief in her entourage. Clémentine's suspicions eventually find confirmation when a treasure chest is unearthed containing a limitless fortune and, more importantly, documentation of her name and family. As it turns out, the secret of Clémentine's origins will also answer the riddle of her mixed-sex body. It seems that Clémentine's mother imprudently fantasized about the visiting Ambassador of Persia during pregnancy, while simultaneously hoping for a daughter, which, following the longstanding "scientific" belief in "maternal impressions," produced Clémentine's half-male/half-female person.[17] Popular scientific belief often linked exoticism and hermaphrodism with the claim that temperature increases affected genital development – a belief that would find its way into racist justifications for France's colonialism in Africa.[18]

Clémentine stands in opposition to literary scholars who generally situate medicalized fictional narratives at the end of the century, for science and medicine play a crucial role in the novel. Likely because of Michel Foucault's enduring influence, along with Busst's temporal and thematic distinction between the "romantic androgyne" and the "decadent hermaphrodite," much literary criticism perpetuates the idea that fictional representations of hermaphrodism are unrelated to clinical discourse until the fin de siècle.[19] Nevertheless, just like the "medico-libertine" genre Foucault identifies in the 1880s, *Clémentine* already rehearses what will become a familiar tension between self-knowledge, on the one hand, and medically imposed knowledge on the other. Yet Cuisin makes no attempt to reconcile these two epistemologies, and his novel does not purport to resolve, or even acknowledge lingering questions about "true sex" preoccupying future writers.

An infant washed ashore in a tempest that swallowed her vessel along with her past, Clémentine is raised by Juan Mathias, a charitable parish priest in a small Spanish village. Too young for language when she is found and too old to remember once she can speak, Clémentine grows up in relative isolation, sheltered from superstitious villagers and the "truth" about her body, which is concealed from her by Juan Mathias. Clémentine's guardian extols the virtues of resignation and monastic life in the hope that his ward will perpetually defer self-awareness by joining a convent. Now an adult, Clémentine the narrator is able to reflect on her upbringing and realize that her inability to decipher Juan Mathias's intentions derived from the fact that "I did not know myself at all during that time" (1: 12). Brutal self-discovery dawns when Clémentine overhears Juan Mathias conversing with Don Anzelmo Maëstro, a famous doctor from Cadix. Alerted by the passing murmurs and prolonged stares of fellow villagers that something is amiss, Clémentine listens in on the men's conversation hoping to learn "the key to the enigmatic behavior" of those around her (1: 17). However, from her hiding spot behind the bookcase, Clémentine is only able to make out part of the phrase "beautiful Clémentine is . . .*dite*" (1: 18). The trauma of Clémentine's eventual realization is such that the mere mention of words ending with "ite" later send her into spasms of terror.[20] As she listens in, Clémentine is filled with mounting anxiety. She learns that despite her extraordinary talents, her body somehow places her at odds with society: "excluded from one sex without belonging positively to the other, nature would have her dedicate her days to piety and silence, while on the other hand her qualities and talents seem to mark her in advance for a distinguished place in the world" (1: 19). Now panicked, Clémentine watches as the doctor hurries to the bookcase, heaving the Académie's dictionary off the shelf to read the entry for "hermaphrodite." Clémentine must learn the meaning of "the word whose frightening ending was *dite*" (1: 20):

> Yes, *Hermaphrodite*, cried out the doctor in turn, here it is, noun and adjective [. . .] from the Greek *Hermes*, Mercury, and *Aphrodite*, Venus, one who participates in Mercury and Venus, who is male and female; who unites the two sexes; it is said of animals and plants. Ah! Continued the doctor [. . .] I remember, he said quite crudely, having seen some of them in my travels in Italy and Germany; I even have one in my dissection amphitheater. (1: 21–22)[21]

Clémentine watches horrified as the doctor, temporarily overwhelmed by exciting potential advances to science, seems at first to "rejoice in my monstrosity," proposing to examine Clémentine's anatomy, but then returns "little by little to human feelings" (1: 22). Later, he spares Clémentine from provincial superstition and narrow-mindedness by spiriting her away to the city of Cadix to live with his family (1: 22–23).

Despite its early publication date, *Clémentine* is rife with (mostly pejorative) references to medicine. To her disgust, Clémentine will eventually discover the "dissected hermaphrodite" in Maëstro's anatomy laboratory, whom she sees as a "sister," and a cautionary tale of placing one's trust in medical men. Later, Clémentine must also refuse a contract for 100,000 francs to be displayed before doctors all over Europe – a practice in which some historical intersex people actually engaged during the nineteenth century in order to earn a living.[22] This frenetic quest for scientific knowledge which temporarily sweeps up even Dr. Maëstro, places the century's early scientific positivism under scrutiny and raises questions about the individual costs of furthering collective knowledge. Once his initial scientific exuberance has subsided, Maëstro offers a humanist counterweight to the sensationalist, money-driven quackery that characterizes the dark underbelly of contemporary medicine as it is presented elsewhere in the novel.[23] Maëstro endeavors to shield Clémentine from more invasive scientific study, and he himself never examines her medically, making it clear that he serves as protector rather than physician. The doctor even abandons his family in order to relocate Clémentine when her secret is discovered in Cadix and a team of local medical men circulate a brochure detailing Clémentine's anatomy around Europe. The humiliation and pain of Clémentine's examination is merely hinted at in the text, but foreshadows Barbin's own description.

Cuisin's clearly pejorative view of medicine and his ambivalent representation of Dr. Maëstro will become a mainstay of realist fiction from Gustave Flaubert's *Madame Bovary* to Zola's *Rougon-Macquart* cycle and beyond.[24] Mary Donaldson-Evans and others have shown that the relatively more complex relationship between writers and doctors in the nineteenth century (than that which existed in the burlesque representations of medicine in Molière's time, for example) reflects medicine's growing respectability during the same period. As the century's early positivism gave way to increasing disillusionment, fictional representations became increasingly skeptical of the abilities of medical men.[25] Cuisin's novel negotiates a somewhat anomalous position with respect to this trajectory, since Dr. Maëstro's miraculous medical abilities exemplify contemporary scientific confidence, while other, more nefarious doctors such as the team in Cadix appear motivated solely by financial gain, or operate with callous disregard for their patients. Dr. Maëstro's art nevertheless outstrips historical ability when he administers a vegetable cream that inhibits the growth of Clémentine's otherwise abundant facial hair (1: 98–99).[26]

Despite Maëstro's medical wizardry, Cadix proves no haven from the libel Clémentine's body attracts. Clémentine's "masculine" vigor and striking profile awaken the aspirations of a homely antagonist named Donna Marcellina, who cannot resist the peerless swordsman. The scorn of the handsome chevalier transforms Donna Marcellina into a persistent enemy whom Cuisin brings back whenever things start to look up for Clémentine. Pursued across Spain and into France by rumor, Clémentine must also dodge prospective lovers, for all who lay eyes on her, it seems, fall hopelessly in love. This proves true regardless of whether Clémentine chooses masculine or feminine attire, imperiling identity and virtue alike.

In one scene, after Clémentine has fled the convent where she had sought refuge following a dazzling display of swordplay that left several policemen seemingly dead by her hand, she intends to marry a French nobleman who has loved her for some time, in the full knowledge of her bodily variation. Clémentine has uncharacteristically let her facial hair grow unimpeded and donned masculine attire in order to facilitate travel, and so when a maid walks in on Clémentine and Saint-Elme in a passionate embrace, she stumbles upon two bearded "men," lips locked (2: 104–5).[27] Surprisingly, this seemingly transgressive tableau merely provides momentary pause and affords comic relief for the lovers who find the maid's shock humorous, and Saint-Elme, who has been professing his love to an apparent man since their escape, seems neither daunted by his androgynous bride/groom-to-be nor by her evident superiority in the masculine realm (she bested him with the sword). This all may seem miraculous given the hostile reaction of the general public to successive revelations of Clémentine's anatomy, but Saint-Elme, who turns out to be Clémentine's long-lost brother – making the above scene doubly transgressive – is not the only lover Clémentine charms. She will eventually marry the Marquis de Saint-Réal whose actions prevent what would have been an incestuous marriage with her brother, and whose unflappable lovelorn attentions will eventually win him a most unusual partner.[28]

If I have lingered over the plot of Cuisin's obscure novel, it is to illustrate its similarities with the classics to follow. Readers will have already detected many of them. Clémentine and Saint-Elme represent early avatars of the semi-incestuous brother and sister pair anchoring Balzac's *La fille aux yeux d'or*.[29] In the same work, De Marsay's long-lost sister, the Marquise de San-Réal, shares a similar name with Cuisin's Marquis de Saint-Réal. Moreover, Clémentine's first governess hails by the intriguing name Séraphine, resonating with Séraphîta for whom Balzac's only novel about a "hermaphrodite" is named, as well as Sarrasine, the castrato of his eponymous novella. Variations of a convent scene in which Clémentine arouses the affections of the Mother Superior also reappear in Herculine Barbin's memoirs and Armand Dubarry's novel, and monastic life plays a part in almost every other work on hermaphrodism from *Fragoletta* to *Mademoiselle de Maupin* to Gaston d'Hailly's *L'hermaphrodite* (see Figure 3.3).

The swashbuckling, androgynous central character from *Clémentine* is inherited by *Fragoletta* and passed on to Gautier.[30] Like Clémentine, Théodore/Madeleine proves irresistible to all who look on them in *Mademoiselle de Maupin* – a constant also observed by Balzac in *Séraphîta*. Yet, in *Mademoiselle de Maupin*, Gautier fully exploits the then scandalous tension of apparent homoeroticism between d'Albert and Théodore rather than glossing over it as does Cuisin. Having already portrayed this trope in *Séraphîta*, Balzac offers the mirror image in

Figure 3.3 Clémentine, in Convent. Frontispiece of vol. 2 of Cuisin, *Clémentine orpheline et androgyne* (1883).

Sarrasine, when an apparently heterosexual attraction is revealed as masked homosexual desire. Moreover, many fictional representations of androgyny rely on some kind of *mise en abyme* to draw out important leitmotivs. In *Clémentine*, *Phaedra* becomes a literary foil intended to alert Clémentine to the potential incest with her brother (which Balzac resuscitates for the same purpose in *La fille aux yeux d'or*).[31] Zola also rewrites Phaedra's tragedy in *La curée* in the incestuous relationship between the "strange hermaphrodite" Maxime, and his stepmother. Both *Fragoletta* and *Mademoiselle de Maupin* incorporate theater as a mirror to reflect the central themes of the novel. *Fragoletta* recruits political satire to address the historical subplot of the Neapolitan Revolution of 1799, while *Mademoiselle de Maupin* relies on a showing of Shakespeare's *As You Like It* to rehearse the cross-dressing and gender-bending crux of the main plot. The Pygmalion myth, no doubt because of the importance of hermaphrodism in the plastic arts, bears mentioning in almost every work.

Relatively little is known about the author of *Clémentine* beyond what can be found in pithy nineteenth-century bibliographies. Born in 1777, he died a pauper around 1845, although even the year of his death is uncertain.[32] He claimed variously to be a former soldier, writer, and curator of an anatomy cabinet – the last of which might explain his fascination with hermaphrodism.[33] An 1883 review of the novel, published on the occasion of a reprint, labels Cuisin "un écrivassier," which translates as a prolific, but terrible writer.[34] The reviewer goes on to describe him as "one of the most prolific plagiarists of the first half of the century," whose over seventy novels assured him "no more immortality after death than they procured him fortune during life" (ibid.). The reviewer deems *Clémentine* a "very unrealistic" novel about a young girl who "unites on her person the attributes of both sexes" (794).

Contemporary bookseller Nicolas-Alexandre Pigoreau, on the other hand, describes Cuisin as "full of cleverness, imagination, and ease" in 1821.[35] Nevertheless, Pigoreau discourages reading Cuisin (along with Rousseau and Voltaire) to all but "mature" men because "such liquor as fortifies old age intoxicates youth" (351). He describes Cuisin as moralizing, but the risk of misinterpretation means the author's work is only safe in the hands of adult men: "all of his works have a moral and useful goal" (174).

Indeed, Cuisin's novel is overtly moralizing, but not in the ways that later fiction has taught us to expect. Rather than killing off his protagonist in a final return to heteronormativity, Clémentine lives happily ever after. Though Clémentine embodies her mother's sin – the kind of preordained suffering or hereditary "taint" that so overshadows Zola's work – the overt homoeroticism of the novel never provokes reprimand or redress. The surprising moral of the story is that God created all creatures of this world, and only God may determine the length of their stay. Living in virtue is the divine commandment to all. Because Clémentine trusts in God's design and doesn't finally end it all in a crisis of dispair, she is rewarded with a happy, albeit sterile hearth.

It is probably Cuisin's notion of morality more than any other inconsistency that secures the ire of his fin-de-siècle reviewer, for by that time, readers had learned to anticipate that an author mete out punishment differently. From Balzac and Gautier, one had come to expect that androgynes had no place in this world: they either ascended or absconded, died or disappeared. No doubt conditioned by previous reading, the reviewer even goes so far as to impose a "true sex" onto Cuisin's protagonist, in what can only be described as a blatant misreading of the novel's enduring insistence on Clémentine's dual identity throughout:

> Nevertheless, at the end of the novel, it seems that she really belongs to the weaker sex. One can see what advantages the author could draw from this physical conformation: inspiring and feeling in turn extraordinary passions, Clémentine, ever virtuous, even in the most unbelievable circumstances, ends up becoming the happy wife of a man whom she had distinguished from the outset, simultaneously recovering immense fortune and a family she had not dreamed up.[36]

It is as if the 1883 reviewer remained stubbornly unable to interpret a novel that, at its most basic level, defied binary sex. Historically, such stubbornness makes sense, given the decades of novels conditioning the belief that intersex desire was always fraught.

Historical Intersex Figures

Because of the role of censorship and the fact that none of the canonical authors mention Cuisin specifically, gauging the influence of *Clémentine* proves difficult.[37] It is perhaps conceivable that later literary representations of hermaphrodism simply drew from the same historical wellspring as Cuisin, in addition to referencing each other in a great intertextual web. Although it is often stressed that Gautier was not preoccupied with historical accuracy, his character Mademoiselle de Maupin of course bears a famous historical precedent. The cross-dressing, dueling, bisexual exploits of Julie d'Aubigny de Maupin (1670/1673–1707) still garnered popular acclaim in the 1830s, judging from the contemporary press.[38] Perhaps "the real" Mademoiselle de Maupin motivated the sword-wielding protagonists from Cuisin to Latouche to Gautier to Gaston d'Hailly. Another historical figure who captured the popular imagination was the "Chevalier/ière d'Éon," whose exploits were memorialized around the turn of the nineteenth century with an edition of Éon's memoirs.[39] An emissary of Louis X, the Chevalier d'Éon fooled foreign dignitaries with cross-dressing, and provoked considerable speculation about sexual identity. The Abbé de Choisy (1644–1724) and the surgeon James Barry (1795–1865) are other potential historical sources.[40] Even George Sand, that female writer who, under a masculine pseudonym, outsold every one of her male contemporaries (including Balzac), was often likened to a "hermaphrodite." In *Les Chants de Maldorer*, comte de Lautréamont refers to Sand with the epithet "the circumcised hermaphrodite" (339–40). Madeleine Fargeaud reveals that Balzac's description of Béatrix, one of his many androgynous characters, borrows from Sand's descriptions of herself as "neither" a "woman" nor a "man," but rather a "being" (l'être), the very same periphrasis that Balzac had also used in *Séraphîta*.[41] Tales of hermaphrodites and gender-bending cross-dressers reappear in nineteenth-century newspaper articles and in pamphlets that may also have inspired novelists. In 1859, for example, Hérail published a brochure on *Mademoiselle Savalette de Lange*, a man who, disguised as a woman, reached the highest echelon of Parisian society and captivated the popular imagination. Hérail's shifting use of pronouns and double-entendre betrays the literary inspiration of his project, while his extensive appeal (he claims 3,000 readers in Paris) suggests that fascination with hermaphrodism extended well beyond literature.

As all of these examples show, however, that even when historical figures may have inspired fictional counterparts, their "real" life exploits had already arrived in the newspapers, spiced with the same imaginative flavor and recounted with the same sensational verve as the great androgyne novels from Latouche on to the fin de siècle. As we saw in the last chapter, if the sexual identity of historical figures sparked intense debate and even complicated legal proceedings, the sexual identity of fictional characters would become an equal source of speculation, and therefore a seemingly perpetual mainspring for plot.

Latouche's *Fragoletta* and the Enigma of the Recumbent Hermaphrodite

Hyacinthe-Joseph Alexandre de Latouche, or simply "Henri" de Latouche (1785–1851), was a poet, novelist, and newspaperman more often remembered for his famous friends than for his own literary corpus. Latouche rubbed shoulders with nearly all the literary greats of the early nineteenth century,

including Lamartine, Chateaubriand, Hugo, Vigny, and Stendhal. He supported both Sand and Balzac before they were known. When Balzac met
Latouche in 1825, the future mastermind of *La Comédie humaine* was no more
than a failed poet, writer of melodrama, and struggling novelist. Balzac
received advice and financial support from Latouche, and they even shared
a home briefly in 1827.[42] Of all of Latouche's volatile friendships (including his
on-again, off-again extramarital affair with the poet Marceline Desbordes-
Valmore), this last one with Balzac has attracted the most attention. This is
due to the ambiguous nature of their friendship, and the resounding influence
of androgyny on Balzac's corpus.[43] It is worth remembering, however, that
contrary to popular belief, Latouche's *Fragoletta: Naples et Paris en 1799* (1829)
is not the first nineteenth-century novel with a protagonist whom we might
today consider intersex.[44] As we have seen, Cuisin's *Clémentine* (1820) claims
that title almost a decade earlier. But unlike *Clémentine*, we know for certain
that Latouche's sprawling historical novel *Fragoletta* did, in fact, influence
both Balzac and Gautier.

Graham Robb describes Latouche as "the man who almost became the
male companion Balzac dreamed of finding."[45] Yet Balzac's lukewarm
evaluation of *Fragoletta* in the early summer of 1829 was a catalyst for the
eventual falling out of the two friends who had been decorating a home
together.[46] In an apparently unsuccessful effort to placate his friend, Balzac
also authored a review of Latouche's novel in December 1829, titled "On
the Historical Novel and Fragoletta."[47] Latouche had been Balzac's financial backer, agent, and editor while publishing his early novel, *Le dernier
Chouan* (later to become *Les Chouans*), and the older author never forgave
the younger his ingratitude. Their relationship would continue to disinte-
grate and was marked by considerable acrimony in later years. Balzac
memorably shredded a copy of Latouche's *Léo* in 1840, and Latouche
would allege that Balzac's "vision had never recovered" from "observ[ing]
the world through the little window of a W.C."[48]

Despite the current obscurity of Latouche's work, *Fragoletta* enjoyed
relative success when it was published in 1829.[49] Several theatrical spin-offs
followed the novel (a sure sign of literary success at the time), and
Latouche's more illustrious contemporaries (Gautier, Maxime du Camp,
Vigny, Maurice Barrès, and even Joséphin Péladan at the fin de siècle)
eulogized the enduring influence of *Fragoletta*.[50] As a journalist, Gautier
covered one vaudeville interpretation of *Fragoletta*, and was struck by the
"grace of the hermaphrodite," a feature he sought to emulate with his own
Mademoiselle de Maupin.[51] The Théodore/Madeleine pair in Gautier's
masterpiece is inspired by the Philippe/Camille pair in Latouche's novel,

and Balzac also cites *Fragoletta* as the catalyst for *Séraphîta*. Beyond the nineteenth century, however, the few critics who do mention Latouche generally confine their observations to a grudging acknowledgment that Balzac and Gautier owe a debt of inspiration to his pioneering use of androgyny in *Fragoletta*. Backhanded compliments about Latouche's beleaguered personal life and sporadic moments of genius ensue, such that the overarching importance of *Fragoletta* on the canon has been for too long overlooked.[52]

Summarizing *Fragoletta* is no easy task. Balzac warned: "May he who has the audacity to write a review of this novel after reading it do so. I shall not dare to do it," and Sainte-Beuve described the novel as "an impossible book to analyze."[53] In the most acerbic contemporary review of *Fragoletta*, Gustave Planche bemoaned the novel's style and organization, describing it as "a royally annoying, disconnected book without logic, without beginning, and without end, written in a pretentious and affected style."[54] Though clearly venomous, Planche's assessment of the novel's coherence is not without a certain element of truth. This expansive, double-volume historical novel recounts the story of d'Hauteville, a French soldier embroiled in the military campaign in Naples at the turn of the nineteenth century, who is, moreover, unknowingly in love with an intersex person. At least that is one interpretation of Latouche's mysterious character, Fragoletta. Seemingly endless digressions, frequent bouts of dialogue, and myriad secondary characters interrupt this central plot. Through it all, Latouche adamantly refuses to spell out the gender of his epicene protagonist. The preface of *Fragoletta* promises "a mystery that is not meant to be understood" – a vow to which the novel will hold.[55]

A sometimes rambling novel, *Fragoletta* nevertheless reveals the occasional nugget of genius in which the novel's entire purpose seems distilled and condensed into one scene. The most poignant of such moments occurs when Éléonore Pimentalé, a famous artist, accompanies friends d'Hauteville and Camille (or Fragoletta) to the Museum of Naples, where they encounter Polycles's statue of a recumbent hermaphrodite.[56] D'Hauteville plays the French military man and brooding romantic hero who gradually falls in love with the androgynous Camille. The latter, at this point, is locked in a loveless and apparently unconsummated marriage with a much older man. She appears flattered by d'Hauteville's advances, but her impressions of him will shift radically once they behold the hermaphrodite sculpture.

In historical fact, Napoleon had purchased the statue from his brother-in-law, the prince Camille Borghèse in 1807, and had it installed in the Louvre, so the work would have been available for Latouche's immediate scrutiny as he penned *Fragoletta*.[57] It is even possible that the recently acquired statue and its Italian origins might have partially inspired Latouche to write his novel about a hermaphrodite and Italian history. In addition to composing "Contralto" in homage to the Louvre hermaphrodite, Gautier was also fascinated by the sculpture, frequently visiting the museum to contemplate it.[58] Allegedly, the sculpture elicited such popular fascination that it had to be protected from "visitors' caresses" with a barrier, because they were actually beginning to wear down the stone.[59]

Once again, Cuisin steals Latouche's thunder by discussing the same statue in *Clémentine* almost a decade earlier. Clémentine and her adoptive sister, Nathalia, read about the sculpture and their discovery prompts a lively discussion about hermaphrodism that signifies differently for each, just as the sculpture will trigger multiple levels of interpretation in Latouche's novel. When Nathalia jokes about hermaphrodites as "monsters," Clémentine is quick to defend herself and those like her: "I limited myself to answering that since our physical appearance is independent from our desires, it would be cruel to mock victims of destiny's bizarreries" (1: 81). Here again, Cuisin infuses his fiction with contemporary scientific discourse. The characterization of hermaphrodism as a "deviation" or "trick" of nature is a hallmark of science predating Geoffroy Saint-Hilaire's theory of arrested or excess development. Nathalia promises instead that if she were a hermaphrodite, "I would fool a thousand pretty girls, and I would make even more male lovers languish" (1: 80, 81). This other sensational plotline is never fully borne out in works on hermaphrodism, although, as previously demonstrated, it cuts to the underlying anxiety in the medical record.[60]

While Cuisin's mention of the statue proves merely anecdotal, Latouche transforms his reference to the famous sculpture into a central plot element. In this scene, Camille, d'Hauteville, and the artist Éléonore approach the statue from behind. D'Hauteville is struck by its graceful feminine beauty – at once mysterious and revealing:

> Leaning on a graceful arm, it looks like it was half asleep. The head, turned in the opposite direction to the body's pose, seems to express at once a smile and sadness. One of the crossed legs lifts a charming foot, and the other is gracefully entwined in the folds of a cloak, which nevertheless leaves almost all of this beauty without veil. (1: 87)

But the statue reserves a shock for d'Hauteville: as he rounds to the front, he lets out an "exclamation of surprise," instinctively turning his head "in order to hide a smile" (1: 88). Camille, on the other hand, follows him, without comprehension: "naively [ingénument], she stopped alongside him, considered the marble for a moment, and then the Frenchman, as if to question him about his surprise" (1: 88). Initially, two possible interpretations present themselves for Camille's apparent incomprehension as she contemplates d'Hauteville's wonderment: either she does not know what an erect member is (and therefore is not surprised by it), or she does not think it is out of place on this marble-bosomed body (1: 88, 89). In a moment we shall see why only the latter of the two possibilities is supported by the text. Whatever the case, however, by watching d'Hauteville, Camille instantly internalizes that this combination is comical, lacks verisimilitude, and, in his eyes, constitutes an unworthy subject of art.[61]

It is to Latouche's credit that this crucial moment of revelation can be read on multiple levels. On the surface, the historical and artistic stakes of intersex are debated from two opposing worldviews. On a deeper level, however, the scene functions in parallel with the dictionary episode for Clémentine by teaching Camille – mediated through d'Hauteville's reactions – about the transgressive nature of her own body.[62] Initially, Éléonore and d'Hauteville debate the merits of "hermaphrodism" as a subject of art. Éléonore, ever the artist, champions the purity of aesthetic expression in all forms, and lambasts d'Hauteville as "one of these men of the north whose imagination is offended by everything, whose appreciation of beauty is preoccupied by a thousand hesitations, or rather whose entire taste consists of endless fears of admiring" (1: 88). Conversely, d'Hauteville, a military man of action, questions the artistic merit of certain corporeal subjects. For him, the "capricious composition" seems "unworthy of art" and he wonders, "why give a body to such a fanciful daydream [fabuleuse rêverie]?" (1: 89). This remark sparks a shift in their conversation to the historical existence of "hermaphrodites," and it becomes immediately apparent that d'Hauteville has conducted a fair bit of research on the subject, despite his prudish airs. He explains to Éléonore that he has read historians "who record that these monsters that your love of the marvelous would have us admire were once thrown into the sea in Athens and the Tiber in Rome" (1: 90). Contemporary reference books evoke similar tales.[63] The narrator further hints at d'Hauteville's bad faith by describing the contradiction between his actions and his discourse. When Éléonore reminds d'Hauteville that such individuals might exist in nature even today, he confesses, having overcome his initial giggles and now unable to wrench his eyes from the statue, that he has read corroborative legal and medical testimony:

> In truth, I believe I remember, continued d'Hauteville slowly, but with his eyes still fixed on the statue, I believe I remember that modern science has sometimes mixed its attestations with your belief. Serious doctors and lawyers have, in faith, intervened on behalf of similar phenomena, but I have always supposed, and I will always believe, that they were taking advantage of our gullibility. (1: 89–90)

D'Hauteville's stubborn refusal to admit the existence of intersex despite the certification of "serious" doctors, lawyers, and historians serves as one metaphor for reading the novel. True to his word, the military man will fumble through the next several hundred pages without ever discovering why Camille refuses his perpetual advances, never really listening for the meaning behind each protestation. D'Hauteville's interpretation is not necessarily wrong; at no point will Latouche clearly disprove him. It is, in fact, possible to read the entire novel à la d'Hauteville, as several critics have, imagining that Camille is no more than a "psychological hermaphrodite" who later lives as a man in order to discover the world differently, much like Gautier's Mademoiselle de Maupin. But the narrator's hints also invite a more attentive reading that is important, not because of the scandal it unleashes, but because it will go a long way toward explaining the fascination with androgyny in works by Balzac, Gautier, and beyond.

In order to understand the subtext of the museum scene, we must again turn to the narrator for clues. Thoroughly engaged by his debate with Éléonore and still transfixed by the statue, d'Hauteville fails to notice that Camille has been backing away from him as he speaks: "Camille distanced herself by several steps, likely because of a natural instinct of prudishness [sans doute par un naturel instinct de pudeur], and Éléonore, more liberated, continued" (1: 90). The secret scandal of the museum scene is that Latouche describes Camille's anatomy with the kind of detail which no novel could permit. Meaning is communicated through the reactions of others, and all the implied references to Camille's person are mediated through a piece of stone. The inattentive reader might think that a naive Camille is not surprised by the sculpture's member because she is in complete ignorance of all human anatomy. The same reader might take the narrator at his word that d'Hauteville is a prude and that Camille backs away from him as if in fear of the ancient "monsters" he invokes. But the attentive reader will notice that Camille is horrified in this scene because she identifies with the statue, and because she learns that the man who has been professing his love to her ad nauseam would abhor her should she reveal her true identity. She is not "liberated" in the way Éléonore is to discuss the theoretical merits her body offers to art, because she is tied to this body that she now learns is a curse. Nor can she dismiss scientific authority or historical narrative with the kind of half-conscious distraction (or perhaps sexual stimulation) as d'Hauteville, because the bodies she imagines coming under scrutiny and hurled off cliffs are bodies similar to her own, similar to the one she sees before her.

Later events support this interpretation. We learn that Camille, in particular, rushed to leave the museum, that she insisted on returning home that very night despite several reasons not to, and that "her mind seemed to have fallen into some painful preoccupation, and one would have said that she was seeking to pull herself away from a thought that was obsessing her" (1: 96, 93–94). Just like Clémentine, hidden behind the bookcase, from the moment that Camille overhears d'Hauteville's thoughts about hermaphrodism, she knows any relationship with him will prove impossible; indeed, that all love is forbidden to her. This will become a leitmotiv in every other nineteenth-century novel about intersex and even in several novels with androgynous main characters. (D'Albert, as we shall see, constantly laments his forbidden and "monstrous" attraction to Théodore de Sérannes, who turns out to be Mademoiselle de Maupin in drag.) Leading up to the museum scene, Camille had seemed interested in d'Hauteville, with her only reluctance apparently stemming from the fact that she was married at the time. Camille's elderly husband, however, has never been her lover or even the jealous type. Instead, he serves as a purely paternal figure, and he will handpick d'Hauteville as his successor before dying. In d'Hauteville's mind, therefore, the temporary obstacle blocking his happiness is Camille's marriage, but Camille has just learned the existence of a more permanent kind of barrier.

Camille becomes so despondent after the sculpture scene that even d'Hauteville eventually notices something is wrong. Yet, despite Camille's veiled confessions, the Frenchman stubbornly refuses to listen. Camille hints that, like the sculpture, she is a "sculptor's daughter" (1: 100). Lamenting her mother's death, she adds, to the chagrin of her interlocutor, that "from today onward I am sure that my mother is the only person who could have ever loved me on this earth" (1: 102). D'Hauteville, as usual, fails to notice the significance of Camille's use of the word "today," or to consider the lessons which might set it apart from all others. Instead, he sentimentally offers to give his life "a thousand times over" to the being whom he had unknowingly called a "monster" only a moment earlier (1: 102). While d'Hauteville drones on with romantic platitudes about the "serenity" and "sweetness" of the night, Camille is deep in thought. Suddenly, s/he announces for the first time that s/he has a long-lost brother, Philippe Adriani, whose identity s/he will assume in the remainder of the novel.[64] After the museum scene, Camille's own body, as Clémentine's had initially seemed to be, becomes the obstacle to his/her happiness. From this point onward, Camille will constantly repeat – both as a woman and a man – that the future holds no promise of happiness (1: 103).

Latouche redoubles clues that Camille is intersex without ever stating it explicitly. On the return ferry from the museum, Camille notices that the ship is flooding, and with the true martyrdom of romantic heroes, both Camille and d'Hauteville clamor to sacrifice themselves to save the other, believing that a lighter load might avoid sinking. At first glance, this scene reads like confirmation of Latouche's inability to coherently organize his novel.[65] But, in fact, it provides another clue to Camille's identity. Only pages earlier, d'Hauteville had described how historical intersex people were once flung off cliffs to drown, so Camille's sudden desire to perish in the waves can be read as a confession of bodily difference. Lest we overlook this clue, Latouche alerts us to the parallel by using the word "monster." (It is worth recalling that the origin of the word "monster" is related to the Latin "monere," meaning "to warn."[66]) Racked by the guilt of having incited the suicide of his former lover, d'Hauteville declares himself a "monster" who deserves death (1: 107). Camille, once again, announces that she is the monstrous one, tellingly without using the painful word itself: "No! It is not you, it is not you, repeated Camille . . . and it is not for you to die" (1: 107). The immediate juxtaposition of these two sentences makes apparent that Camille believes s/he is the "monster" and that, rather than d'Hauteville, it is his/her place to die. Unsurprisingly, d'Hauteville remains too preoccupied with his heroic posturing to listen.

In a letter addressed to d'Hauteville, Camille later admits to having read up on hermaphrodism (like the fictional Clémentine and historical Marie B.), and that studies confirm s/he is doomed:

> I have reflected on my fate; I have been enlightened by meditations and readings; I have nothing to hope for or to fear. I am therefore going away from a country given over to the anger of unjust men. God himself is unjust because the existence that he gave me would bring misfortune to whoever might place hope in a bond with me. (1: 164)

D'Hauteville is crestfallen. By this time, Camille's elderly husband had died, and d'Hauteville hoped that any impediment to his love would disappear with the old man. Instead, Camille's persistent hints leave d'Hauteville only with a growing awareness of some impenetrable mystery: "therein lies some horrible secret that must be discovered" (1: 164). This secret – which is in some ways an open secret – and d'Hauteville's mission to uncover it become the motor driving the plot forward. As we have seen, Barthes called this enigma propelling the narrative the "hermeneutic code," and often it remains incompletely resolved at the denouement.[67] Our goal as reader is the same as d'Hauteville's, but just as he never really "gets it," neither does Latouche fully unveil the mystery to the reader. If we were waiting for Latouche to spell out the riddle, to confirm that Philippe was really Camille all along, that s/he is intersex just like the sculpture, we will be frustrated.

Dangerous Interpretations

Understanding the statue scene will become the key to deciphering the trauma of a later scene that literary critics have remained unwilling to interpret in its shocking totality. This is the scene in which Philippe Adriani, having been banished for attempting to seduce d'Hauteville's younger sister Eugénie, is really lurking behind the bushes of d'Hauteville's family home and watching from the shadows, like Madame de Lafayette's lovesick Nemours. Philippe, the long-lost "brother" Camille suddenly claimed to have immediately following the museum visit, appeared at d'Hauteville's family estate in France just as Camille disappeared from d'Hauteville's life in Italy. Back in the garden, Philippe now suddenly springs from the foliage and begins spouting amorous prose calculated to overwhelm Eugénie. The scene's every detail contributes to the overall conclusion that Philippe intends to harm her. Initially, Philippe is compared to the "demon of the celestial garden," and then the "perfidious and terrible child" lures her into a secluded section of the garden to rape her (2: 180–81). Not only does Philippe commit violence on Eugénie's person, but the rapist also masterfully manipulates her, so that in the end, Eugénie will believe that what happened was her own fault. In a reference to the hermaphrodite sculpture, Philippe's lust is compared to some kind of Greek wonder: "This love resembled only the emotions that the Greeks knew, a drunkenness of feelings foreign to the soul, a desire more excessive than ideal. But their emotions also allegedly created miracles, gave sex to a cloud, and life and love to Pygmalion's marble" (2: 184). The fierce desire awakened in Philippe's breast is excessive and immoderate, powerful enough to animate stone or vapor.

The rape scene is triggering and difficult to read. Eugénie pleads for Philippe to stop, and s/he almost does: "Adriani hesitated nevertheless: for a moment he wanted to respect his still pure victim; the imploring whining of the poor and tender girl would have rattled a human soul" (2: 185). As s/he pins her to the ground though, Philippe imagines that Eugénie's arms pull him/her close, which s/he willfully interprets as consent: "But either by an involuntary movement of tenderness, or a convulsion of terror, he believed he felt one of Eugénie's arms holding him and squeezing him. Then ... all of his blood spilled and the threat of eternal punishment would have been too little to separate him from his idol. He remained" (2: 185). When Eugénie's mother awakens at two in the morning, she searches frantically for her missing daughter, only to find her unconscious, soaked from the downpour, resting on the folds of her dress (2: 187). Having been violated, Eugénie's own body now becomes a transgression and is transformed into a statue. Eugénie is compared to "one of those white statues that rest upon a cenotaph," which both prefigures her imminent death and gestures to the one who has caused it (2: 187).

Despite the fact that Latouche leaves out the actual rape, employing instead ellipses and the euphemism "he remained" to silence the act, no room for doubt remains in the other characters' minds. Eugénie's mother knows for certain when she undresses her daughter: "she undressed poor Eugénie slowly; and, suddenly, forgetting her carefulness, her tenderness perhaps, she took a few steps back in order to ask her questions without pity" (2: 187).[68] Even Philippe Adriani, who has made several allusions to his/her innocence, seems to tacitly admit guilt in the final duel scene of the novel. Moments before d'Hauteville runs Philippe through, s/he pleads: "Who knows if Eugénie and I are not innocent?" (2: 330). "Coward! You do not want to die and you are pleading," reasons d'Hauteville. Philippe confesses guilt by refusing to deny d'Hauteville's accusation: "And even so – cannot missing life be permitted to me? I am still so young" (2: 330).[69]

The rape scene is rarely mentioned by the few critics who have discussed *Fragoletta*.[70] Frédéric Ségu only refers to the scene in passing, insisting that nothing happened: "Surprised by her mother, she faints, and, over the course of the serious illness that results from this emotion, Eugénie, chaste soul who believes herself sullied, recounts her mistake to her brother while exaggerating it."[71] Yet, Eugénie does not limply fall to the ground when surprised by her mother. Her mother finds her in the middle of the night, already unconscious; her immobile, rain-covered body compared to a marble statue. Nevertheless, Ségu is not alone in his belief that Eugénie just "imagines" being violated. Even though M. Paul Pelckmans acknowledges the incontrovertible violence of this scene, he cannot admit a rape took place, since for him, rape can only be perpetrated on a woman by a man, and he is sure that Camille is no more than a woman in disguise: "Eugénie believed herself to be dishonored but it is impossible that Adriani-Fragoletta actually had sex with her [l'ait vraiment possédée]."[72]

The fact that readers seem unwilling to acknowledge the full horror of this scene may partially be owing to the longstanding critical belief that "romantic androgynes" were idealized figures and that the damned "decadent hermaphrodite" did not make its debut until the fin de siècle. If Philippe Adriani were the creation of Rachilde or Huysmans, one might have less trouble interpreting the rape scene. But because Ségu, like Nigel Smith, endeavors to show the foundational influence of *Fragoletta* on Balzac's *Séraphîta* and Gautier's *Mademoiselle de Maupin*, in which the androgynous characters are supposed to be idealized, they seem unwilling to confront the darker side of Latouche's character. However, this argument underestimates the importance of Balzac's more unsettling use of androgyny in *Sarrasine* and *La fille aux yeux d'or*. The latter, which he wrote at the same time as *Séraphîta*, makes the link *Fragoletta* establishes between desire and violence explicit with Paquita's murder, and the androgynous brother-sister team echoes the sexual domination present in Latouche's rape scene. As I will show, even in Gautier and Balzac's more idealized works, bodily desire remains latently present.

Ségu's perfunctory dismissal of anything untoward occurring in this scene also has to do with the way Latouche has chosen to recount it. Just as with the statue, Latouche displaces "certainty" from the bodies in question. "Truth" is not fully articulated, and just when it seems most clear, new evidence will emerge to further obfuscate it. If frustrating for the reader, this strategy pays dividends when it comes to confounding censorship, and it echoes the central mystery of the novel surrounding Camille/Philippe's sex and sexuality, so that ultimately the lack of resolution is consistent with the plot. In this way, *Fragoletta* is diametrically opposed to its predecessor *Clémentine*, for while Clémentine and the reader both learn that she is intersex simultaneously, Latouche stops short of fully revealing Camille/Philippe. And there is something deeply disquieting about the finale of *Fragoletta*, partially because contemporary readers have learned to expect "true sex" to dawn, and partially because, though we are left with no certainty, we feel that Latouche ends with a lie.

In the final duel, Philippe reiterates Camille's proclamations about being a monster and deserving death: "Who told you that I had a conscience, a heart, and humanity? What do I have in common with human creatures? I am not of their species" (2: 326, 328–29). After d'Hauteville runs his sister's attacker through with a sword, "Philippe" tries unsuccessfully to cast himself/herself into the sea (a second echo of the ancient tales) in the hope of disguising "the truth" of his/her body forever.

Nevertheless, Philippe/Camille's body is recovered and brought to a neighboring monastery, where "the oldest of the priests trained to practice medicine" begins an autopsy by opening Philippe's blouse (2: 340). The novel's last enigmatic line reads: "My brothers [. . .] we must bring the body to the Sisters of Mercy" (2: 341). At first reading, this is one of the more perplexing conclusions French literature has to offer. Could Camille really only ever have been a woman who disguised as a man in order to avoid d'Hauteville for some undisclosed reason? Such a conclusion cannot account for the way Camille suddenly refuses d'Hauteville's attentions after the museum trip. Even though Latouche's entire novel fundamentally resists certainty, resonances send us back to the sculpture scene for a second interpretation.

In the final pages, the priest abandons his autopsy table the moment he discovers Philippe/Camille's breasts. These breasts represent a fleshy parallel to the sculpture, and like the stone member that scandalized d'Hauteville, they are startling because of their context. The male genitals were shocking on what d'Hauteville believed to be a female body, just as the breasts are shocking because they were discovered on what was thought to be a male corpse, by a man who is, moreover, forbidden to see them. However, the scene is also a lie since the post-mortem was never completed. Upon finding breasts, the befuddled religious doctor retreats: "he was shaking. He nevertheless quickly put down a first instrument before going away, and he did so with his eyes down, his forehead red, and his countenance troubled" (2: 340). The priest's shock recalls d'Hauteville's initial embarrassment before the sculpture. His is another metaphor for reading, but one that stops short of examining the whole text. Both reactions tell cautionary tales about readerly response that provide insight into why Latouche chose to tread so lightly in his bodily descriptions of Fragoletta (and why Balzac was so reluctant to summarize the novel). Although we assume Camille/Philippe's trousers reserve the same surprise as the sculpture, we cannot know because Latouche does not disclose this information. Perhaps he feared that redoing the scene once the body reached the convent would tip the balance of his novel toward farce; that his prudish reader, like d'Hauteville before the sculpture, might turn away.

At the same time, however, to overly insist on a reading of Camille/Philippe as intersex would be tantamount to missing the point. At some level, the reader's desire to see the full "truth" revealed commits the same essentialist assumption as the fearful priest: it suggests that sex is everywhere inscribed on the body. It is only a matter of knowing where to look and how to tally up the parts. The beauty of Latouche's denouement is that he exposes that belief as mere cultural myth. By refusing to fully undress Camille/Philippe, Latouche effectively deconstructs any essential notion of sex by dissociating it from the presence of a given body part. Instead, we learn that peering underneath clothing does not necessarily reveal any truth at all. It tells us only about ourselves, perhaps about our own voyeurism, or what we allow ourselves to see, like the priest, who discovers only a mirror for his own shame. By refusing to reveal the "truth" of bodies, *Fragoletta* introduces the possibility that there is no "true sex," or, at least, that medicine, like the inobservant doctor, can only clumsily decipher it. As we saw in Part I, contemporary medical literature on historical intersex related similar difficulties and sexing errors.

At the same time that Latouche's priest/doctor was botching his autopsy, contemporary medical men and forensics experts were faced with incontrovertible difficulties when attempting to reconcile cases of intersex with a system of binary gender. Time and again, we saw famous doctors disagree about which sex (if any) to ascribe to their patients, and on what characteristics such determinations should be based. No one method could escape the danger of later reversal, and the rapid pace of evolving scientific technology seemed only to further obfuscate the issue, as biopsies began to reveal that individuals who appeared outwardly to harmonize perfectly with the female sex might, in fact, harbor internal organs of the "male sex."

Even more surprising then, is an article from the *Gazette des tribunaux* of August 23, 1833, in which the journalist instructs readers to consult *Fragoletta* in order to glean the truth for a legal proceeding. Crafting a euphemistic and elided style to pique the reader's curiosity, the author offers a mysterious rendition of a recently ended marriage between a woman and her intersex husband:

> The Civil Tribunal will soon try a case of which there are few examples in judiciary annals. Several years ago, Mademoiselle D... married Sir L... She was young, naive, and imagining nothing in a husband except a cashmere and the name *Madame*, she did not understand right away what position she was in, and did not realize that something could be missing. Nevertheless, she was soon enlightened by her confidences with a few young female friends and by her mother's instructions. Indeed, her *husband* had a sweet and feminine face, the rounded forms that did not seem to belong to his sex, etc. In short, a thousand other unmistakable remarks came to convince the young lady (or demoiselle) that her spouse could have just as easily been the wife of another as he was her husband. Monsieur L... was ... read the last chapter of *Fragoletta*. (1047)

Readers will no doubt relish the inversion of a newspaperman sending us to a novel in order to glean the facts about a historical case. According to the *Gazette* author, the last chapter of *Fragoletta* will elucidate this mystery, but, as we have seen, the novel itself does not reveal the promised truth. Despite Latouche's ambiguity and the traditional scholarly unwillingness to identify Fragoletta as intersex, it is clear from this article that some readers had no trouble deciphering the scandalous enigma of the novel. However, the journalist's reading of *Fragoletta* interprets the androgyne as an individual equally endowed to become "wife" or "husband," whereas the entire drama of the novel stems from the impossibility for the intersex character to fit into those social roles. Indeed, it is this crisis which most likens Fragoletta's plight to the legal case evoked by the *Gazette des tribunaux* writer. Balzac understood this tension. In his review of Latouche's novel, he described Fragoletta as an "an inexpressible being, who does not have a complete sex, and in the heart of whom battled a woman's timidity and a man's energy, who loves the sister, is loved by the brother, and can give nothing to either one."[73] While insisting on Fragoletta's position outside of binary gender, Balzac glosses over bodily sexuality in favor of more platonic sentiments, a choice prefiguring his own *Séraphîta*.

That Cuisin's Clémentine embodies the best of both man and woman fits with the consensus among literary critics that earlier representations of hermaphrodism are often idealized. (We have seen that *Fragoletta* problematizes this distinction.) Both *Mademoiselle de Maupin* and *Séraphîta* portray androgyny as the combined superlative of both sexes rather than a compromised amalgam falling somewhere in between. Several later decadent works like *Les demi-sexes* by the popular author Jane de La Vaudère, or *Monsieur Vénus* by the more famous Rachilde, describe their androgynous protagonists as less than perfect exemplars of both sexes. In *Monsieur Vénus*, Raoule de Vénérande is a masculinized woman who transitions away from femininity. Similarly, her partner, Jacques Silvert, is an effeminate man progressively emasculated by Raoule until he can no longer perform the "active" role during sex, a defining characteristic of masculinity.[74] In these works, androgynous characters become neither rather than both, and the calculus by which Raoule and Jacques "switch sexes" implies that masculine and feminine lie on opposite ends of the spectrum. To approach one is, by definition, to move away from the other.

However, as we have seen, Latouche's *Fragoletta* disrupts this neat temporal separation between the "romantic androgyne" and the "decadent hermaphrodite" in ways which critics have not always been willing to acknowledge. Despite *Fragoletta's* early publication date, Philippe Adriani's inferior ability as a swordsman along with his cowardice and cruelty hardly qualify him as an exemplary male by nineteenth-century standards. Similarly, Philippe's alter ego, Camille, is too poorly developed for the reader to know if she embodies the "feminine" sensibilities of Mademoiselle de Maupin. As Balzac observed, Fragoletta is neither fully female nor fully male. S/he appears in the 1830s already tinged with the sexual cruelty of the decadent Raoule. As we shall see, Latouche's influence on Balzac is legible in Balzac's own ambivalent depictions of androgyny in *Séraphîta*. Given that Balzac credits Latouche as a source of inspiration, it is even conceivable that Latouche's vexed portrayal of hermaphrodism as both beauty and violence goes a long way toward explaining Balzac's own ambivalent use of androgyny throughout his career. And this richness in Balzac's characters, in turn, helps to explain the lasting influence of androgyny throughout the century, and why later authors like Zola, who are thought only to portray "evil," decadent "hermaphrodites," continue to allude to Balzac and Latouche.

The Pure and the Impure in *Séraphîta*

Readings of *Séraphîta* have been conditioned by the belief that Balzac's use of androgyny stems from Swedenborgian mysticism, but our review of earlier works on intersex invites us to see Balzac's novel in a new light.[75] In a letter to Madame Hanska, Balzac reveals that a sculpture of a hermaphrodite initially inspired him to write *Séraphîta*.[76] In the same letter, he also admits his debt to Latouche's *Fragoletta*: "Séraphîta will be both natures in a single being, like Fragoletta, but with this difference that I imagine this creature as an angel arrived at its last transformation, and breaking its envelope in order to arrive at the heavens" (88). Because of Balzac's description of an angel and his avowed adherence to Swedenborgian mysticism, most critics have read Séraphîta as a being entirely divorced from material and historical context.[77] Yet since Balzac alludes to *Fragoletta* (1829) as a point of departure for his novel, and since it is not revealed that Séraphîta/Séraphitüs is an angel virtually until her/his ascension to heaven, it is also imperative to examine Balzac's use of androgyny in the context of Latouche's story about a physiological hermaphrodite (as was the case when Balzac began writing it in 1833).[78] Reading *Séraphîta* in this way reveals the novel to be fraught with previously overlooked tensions between material and spiritual epistemologies and desires, and is important because it uncovers a radical subversion of gender norms where we would least expect to find one.

Even though Balzac claims that *Séraphîta* perfectly reflects Swedenborg's teachings, scholars have been quick to point out that the author's knowledge of the mystic actually originates from Daillant de La Touche's abridged rendition of Swedenborg's works.[79] Analysis of Balzac's early drafts of the novel reveals that his insistence on the androgyny of Séraphîta/Séraphitüs was added later, in revisions that excised material references that could have ascribed a gender to the angel (II: 721). Yet this sexual indeterminism, which displaces "true sex" from the veiled sexual organs to what contemporary doctors called "secondary sexual characteristics," does not succeed in removing Séraphîta/Séraphitüs as a target of the sexual advances of other characters.[80] According to Henri Gauthier, both female and male characteristics are idealized and symbolize the purity and superiority of the angel (II: 722). But this reading overlooks the bodily yearnings which Séraphîta/Séraphitüs experiences, much to her/his chagrin. In other words, Balzac will preserve not only the gender indeterminism of Fragoletta with his character Séraphîta/Séraphitüs, but also the material yearnings his androgyne awakens in others and experiences firsthand.

Although the novel is titled *Séraphîta*, the reader's initial glimpse of the androgyne is of Séraphitüs, as *he* nimbly scales snow-covered peaks with Minna, "a pale young girl."[81] The narrator attempts to describe Séraphitüs ambiguously as "the person Minna called Séraphitüs," "the being" (l'être), or "the singular being" (l'être singulier), but he also occasionally resorts to the masculine pronoun "he" (il), and it is clear from Minna's early declarations of love that she believes he is a man (II: 736, 738). The unintentional humor of this scene is that while Séraphitüs persistently spouts lofty aspirations of coming nearer to God, Minna professes her worldly love for him. With aplomb flying in the face of propriety, Minna endeavors to make her feelings known, undaunted by her would-be lover's reluctance. Séraphitüs, on the other hand, generally feigns incomprehension or else deflects Minna's attentions by recommending that she lavish her affections on Wilfred – a boy who, we will soon discover, is also in love with Séraphîta, but who regards the epicene character conversely, as the epitome of femininity.

Nevertheless, Séraphitüs's religious fervor is, at some level, tainted with worldly materialism, and it is clear s/he is not entirely deaf to Minna's declarations: "I don't know if it is the moment to speak in such a way, but I want so much to share with you the flame of my hopes! Perhaps we will be together one day, in a world in which love does not die" (II: 743). Séraphitüs's amorous diction strikes a discordant note in an idealized description of heaven. Minna's impatient quip, "Why not now and forever?" renders this sexual tension explicit (II: 743). Staring morosely at a rare flower, Séraphitüs also appears to regret sacrificing his material purpose for a spiritual one: "Séraphitüs contemplated with melancholy, as if its smell expressed to him plaintive ideas that he alone understood" (II: 739). Séraphitüs later blushes when Minna unintentionally asks him about his own sexual potency while referencing the flower: "Why would it [the flower] be unique? It will no longer reproduce? Said the young girl to Séraphitüs" (II: 737). Like the lonely, hybrid flower, Séraphitüs is not destined to procreate.[82]

Given Minna's barrage of flirtation in the mountain scene and evident hope that Séraphitüs will marry her, their reception into civilization will prove astonishing. Upon their return, Minna's father suddenly addresses Séraphitüs as a young woman: "Thank you, mademoiselle, answered the old man while placing his glasses on the book. You both must be tired" (II: 742). The feminine plural form of the adjective "fatiguées," confirms irrefutably that Pastor Becker believes he is addressing two women. Balzac attempts to mitigate the blow of this shock for his now disoriented reader by describing Séraphitüs/Séraphita as incomparable and other-worldly, the embodiment of both male and female perfection. The narrator explains that "No known type could offer an image of this face that was majestically male for Minna, but who, in the eyes of a man, would have eclipsed the most beautiful heads attributed to Raphaël" (II: 742). Here reappears Latouche's theme of heteronormative desire projected onto an androgynous body. While Minna looks on Séraphitüs's "majestically male face," men perceive Séraphita as feminine grace incarnate. Yet, unlike Latouche, who never fully exposed his character as intersex, or even Gautier, who explains early on to readers that his protagonist is a woman in drag, Balzac describes his creation as a hermaphrodite of both mind and body. But because this hermaphrodite is revealed to be an angel, the social and cultural difficulties that this dual identity creates are eventually tran- scended, and in this way, intentionally smoothed over. Over the period of several chapters before this revelation, the seraph plays a familiar role in the unknown gender plot as an object of both masculine and feminine desire. Indeed, *Séraphita* raises many of the questions Balzac had treated earlier in his 1830 novella *Sarrasine*, and while on earth, his androgyne experiences much of the anguish described by both fictional characters and historical figures – most notably that of Herculine Barbin, whose memoirs, as we have seen, offer the only autobiographical account of intersex in nine- teenth-century France.

At least for the first three chapters, when Séraphita becomes the target of first Minna and then Wilfrid's affections, the reader is meant to suspend disbelief while acclimating to the very fluid gender identity of Balzac's main character. In some ways, then, Balzac expects his reader to inhabit the same "happy limbo" of sexual indeterminism that Foucault reads into Barbin's memoirs in the period before legal sex revision, and that Judith Butler has so astutely critiqued. According to Butler, Foucault "fails to recognize the concrete relations of power that both construct and condemn Herculine's sexuality. Indeed, he appears to romanticize h/er world of pleasures [...], a world that exceeds the categories of sex and of identity."[83] A second problem with Foucault's "cursory reading," as Butler sees it, is that it contradicts his argument in the *History of Sexuality*, in which Foucault suggests that sexuality cannot exist outside of the matrices of power. "Foucault invokes a trope of prediscursive libidinal multiplicity that effectively presupposes a sexuality 'before the law'" (131). Similarly, Balzac wants to romanticize androgyny that exists not "before the law," as Butler writes of Foucault, but rather "outside of worldly law," which proves just as problematic because he situates his androgynous character within the worldly matrices of power by construct-ing indeterminism using the discursive realm of the novel.

The novel's very structure mirrors the sexual ambiguity of the main character, alternating between descriptions of the "male" and "female" gender identities, if not of Séraphîta/Séraphitüs, then at least of those projected onto her/him by other characters.[84] Chapter two, titled "Séraphîta," opens with Wilfred's amorous declarations to the same char-acter whom Minna sees as a perfect man, but whom Wilfrid suddenly addresses as "my beloved woman" (ma bien-aimée) (II: 748). With the womanizing Wilfred, Séraphîta becomes flirtatious and cruel: "Have I not spoken these words just as the Parisian ladies about whom you tell me the love stories? [...] You desire me and you do not love me. Tell me, do I not remind you of some flirtatious woman?" (II: 749, 751). Séraphîta recognizes that this corruption comes from contact with this world: "I am always wrong to set foot upon your earth" (II: 751). It should also be added that Séraphîta/Séraphitüs's disparate personalities, which shift depending on whether the androgyne is acting the role of a man or a woman, echo (although with inversed genders) Latouche's bipolar creation of the cruel Adriani and timid Camille in *Fragoletta*. Moreover, as Wilfred admires Séraphîta's sensual form, he subtly acknowledges that her body harbors a mystery, much like that of Latouche's androgynous protagonist, and one that somewhat recalls the Louvre hermaphrodite sculpture: "He slowly came closer in order to better behold the seductive creature that was lying stretched out before him, softly reclined, head resting in hand and with the elbow in a deceptive pose" (II: 751). This charge of "deception" is fre-quently leveled against historical intersex people in medical literature.[85]

Séraphîta responds to Wilfred's projected desire in kind. Although she has begged Wilfred to marry Minna (as she asked Minna to look on Wilfred in the opening mountain scene), Séraphîta now admits that she would feel jealous of this union: "Well, Wilfred, listen, come close to me, yes, I would be angered to see you marry Minna; but when you will no longer see me, then … promise me to unite yourselves, heaven destined you for each other" (II: 753).

Like Clémentine and Fragoletta, Séraphîtüs repeats that he is not fated for love: "I am like an outcast, exiled from heaven, and like a monster, with no place on earth" (II: 746). Recall that Camille had evoked almost the same terms when rejecting d'Hauteville. Similarly, in Gautier's *Mademoiselle de Maupin*, published the following year, Théodore de Sérannes (Mademoiselle de Maupin in disguise) cites a mysteriously impossible love when refusing Rosette's advances: "It is not that I do not love Madame Rosette at all, I love her infinitely, but I have reasons to not marry that you yourself would find convincing, if it were possible for me to tell you."[86] As in *Séraphîta*, the unstated motivations in Gautier's novel are also the mystery propelling the plot forward, or the "hermeneutic code," to use Barthes's terminology. Even if the doubtful sex novels mentioned (*Fragoletta*, *Séraphîta* and *Sarrasine*, and *Mademoiselle de Maupin*), do not fully resolve the mystery at the denouement, they invariably lay bare the limitations of binary sex.

Several critics have outlined the ways in which Gautier's *Mademoiselle de Maupin* anticipates Butler's notion of "gender performativity," but not, to my knowledge, Balzac's *Séraphîta*, even though the two novels (published within a year of each other) both deal with sexual indeterminism and both draw their inspiration from Latouche's *Fragoletta*.[87] Likely because of the overarching importance of the "myth of the androgyne" in literary studies, coupled with Balzac's efforts to dissociate his androgynous protagonist from corporeal sex, critics have for too long overlooked the ways in which *Séraphîta* engages with the historical debate surrounding "hermaphrodism."[88] In a sense, this engagement should come as no surprise, owing to the large number of gender nonconforming or androgynous characters in Balzac's realist writings, and his other mysterious gender novel published four years earlier, *Sarrasine* – a story in which homosexual desire constitutes an infraction against the heterosexual matrix made punishable by death. *Séraphîta* is, in fact, more like *Sarrasine* and Balzac's realist corpus than has been previously acknowledged. This realization is crucial in order to understand his radical subversion of gender paradigms in *Séraphîta*.

Butler famously defined gender as "a stylized repetition of acts" (191), meaning that it is "a construction that regularly conceals its genesis; the tacit collective agreement to perform, produce, and sustain discrete and polar genders as cultural fictions is obscured by the credibility of those productions – and the punishments that attend not agreeing to believe in them" (190). It is clear from the scenes analyzed previously that gender is performative in Balzac's *Séraphîta*: both Minna and Wilfrid perceive the gendered object of their desire based on a stylized repetition of acts and those secondary sexual characteristics that were, in nineteenth-century France, and that still, in part, continue to be associated with femininity or masculinity to this day as a result of cultural construct. Séraphitüs embodies boldness, athleticism, physical strength, and the ability to protect; whereas Séraphîta is seductiveness, beauty, and the desire to nurture incarnate. Furthermore, the narrator often renders explicit the link between gender and actions, as if to reinforce social norms. When Wilfrid greets Séraphîta as a woman in the opening sentences of the second chapter, the narrator interprets her gestures as indicators of femininity: "She turned slowly toward him, after having tossed her hair back as does a beautiful woman who, suffering from a migraine, no longer has the strength to complain" (11: 748).

Stereotypes about women with headaches aside, what is especially interesting about Balzac's use of "gender performativity," then, is that it depends almost less on the gendered performances of Balzac's main character than on the projected desire of those that behold him/her and their belief in binary sex. In hearing her feminine name called out by Wilfrid, Séraphîta responds, the narrator reminds us with a simile, "as would a pretty woman" (ibid.). Later, when Wilfrid expresses wonderment at Séraphîta's behavior as a "coquettish woman," rather than "the pure and celestial young girl" he beheld for the first time in church, Séraphîta demonstrates her chameleon-like ability to perform a radically different identity: "Séraphîta passed her hands over her forehead, and when she revealed her face, Wilfred was surprised by the religious and holy expression that was spread over it" (751). One could interpret this scene as a confirmation of Séraphîta's supernatural ability to radiate a pure, celestial identity. Alternatively, it could be read as evidence that Séraphîta's "saint expression" was one performance among many.

While Minna persists in considering Séraphitüs as a man, remaining unperturbed when other characters address her companion as a woman, Wilfrid becomes increasingly exasperated by Minna's consistent use of the masculine pronoun "he" (il), perhaps because it would imply homoerotic desire on his part. Irritated, he finally quips: "He? asked Wilfrid, who?" (11:

802). If "they" had been the word of the year in 1834, (and it was gender-neutral in French), Balzac might have written a very different novel. Wilfrid's impatient jibe effectively shames Minna into silence, even though his outburst might well stem from the fear of homosexuality: "The young girl lowered her head while casting him a look full of sweet malice" (11: 803). Wilfrid's frustration suggests that Balzac anticipated how difficult it would be for nineteenth-century readers to reconcile a nonbinary, supernatural being with the worldly heterosexual matrix.

To the extent that performative gender opens up the space necessary for action that destabilizes normative notions of gender and sexuality in Balzac's novel, the instability of Séraphîta/Séraphitüs's gender identity (and the tricky "limbo" Balzac asks the reader to inhabit in order to understand it) accomplishes the political work advocated in Butler's theory. It is true that Séraphîta/Séraphitüs's ascension in the final chapter will ultimately sublimate danger to worldly binaries and tidily resolve the "threat" of homosexual desire by replacing it with the heterosexual and normative union of formerly "transgressive" figures, Minna and Wilfrid. However, large sections of the novel expose the "tenuous construction" (to use Butler's terminology) of gender norms even in nineteenth-century France (192). A mystical novel about an androgynous angel loved by both a man and a woman, who rises to heaven as pure light in the final chapter may seem a strange choice for the author of *The Human Comedy*; but Balzac's representation of unstable gender identity both ties the novel thematically to his larger corpus, and renders the text more strangely subversive than we might have ever thought.

Mademoiselle de Maupin and Medicine

Mademoiselle de Maupin recounts a relatively banal love triangle with a few spicy innovations. The Chevalier d'Albert, a young, epicene dandy, searches listlessly for his ideal woman. D'Albert will eventually take a lover whom he calls "Rosette" – charmingly after one of his dogs – and although she is extraordinary in every way, she nevertheless falls short of his ideal of perfection. Rosette, the reader learns, is also using d'Albert to palliate an unrequited love for her old flame Théodore de Sérannes, who conveniently returns just when d'Albert and Rosette are beginning to become intolerably bored with one another. Much to d'Albert's horror, Théodore, Rosette's former love interest, embodies everything d'Albert had so ardently desired in a lover, and he spends the rest of the novel in anguish, hoping Théodore might be a woman in disguise and despairing that he would love Théodore as a man just the same. Just as d'Albert bemoans his impossible desire for Théodore, the reader learns that Théodore had earlier refused Rosette's affections for some still unknown and apparently incontrovertible reason. Through Théodore's letters, we eventually discover it: Théodore is none other than Madeleine de Maupin, who has taken on a masculine identity. It is only in the final pages of the novel that Maupin reveals themself to d'Albert by spending half a night of passion with him before retiring to Rosette's room for the second half.[89] Maupin disappears by dawn, leaving a final letter to explain that separation is the only way forward. The lovers would only inevitably tire of each other otherwise.

No doubt because the preface to *Mademoiselle de Maupin* is almost more famous than the novel itself, Gautier's use of androgyny has most often been analyzed in relation to his philosophical aesthetics.[90] I would like to focus, however, on the ways in which the narrative engages with the historical debate surrounding unknown, or "doubtful" sex. The justification for what might otherwise seem like an eccentric comparison can be found in Mademoiselle de Maupin's own project. In chapter 10, we finally learn that Maupin transformed themself into Théodore de Sérannes in order to determine what men were really thinking, so that they might find one worthy of loving.[91] Maupin explicitly defines this endeavor as medical in nature: "I wanted to study man in depth, to dissect him fiber by fiber with an inexorable scalpel and to hold him alive and palpating on my dissection table" (1: 385). Gautier's use of the scalpel here situates *Mademoiselle de Maupin* within the realm of what Lawrence Rothfield terms "medical realism," and what Foucault identified as part of the "clinical gaze."[92] In addition to anchoring the plot to a new field of inquiry (medicine), this fascinating formulation determines the novel's focus as a study or *dissection* of human nature, while placing Maupin squarely in the role of the doctor/author.

In this way, Gautier's novel can be seen as more subversive than its predecessors, since the transgressive figure (Maupin) discursively takes up the tools of scientific inquiry in order to use them against men, and, by extension, heteronormative institutions of power.[93] Unlike Maupin, Clémentine was victimized by medical examination, and doctors generally appear in Cuisin's novel as cruel and opportunistic. Fragoletta's nervous priest hastily drew a faulty conclusion about the identity of Adriani's corpse owing to his essentialist equation of breasts with femininity. Similarly, in *Séraphîta*, Pastor Becker spends his days perusing scientific literature in the hope of finding precedents which could account for the strange androgyny and mysterious abilities of Balzac's main character. Of course, Becker's explorations are powerless to explain Séraphîta/Séraphitüs, since the identity as an angel lies outside the scope of scientific investigation.

In addition to the medical overtones of Maupin's project, the novel rehearses a preoccupation with scientific scrutiny in a vain attempt to determine the "true sex" of Théodore/Madeleine.[94] D'Albert describes studying their every contour, movement, and body part in a passage sharing a number of similarities with historical case histories of intersex:

> If you only knew [. . .] how carefully and with what breathless anxiety I observed you, down to your slightest movements! Nothing escaped me; how I ardently looked at the finest revelation of skin that appeared on your neck and wrists in order to try to ascertain your sex! [. . .] I analyzed the undulations of your step, how you placed your feet, how you swept back your hair; I tried to discover your secret from the habits of your body. [. . .] Never has anyone been looked at more ardently than you. (1: 475–76)

Yet, for all his intense observation, d'Albert remains powerless to discover Maupin's gender and his analysis results merely in vacillating interpretations: "I said to myself: surely, she is a woman" – then suddenly a brusque and daring movement, a virile accent or gesture would destroy my flimsy edifice of probabilities in an instant and throw me back into my initial doubts" (1: 476). Maupin realizes that d'Albert is visually dissecting them: "he must recognize each one of the hairs on my head and know exactly how many eyelashes I have on my eyelids; my feet, my hands, my neck, my cheeks, the slightest hairs at the corner of my lips, he has examined everything, compared everything, analyzed everything" (1: 507). Unlike Maupin, who remains in control, d'Albert cannot muster any clinical certainty, doubting Maupin's sex virtually until they go to bed together (1: 511).

As was illustrated in Part I, this visual scrutiny in order to reveal the mystery of doubtful sex is shared by medical publications of the time. In case studies of "hermaphrodism" not just body parts, but also gestures, tonalities, and mannerisms all became objects of intense study. Even as the genre of the case history became increasingly codified, doctors often relied on the same narrative techniques found in contemporary literature, including the "descriptive imperative" identified by Brooks as a hallmark of the nineteenth-century novel, which is evident in d'Albert's visual dissection of Maupin above.[95] Because d'Albert's analysis centers on determining Maupin's gender through visual scrutiny, this passage shares more with case studies of hermaphrodism than the popular genre of physiognomy, which relies on observation in order to describe typology rather than to reveal hidden "true sex."

Foucault recognized this method of decipherment as a hallmark of the nineteenth century in particular, when doctors began "deciphering the true sex that was hidden beneath ambiguous appearances."[96] Part I of this book demonstrated that the assertion of "true sex" was more a claim borne out through narrative case histories than an objective scientific reality, and that many doctors either did not believe it always existed or were unable to determine its nature in ambiguous cases. Like d'Albert's scrutiny of Théodore, medical examination was often powerless to reveal "true sex," and much like Maupin's own self-identification as a member of a "third sex," a number of doctors believed that a third sex did, in fact, exist, with many even attempting to modify the Civil Code to reflect this fact.

The very same year that *Mademoiselle de Maupin* appeared, in 1835, Dr. Dany published a remarkable case history of Joseph/Josephine Badré, which opens with a novelistic rendering of Badré's upbringing and youth composed in the literary *passé simple*.[97] The account includes mistaken identity, cross-dressing, a number of peripeteia, sexual exploits, dishonesty, and penetrating visual analysis. The considerable suspense cultivated by Badré's story is resolved only at the denouement, when the patient, having succumbed to a sudden bout of pneumonia, is autopsied, revealing a single atrophied and undescended testicle that appeared to doctors to have stopped developing early in gestation. Badré had formed the basis of an earlier medical examination and resulting publication, and both case histories combine technical, detached clinical analysis with the kind of creativity that one associates more with literature.[98] For example, Badré's dishonesty about his ability to ejaculate garners almost as much speculation as the description of the autopsy itself, and which Dr. Dany ultimately hypothesizes was motivated by "a feeling of vanity or the desire to generate more interest" (1835, 462). Meegan Kennedy has shown that such "discursive hybridity," especially in early nineteenth-century case histories, contributed to the genre's natural structure of suspense and resolution by highlighting the physician's insight as much as his clinical observation and command of medical technology.[99]

As we saw in Part I, doctors (like Guermonprez and the medico-legal expert Tardieu) sometimes relied on their professional reputation as observers in order to justify their authoritative claims, even when evidence was lacking. In addition to sharing a narrative structure that privileged close observation as a means to decipher – as much as to cultivate suspense – certain of the terms used in Gautier's novel to assess Maupin's sex reappear in Badré's case study (such as the French word "duvet" for slight facial hair). The medical case includes, moreover, a novelistic rendition of how Badré came to believe that his sex had been incorrectly determined at birth:

> Age, as it were, by developing the organs, soon made hair [duvet] appear on the upper lip and chin, which, light at first, soon took on a certain thickness. The young Badré had already noticed, while frolicking with his female companions, that they did not offer the same characteristics that he observed in himself, and by examining himself with renewed attention, he confirmed his belief that an error had been committed in his case. Ashamed to appear among women in a costume that so singularly contrasted with his pronounced signs of virility, he adopted the resolution to switch clothing and to arrive in Paris under the name of *Joseph Badré*.[100]

Like the fictional character Maupin, Badré changed clothing and embarked on a fresh start, hoping, like Abel Barbin after him, that the anonymity of the capital would mean a new beginning.

Gautier's "Monstrous Genre"

Relying on a kind of hybrid epistolary form, Gautier is able to defer the revelation of Mademoiselle de Maupin's "true sex" until nearly the end of the novel. This unique rhetorical strategy involves both letters in the traditional form of the epistolary novel – in which characters describe their inner thoughts and feelings to a close friend – and a narrator who summarizes events, as he puts it "in the ordinary shape of a novel" (1: 332).[101] As Gautier himself remarked by describing the novel as a "monstrous genre" (genre monstre), the novel's structure mirrors the dual gender identity of its central protagonist (1: 244). This hybrid approach allows Gautier to project the illusion of mystery long after the reader discovers that Théodore de Sérannes and Mademoiselle de Maupin are the same person. In chapter 6, the narrator already hints that Théodore might be a woman when a partially unbuttoned blouse reveals unusual contours:

> [. . .] the beginning of a certain rounded line difficult to explain on the chest of young boy; looking at it closely, one might have also found that the hips were a little too developed. The reader will think of it what he will; these are mere conjectures that we offer to him: we do not know more about it than he, but we hope to learn more in a little while, and we promise to faithfully keep him informed of our discoveries. May the reader, if he has a better view than we, penetrate his gaze under the lace of this blouse, and decide in good conscience whether the contour is too much or too little pronounced. But we warn him that the curtains are drawn and that only a twilight ill-suited to these sorts of investigations reigns in the room. (1: 334)

Gautier's narrator flirtatiously invites readers to test their own skills as observers and to decipher bodily signs, but there is nothing clinical about the erotic overtones of his diction. Even though the narrator coyly writes shadows into his scene in order to force the reader to read on to discover Maupin's identity, the novel itself will ultimately highlight the difficulty of interpreting the human body in a fashion akin to Latouche's *Fragoletta*, and to medical case studies.[102] This "warning" or "introduction," as "avertissement" can sometimes mean, foreshadows the end of the novel in its refusal to restore the protagonist to binary gender.

Although the reader now knows Théodore's secret, the mystery persists for Rosette and d'Albert, and the latter, especially, waits in torment, vacillating between the belief that the person he loves must be truly a woman, and the knowledge that, even "If I came to know with certainty that Théodore is not a woman, alas! I do not know at all whether I would not still love him" (1: 381). Right up until the second to last page of the novel, d'Albert is not sure if Théodore is a woman at all (1: 511). Here lies another of Gautier's innovations. Not only does Maupin take over the role of doctor; Gautier displaces the familiar label of "monster" from the androgynous, main character onto d'Albert.[103] The "monster" is no longer a perceived threat to the binary, but rather to heternormativity. Finding himself sexually attracted to Théodore, d'Albert is forced to confront his own inner "monster" by acknowledging that the apparent young man is the exact embodiment of his ideal lover. As Kari Weil finely puts it, Madeleine de Maupin is the "mirror to the sexual ambivalence he must recognize in himself."[104] Weil has intuited a hallmark of representations of androgyny that was originally introduced by Latouche. Unlike d'Albert, however, d'Hauteville is unable to evolve as a character and remains equally blind to his own attraction to androgyny. Incapable of recognizing his own role in Camille's disappearance, he is instead condemned to interpreting "her" absence as an impenetrable mystery.

All the novels that use unknown gender as a motor for the plot underscore the difficulty of interpreting the naked body, and they often reference one another in an intertextual web. Gautier alludes to the multi-layered ambiguities of the final scene of Latouche's *Fragoletta* in *Mademoiselle de Maupin*. In Gautier's rendition, Rosette unbuttons the blouse of Théodore's young page, Isnabel, in an attempt to revive him after a riding accident (1: 355). Discovering a "fine pair" of breasts on the young Isnabel, Rosette immediately assumes that the adolescent is Théodore's lover rather than applying her discovery to a reevaluation of the mysterious Théodore: instead of imagining that Théodore's own bosom might reserve a similar surprise, the scorned lover apparently berates Théodore for the impropriety of parading *his* young lover around with *him*. Again, interpreting the body reveals as much about the interpreter as the body under scrutiny. Here we learn of Rosette's unfounded jealousy and vivid imagination rather than about the "true" identity of Isnabel. (Isnabel is not Théodore's lover; she is a child rescued from a would-be pedophile.) Moreover, the ensuing fight between Théodore and Rosette provides further caution about the dangers of interpretation. The reader witnesses their disagreement from afar, and cannot listen in, but Théodore seems shamed, since they "changed color several times throughout Rosette's story" (1: 456). Théodore's legible discomfort mirrors the priest's visceral response in *Fragoletta*. While Rosette might interpret Théodore's blushing cheeks as confirmation of her fears about Isnabel, Théodore may just as likely feel embarrassment or fear because of how close Rosette is to discovering a bodily secret. Because Gautier credits Latouche's *Fragoletta* as the inspiration for his novel, there can be little doubt that he intends this scene as a homage to the earlier work, and that he thereby voluntarily inscribes a place for *Mademoiselle de Maupin* in a long line of intersex novels. What is most fascinating about this choice is that although Maupin is the only character among those novels who is not intersex, but rather a transing person, Gautier nevertheless refuses to assign Maupin a "true sex."[105] Instead, Maupin famously describes themself as a member of the "third sex":

> Neither one nor the other of these two sexes is my own; I have neither the foolish submissiveness, nor the timidity, nor the pettiness of women. I do not have the vices of men either, their disgusting, vile nature and their brutal tendencies; – I am of a third sex altogether that does not yet have a name; higher or lower than them, inferior or superior. I have the body and the soul of a woman, the mind and the strength of a man, and I have too much or not enough of one or the other to be able to pair up with either. (1: 505)

Like fellow literary hermaphrodites Clémentine, Camille, and Séraphîta/Séraphitüs, Maupin shares their inability to fully integrate into society.[106] Like Badré, Maupin does not feel that their clothing reflects their identity. Although their body is not the obstacle, Maupin disavows belonging to either sex. For Maupin, this rejection of the binary is a conscious choice rather than a forced punishment: both sexes are fraught with undesirable flaws such that choosing exile amounts to intentional rebellion and the only tolerable solution. Maupin's triumphant reclaiming of the term "third sex" is also a political act that turns away from doctors like Bouillaud, who, as we saw in the second chapter, had attempted to use it as a way to secure a civil death sentence for individuals who could not be neatly categorized as either male or female. By suggesting that Maupin's identity "does not yet have a name," Gautier both signals the current insufficiency of language to describe nonbinary gender and gestures hopefully to a future when perhaps it will. Understanding *Mademoiselle de Maupin*'s place among the unknown gender novels reveals the stakes of Gautier's initially surprising refusal to deny nineteenth-century readers the satisfaction of fully revealing "true sex." If Latouche took the first step by dissociating "true sex" from a tally of body parts in *Fragoletta*, Gautier takes the next by questioning the social and cultural underpinnings of binary gender.

Seen in this light, Gautier's refusal to recount Théodore/Rosalinde's final night might also constitute an allusion to Latouche's novel. This scene marks the novel's famous culmination when Maupin consummates their love with d'Albert and then slips into Rosette's room to spend the rest of the night with her. Just as Latouche never fully unveils Fragoletta's body, the narrator never gains access to what happened in Rosette's bed: "What [Maupin] said and did there, I never could figure out [. . .] I have made a thousand conjectures on the subject, each more preposterous than the one before, and so outrageous that I really do not dare to set them down on paper, even with the most respectable, euphemistic style" (1: 372). Of course, this titillating rhetorical strategy offers a convenient way to insinuate lesbianism without getting into trouble for describing it too clearly. Not only is the body difficult to read; Gautier suggests more radically that gender identity does not determine sexuality. To the end then, Maupin remains faithful to their initial project of experimentation and discovery. The nineteenth-century confines of literary decorum dictate, however, that the reader be denied those insights.

Gautier's rehearsal of the unattainability of bodily truth in *Mademoiselle de Maupin* echoes *Fragoletta*. Even though Madeleine/Théodore is more idealized than Camille/Philippe, the impenetrable mystery remains. Gautier has simply transferred the dilemma to an aesthetic one. If Madeleine de Maupin cannot wake up next to d'Albert, it is not because their love represents some kind of "monstrosity" by nineteenth-century standards, as was the case in *Fragoletta*, but because to be with him more than the one night would be to wreck the illusion of perfection that Maupin exudes. This is an extension of the often-repeated line from the novel's preface: "There is really nothing beautiful unless it can serve for nothing; everything that is useful is ugly."[107]

Despite the diversity of their techniques, all of the doubtful sex novels share a description of the human body that resists full interpretation. Barthes's hermeneutic code, which displaces revelation to motivate further reading, remains incompletely resolved at the denouement. Just when it seems that "true sex" has at last been revealed (when Fragoletta's blouse is unbuttoned, Mademoiselle de Maupin spends the last night with d'Albert, or Séraphîta ascends to the heavens), that very moment ends up prolonging the mystery of their identities. In its own way, each novel suggests that binary sex is unable to circumscribe bodily diversity. Yet, lest we assign too revolutionary and subversive a status to our novelists, it is important to remember that they also announce that non-normative identities have no place in nineteenth-century France. Maupin absconds in the night; Fragoletta dies by the sword; Séraphîta rejoins heaven. Even Clémentine, the only androgyne allowed to live happily ever after, still must do so in relative obscurity, forgotten to the world.

By reading canonical literature in the context of overlooked or popular fiction, we can come to better appreciate the historical significance of classic literary texts. *Fragoletta* enables us to decipher the meaning behind the hermeneutic code's unresolved nature in *Mademoiselle de Maupin*. And yet, because of the enduring critical belief in an ahistorical "myth of androgyny" that is unrelated to intersex, this parallel has remained uninvestigated for too long. Latouche teaches us something about the illegibility of bodies that is crucially important for understanding what is at stake in Mademoiselle de Maupin's articulation of a third sex. Gautier's appropriation of medical discourse reveals the limitations of the clinical gaze while calling into question the very meaning of "monstrosity." Throughout nineteenth-century French literature, the mystery of uncertain sex teaches us as well that sexual economy remains everywhere closely tied to textual economy, so that reading the one becomes inextricable from deciphering the other.

CHAPTER 4

Inheriting *"Hermaphrodism"*
How Degeneration Theory Changed Literature and Medicine

Fig. 12. — Marie-Madeleine Lefort à l'âge de 16 ans.

Figure 4.1 Marie-Madeleine Lefort, Sixteen Years Old, from Debierre,
L'hermaphrodisme [. . .] (1891).

"At the beginning of the century," a child was born into "an opulent family on the verge of disappearing." The birth represented the family's last chance to preserve their ancient name, and the infant would be blessed with both fortune and title.[1] The child, however, was registered as a girl on the birth certificate, meaning that the line would live on even if the great name would not. But fourteen years later, a prominent Parisian doctor was called to the family estate to examine the girl, who seemed to be growing more masculine with each passing day. It was determined that an error had been made; the civil status was hastily revised in a hushed proceeding, and hope that the family name would live on was unexpectedly rekindled. Then, for a second time, the family summoned the famous doctor. Although the boy began to grow facial hair and enjoyed "boyish" sport, his body looked different, and his parents worried that another mistake had been made. The doctor was adamant: the child was indeed a boy, but his testicles would likely remain forever in his abdomen. Again, the doctor returned, this time to conduct a minor surgical procedure intended to "improve" the outward appearance of the boy's genitals. Years passed. Reassured that their son, now of age, could marry, the next task was locating a suitable bride – one who either had not heard of his astounding transformation or for whom a lavish lifestyle would outweigh any misgivings about it. Just such a young woman was soon found, and the newlyweds were spirited to Italy for a two-year honeymoon. The extended trip served as a pretext during which time a pregnancy was simulated through a prosthetic bump placed under the bride's gowns, the size of which "grew" at regular intervals (47). A false birth was orchestrated. "The child that was produced as an heir to the name and title of the noble family was that of a carpenter, whose poverty had reduced him to separating from the newest arrival into his already large family." At first, it seemed as if "everyone's wishes had been fulfilled – but nothing could dispel the young woman's remorse for accepting to become an accomplice to her husband and new family." Moreover, her husband's "mood swings" "compounded the sadness, deception, and bitterness of married life. It was widely said that the young woman died of a broken heart after a few years of marriage." Unexpectedly, the "son" whose adoption had been so sinisterly orchestrated was later disowned by his own "father," undoing years of careful planning, and ensuring that the family name would die with him. As if in perfect concordance with a Zolian universe, the "depraved" and "degenerate" widower eventually succumbed to incurable venereal disease (47).

Like Joris-Karl Huysmans's androgynous protagonist Des Esseintes from *À rebours* (1884), the epicene man was the "last descendant" of a formerly great house (1).[2] This novelistic rendition of the dying breath of a noble family was not, however, written by a long-forgotten naturalist or decadent author. It was recounted by young medical student Georges Dailliez, in his thesis from 1892 entitled, *Subjects with Doubtful Sex: Their Psychological State; Their Condition Relative to Marriage*. The famous doctor thrice called upon by the wealthy family was Philippe Pelletan, "one of the most capable surgeons in the early part of the nineteenth century," whose unpublished notes from each of his successive visits Dailliez reproduced with care, along with his own novelistic framework of a near-spent family and their sordid maneuverings to contrive an heir (37). Dailliez's knack for storytelling is not the only thing that likens this case to contemporary fiction. As the title of his thesis indicates, the young doctor was preoccupied with the relationship between "doubtful sex" and degenerate heredity, and his writing confirms the prevalent belief at that time that those presenting with genital variations were likely "degenerates" with weakened mental faculties or dangerous tendencies toward debauchery, mental illness, and even suicide.

This chapter traces the nebulous narrative of degeneration theory in Émile Zola's *La curée* (often translated as *The Kill*), from its origins in medicine to its influence in fiction, and then back to case studies of "hermaphrodism". This trajectory will reveal how the degeneration diagnosis fundamentally shifted relationships between doctors and their patients. Dailliez's case is especially telling because of the contrast between the detailed, clinical notes Pelletan took in 1823, and the way Dailliez would recast them (à la Huysmans) in 1892 as a sinister expression of degenerate heredity in a family on the brink of extinction. *La curée* (1872) is a pivotal text because Zola's understanding of "hermaphrodism" anticipated and may have even partially inspired what became the central focus of works on sexual "perversion" during the fin de siècle. Zola's obsession with androgyny is merely a partial reflection of what became a widespread cultural anxiety, echoing the mounting terror inflected in the writings of numerous authors and doctors, from the well-known Rachilde and Huysmans to the more obscure Armand Dubarry and Dr. Laupts. In *La curée*, "hermaphrodism" becomes a scary confluence of scientific, moral, and social anxiety that prefigures its treatment in later nineteenth- and early twentieth-century sexology. In this way, Zola's novel serves as a harbinger of fictional and medical representations to come that popularized a pejorative view of "hermaphrodism" resulting from degenerate heredity. It is perhaps the darkest chapter in the nineteenth-century prehistory of intersex. At the same time, however, I also argue that Zola's use of androgyny in *La curée* unexpectedly subverts his normalizing use of science. Zola's representation of acquired androgyny and transient homosexuality in *La curée* not only relies on contemporary "scientific" theories; it also invites a new reading of Zola's hereditary determinism that moves beyond traditional criticisms of the experimental novel by inviting us to rethink Zola's naturalism. By portraying unstable gender identities, *La curée* undermines the seemingly inexorable calculus of degenerate heredity inherited from medicine and recasts literary naturalism in a new light – less as a derivative of science than as a critic of it.

"The Man-Woman" of a Rotting Society

First published in 1872, *La curée* became Zola's second novel in the *Rougon-Macquart* series – the author's great "natural and social history of a family under the Second Empire," intended to rival Balzac's *Comédie humaine.*[3] *La curée* tells the story of Aristide Saccard, an ambitious and corrupt employee at the Hôtel de Ville who feverishly leverages connections while taking advantage of insider information in order to profit from the great Paris housing speculation of the 1850s and 1860s. Saccard's androgynous sister, Sidonie, plays a central role in the plot by uniting Saccard with his second wife, Renée – a marriage securing the assets and capital he needs in order to launch his career as a real-estate mogul. While Saccard relies on his business acumen to embezzle from Second Empire France, he also exploits his young and fashionable wife by progressively dispossessing her of her landed assets and encouraging her to spend recklessly on clothing and jewelry, thereby increasing his social capital. Now a trophy wife bored with her lavish lifestyle and insipid lovers, Renée falls into an affair with her stepson, Maxime – Saccard's son by a previous marriage and one of the novel's many "hermaphrodites." Renée spirals deeper and deeper into debt and debauchery – overtly symbolized by her increasingly outrageous outfits – eventually suffering a nervous breakdown before finally dying of meningitis, leaving her conservative father to cover a staggering bill to her couturier.

Zola published the first edition of *La curée* with a short preface dated November 15, 1871, that serves both to justify and explain the work in the wake of its widely disparaged serial publication:

> I wanted to show the premature exhaustion of a race that lived too quickly and that resulted in the man-woman of rotten societies; the furious speculation of a period embodied in an unscrupulous temperament, disposed to adventures; the mental breakdown of a woman whose milieu of luxury and shame magnifies tenfold her innate appetites. And with these three social

monstrosities, I tried to write a work of art and science that was at the same time one of the strangest chapters of our social customs.[4]

Zola's "strange" marriage of art and science in *La curée* amounts to a novel teratology that categorizes three social monstrosities: the "man-woman of rotten societies," the unscrupulous and frenetic speculation during Haussmannization, and the nervous illness of an unhinged woman, depraved by her milieu.[5] In this way, Zola resembles the doctors explaining the origins, symptoms, and diagnosis of hermaphrodism. Like all good teratologists, Zola includes a case study for each category: Maxime, Saccard, and Renée. Unlike these scientists of monstrosity, however, Zola's categories are not intended to be universally true, but instead result explicitly from the diseased climate of Second Empire France. Zola's "man-woman" is the ineluctable product of a putrescent society; Saccard's greed is the metonym of an entire generation of furious speculation; Renée's madness is triggered by her environment. Zola's preparatory notes suggest careful meditation on what he eventually termed "the man-woman of rotten societies," and even though the published edition of *La curée* omits its preface, the author's later description of Maxime as a "strange hermaphrodite" perseverates on central elements taken from the earlier manuscript. Zola rewrote the term "man-woman" three times while reworking his preface to *La curée*, before deciding that it was the "result" of the family's degenerate "race," rather than simply a feature of it.[6] Zola later salvaged key fragments from his abandoned preface to elucidate their meaning:

> He [Maxime] was a defective offspring, in whom the parental faults worsened and became complete. This family lived too quickly; it was already dying out in this frail creature, in whom sex must have hesitated, and who was no longer a greedy will for gain and pleasure as was Saccard, but rather a coward devouring entire fortunes; a strange hermaphrodite arriving at the appropriate moment in a society that was rotting. (1: 425)[7]

An inevitable corollary of social decay, the androgynous Maxime arrives preordained. Zola's representation of Maxime as the epicene product of both his family and times resonates clearly in both passages and he insists on Maxime's androgyny with characteristic fervor. As a child, Maxime exhibits an early flair for fashion and resembles a "tall, thin rascal with a girlish face, a delicate and insolent look, and very soft blonde hair" (1: 404). His stepmother plays with him like a "doll," calls him "mademoiselle," and characters constantly liken him to women. Maxime's gestures belong to "that feminine look of schoolgirls" and "he had the thin waist, the swaying hips of a grown woman" (1: 407, 408). For these reasons, most critics identify Maxime as Zola's token "man-woman," but his "hermaphrodites" prove considerably more numerous and varied.[8] Although Maxime's degenerate heredity already marks him as a "strange hermaphrodite," it is his passing homosexuality in boarding school that "must have crippled his virility for good" (1: 408). Experimentation in convent school also "taints" Renée with "virility," and many other characters display some degree of androgyny, either congenitally (in the case of Maxime's future wife, Louise) or because of hard life in Paris (in the case of Maxime's aunt, Sidonie). Roughly twenty years before Dailliez's medical thesis, Zola's portrayal of hermaphrodism as an expression of degenerate heredity and the corrosive effects of modern society anticipates the popularization of psychological models of "perverse" sexuality in the 1880s and 1890s that attributed gender and sexual noncon-formity to degenerate heredity.[9]

Degeneration Theory, Zola, and Social Decline

> In the mystery of conception, so obscure, does one think of that? A child is born: why a boy, why a girl? One knows not. But what a complication of obscurity and misery if nature has a moment of uncertainty, if the boy is born half girl, if the girl is born half boy! It happens every day! The uncertainty can begin simply at the level of physical appearance, of the general qualities of character: an effemin-ate man, delicate, cowardly; a masculine woman, violent, without tenderness. It can extend to outright monstrosity, the hermaphrodism of organs, feelings, and passions that go against nature. Certainly, morality and justice are right to intervene, because they are responsible for keeping the public peace. But by what right nevertheless, if free will is in part abolished? One does not condemn a hunchback from birth, because he is a hunchback. Why think less of a man who acts like a woman, if he is born half woman?[10]

In an 1895 letter that became the preface to the anonymously authored *Roman d'un inverti-né* (*Novel of a Born Invert*), quoted above, Zola describes "hermaphrodism" as a woeful by everyday fact of life ranging from individuals born with sexually "uncertain" physical appearances to ambiguous body parts or even "unnatural" same-sex desires.[11] He stakes his claim of widespread "sexual uncertainty" on a fundamental ambivalence. On the one hand, Zola argues that sexuality is innate, like congenital "hermaphrodism" or being a "hunchback," which works to exculpate sexual "deviants" (albeit in a tellingly unkind manner). On the other hand, public morality and justice must sometimes meddle in private sexual matters, and Zola makes his intolerance of behavior outside the heterosexual matrix manifest by peppering his discourse with normalizing qualifiers like "monstrosity," and "against nature." In fact, Zola claims not to condone sexuality at all, except with the express purpose of procreation. In the same work, he insists that "Man and woman are surely only here on earth to make children, and they are killing life the day that they no longer do what it takes to make them" (4).

More than any other of his novels, *La curée* fleshes out the contours of Zola's ambivalence about sexuality. Given Zola's teratological aim to reveal "social monstrosities," it seems fitting that the experimental novelist would include a category for "hermaphrodism," since the father of teratology, Isidore Geoffroy Saint-Hilaire, had dedicated so much of his life to the subject. As we saw in Chapter 1, Geoffroy Saint-Hilaire wrote what was widely considered the definitive work on hermaphrodism for much of the century.[12] Zola's remark that Maxime's sex "must have hesitated" also resembles Geoffroy Saint-Hilaire's explanation of hermaphrodism, which he hypothesized as a result of over- or under-development in the typical growth pathways of a human fetus.[13] But unlike Geoffroy Saint-Hilaire, preoccupied foremost by anatomy, Zola's experimental novel relies on the governing principle of heredity, and it is the theory of degenerate heredity that explains Zola's plethora of "hermaphrodites."

Prosper Lucas's *Traité philosophique et physiologique de l'hérédité naturelle* (1847–50) became Zola's primary scientific authority on heredity in the *Rougon-Macquart* cycle, but psychiatrist Bénédict Morel's 1857 *Traité des dégénérescences* also profoundly impacted the novelist, and was largely responsible for popularizing degeneration theory in France.[14] Relying on a pre-Darwinian concept of evolution, Morel's treatise alleged that environmental, biological, and behavioral factors influenced heredity, producing a vast array of pathologies in offspring.[15] Over time, the collective impact of these hereditary taints resulted in sterility and the dissipation of entire family lines. After the publication of *On the Origin of Species* in 1859, elements of Darwinian evolution were also gradually assimilated into the theory of degenerate heredity, but France was notoriously reticent about Charles Darwin's research for far longer than its neighbors. A prominent exception to this trend, Zola was an avid Darwinist who titled his first book in the *Rougon-Macquart* saga "The Origins," and exclaimed in 1868 – just two years before he began writing *La curée* – "our characters' personalities are determined by genital organs. It's from Darwin! That is literature."[16] Zola's exuberant belief in the explicative power of genitals is worth noting given his fascination with intersex.

Vernon Rosario explains that, because of its "vagueness," hereditary degeneration was cited to explain "a bewildering variety of social 'diseases': criminality, anarchy, depopulation, immorality, foreign national characteristics, urban poverty, and so on."[17] No doubt the mysterious, even mythic power of heredity held the novelist in a trance. Heredity was the new cosmic force in the universe, silently shaping the future with degeneration as its henchman, cutting down the wicked and the weak. Along with Rosario, Daniel Pick and Robert Nye have carefully analyzed the social and cultural work carried out by its diagnosis, but the relationship between hereditary degeneration and case studies of hermaphrodism has not been explored, even by historians studying fin-de-siècle hermaphrodism.[18]

The term "degenerate heredity" implies that hereditary "defects" will be conferred upon future generations with increasing detriment. As Morel writes, "The offspring of degenerate beings demonstrate progressive degradation" (1857, 5). In his 1896 *Perversion et perversité sexuelles* (*Perversion and Sexual Perversity*), Dr. Laupts echoes this point:

> When one finds a slight form of degeneration of the central nervous system among ascendants, hysteria, for example, one can encounter among descendants grave psychological problems [...] In all of the cases of sexual inversion, whether it be acquired perversion or congenital perversion, one finds a very charged heredity. (219)

Chief among the "grave psychological problems" Laupts identifies is "perverse sexuality." Its etiology, or potential causes, are multiple. In addition to a family history of nervous or mental illness, alcoholism, and suicide, Laupts also lists intermarriage, and even large age differences between spouses (220). From Lucas, Zola finds the idea to "kill off" a few of his characters with hereditary illnesses – a plan zealously executed in *La curée*.[19] In 1857, Morel described unusual genital variations as another expression of degenerate heredity: "The extreme limit of degeneration exists when the individual is not only incapable of propagating his kind in normal conditions, but shows himself completely impotent, whether in consequence of the non-development of the genital organs, or from the absence of all prolific power."[20] *La curée* might be seen as Zola's test case for Morel's "extreme limit."

The Rougon-Macquart's hereditary taint originates from Adélaïde Fouque, or "Tante Dide," whose hysteric fits eventually reduce her to near mute paroxysm in the final novel of the series. Zola's efforts to link the entire family's "fracture" (fêlure) to one individual and his goal to study a single tainted family anticipates the hallmark of later works on heredity, such as Charles Féré's *La famille névropathique* (1884). Zola's *Dossier préparatoire* credits Lucas with the influence of relative age differences between parents on the sexuality of their children.[21] A disciple of degeneration theory, Zola explains Maxime as the cumulative and degraded product of his ancestors' lesions, worsened still by his mother's extreme youth at the time of his birth:

> The Rougon blood ran thin in his veins and became delicate and depraved. Born from a too-young mother, he was a singular and somehow incoherent mixture of his father's frenetic appetites and reckless abandon and his mother's weakness; he was a defective offspring in whom the parental faults worsened and became complete. (1: 425)

With mathematical precision, Zola pushes this logic to horrific culmination with the birth of Maxime's son, Charles, in *Le Docteur Pascal* (1893). Maxime passes his androgynous beauty to Charles, but by the seemingly inescapable laws of degeneration, he is a weak-minded hemophiliac unable to survive childhood.

Charles's death mirrors the fear of population stagnation or decline which became entangled with the theory of degenerate heredity and was rapidly termed a national crisis in France. "One is struck with terror at seeing the birthrate decline everywhere in France," wrote Pierre Garnier in his 1883 opus, titled, importantly: *The Hygiene of Generation: Human Sterility and Hermaphrodism* (4). Garnier's title illustrates how in the last decades of the nineteenth century, hermaphrodism, formerly perceived as an individual anomaly, was recast as a social malady heralding grave consequences for all. As we shall see, case studies of hermaphrodism also reflect this navigation away from the individual toward the impact on greater public welfare.

At the forefront of the shift from the individual to the collective was the advent of surveys revealing alarming statistics. France's birthrate began to plummet in 1825, and would not bottom out until 1939.[22] At the same time, the birthrates of other European countries did decline until around 1900, and while France's neighbors maintained a steady population growth of at least 30 percent between 1872 and 1911, France's population only mustered a 10 percent increase over the same period.[23] In fact, between 1891 and 1895, deaths actually exceeded births in France – an alarming situation that was reproduced during several individual years.[24] Dr. Laupts's discussion of the falling birthrate in *Perversion et perversité sexuelles* demonstrates both an acute awareness of these distressing statistics, and underlines how specialists blamed "deviant" sexuality for the crisis. For Laupts, "Among the revealing signs [of perversion], one of the most serious [. . .] is population stagnation, the stoppage of its growth, the decreased birthrate. This decrease [. . .] has hit France harder and earlier; therein lies a serious symptom, perhaps the indication of a grave lesion" (1896, 361). According to Laupts, both late marriages and contraception meant that "perversion has stained marriage itself, and it is no surprise that many children are born tainted with more or less abnormal inclinations that they inherited from their ascendants' bad habits" (361–62). At least in popular imagination, degenerate heredity was producing a crisis of both quantity and quality in the general public. Faced with stagnant population growth and a feeble birthrate, some concluded that France was limping toward the last moments of what had been a great civilization, but was now decadent, diseased, and doomed.

Boarding School, or Accidentally Becoming Gay

Maxime's androgyny results from his degenerate heredity, which might also predispose him to "inversion" according to nineteenth-century scientific beliefs, but it is his behavior and environment during childhood that seal his fate:

> The school in Plassans, like most provincial boarding schools, a den of young bandits, thus proved a hotbed of corruption that developed Maxime's neuter temperament in unusual ways, fostering the evil that had come down to him from some unknown heredity. Age would fortunately correct it. But the mark of his childhood indiscretions, this effeminization of his whole being, of the moment when he believed himself to be a girl would stay with him, crippling his virility. (1: 407–8)

Boarding school, that "place of sin," is a familiar target of Zola's invectives.[25] Yet the author's enduring fear that one could "become hermaphroditic" is somewhat at odds with his model of ineluctable hereditary determinism, even in characters often considered to be the most predetermined, like Maxime. Moreover, by explaining Maxime's "passing homosexuality" as a result of his cloistered adolescence, Zola's plot may serve as a fictional model for medical discourse. Citing a situation similar to Maxime's, Laupts writes twenty years later: "Quite often, such an invert was only predisposed; a confined education in high school, the lack of a female entourage at the moment of puberty made him into an invert. He is not incurable" (1896, 14).

Even though Maxime is predisposed to "inversion" through degenerate heredity, his case illustrates that Zola, like Laupts, does not believe that all kinds of sexuality are innate. In a newspaper article in *La Cloche* from 1870, Zola fulminates on the evils of boarding school using almost the identical words as Laupts: "All cloistered association of people of the same sex is bad for morality."[26] Zola describes boarding school as a festering social wound that ought to be cauterized "with red-hot iron," and he advocates abolishing the institution once and for all.[27]

Schooling also explains, in part, why Renée ends up as debauched as her stepson even though she comes from "good stock" and a conservative home (unlike Maxime). Zola insists on this point when planning to illustrate how Renée's sister, delivered from the evils of convent school, would elude her sister's terrible fate, and further reinforces it in the preface, by indicating that Renée's environment is "ten times" worse than her "natural inclinations."[28] For Zola, convent school will have lasting nefarious effects on adult sexuality: "If she went to convent school, it is certain that she is not innocent. It is not a virgin that one is marrying. Perhaps, if she has a calm temperament, she will be able to live honestly; but within her honesty itself, her entire life will be sullied by memories of her childhood."[29] Just as the cumulative weight of Maxime's son's degenerate heredity assures his untimely death, the narrator considers Maxime and Renée's incest a foregone conclusion given their early childhood initiation into homosexuality at school and their later confidences on the subject, as well as Maxime's strange, effeminate upbringing. Since first meeting, they had been drifting toward incest:

> Every minute that had passed between them since that moment had been a minute of perversion. The peculiar way in which the young woman had raised the child; the familiarities that had made them friends; and, later, the ribald audacity of their shared confidences – all that dangerous promiscuity had ultimately formed a singular bond between them, one in which the joys of friendship became almost carnal pleasures. They had given in to each other years ago. The brutal act was only the acute crisis of this unconscious malady of love. (1: 481)

In fact, Zola indicates that we should have anticipated this outcome after the first chapter, but just in case we lapsed into inattention, he includes several instructive passages like the one above.[30] The snowballing effect of these assertions creates the overall impression that Maxime and Renée's incest was preordained, much in the way of a tragic flaw. Indeed, the overdetermined nature of their relationship is reinforced by Zola's frequent references to the Phaedra myth.[31]

In a twist to the gender-bending of Théophile Gautier's novel (in which d'Albert finds himself falling in love with an apparent man), after sleeping with Renée, Maxime blames the fact that he almost mistook her for a boy as a kind of exculpatory explanation for their semi-incestuous tryst:

> The affair had angered him. He blamed the black satin domino. Had anyone ever seen a woman dressed like that? You could not even see her neck. He had taken her for a boy; he was playing with her, and it was not his fault if the game had become serious. He certainly would not have laid a finger on her if she had just shown a bit of her shoulder. He would have remembered that she was his father's wife. (1: 459)

This passage has often given critics pause. Hannah Thompson reads it as evidence of the power of disguise in Zola's work, interpreting Renée and Maxime's sex as the "central deconstructive moment in *La curée*," because "in terms of plot development, her adulterous and semi-incestuous act undermines Saccard's role as her husband and Maxime's father and places her outside the realm of normative sexuality."[32] Roddey Reid, on the other hand, expresses shock: "One transgression seemingly contains another. The secret outrage of their carnal incest is that it also constituted a violation of the heterosexual matrix; Maxime was caught off guard, for he thought he was playing with a 'boy'(!)."[33] When placed back into its historical context, Maxime's action seems less shocking. That Renée is drawn to the "woman" in Maxime, and Maxime the "man" in Renée, as Reid judiciously remarks, can be understood in the context of Zola's scientific research to reflect both their exposure to homosexuality while away at school, and the widespread societal "decline" toward sexual indeterminism.

In a warning owing more to fiction than science, Dr. Laupts cautions explicitly against an upbringing like Maxime's because it may cause grave psychological problems: "You must not lose sight of the fact that, in all cases except innate inversion, to separate any young child from his family and surround him with other children is to put him truly at risk" (1896, 341). With "inversion" lurking behind every corner, the best way for boys to distract their weak minds is by exercising their bodies: "Simple fencing, gymnastics, playing boule, horseback riding, happiness, and activity suffice to chase away obscene obsessions that lie in wait for the schoolboy at every moment of his life at school" (342).

In Jean Racine's noble realm of honor, Phaedra's confessed love for her stepson becomes a damning speech act that equates saying with doing and that therefore seals her death warrant. By contrast, Zola's characters consummate their boredom-inspired desire with little initial guilt or afterthought. Only in one of the final scenes of the novel does the crushing weight of Renée's transgressions become apparent to her as she beholds her naked body in the mirror. Numbed by continual exposure to decadent debauchery, the "incest" invites retribution not for the transgressions of generations past (the Rougon-Macquart family taint) as in Racine's tragic flaw, but even more so because of the way that Maxime and his stepmother are shaped by personal experience. This sense of "becoming" is the very antithesis of the notion of Racinian tragedy, in which Phaedra's punishment results purely from her mother's transgressions. (Phaedra's mother incurred Venus's wrath by boasting of her beauty, and it is for her mother's vanity that the goddess castigates Phaedra by making her fall in love with her stepson.)

Even after being "cured," a homosexual experience represents a latent danger for Zola. In divulging their childhood indiscretions, Renée and her stepson form a kind of pact and are sexually stimulated as they relive past moments:

> The joy that children feel when whispering about forbidden things, the attraction that draws a young man and a young woman together into sin, albeit in word only, kept bringing them back to salacious subjects. [. . .] Renée confessed that the little girls in her school were very naughty. Maxime outdid her and dared to recount some of the shameful things that went on at his school in Plassans. Then she leaned toward his ear, as if the sound of her voice was the only thing that would make her blush, and she confided to him one of those stories about convent school that are common in bawdy songs. (1: 429)

Renée's whispered confession suggests she may have partaken in the lesbianism of her school friends, "the inseparables."[34] No matter the degree of her involvement, Renée is evidently "tainted" with virility from her experiences in convent school to the point where, as Nicholas White puts it, "she plays the role of the leading male" in their relationship.[35]

But while savoring the memory of a guilty pleasure might lead to recidivism, the real danger for society at large, according to degenerate heredity, was that future generations would be born with a taste for it. This is the problem with Louise de Mareuil, Maxime's ill-fated fiancée. Louise bears the same androgynous "stigmata" (Morel's term) of degenerate heredity as her fiancé (1: 353).[36] In his *Dossier préparatoire*, Zola intends for Louise to suffer from what he calls the "naivety made knowledgeable by heredity," by which he means that she is born with her mother's debauched memories ingrained on her virginal body (1: 370):

> Carried in this unhealthy womb, Louise emerged with anemic blood, misshapen limbs, and a diseased brain, her memories already filled with a filthy life. At times she believed that she possessed vague memories of another existence and imagined bizarre, shadowy scenes of men and women embracing, a whole carnal drama that titillated her childish curiosity. [. . .] It was her mother speaking in her. (1: 434)

Because individuals like Louise and Maxime would represent a threat to future generations for as long as they survived, Laupts ominously cautions doctors against trying to cure them all. When a "débauché" comes to you, he urges his fellow doctors to "think about what this sick person will represent as [. . .] a germ of perversity for humanity" (1896, 281). In the case of the "occasional introvert," who only engages in homosexuality briefly, out of "necessity" because he was separated from women, as with prison inmates or school boys, Laupts adds: "the fall of this young man certainly does not seem justifiable, but it is understandable" (102). But even years after his "fall," such a man represents a latent threat: "restored to healthy habits, if this individual marries, he will probably pass on to his children an unfortunate predisposition, a penchant for inversion that, without being accompanied by physical signs, will make them into types that we could call born cerebral inverts" (102).

Yet by insisting on Maxime's transient homosexuality and Renée's acquired virility in boarding school, Zola unwittingly introduces an instability that is fundamentally at odds with his hereditary determinism. The introduction of behavior and environment erode the foundations of a mythological reading of the novel and undermine the predestination of any tragic flaw. This threat of unforetold "becoming" cannot come from myth, but only from science. Yet, at the same time, the preordaining power of science – the very heart of Zola's novelistic project – is fundamentally upset. This incompatibility is a feature of the circular logic of degeneration theory itself. As Charles Bernheimer wrote, tautology characterizes the very narrative of degeneration: "the discourse of degeneration [. . .] reads physical stigmata as signs of moral corruption and interprets moral infirmities as symptoms of bodily disease."[37] Paradoxically, Zola's strategy of employing science to create fiction lays bare the unsatisfactory nature of science's explanatory narrative. This observation invites us to move beyond traditional criticisms of the experimental novel that have alternately focused on either Zola's flawed application of literature as a scientific tool of investigation or on the flawed nature of the outdated "scientific" theories of heredity on which his fiction relies. In other words, a frustration with science's inability to explain the ills of modernity finds expression in Zola's narrative where we would least expect it.

Hermaphroditic "Inverts"

Vernon Rosario illustrates that the term "inversion of the genital sense," first introduced in France in 1882, was actually an amalgam of earlier nosological and diagnostic characteristics used to describe "pederasts" and "effeminate hysterics."[38] In fact, the inversion diagnosis was tied to "hermaphrodism" in several ways, demonstrating how much the meaning of the term itself was unstable, and had already shifted in the second half of the century. While German sex reformers like Karl Ulrichs called for a "third sex" deserving medical and legal tolerance, Nye shows that the French associated inversion with effeminacy and impotency.[39] For Dr. Garnier, impotence and sterility inextricably linked "inverts" and "hermaphrodites": "Hermaphrodism [. . .] is the necessary corollary of impotence and sterility, by simultaneously uniting imperfect, incomplete, or rudimentary attributes of both sexes on the same individual" (1883, 5). Even though sexologists outside of France "could readily conceive of homosexual men who were masculine in every visible way and differed from other men only in their interior psychic constitutions," contends Nye, "the French maintained that inverts were men with weakened sexual economies if not with androgynous secondary sexual characteristics."[40] In 1893, Julien Chevalier argued that inversion was the result of an atavistic return toward the embryonic state of hermaphrodism, and, as we saw in Chapter 2, Tardieu's earlier work in the 1870s stressed the importance of "abnormal" genital morphology in the diagnosis of "pederasty."[41] According to Émile Laurent, hermaphroditic genitalia, exhibiting secondary characteristics of the opposite sex, and same-sex desires all constituted evidence of a degenerate slide toward lesser animals (1894, 138). In the French model, degeneration placed homosexuals at the androgynous low-end of the evolutionary spectrum. In fact, in the first French case study of "inversion," Drs. Magnan and Charcot importantly link "perversion" to "the degrading consequences of a weakening of morals in a profoundly vitiated society."[42] Like Zola's hermaphrodite Maxime, "inverts" were considered physical *and* moral degenerates.

It has been argued that this "old teratological" view of inversion stretching all the way back to Geoffroy Saint-Hilaire is what prevented the French from making lasting contributions to sexology. Citing Geoffroy Saint-Hilaire's comments about the "abnormal" genitals of "dwarfs" and "giants," Nye suggests that for Geoffroy Saint-Hilaire, "sexual appetite and genital conformation were the markers par excellence of human anomaly on account of their particular sensitivity to the vitality of the internal economy."[43] Yet, in the case of hermaphrodism, Geoffroy Saint-Hilaire did not claim that genital variations correlated with mental health issues, and even in the case of "giants," the teratologist admitted that not all of the subjects he examined presented with unusual genitals.[44] In Geoffroy Saint-Hilaire's system, hermaphrodites were not considered "monsters," strictly speaking, but rather their own "distinct" branch that "should be classed immediately before monstrosities" (1832–37, 2: 32). For Geoffroy Saint-Hilaire then, hermaphrodism occupied a "intermediary rank" between monstrosity and lesser anomalies (2: 33).

Nye has suggested that Geoffroy Saint-Hilaire believed that "all individuals" were "necessarily of one sex or the other."[45] As evidence, he quotes the scientist's statement that the classes of men and women "belong to not only different but nearly *inverse* functions in the family and in society. In that sense there are no intermediaries; our laws do not admit their existence or foresee their possibility."[46] But this just means that Geoffroy Saint-Hilaire recognized that social and cultural practice sanctioned binary gender roles, and that no legal category existed for those individuals who fell outside the limits of "men" and "women." Not only did Geoffroy Saint-Hilaire understand this, but his research had proven that the two social and legal categories could not confine the full range of human diversity, and he even argued that some "hermaphrodites" formed part of a "veritable third sex."[47] Time and again, Geoffroy Saint-Hilaire asserted that "the reproductive system can [. . .] present such an association of characteristics of both sexes, and these characteristics can be so combined, that the determination of true sex is difficult or even entirely impossible" (2: 36). In fact, Geoffroy Saint-Hilaire hoped that his research would alert forensic experts to the extreme difficulty" and even sometimes "absolute impossibility" of determining the sex of hermaphrodites (1832–37, 3: 575). As we saw in Chapter 1, Geoffroy Saint-Hilaire's taxonomy described several types of hermaphrodism in which the patient would have no binary "true sex," and he stressed that sex assignment was, at best, "approximate." He repeated derivatives of this word three times in the space of two pages:

> Sex determination can often only be a simple approximation, hermaphrodites that authors call male or female truthfully do not have, in many cases, the characteristics of the sex that one attributes to them, but are simply less far removed from those of the other sex. Finally, it can be the case that the conformation of their reproductive system places a hermaphrodite at equal distance from both sexes, and consequently, remains completely unreducible to one or the other. (1832–37, 576–77)

As we saw in the Chapter 2, Geoffroy Saint-Hilaire claimed that cutting-edge research (like his own), revealed both that outdated models and the Civil Code wrongly asserted that binary gender was universally applicable:

> According to old physiology, and our current legislation, the male and female types were two sexual states that were not only distinct, but opposite: no analogous relationship existed between them, nor any intermediary states [. . .] and one could only see in a hermaphrodite a male simulating a female (or the inverse) [. . .]. (1832–37, 3: 575)

Thanks to new science, it was finally understood that "The male and female systems are not two essentially and elementarily different systems, but rather, if one can put it in this way, are two different forms of a single, identical system" (1832–37, 3: 576). According to Geoffroy Saint-Hilaire, the female and male reproductive system differed by "degree of development" rather than nature: "There are the same materials in both cases, they are only differentiated between one sex and the other by the degree and the mode of their development" (ibid.). By arguing for the androgynous origins of the sexes, science posited a fundamental "sameness" that undermined essential sexual difference. In other words, if fin-de-siècle doctors linked what they saw as "abnormal" genitals and "abnormal" sexuality, that idea had little to do with Geoffroy Saint-Hilaire's 1830s taxonomy of hermaphrodism. Or rather, it had to do with a reappropriation of only a small part of Geoffroy Saint-Hilaire's research that had been reimagined in the new context of degeneration theory.

Geoffroy Saint-Hilaire had shown that all embryos start off as nonbinary, and argued that arrested or excess development could prevent complete sexual differentiation in some individuals. In 1891, Dr. Debierre (one of the proponents of "true hermaphrodism" hoping to revise the Civil Code to add a "third sex") details the development of genitals from their hermaphroditic origins, following Geoffroy Saint-Hilaire (see Figure 4.2). Degeneration theory posited an atavistic return to the androgynous origins of sexual difference that Geoffroy Saint-Hilaire had revealed decades earlier. For Geoffroy Saint-Hilaire, by contrast, there was no causal relationship between hermaphrodism and mental illnesses, or between sexual indeterminacy and sexual "deviance."

It is more likely that the overlapping history of hermaphrodism and homosexuality around the turn of the twentieth century is related to medical collaboration between doctors studying sexual inversion and those who encountered cases of hermaphrodism combined with the

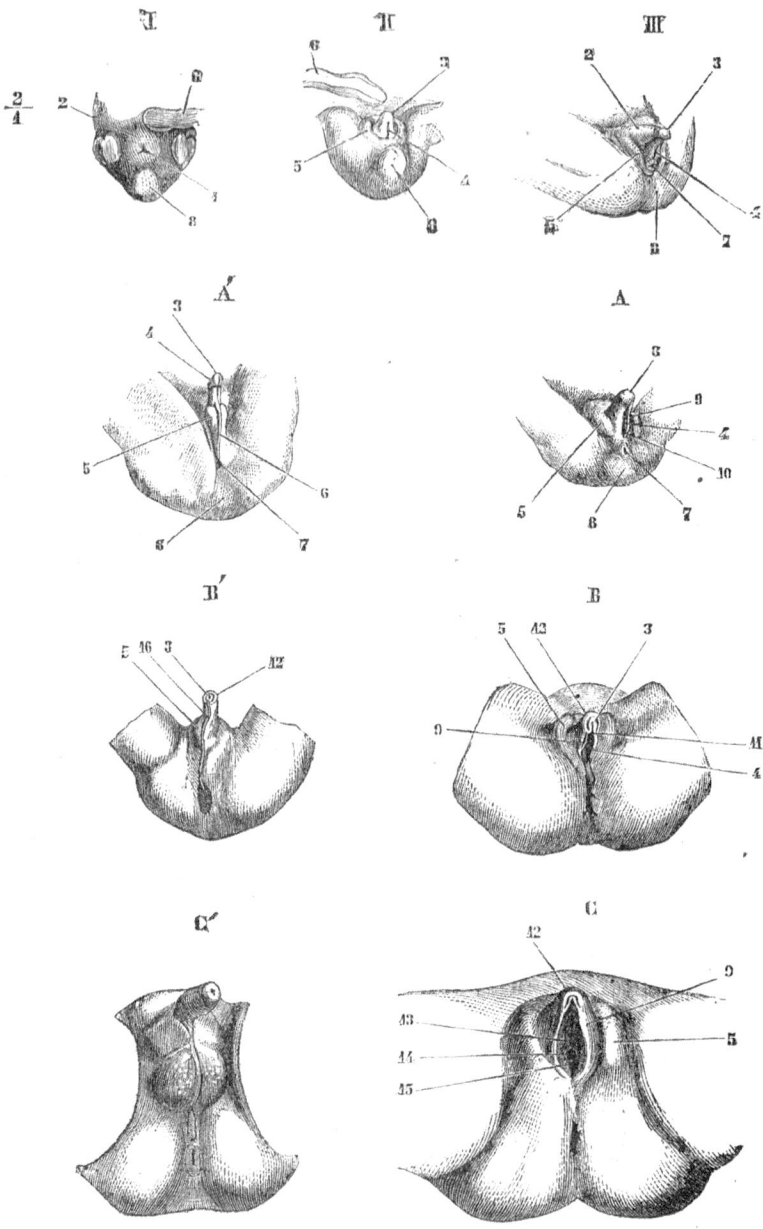

Fig. 9. — Développement des organes génitaux externes.
Ch. Debierre. — L'hermaphrodisme.   3

Figure 4.2 Development of the External Genital Organs, from Debierre,
L'hermaphrodisme [. . .] (1891).

widespread influence of degeneration theory.[48] For example, Dr. Samuel Pozzi, France's most well-known expert on hermaphrodism after Geoffroy Saint-Hilaire, worked with Dr. Magnan, possibly the "most influential neurologist of the Third Republic."[49] Pozzi coauthored a 1911 article with Magnan titled, "Inversion of the Genital Sense in a Feminine Pseudo-Hermaphrodite."[50] After detailing the intimate landscape of their inner and outer anatomy, Pozzi also appears to have redirected certain of his intersex patients to his alienist colleagues who would then publish the same patient's equally fascinating psychological portrait.[51] Other doctors passed their patients around as well.[52]

In an 1887 paper on "abnormal" genital morphology, Magnan draws a parallel between psychological "stigmata of degeneracy" like inversion, and physical "stigmata of degeneracy" like hermaphrodism.[53] In this article, Magnan describes "inverts" as male minds caught in female bodies, and vice versa.[54] He will venture a similar claim about the "hermaphrodite" in his joint publication with Pozzi, describing the patient as "a male brain in a female body" (1911, 229). Magnan's formulation also echoes Zola's preface to the *Roman d'un inverti-né*. Despite their apparent refusal of the German call for tolerance of inversion, French doctors obviously have recourse to the German model of "psychological hermaphrodism" when explaining some cases. Pozzi even classifies another patient as a case of "psychological hermaphrodism," following Hirschfeld's expression.[55] Laupts, for his part, believes that the "invert" whose confessions he publishes is in every other way a woman, who happened to be born into a man's body, even going so far as to qualify the patient as a "wannabe" hermaphrodite:

> It's the classic type of a malformed person, of a sick person. This being is a woman both physically and morally . . . Without doubt, the genital organs are those of a man, but all the secondary sexual attributes are those of a woman, and therein lies the visible hesitation, incertitude, and error that have presided over the constitution and development of such a being. It could be said: "s/he's a wannabe hermaphrodite" ["c'est un hermaphrodite manqué"]. (1896, 96–97)

Magnan was no stranger to Zola. They frequented the same social circles and both famously attended Charcot's presentations at the Salpêtrière. Additionally, five years after *La curée*, in *L'Assommoir* (1877), Zola based the doctor who interviews Gervaise about her husband's family history of alcoholism, before admitting him to Sainte-Anne, on the psychologist himself.[56] Magnan had published multiple treatises on alcoholism in the early 1870s that influenced Zola, but he was most well remembered for his

1885 work, *Anomalies, Aberrations and Sexual Perversions*, and his role of helping to popularize degeneration theory. Chronologically, it is possible that Zola's representation of hermaphrodism in *La curée* informed Magnan's thoughts about sexual ambiguity and degeneration theory.

Daniel Pick explains that by the 1890s, skepticism of degeneration theory was "gathering pace" and drawing new doubters, including Sigmund Freud, who had earlier studied in France: "The word was slowly losing its specificity and its mystique, its point of difference from heredity in general, in serious medicine and psychology."[57] As we shall see, however, this timeline does not reflect the influence of degeneration theory in case studies of hermaphrodism themselves, which continued to cite the theory for a long time after it came under suspicion in wider psychology.

The Plight of "Degenerate Hermaphrodites"

With such weight given to hereditary antecedents in the explanation of "sexual perversion," it is of little surprise that doctors begin almost methodically to include family history in their case studies of hermaphrodism and homosexuality that fell under the catch-all term of degenerate heredity. In the *Archives d'anthropologie criminelle*, in which Laupts first published the *Roman d'un inverti-né*, with all the titillating stratagems of a serialized novel, the doctor invites his colleagues (and novelists alike) to contribute their case studies of inversion according to a prescriptive format with special attention given to personal and familial antecedents.[58] Laupts recommends creating a family tree, noting any nervous or psychological taints, signs of degeneracy, risk factors like alcoholism, intermarriage, and even traumatic events or emotional disturbances during pregnancy (1896, 40–44). Zola's character based on Dr. Magnan will ask some of these very questions to Gervaise in *L'Assommoir*.

With the addition of detailed psychological information along the lines of Laupts's prescription, case studies of hermaphrodism in France from the second half of the nineteenth century appear increasingly different from their predecessors, which had focused more on anatomical descriptions.[59] In the wake of Morel's popularization of degeneration, medical representations of hermaphrodism increasingly include clues to the familial origins of "doubtful sex," and often explicitly cite degenerate heredity as the central cause. In this way, "hermaphrodites" who were once a kind of medical curiosity, instructive in the teratological model for what the "abnormal" could teach us about the "normal," were now progressively transformed by medical beliefs into radically different beings.

Dailliez's novelistic case of an intersex child born to a near-spent family that opened this chapter illustrates this shift well. Written long before degeneration theory, Dr. Pelletan's notes taken in the early part of the century draw no parallels between the boy's body and his mood swings or eventual debauchery, but when Dailliez records them in his thesis from 1892, he does so under the heading "demoralization and duplicity," grouping the case alongside others of degenerates in which "genital abnormalities" supposedly led to sexual deviance (35). Focusing on a detailed anatomical description of his young patient, Dr. Pelletan was not preoccupied with family history or heredity in 1823, and one of his relatively impartial signed certificates indicates that the patient was highly intelligent, noting his special aptitude for Latin and mathematics (37). Dailliez, on the other hand, added the novelistic framing about a birth in a nearly extinct family that would inevitably link the child to decadent literature for contemporary readers. It was the young medical student who divulged the sordid details of the family's duplicitous machinations in order to procure an heir by placing them alongside Pelletan's more neutral writings, in a transparent effort to imply that the family was tainted with degeneracy. Dailliez all but states that degeneration had rotted the family tree from the roots: "It is therefore proven that, in the opulent class, congenital defect leads to psychological troubles and to perturbations of the reproductive sense amounting to abuses, and that result in terminal chronic myelitis" (1892, 47). Although Dailliez is unable to determine the exact nature of the man's debauchery, he hastens to add that "people worthy of our trust" "categorically affirmed" that he was so, and that doctors believed that the neurological disease attacking the patient's spinal cord (myelitis) had been caused by a sexually transmitted disease. It was Dailliez, finally, who attributed the guilt-ridden woman's heartbreak and death to her husband's mental instability.

Like their "degenerate" cousins the "inverts," the new diagnosis of hermaphrodism as an expression of degenerate heredity contributed to a pejorative view of patients with genital variations in late nineteenth-century medical literature like Dailliez's thesis. Given the large number of French cases citing hereditary degeneration as a cause for hermaphrodism, it is surprising that the theory's decisive role in both diagnosis and prognosis has been overlooked.[60] Examining a few representative cases reveals how degeneration theory distorted case narratives of "hermaphrodism."

When, in 1906, the patient known only as "G. M." confronted Drs. Roubinovitch and De Beurmann in the hopes of obtaining a legal sex revision, they felt unsure how to proceed. G. M. posed "diverse practical problems," and the doctors admit, "we had to hesitate for a long time before making a sex determination" (49, 48). Raised as a girl, G. M. sought a medical opinion that would allow him to amend his civil status to male when doctors treating a skin condition had inadvertently discovered ambiguous genitalia.[61] According to his doctors, G. M.'s genitalia resembled those of a male fetus, while his body type and breasts likened him more to the female sex. The patient also exhibited "male psychology," characterized by doctors as sexual attraction to women, interest in sports and politics, and "disdain" for sewing (48–50). Ultimately, the doctors determined G. M. was a man – a finding confirmed by medical authorities of considerable repute, but they hesitated before providing him with new civil liberties under the auspices of a legal sex revision (48).[62] Despite the difficulties of determining G. M.'s sex, it was his "degeneracy" that proved the most troubling to experts. The good doctors remark that their "Saint-Denis androgyne" has a family history of hermaphrodism, suicide, prostitution, and mental inferiority, which they cite, "once again," as corroborative evidence for the hereditary transmission of hermaphrodism: "Suffice it to say that G. M...'s case demonstrates once again that pseudo-hermaphrodism is a serious stigmata of hereditary degeneration that is nearly always accompanied by diverse psychological problems, among which sexual psychopathies seem to occupy a preponderant majority" (58). In fact, a host of French research in the late nineteenth and early twentieth centuries attributed "hermaphrodism" to degenerate heredity – a diagnosis linked, moreover, to insanity. But this idea did not come into being overnight.

Multiple cases of intersex within a single family had alerted earlier doctors to its potentially hereditary origins, but the advent of degeneration theory produced a shift in the way doctors reported these facts. As with "inversion," doctors began to incorporate family histories into case studies of hermaphrodism, which they scrutinized in order to speculate on its origins. In 1887, Dr. Sentex purposefully adds that the parents of his intersex patient are cousins, and "consanguinity cannot be left unmentioned in a case such as this" (55). Dr. Guermonprez makes a similar discovery in his patient's genealogy, and insinuates that the apparent celibacy of a different relative – "unheard of in the region" – was probably fabricated to disguise some genital "abnormality."[63] In another case, Dr. Motet announced that the patient's parents "must" be cousins (even though they ardently denied any relation) because of their child's developmental delays.[64] Owing to the perceived link between genital variations and mental illnesses, Dr. Marandon de Montyel published "On Anomalies of the External Genital Organs of the Mentally Ill and Their Relationship to Degeneracy and Criminality" in 1894. The elaborate classification system provides a broad spectrum of genital variations. Faucher and Bourdin's case from 1899 offers another striking example of how the compelling narrative of degeneracy inflected representations of hermaphrodism.[65] In the absence of a family history or any biographical information whatsoever, the doctors manifest such profound conviction in the theory of degenerate heredity that they attribute their patient's developmental delays to her sexual ambiguity, while concluding that both are expressions of degenerate heredity: "It is generally accepted that idiocy and hermaphrodism are two effects of the same cause: hereditary degeneration [. . .]. It is therefore necessary to admit that the coincidence is not mere chance and that hermaphrodites are dotards from a mental point of view" (303).[66] As evidence, the doctors quoted Émile Laurent: "From an intellectual standpoint, hermaphrodites are nearly always inferior beings. Physical degeneracy nearly always corresponds to psychological degeneracy" (303).[67]

In 1890, Dr. Pozzi – the leading French expert on hermaphrodism, referenced above for his work with prominent psychologists like Zola's friend Magnan – describes hermaphrodites as "either weak of mind, or, if they are intelligent, mentally unstable. They most often have, moreover, hereditary antecedents affecting the nervous system" (354). Little suggests that Pozzi's beliefs evolved more favorably over the years. Although he encountered many intelligent patients and even described one with apparent admiration, his final comments on the case betray the larger cultural belief that "hermaphrodites" were untrustworthy: "Certainly, it would be poor form, after such an example, to only speak ill of hermaphrodites' morality" (1911, 335). In fact, "hermaphrodism" was so widely believed to result from degenerate heredity that doctors unable to discover any kind of hereditary antecedent in their patient's family history often expressed genuine surprise. This, however, did not always prevent them from discussing the prospect of "hereditary hermaphrodism" in their conclusions.[68] Because doctors believed so intensely that "hermaphrodism" resulted from degenerate heredity, and because they blamed degenerate heredity for a vast array of mental "deficiencies" and "perversities," some physicians began to regard their patients as dangerous and untrustworthy.

In his 1912 case study, Auvray infuses his observations about a patient with judgmental assumptions: "It is clear that she is aware of her anomaly and wants to pass as a woman at any cost" (323). Whereas in the past doctors had often relied on a patient's sexual desires in order to determine their sex, Brouardel writes in 1887: "I bid you do not allow yourself to be swayed by the often-misleading moral orientation of an individual" (57). In fact, increasingly, fin-de-siècle doctors causally linked mental and genital "deviations," so that because their external genitalia were different, their mental capacities too were thought to be affected. Brouardel continues: "when genital aptitudes are not normal the mental state takes on a singular, generally melancholic state" (57). In his 1892 case study of Louise-Julia-Anna, Guermonprez echoes Brouardel:

> Her perversity has become so profound that questioning her can only lead to useless answers because it is impossible to afford them the slightest confidence. [...] Her moral sense is so degraded, so profoundly fallen, that it is impossible not to put them in comparison to her anatomical deformities. (370)

Geertje Mak has argued that Guermonprez's case is "one of the most rigid, moralistic, and denigrating accounts of a clinical encounter between a hermaphrodite and a physician of that era" and is "not very representative of other case histories."[69] Mak is right when one considers cases spanning the entire century, but it is sadly much more representative of other case studies from the heyday of degeneration theory. Doctors in the last quarter of the nineteenth century frequently cite degenerate heredity as an explanation of hermaphrodism, and when they do, moral judgments nearly invariably ensue.[70] Degeneration theory and moralistic and vilifying accounts seem to bear a direct correlation in France. In this way, Guermonprez's report is actually representative of cases in which doctors cite degenerate heredity in a patient's etiology. Guermonprez calls Louise-Julia-Anna "a teratological being both in the moral and the psychological sense," and further alleges, "beings of this sort are degenerates" (1892, 370, 368). The preconceived equation of "hermaphrodites" with sexual deviants (therefore not trusted to relate their own experiences) is notably absent from nineteenth-century French case studies predating the advent of degeneration theory.[71]

Although doctors doubt their patients' veracity in some early case studies, these instances appear to form the exception rather than the rule.[72] Often they reference the idea that some individuals were using their bodies for financial gain, and so had pecuniary motivations for dishonesty. As one doctor wrote: "One should take the declarations of a hermaphrodite or of people who have close relationships with him with a grain of salt. One should first examine whether these declarations are occasioned by an ulterior motive."[73] In this instance, doctors were referring to Charles Durge, who made a living in Europe by traveling around and displaying himself as a "hermaphrodite" at fairs and in medical schools. Many cases make mention of this phenomenon, although doctors demonstrate little self-reflective criticism about their role in the industry.[74]

The perceived causality between genital variations and mental illnesses would become so widely accepted in France that some doctors even read malicious and deceptive intentions into statements that they otherwise found wholly true and reasonable. When G. M. (whose request for a legal sex revision was referenced above) asked doctors to convert his civil status to that of a man because he could earn twice as much in his job as a man, they concluded that he must be lying. Descended from a line of "deviants," sexual desire, not economic benefit, must motivate G. M.'s request, they alleged.[75] Although their patient *was* male, and would benefit financially from a change in civil status, the doctors refused to help in the name of the greater good:

> From a salary perspective [...] G. M. . . . only makes three francs a day as a female laborer whereas as a male laborer, she could expect a gain of at least double that [...] moreover, G. M. . . . could invoke the right to vote. G. M. . . . as a man, could also hope to marry a woman [...] In conclusion, one easily sees all the individual advantages that G. M. . . . could hope to draw from a modification of civil status. [...] The conformation of the external genital organs supports, moreover such a change. [...] But can the same be said for the community's interest? What can society gain by increasingly promoting the widespread evolution of beings like G. M. . . . struck with degeneracy and sterility? What are they worth socially? What is the marriage of such subjects worth? (1906, 57)

In the same sentence in which his doctors declare G. M. sterile, they also paradoxically fear that his "kind," if left unchecked, will contaminate the larger population. Even though he cannot procreate, G. M. has suddenly become a threat to social welfare.

G. M.'s case is atypical in that his doctors are not thwarting his efforts of legal sex revision in order to curb what they saw as homosexuality, as was true in Guermonprez's case. As a male, nineteenth-century society sanctioned G. M.'s attraction to women. Instead, G. M. was "problematic" because of his "degeneracy." His doctors admit this regarding their patient in particular, but suddenly shy away from the eugenic implications of their actions in general: "This touches upon a question of social organization and legislation relative to degenerates in general. It is not our intention to broach such a subject" (58). Ultimately, however, by weighing G. M.'s individual rights and needs against those of the larger society, that is exactly what the physicians were doing. Unfortunately, for G. M. and others like him, prominent contemporary doctors promised little hope for a bright future:

> Being very unstable because of his defective hereditary organization, one can see in G. M. a being predisposed to diverse sexual psychopathies, [...] to suicide, etc. ..., in a word, to all of the morbid varieties that can present among hereditary degenerates. Observations made by Legrand du Saulle, Magnan, Christian, to cite only the French alienists, authorize us to pronounce a severe prognostic concerning G. M.'s mental future. (57)

Medical men regard G. M. almost as a lost cause, his future already crushed under the weight of hereditary determinism; the onset of insanity was merely a matter of time.

Blaming Mothers

As Zola relates in his preface to the *Roman d'un inverti-né*, the actual moment of conception was shrouded in mystery from a nineteenth-century scientific perspective. When and how sex was determined was hotly debated, and in the neo-Lamarckian theory of degenerate heredity, it was widely believed that a mother's state of mind during pregnancy could manifest itself physically in her unborn child's body.[76] Following the "theory of maternal impressions," doctors encountering intersex began accordingly to interrogate mothers about their experiences during pregnancy and to regard their responses as explicative. Pozzi records in his 1896 case that his patient's mother "became frightened during her third month of pregnancy when she saw a man crushed."[77] More frequently, a mother's hysteria or nervous anxiety was believed to have caused her child's bodily difference. For example, in 1891, Paul Petit significantly lists "hermaphrodite" Eugénie Remy's mother as a "a neuropath [...] who allegedly had, throughout her second pregnancy, nervous attacks" (130). In another case, Pozzi zeroes in on a mother's "sadness" as a potential cause for her child's sex variation, while he exculpates the father (276).

Just as Lucas had argued decades earlier, the circumstances surrounding the moment of conception were still believed vital to fin-de-siècle doctors confronting cases of doubtful sex.[78] Lucas had also hypothesized that insanity was passed through the mother, which may be why the Rougon-Macquart's "fêlure" originates with Tante Dide.[79] Yves Malinas notes three instances in Zola's cycle in which congenital defects are attributed to a mother's physical or mental state during conception, but the concept also proves a fruitful source of plot in a number of other fictional representations of intersex.[80] Several literary "hermaphrodites" have been born of the scientific belief that a mother's emotions caused her child's sex difference. Briefly contrasting J.-P.-R.-Cuisin's interpretation from 1820 to that of Armand Dubarry in 1898, will illustrate the vilification of hermaphrodism in the wake of fin-de-siècle sexology.

In the preface to his novel *Clémentine orpheline et androgyne*, Cuisin announces that his work will answer the question "what will have been the mother's influence on a hermaphrodite's ideas?"[81] Half a century before Zola's experimental novel *La curée*, Cuisin puts this question of maternal impressions to the test, and determines quite simply that the ambivalence of Clémentine's mother during pregnancy must have manifested itself physically in the form of her child's half-male/half-female body and psychology. Struck by the beauty of the visiting Ambassador of Persia, the Countess of Sombeuilles involuntarily molds her child after his physical traits by reading *A Thousand and One Nights* and imagining the ambassador's exotic features:

> It is in the seductive poison, my daughter, that I was imprudently shaping your being with the most singular elements. [. . .] Indecisive nature, not knowing which wishes to obey, accorded a daughter to my desire, (because in the beginning of my pregnancy, I passionately desired to have one), while bending simultaneously to my caprices and wants, so she indecently melded with this former sex other attributes which came to me from my fatal ambassador. You were no less dear to me for it [. . .]. (2: 181)

As we saw in the previous chapter, hermaphrodism was linked to exoticism in the medical record as well, with genital development allegedly linked to temperature increases. And, indeed, Marie-Madeleine Lefort is stylized with the trappings of "Orientalism" on display along with her naked body in the opening illustration of this chapter (see Figure 4.1). All's well that ends well for Clémentine, who, as we saw in Chapter 3, marries an open-minded nobleman unconcerned by the fact that they will not be able to have children. The tone of the entire novel is light-hearted and fantastic.

In Armand Dubarry's fin-de-siècle novel *L'hermaphrodite* (1898), doubtful sex takes a fatalistic turn for the worse.[82] Dubarry's "hermaphrodite" Brigitte from *Les déséquilibrés de l'amour* embodies the inevitable result of degenerate heredity and her mother's violent rape at the hands of the murderer "La Terreur de la Villette." Like Barbin's journal, Brigitte's tale of woe is narrated in the first person: "I am an illegitimate child conceived in the most lamentable circumstances, and heredity has given me such sad oddities making me a marginalized being, a sort of monster without defined sexuality" (1). She discovers scientific beliefs about her body by reading medical literature (like fictional Clémentine and Camille, and historical Marie B. before her), which proves horrifying. Brigitte learns from the medical authorities of the time (Legrand du Saulle, Christian, Garnier) that she is doomed: "Hermaphrodism, which most often derives from heredity, leads to melancholy, that I knew, and also, to madness" (58). Here, fictional Brigitte cites by name some of the same doctors referenced in G. M.'s historical case study discussed above.

Dubarry's bizarre hybrid genre, often called a *roman de mœurs*, conflates medical treatises and fiction in a fashion akin to Zola's *La curée*, but with the erotic twist of pornography.[83] As we have seen, the boundaries between fiction and medicine were long since blurred in the messy reality of cultural exchange. Dr. Laupts, as it were, is a *nom de plume* for Dr. Georges Saint-Paul – a man who dabbled in literature and would fondly reflect on his friendship with the great Émile Zola for years to come.[84] He also labeled the autobiographical writings of the Italian "invert" a *novel*, which led some to wonder whether he had made the whole thing up. Michael Rosenfeld's recent discovery of the full manuscript of the *Roman d'un inverti-né* reveals that Saint-Paul exercised considerable editorial liberties, excising large sections in order to make the memoirs better fit with his theories about homosexuality.[85] Zola's representation of hermaphrodism as an expression of degenerate heredity and the corrosive effects of boarding school anticipates, and may have even contributed to, the popularization of psychological models of perverse sexuality that were so abundant in the 1880s. After all, the anonymous author of the *Roman d'un inverti-né* sent his confessions to the novelist Zola instead of to a doctor (although he was delighted to discover them in the window of a medical bookshop). With all of these doctors who styled their case studies with the codes of fiction and novelists who conducted "literary experiments," the narrative appeal of degenerate heredity is worth noting. The need for narrative forms a palpable entity in case studies of hermaphrodism in which doctors attribute their patients' ambiguous genitalia to sordid family history or, when evidence lacks, to fantasy and fictional experiences *in utero* and beyond.

A Subversive Reading of Degeneration in *La curée*

Zola's bold mix of art and science in his experimental novel has attracted criticism from its inception, either for the author's spotty fieldwork, deep conceptual contradiction, or simply poorly chosen sources.[86] Yet it is partially the state of nineteenth-century medicine that explains why Zola's representation of hermaphrodism in *La curée* is at once cutting-edge science for the time and a hopelessly outdated remix of ancient folklore.[87] Zola's portrayal of Maxime and his son's physical androgyny as resulting from their degenerate heredity relies on contemporary "science." In 1859, Moreau de Tours described hermaphrodism as a kind of "sexual uncertainty" and "hesitation," which Zola portrays in *La curée* and describes in his preface to the *Roman d'un inverti-né*.[88] We know that Zola read Moreau de Tours, and his reading notes betray his interest in hermaphrodism.[89] By alleging that the telltale signs of degeneration could be detected through physical as well as psychological "stigmata," Morel had paved the way in 1857 for later doctors and psychologists who would claim that genital variations signaled mental inferiority.[90] In this way, Zola anticipates the pathologizing of hermaphrodism *and* homosexuality in the 1880s and 1890s by doctors like Legrand Du Saulle, Magnan, and Christian, whose damning predictions were cited in G. M.'s case and in Dubarry's novel.[91] Zola's fear of the "man-woman" as the inevitable product of decadent and near-spent societies prefigures a trope that will be repeated in the discourse of well-known sexologists, psychologists, criminalists, and doctors. For example, Cesare Lombroso (1835–1909), a prominent criminologist who argued that miscreants could be identified through physical "defects," averred in 1896: "The influence of degeneration tends to bring the two sexes together and to confuse them, through an atavistic return to the period of hermaphrodism."[92] Much criticism of Zola focuses on his reliance on mythology or allegory, and tends to ridicule his fascination with science and efforts as an experimental novelist. Yet if Zola's science is so often relegated to the realm of myth, it is as much because nineteenth-century medicine often bordered on the mythical, as because Zola used his family of degenerates as a metaphor in order to cast aspersions on the social body of the entire Second Empire.

An extensive review of the medical literature on "hermaphrodism" reveals that the widely perceived connection between "abnormal" psychology and "abnormal" genitalia postdates Morel's popularization of degeneracy. It is not until the 1880s that the word "degeneration" appears in numerous case studies as an explanation for sex variations. With this new etiology comes a shift in the representations of "hermaphrodism", which has been overlooked by recent historiography. Falling under the shadow of Morel's popularized degeneration theory, case studies increasingly document the familial origins of sex differences and list degenerate heredity as the underlying cause. In a way, medical beliefs transformed "hermaphrodites" from scientific "curiosities" into sinister expressions of social decay. The meaning of the term itself had shifted radically. "Hermaphrodism" now implied something about sexuality, and not just sex.

I have argued that Zola's *La curée* represents an early avatar of this phenomenon. Whether or not the novel itself influenced doctors, it offers a powerful example of how cultural and popular beliefs are often incorporated into medical and scientific narratives. In a newspaper article from 1870, Zola fulminates on the sexual experimentation of Second Empire France, with its pursuit of new pleasures in the effacement of sexual difference: "Truly, the Empire made us into a great nation. Now our men are becoming women. When Rome was rotting in its greatness, it accomplished the same miracles. The beautiful nights of ancient orgy have returned, the ardent nights in which creatures no longer have a sex."[93] All around him, Zola sees men dressing as women; women dressing as men, and detects the ever-present danger that their "true sex" will become unrecognizable behind their disguises.[94] This is precisely what happens in *Germinal*, when Étienne mistakes Catherine for a boy because of her dingy miner's uniform and the shadowy underground.[95] Yet by suggesting that clothes make the woman, Zola paradoxically sets up gender identities as mutable facades – easily donned and easily discarded. This is what Hannah Thompson means when she says Zola prefigures Judith Butler's notion of "gender performativity."[96]

Thompson's argument fits with our reading of Renée. Yet for characters like Maxime and Louise whose degenerate heredity finds expression in near-sterile androgyny, "hermaphrodism" is about more than appearances. Maxime's androgyny is inscribed upon his body, not just dictated by his dress, and his fiancée Louise is described as a "boy dressed as a girl," as if her ambiguity emanates from her features rather than her frock (1: 353). In fact, *La curée* subverts Zola's staunch belief in the need for clear binary distinctions even more radically. Not only can someone become "hermaphroditic" in boarding school, but with the character Sidonie, Zola suggests that sex can be lost all together. Sidonie becomes nonbinary:

> The woman in her died; she became nothing but a business agent, a dealmaker rushing around Paris at all hours with her legendary basket full of the most dubious merchandise, ready to sell anything and everything [. . .] to see her rush past a row of houses, one might have mistaken her for an errand boy disguised as a girl. [. . .] Thanks to the milieu in which she had grown old, [. . .] the common temperament had been warped to produce this strange hermaphrodism of a woman who had become neuter, at once businessman and procuress. (1: 371–73)

Because Sidonie's dual masculine and feminine identity as a "businessman" and a "procuress" seems to define her neatly within what Butler terms the "heterosexual matrix," Roddey Reid argues that "the figure of androgyny is a conservative trope, a controlling rhetorical device that returns Sidonie to a simple male/female, masculine/feminine opposition in which the truth of sex and gender remains unproblematically and symmetrically male or female."[97] Thompson tenders a parallel argument: there is no homosexuality for Zola since all homosexual men are "women" trapped in a man's body, and vice versa. The sentence above, however, could just as easily be interpreted to mean that Sidonie's status as both businessman and procuress pushes her beyond the male/female dichotomy into a third, nonbinary category, which Zola calls "neuter" following the teratologists studying hermaphrodism. In this case, the effectiveness of Zola's conservative attempts to recover his transgressive and androgynous characters and fully inscribe them within the heterosexual matrix is highly questionable.

In many ways, Sidonie does appear to inhabit a limbo space.[98] Visually, she defies categorization. Her "signature black dress" obscures her body like the hat which covers her hair and forehead, and, writes Zola, "in truth she was ageless" (1: 369). Her shop is a three-level "unknown temple" with secret stairways and discreet doors, in which her name changes according to floor: "Upstairs, she went by the name Madame Touche, after her husband, while she had only listed her first name on the shop door, which meant that she was generally called Madame Sidonie" (1: 369). Sidonie does not speak of her past; her means and motivations remain unfathomable, and no one ever figures out how she hatched the plot to deliver Renée to her brother. When Saccard arrives in Paris just after the *coup d'état*, he discovers his formerly married sister, Sidonie, living alone, unwilling to mention her absent husband, and using her shop as a front for a hodgepodge of illicit commerce that remains as shrouded in mystery as its proprietor (1: 372).

It is often argued that Sidonie is a closeted lesbian, but I suggest that Sidonie's amorous attentions to women are more often the deeper expression of her love for intrigue than a reflection of sexual desire. Sidonie plots for the sheer love of plotting: "If Madame Sidonie did not become rich, it was because she often worked for love of the art of working" (1: 371). Furthermore, the narrator describes her as asexual since she cannot imagine herself as potentially sexual: "There was only one thing that she did not sell, it was herself; not that she would have had any scruples about it, but because the idea of such a contract would not have occurred to her" (1: 372).

Despite Zola's clearly pejorative vision of hermaphrodism, Sidonie's androgyny actually appears to leave her well-positioned for competition in the urban setting. Her self-effacing gender enables her to serve as an intermediary in diverse transactions, allowing her to slip effortlessly between male and female social spheres; "high" and "low" classes. Undoubtedly, she is a ruthless businessperson, negotiating Saccard's marriage with Renée as his wife Angèle lies dying in the other room, attempting to pimp out Renée later in the novel, and then eventually betraying her to Saccard. She is a schemer, a plotter, and even, it seems, a kind of author.[99]

A double for Zola in the text, it is she who orchestrates the union between Renée and Saccard, justifying the entire plotline. Like an omniscient narrator, Sidonie "confidently predicts" both Angèle's death and Renée's miscarriage, and so is at the heart of the merger that provides Saccard with the prize real-estate he needs for his speculative exploits and which thrusts Renée into the arms of her stepson – the novel's two major plot devices.[100] Like Gustave Flaubert's godly author, Sidonie is "everywhere present and nowhere visible," knowing everyone's most intimate secret – from pedophilic old barons to misunderstood young brides (1: 370). Sidonie even authors the novel's denouement by exposing Maxime and Renée's affair to Saccard, who, in one of the more brazenly scandalous moves of the entire novel, ignores it completely in exchange for the last shred of property in his wife's possession. Sidonie becomes so enmeshed in the lives of others that she lives vicariously through them, literally blending in with her surroundings: "the businesswoman had one of those unremarkable appearances that are easily lost in a crowd" (1: 373). Reduced to the metonym of her giant basket full of papers and receipts, Zola defines her as "Living in other people's homes, in others' affairs, she was a veritable catalog of supply and demand" (1: 370). Her basket, like the novel itself is "an entire world" full of odds and ends and "especially handfuls of stamped papers on which she deciphered the illegible writing with particular dexterity" (1: 370). True, her life goal of recovering three billion from an old debt proves illusory, but she represents an incredible will to survive that should not be underestimated given the other doomed branches on the family tree; and what is an author without a pipedream anyway? After all, Zola nursed several of his own, including his belief that once the "laws of heredity" could be fully understood they might one day lead France away from what the narrative of degeneration foretold would otherwise be a diseased and doomed future.

While it is unlikely that Zola intended for parallels to be drawn between himself and Sidonie Rougon, his text allows for such a comparison. This may be a sign that La curée has slipped entirely out of Zola's control. If he had set out to show heredity's clear, inviolable rules, he has failed. Sidonie's degenerate heredity doesn't strike her down in the novel. She thrives, and on the level of storytelling, it is thanks to her efforts that we have any plot at all. Zola's representation of unstable gender identities in *La curée* thus undermines the seemingly relentless force of degenerate heredity inherited from scientific theory and invites us to see literary naturalism more as a critic of science than as an expression of it. Zola's ambivalence toward Sidonie's androgyny is the embodiment of ambivalence about the very science on which his method is based. Reid defines the "fundamental tension" in *La curée* as "the need and desire to designate a transgressive 'outside' to the sex/gender system of familial discourse (in order to inscribe the norm), but an 'outside' that nonetheless does not stand altogether 'beyond' the horizon of normalizing discourse."[101] But by entrusting so much of his novel's genesis to Sidonie's trademark basket, Zola's normalizing discourse risks becoming empty rhetoric.

In a bizarre irony, Zola's myriad of "outside" characters might even have contributed to the popularity of *La curée* among marginalized individuals. The anonymous author of the *Roman d'un inverti-né* (who dispatched his autobiographical writings to the great author in the hope that he might one day read about himself in the pages of a novel) cites *La curée* as his favorite of Zola's novels, because in it he finds "some of my feelings and the sphere in which I nearly always inhabited, in which I was born and lived."[102] Still, there was room for improvement, he informed Zola: "It goes without saying that I'm crazy about your works, that I read them with admiration, even though, in my opinion, the subject of the last ones was not very agreeable" (1896, 89).

Zola's "hermaphrodites" are not simply "homosexuals." They are instead degenerate beings (predisposing them to homosexuality, in Zola's view) whose ambiguous bodies both epitomize and result from the diseased atmosphere of Second Empire France. Maxime, Sidonie, and even Renée seem neither wholly female nor fully male. They are doubly lacking rather than doubly endowed. Here, Zola is both on the wrong side of history and strangely "ahead" of his time, since, as I have shown, degeneration as an atavistic return to androgynous origins only becomes ubiquitous in case studies of hermaphrodism in the 1880s and 1890s.

In the preface to *La fortune des Rougon* (1871), Zola writes that just like gravity, heredity has inviolable laws explaining the link between related individuals with "mathematical" precision.[103] Unfortunately for Zola, the laws of heredity, like some "mysteries of birth," were not quite so transparent in the nineteenth century (and still, in many ways, evade us today). Perhaps this is why Dr. Pascal's great life work on heredity is burned at the end of the *Rougon-Macquart* series in *Le Docteur Pascal* (1893). Pascal, like Zola, had promised to unveil the complete truth behind heredity, but after reading forty years' worth of scholarship on the subject, it is as if Zola realized no such truth were to be had. In the same way that Zola's portrayal of in-between figures embodying multiple or shifting sexual identities and genders undermines his belief in the binary, his use of heredity is conveniently explicative and evasive. Critics have argued that Zola cannot step outside the binary gender divide, but his works clearly do.[104] He is often seen as hopelessly deterministic, but determinism cannot be reconciled with mutable, in-between, and multiple.[105] The moral determinism of Zola's version of heredity is, at best, inconsistent, like "rolling the hereditary dice."[106] How else could the Rougon-Macquart's entire hope for regeneration be incarnated in the incestuous child born of Pascal's marriage to his own niece?[107]

It is important to remember that while heredity is the governing principle of the entire *Rougon-Macquart* series, the science of genetics is not, because Gregor Mendel's work on the inheritance of genes from 1865 was not rediscovered until 1900. This means that the scaffolding for understanding heredity in the Rougon-Macquart line was constructed without even the most rudimentary understanding of recessive and dominant genes. The science of genetics was not born until Mendel's work was understood and Hugo de Vries had introduced the concept of mutation.[108] Allen Thiher suggests that part of the reason Zola's "science" has been so criticized is because he is "on the other side of that moment, before Mendel's work on genetic distribution was rediscovered, and after which no earlier model of heredity could be recycled."[109]

The story of Mendel's "lost" work reveals the role of chance as much as that of science in the shaping of hereditary models. *La curée* popularized degeneration theory in the early 1870s, a decade before it would make a sinister appearance in case studies of hermaphrodism, spurring a radical shift in doctor/patient relationships and in the meaning of the term itself. Paradoxically, using decades-old science, Zola's novel was on the cutting edge of literary experimentation that may have actually influenced medicine. But it is also important not to imagine that if only Zola had read Mendel, his fiction might have come closer to the truth. In the final section, we shall see how twenty-first-century medicine and science are still far from revealing all of the mysteries of intersex, and how a nineteenth-century belief in the binary caused irreparable damage when doctors subjected intersex children to irreversible surgeries, until the intersex movement shed light on their practices and led to a major overhaul of medical protocols in the 1990s. Then, as was the case in the nineteenth century, the rising power of psychology was at the origin of damaging medical practice. Finally, we shall see how the contemporary trans rights movement is also shifting toward a more dynamic and inclusive gender spectrum, circling back to tiny moments of nineteenth-century resistance to "true sex."

The Nineteenth-Century Roots of Contemporary Resistance to "True Sex"

In 1859, Dr. Debout scandalized several members of the Society of Surgery by proposing to create an "artificial vagina" for one "Louise D."[1] It was not the dangerous and difficult nature of this operation that concerned Debout's colleagues. Rather, some of them worried that "Louise D." was not, in fact, a woman. Twenty years old, Louise D. had been sent to Debout "for a congenital defect of the external genital organs that caused this young girl to be seen as an example of hermaphrodism" (1859, 115).[2] The debate stemmed from Debout's inability to verify the presence of a uterus, and disagreement about the ovoid mass in Louise D.'s groin, which doctors could not identify as either testicular or ovarian in nature (116–17). Persuaded that Louise D. was a man, Dr. Richard advised against operating, but in the end an initial exploratory surgery was agreed upon, which was intended to create a vaginal opening (116). No small measure of professional pride was wrapped up in the remarkable operation. Le Fort boasts: "because she dearly desired to marry, and since her family doctor had stated that he could attempt nothing useful in order to satisfy her desire, she consulted me" (1863, 204). The case was presented to the Society of Surgery on three occasions, and according to Trélat, doctors felt "rushed and bothered by the patient's incessant obsession" to operate (1880, 59). In the end, it was Dr. Hugier who performed exploratory surgery following another physical examination. Despite finding what "could well be a testicle," Hugier did not suggest Louise D. was *really* a man, but instead insisted on her complex mix of sex traits, including regular menstruation, an enlarged clitoris, and what he thought might be a uterus (1860, 6–7). At long last, Hugier successfully created the vagina that Louise D. had so adamantly desired from the outset, and she survived to tell the tale.[3]

Louise D. appears in a number of case studies that document her years-long relationship with medicine up until the hour of her untimely death. Le Fort's dissertation from 1863 mentions that three years after the construction of her new vagina, Louise D. had written back confirming that she was fully recovered and doing well (207).[4] In 1880, Dr. Trélat followed up again, revealing that "thanks to her artificial vagina," Louise D. had been able to marry, but tragically later succumbed to "metroperitonitis," an inflammation of the uterus and peritoneum, which, he hastened to add, was "unrelated to the operation" that had created her vagina a few years earlier (59).[5]

We have seen that others like Louise D. were sometimes operated upon in nineteenth-century France because, like her (and Louise-Julia-Anna from Chapter 1), they requested those surgeries. Other times, gonads were removed without their owner's knowledge, sometimes for medical, but more often for social reasons. But what fundamentally differentiates nineteenth-century "hermaphrodism" from contemporary "intersex" is that such surgeries were relatively rare and generally performed on adults. In nineteenth-century France, the medical management of hermaphrodism did not systematically render it invisible by attempting to shape the body to fit with cultural beliefs about binary gender. For starters, most of the technology did not yet exist. In the period before it became available – much of which was later necessary for those trans people who *desired* to modify their bodies in order to reflect their own gender identities – doctors' responses to ambiguous sex and the sex determinations they made varied almost as much as the bodies of the people who came to see them, and, in some ways, technological limitations, a legal blind spot, and the lack of medical consensus on "hermaphrodism" afforded some individuals freedom to live their lives outside of medical control in a way that would become virtually impossible in the twentieth-century West.[6]

Changing Medical Protocols

On average, hospitals around the United States perform five surgeries per day on intersex babies and children, and, by the most conservative estimate, between two and four thousand infants are born each year in this country with anatomies differing from those most commonly associated with male and female.[7] Melanie Blackless and Anne Fausto-Sterling argue that the frequency of intersex traits is closer to 1 or 2 percent.[8] Even the most moderate estimates suggest that the incidence of intersex falls somewhere between those of very well-known chromosomal variations like Down syndrome (1 in every 750 births) and Cystic fibrosis (1 out of 2,500 to 3,500 births).[9] Yet, intersex, which only sometimes involves a chromosomal variant, is widely perceived to be much less common than either genetic variation. This is due to medical protocols for managing intersex – protocols that have come under increasing scrutiny since the advent of the grassroots intersex movement of the 1990s.

In what follows, I suggest that the debate surrounding "hermaphrodism" in the nineteenth century can teach us something about the current medical management for intersex. But rather than focusing on the ways medicine can and has reified normalizing notions of sex and gender through its own authoritative discourse, I will instead argue that the surprising resistance to "true sex" in both nineteenth-century literature and medicine prefigures the contemporary resistance to medical sex assignment surgery for patients born with intersex traits.

I have shown in this book that the paradigms for establishing sex in ambiguous cases were highly contested and constantly evolving (or at least reappearing cyclically) in the nineteenth century. By the end of the eighteenth century, Foucault tells us, hermaphrodism was thought to be impossible, and doctors predicated sex assignments on the belief that essential bodily differences distinguished men from women. Early in the nineteenth century, doctors began to allege that certain organs counted more than others in the arithmetic of sex determination, and they hoped that histology might resolve the doubt once and for all with the aid of microscopic analysis. But without anesthesia or sanitary conditions until nearly the turn of the twentieth century, exploratory abdominal surgery in order to examine internal reproductive organs was fortunately a relatively rare occurrence.[10] At best, autopsies could merely vindicate or disprove doctors who had debated a patient's sex during life. At worst, they too were inconclusive, which of course changed nothing for the deceased patient. But, in the 1830s, Isidore Geoffroy Saint-Hilaire averred that some individuals existed whose sex was either impossible to determine or remained irreconcilable with binary sex. For him, the theory of arrested or excess development explained why androgynous bodies fell on a sliding scale, somewhere between male and female. Determining the sex of hermaphrodites was a tricky business, he warned, and even the best doctors might not be able to tell. True to Geoffroy Saint-Hilaire's prediction, medical men fervently contradicted each other about the sex of their patients for the next hundred years, and even beyond. Many rallied again to a gonadal definition. Others based sex determinations on idiosyncratic criteria. Some acquiesced to their patients' wishes, and many more believed, as did Geoffroy Saint-Hilaire, that human diversity exceeded the confines of the social and legal categories for sex. Hermaphrodism then became a test case for the ethical ramifications of doubt. Should individuals outside of the binary be allowed to marry? How could "doubtful sex" be reconciled with a legal system that refused to acknowledge it? Should surgeons intervene to make sexual relations possible? What if the patient threatened suicide without it? Who should be informed when cases of "hermaphrodism" were discovered – the patient, the spouse, the authorities, or no one at all? Should a happy hearth be troubled by medical revelations? Was homosexuality *really* homosexuality if the participants were not aware of it? What if a man who looked like a woman wanted to marry a woman? I have shown how these questions gained pressing urgency during the natality crisis in fin-de-siècle France, and how novelists seized on the mystery of doubtful sex as a motor for fictional plot. Just like the medical record, literature often reveals blurred boundaries between the sexes in spite of seemingly heteronormative denouements.

By the early twentieth century, doctors like Louis Ombrédanne acknowledged that histology was not foolproof either. Instead of solving the mystery, new technology revealed an even more complex picture of the factors affecting sex variances, and by this point, so many cases of "ovotestes" – gonads uniting both ovarian and testicular cells – had been seen under the microscope that Ombrédanne called Pozzi's earlier dismissal of them "indefensible" (1939, 33).[11] Ombrédanne inveighed against doctors claiming that "true sex" should be determined by the gonads. "There is no true sex," he averred in 1939, and circling back to Geoffroy Saint-Hilaire, he stressed that "every human was a hermaphrodite at one point of life in utero" (36). Dr. Pozzi and others had been wrong to doubt "true hermaphrodism," because "there are numerous observations of subjects who have both ovaries and testicles that have been determined such by histology" (30, 33). Ombrédanne had, himself, identified five cases in this way. In a near verbatim reversal of doctors who had claimed that each person had one "true sex," even if it was difficult to determine, Ombrédanne insisted that "*True sex* is the word behind which only errors of appreciation are hidden" (36). What Pozzi and others had missed, was that "function," not just "forms" needed to be counted, and tastes and preferences mattered too. Ombrédanne recommended a tally of multiple different factors, which he called a "bilan" or "balance sheet," that weighed sex traits, but also sexuality, and the patient's gender identity (a new concept at that time). He also advocated helping the parents of intersex children to understand that decisions about how to raise them should not be rushed, and, in some cases might wait until puberty (171). Ombrédanne's counsel would soon be reversed in the United States, and while his prescription of patience might seem forward thinking to us today, his insistence on function was actually laying the groundwork for the damaging medical management of intersex in the future.

By the time Ombrédanne published his treatise in 1939, new technologies were coming to the fore that reshaped the realm of the medically possible.[12] By the midcentury, surgery and endocrinology made it increasingly feasible to sculpt intersex bodies to conform to cultural expectations for binary sex categories. The question was no longer: "to which sex does the patient belong?" but rather: "to which sex is it possible to create the outward semblance?" At that time, the medical management of intersex was "pragmatic," and based on a psychosocial gender-identity theory established in the 1950s by the psychologist John Money.[13] This now-discredited theory asserted that an infant's anatomy had to match the "standard" anatomy for his/her gender in order for the individual to adjust "normally"; which meant that boys needed "adequate" penises (and no vagina) and girls needed to have penetrable vaginas and small clitorises.[14]

Contrary to a commonly held cultural misperception, even today, sex is not simply a matter of chromosomes, and is not determined in ambiguous cases based on chromosomes alone.[15] Fausto-Sterling, Alice Domurat Dreger, Katrina Karkazis, and Sharon Preves, among many others, have shown how sex assignment surgeries on intersex children are based on cultural beliefs about sex and gender. Because of the social value placed on a man's ability to urinate while standing and to use his penis in order to penetrate a vagina, in the twentieth- and twenty-first-century West, a genetic male (an infant with a Y chromosome) whose penis is deemed "inadequate" at birth would be assigned the female sex/gender and be reconstructed to "appear female."[16] According to Money's paradigm, gender identity was fixed very early in life, so sex/gender was often assigned within the first twenty-four to forty-eight hours after the birth of an intersex child, and then was created and maintained in the most convincing way possible by means of hormone treatment and/or surgery.

Money believed that gender identity was established in the first eighteen months of life, and that any perceived doubt regarding assigned sex by a child would be disastrous for psychological development. Doctors were therefore encouraged to convey to parents with absolute conviction that the assigned sex was the "true sex" of the child. Uncertainty could be transferred to children and lead to serious psychological "problems," not the least of which, in Money's view, figured homosexuality.[17] Much like the gonadal paradigm for determining sex, which rose and fell on a wave of technological innovation, Elizabeth Reis has revealed that Money's psychosocial sex assignment theory only gained critical purchase because of the increasing power of psychology and the perceived belief that psychological evaluations constituted objective techniques for collecting scientific evidence. This power was one psychologists and doctors played a role in cultivating for themselves using their own narratives of scientific authority, just as Guermonprez or Tardieu, or any of the other influential medical men of yore.[18] And just like the "alienists" who were instrumental in propagating degeneration theory, Money's theory caused lasting damage.

In 1993, the Intersex Society of North America (ISNA) was founded in response to the medical management of intersex. ISNA advocated for patients who were harmed by their early sex-assignment surgeries and treatments. The organization argued that Money's psychosexual theory of gender assignment fostered shame. ISNA would evolve into an important resource for intersex people, their parents, and their doctors, and played a decisive role in the debunking of Money's theories. Intersex activists argued that since most intersex variations were not life-threatening, there was no need to treat intersex as a medical emergency. Why inflict irreversible medical operations with permanent side effects on children too young to make their own decisions? Especially when many of these "treatments" caused physical and psychological trauma, and, some argued, were tantamount to genital mutilation. Long-term infrastructure needed to be created in order to disseminate information and provide patients and their families with mental health care. As an alternative to Money's policy of keeping intersex a secret, ISNA advocated full disclosure, and they disseminated information broadly. Thanks to ISNA's efforts, health care professionals slowly began to change the care they provided for families.

In 2008, the now defunct ISNA was replaced by a series of nonprofit organizations charged with implementing new ideas about appropriate care for intersex across the country. As a result of the efforts of ISNA and Accord Alliance, and, most recently, InterACT, the medical management of intersex is shifting. Doctors have acknowledged that information regarding intersex is lacking to guide parents, clinicians, and patients, and in 2006, a new standard of care was published in *Pediatrics*. The "Consensus Statement on Management of Intersex Disorders" was groundbreaking because patients contributed to its creation, and although ISNA acknowledged at the time that it was not without flaws, the document championed many of the hard-fought tenets of the grassroots intersex movement. Notably, the consensus calls for more patient-centered care, including a focus on mental health rather than on gender assignment and outward genital appearance. Herculine Barbin might have been pleased to learn that genital examinations and the dissemination of medical photography are to be limited.[19] The statement also outlines a more conservative approach to surgery, including the elimination of certain types of pediatric surgery, and doctors now stress that the goal of surgery should be functional outcome, rather than cosmetic appearance. The report reveals that no evidence supports the claim that early surgery alleviates parental anxiety surrounding intersex.[20]

Raising societal awareness about intersex engendered its own set of problems, including controversial new medical nomenclature.[21] The acronym "DSD," which stands for "Disorder(s) of Sex Development," was meant to infuse neutrality into gender variations that have been stigmatized by the shame associated with medical practices. Some critics, including many intersex people, activists, and scholars, however, are troubled by the word "disorder," and believe the term DSD unnecessarily pathologizes a gender variation that should not require medical treatment. Early on, Reis and others suggested that the term DSD be repurposed to stand for "Divergence of Sex Development," and today, the NHS in the UK defines DSD as "Differences in Sex Development." Many have instead demanded that the term DSD be abandoned entirely. Georgiann Davis has recently argued that the "disorder" nomenclature is a linguistic tool used by the medical profession to "reclaim their authority and jurisdiction over the intersex body, and, in that respect, it is no better than 'hermaphrodite.'"[22]

The nineteenth-century concept of "true sex" is still bound up in debates over how to name all sorts of experiences that challenge the binary (whether they originate from the body or one's sense of self), and the system for naming gender variations is as dynamic and historically contingent as ever. The comparatively recent term "intersex," is itself unstable, and its future uncertain. For many, "intersex" is a medical term and, so, like past medical nomenclature, it misleadingly suggests that doctors need to be involved. Some whom doctors labeled "intersex" reject this word because, like the outdated "(pseudo)hermaphrodism" terminology, it implies incompatibility with binary gender that is out of synch with their own identification as men or women. Being born "intersex" does not mean they aren't *truly* men or woman. Similarly, for some binary-identified trans people, gender identity *is* their "true sex." Unlike birth sex, it is the one they know to be true for themselves. Even now, trans people who want to transition their bodies to reflect their gender identity are required to demonstrate a stable gender identity over a long period of time and "gender dysphoria" in order to attain the gender-affirming medical treatment they want. Increasingly, there are intersex (and trans and many other) people who identify as nonbinary, and for them, "true sex" lies beyond male and female. Nonbinary intersex people have sometimes felt marginalized from within their own minority communities, and some intersex rights groups still stress, as did ISNA, that all intersex children should be assigned a gender until it is safe for them to live in a world without one, if they so choose.

No one knows how long the word "intersex" will be around, or if, like "hermaphrodite," it will become a historical artefact of discourse. There was a time when it looked like "DSD" might replace it (it still has in clinical settings), but "intersex" seems to have gained a cultural foothold for the time being. Regardless of the word they choose to describe themselves though, people whose bodies open up the binary will continue to be born, because what we call today "intersex" and what was called in the past "hermaphrodism" are just umbrella terms for a range of naturally occurring gender variations. Umbrella terms (like "masculine" and "feminine") are always problematic, because lumping people together obfuscates their differences.

Historians have long described the nineteenth century as a period of increasing medicalization during which "true sex" won out over doubtful sex. The Foucauldian paradigm asserts that doctors believed that all individuals had a "true sex" that was either male or female, but that was merely obscured in cases of hermaphrodism. There was no such thing as a "true hermaphrodite," according to nineteenth-century medicine. I have shown that this was not always the case. Many doctors recognized that their patients were neither "male" nor "female"; that they fell somewhere in between, had no discernable sex, or belonged to a third category deserving of its own legal status. While a number of doctors rallied round a gonadal definition of sex that all but engendered the practical elimination of "hermaphrodism," others stubbornly insisted that "true hermaphrodism" existed, citing case after case to support their claims. Some patients read medical cases and made their own sex determinations, while others sought medical treatment elsewhere when their doctors did not meet their needs. Periodically, throughout the entire length of the century, doctors and jurists even called for a third sex to be added to the civil registry. Of course, they did not do so because they hoped to destabilize the foundations of binary gender or heteronormative society. Rather, they did so because they thought French law either did not reflect the current state of scientific knowledge, or because they feared that it was not doing enough to protect citizens from those born with what was then termed "doubtful sex." But they nevertheless *did* destabilize the foundations of binary gender *and* heteronormative society, which is precisely why no one could stop telling stories about "hermaphrodites."

The advent of sex assignment surgery upped the stakes of ambiguous sex. The systematic endorsement of irreversible medical procedures in the treatment of intersex only became endemic with Money's work in the mid-twentieth century. Money's anxiety surrounded the question of nonbinary doubt – how much of it could be tolerated and for how long. The solution he posited for the "problem" of intersex was to eliminate doubt. Doctors should convey no doubt to patients about their decisions (even if it meant hiding information from them), parents should convey no doubt to their children, and bodies should be shaped to make sex appear less doubt-provoking.

Nineteenth-century medicine already foretold this model's predictable failure. We have seen that doctors announcing the impossibility of hermaphrodism only seemed to invite refutation. The legal blind spot for individuals outside of binary sex only served to provoke greater scrutiny of the question. And the message reverberating through the pages of the novels that relied on "doubtful sex" as a motor for plot was invariably that the naked body was difficult to interpret – searching for bodily "truth" only engendered fiction.

But the uncertain environment with which nineteenth-century novelists conditioned us to be comfortable through their use of suspense and their promise of resolution on the final page has often ended violently for intersex and gender nonconforming people, and I am acutely aware that an academic discussion is woefully insufficient to address the lived experience of intersex children and adults. We have seen that since the nineteenth century, bodies that challenged the binary were othered and became sites of imperialism upon which medicine staked its own claim of mounting authority, and that this tradition is still very much alive in spite of some recent shifts. Yet, if the nineteenth-century resistance to "true sex" and the fall of John Money can teach us anything, it is that the best medicine is patient-centered, and listens to its own uncertainties.

I have tried, in this book, to avoid imbuing nineteenth-century resistance to "true sex" with transhistoric weight by lending it anachronistic agency over unforeseen changes. It is not because some nineteenth-century doctors believed their patients did not possess binary "true sex" that contemporary doctors are collectively reevaluating "medical management" of intersex. Nineteenth-century patients like Louise-Julia-Anna, who refused to listen to unhelpful doctors, probably did not do so because they hoped their actions would inspire a grassroots intersex movement a century later. At the same time, however, to say that nineteenth-century medical men believed patients always had a "true sex," or that patients did not sometimes determine their own, remains equally inaccurate. More importantly, it is equally dangerous, because it has worked to silence the individual voices that have called binary sex into question. Certainly, this is the opposite effect to what the social constructionists like Foucault intended when describing the cultural under-pinnings of sex in the nineteenth century. Finally, I believe it is possible to acknowledge what we have inherited from the way that nineteenth-century doctors, patients, and novelists challenged the idea of "true sex" without ascribing a revolutionary politics to their individual struggles, and while still fighting against the violence that nineteenth-century models have inflicted and continue to exert in contemporary society. Recently, contemporary intersex activist Pidgeon Pagonis started a hashtag advocating "intersex stories not surgeries."[23] This book has argued that these stories go back centuries, and they will continue for centuries more.

Notes

Introduction

1 The lover identifies the patient as a man with "un des ses amis" (Poppesco, 1874, 44). The case figures in Poppesco's medical thesis, presented to the Paris Faculté de médecine in 1874.

2 Poppesco's French dissertation was translated into English in 1875 by Dr. Edward Warren Sawyer of Harvard (1875, 39). Further references are to this translation.

3 Here, I cite sensitive historical terminology explained further below. Although "hermaphroditism" is a common variant to "hermaphrodism" in the anglophone tradition, the French equivalent was almost never used.

4 In his preface to the English edition of Herculine Barbin's memoirs, Foucault identifies what has come to be known as the "one-body-one-sex rule": "Henceforth, everybody was to have one and only one sex. Everybody was to have his or her primary, profound, determined and determining sexual identity; as for the elements of the other sex that might appear, they could only be accidental, superficial, or even quite simply illusory." Foucault, ed., *Herculine Barbin*, trans. McDougall, viii.

5 Meyerowitz, for example, writes that the "nineteenth-century vision of binary sex [. . .] saw female and male as distinct, immutable, and opposite" (*How Sex Changed*, 5). Although true as a general assessment of cultural and societal beliefs about binary sex, this book reveals that doctors encountering cases of uncertain sex often drew different conclusions.

6 Dr. Charles Debierre's 1891 treatise offers an example, alongside an illustration taken from Heppner's 1872 study of another "true hermaphrodite" (see Figure 0.1) (1891, 108–9). Because the infant in Heppner's case only survived seven weeks, Granier claims that "true hermaphrodites" were not viable (1894, 332). Heppner's case illustrates the highly contested nature of both "true sex" and hermaphrodism, and the ways that nineteenth-century technology could not always solve the riddle of unknown sex. At that time, intersex was often invoked as "doubtful sex."

7 This definition comes from InterACT: Advocates for Intersex Youth (interactadvocates.org). InterACT maintains the website for the now-defunct Intersex Society of North America (ISNA), which popularized a much lower

figure for the incidence of intersex, as well as the controversial DSD nomenclature, discussed in the Epilogue.

8 Fausto-Sterling made this claim based on medical literature between 1955 and 1998. In the 2020 updated reprinting of *Sexing the Body*, Fausto-Sterling found only two follow-up attempts to assess the incidence of intersex in the general population in the twenty-year span since the book was originally published. Both found the incidence to be closer to 1 percent, but also that they were based on genital variations rather than on chromosomal variations, so Fausto-Sterling concludes that "the numbers are not that far off" from her original findings (324). InterACT makes the comparison between the likelihood of having an intersex child according to Fausto-Sterling and the radically lower likelihood of having identical twins (interactadvocates.org).

9 Some intersex people have reclaimed "hermaphrodite" for themselves, but it is considered a slur to others and should never be used in a contemporary, human context. Early in the twentieth century, the word "intersexual" began to replace "hermaphrodite." More recently, "intersex people" has often replaced "intersexuals," which misleadingly suggested that intersex was related to sexual orientation. Intersex (-ed; -ual; -uality) describes individuals who are born with reproductive characteristics or sexual anatomy that are different from, or combine traits commonly associated with, both the male and female sexes. For example, an XXY chromosomal karyotype. InterACT defines intersex more broadly as "differences in sex traits or reproductive anatomy that people are either born with or develop early in life" (interactadvocates.org). Since 2006, doctors and some intersex activists have suggested the term DSD, "Disorders of Sex Development," as an alternative to "intersex." Many have argued strongly against it. As Holmes and others have remarked, no one knows how long the word "intersex" will remain, especially considering the disputed medical nomenclature (see Holmes, *Intersex*). Intersex is not a synonym for transgender (or trans). A person who identifies as trans is often a person whose gender identity (self-identified gender) is different from the sex assigned at birth. For Bornstein, "Trans may refer to *anyone* for whom the conscious management of their gender identity and/or expression takes up a significant part of their lives" (*Gender Outlaw*, 83).

10 Geoffroy Saint-Hilaire (1832–37, 2: 31). According to Dr. Ombrédanne, Geoffroy Saint-Hilaire's broad definition dominated from the 1880s on, sanctioned by the Academy's 1878 definition: "Hermaphrodism is the union of certain characteristics of both sexes in a single individual" (1939, 19).

11 Here, Halberstam quotes Martínez to argue that we should not try to reclaim past figures using contemporary terms, since those individuals did not have the vocabulary or technology to claim themselves (Halberstam, *Trans**, 25).

12 Second-wave feminists of the 1970s argued that sex was separate from gender, and that social institutions created most differences between men and women. They often defined "sex" as the primarily physiological and anatomical characteristics distinguishing an individual as either male or female, whereas

"gender" described the social attributions of femininity or masculinity. More recently, queer and gender scholars such as Judith Butler, Henrietta A. Moore, Anne Fausto-Sterling, and Morgan Holmes, among others, have questioned the meaningfulness of the sex/gender distinction, since the ways in which we determine sex are already entangled in our ideas about gender. "Sex," they remind us, is not a static category, and its determination is often wrapped up in preconceptions about "gender." Finally, the term "gender," or "*genre*" in French, as we understand it today, is largely anachronistic when describing the nineteenth century. At that time, the term "*sexe*" implied both the social expression of masculinity and femininity and their physical underpinnings.

13 Mesch, *Before Trans*, 296. Mesch's approach to historical sources builds on Halberstam's method in *Female Masculinity* and Halperin's theorization in *How to Do the History of Homosexuality*. Counter also deftly uses contemporary theoretical frameworks to explore the intersections between sexuality and politics during the Restoration in his *The Amorous Restoration*, and *Inheritance in Nineteenth-Century French Culture*. My method is indebted to the work of all these scholars, who have helped to sharpen my thinking and foreground my approach to historical materials.

14 Manion, *Female Husbands*, 14.

15 Halberstam makes this claim in *Trans** when discussing early cinematic representations of trans identities.

16 Unless otherwise noted, translations are my own.

17 Zola, *Les Rougon-Macquart*, dir. Lanoux, 1: 425.

18 Contemporary scholarship has often drawn a tempting, but somewhat artificial boundary between "androgyny" and "hermaphrodism," which was not consistently honored by nineteenth-century authors. For Hargreaves, "the material fact of the body" is what is most at stake in the distinction between the two (*Androgyny*, 6). Nineteenth-century medical discourse frequently describes bodies as androgynous – a term also used to describe the effect of cross-dressing, whether or not the body itself was affected. Moreover, literature from that time rarely fully unveils the body. For these historical reasons, I employ both words nearly interchangeably, although "hermaphrodism" appears more frequently in medical texts than derivatives of "androgyny," which more often evoke mythology. Intersex activists and scholars, including Thea Hillman and Morgan Holmes, stress that the myth and fantasy surrounding the word "hermaphrodite" are a large part of the problem with public misperceptions about intersex, and that Jeffrey Eugenides's Pulitzer Prize-winning *Middlesex* (2002) was one of the biggest offenders in spreading misinformation. See Holmes, *Critical Intersex*, and Hillman, *Intersex*.

19 Lucien's feet liken him to a woman in *Les Illusions perdues*, and "he had hips shaped like those of a woman." In *Splendeurs et misères des courtisanes*, Lucien is described as a "femme manquée." Balzac, *La Comédie humaine*, dir. Castex (5: 145; 6: 898). Further references to the Pléiade edition directed by Castex are in the text.

20 Raoule de Vénérande in *Monsieur Vénus*, Marcelle Désambres in *Madame Adonis*, la duchesse de Pluncey in *Nono*, Mary Barbe in *La Marquise de Sade*, and Eliante Donalger in *La jongleuse*. On the tension between Rachilde's gender-bending characters and personal rejection of feminism, see Mesch, *The Hysteric's Revenge*. For her analysis of Rachilde as a precursor to trans identity, see *Before Trans*.

21 See, for example, Massardier-Kenney, *Gender in the Fiction of George Sand*; Nesci, *Le flâneur et les flâneuses*, and Prasad, "Deceiving Disclosures."

22 The short story describes "unhappy Lantosque, a well-born, clever man, who might have exhibited himself in some travelling booth, for he was a hermaphrodite – do you understand? – a hermaphrodite. And his whole life was one of long, incessant torture, of physical and moral suffering" (Maupassant, *Short Stories*, 3: 84). When Lantosque falls ill with influenza, he refuses to be seen by a doctor, and "he would cover himself with bedclothes up to his chin, find strength enough to tear up the prescriptions, and to drive away everyone" (86). In his will, Lantosque commands his cousin to wrap him up in his sheets and place him in his coffin directly, adding: "I wish to be cremated at Père-Lachaise and not to be subjected to any examination, or post-mortem, whatever may happen" (88). The news that Lantosque was a "hermaphrodite" only escapes when his cousin betrays the secret. In reality, the short story "L'hermaphrodite" was written by baron René-Jean Toussaint under his most popular penname, René Maizeroy, and published as part of *La fête* in 1893. Toussaint's short story gained unexpected longevity when it was falsely attributed to his much more famous friend and neighbor, Maupassant.

23 Quoted by Graille, *Les hermaphrodites*, 9. The Flammarion edition edited by Dord-Crouslé merely states: "Try to see some" (423). The dictionary was published as part of *Bouvard* and *Pécuchet* (1911–13).

24 See Grosz, "Intolerable Ambiguity," and Dreger, "Jarring Bodies."

25 Busst, "The Image of the Androgyne," 4.

26 See also Péladan's *De l'androgyne: Théorie plastique* (1910). On Péladan's *L'androgyne*, see Albert, *Saphisme et décadence*.

27 This book analyzes narrative discursively. For discussion of the "narrativist turn," see Polkinghorne, *Narrative Knowing*. The importance of narrative in medicine is well documented. For instance, doctors rely on patients' narratives in order to diagnose illness, the case study is a narrative genre, and illness and healing are situated in narrative time for the patient and doctor. For analysis of the relationship between realist and medical narratives, see Rothfield, *Vital Signs*. Contemporary bioethicists Rita Charon and Martha Montello describe a paradigm shift in today's medicine as "narrative ethics." See Charon and Montello, eds., *Stories Matter*, and Charon, *Narrative Medicine*.

28 See Albert, "Du Mythe," which conflates homosexuality and hermaphrodism. I investigate what is at stake in this pairing in Chapter 4. Murat's excellent *La loi du genre* presents a history of the emergence of the "third sex," a broader term than "hermaphrodism," predominately in early nosological categories for

homosexuality. Murat relies mainly on police archives rather than on medical records, meaning that my research is based on a different corpus of archives. Crahay's dissertation investigates androgyny and masculinity in both literature and medicine during the narrow window of time of the July Monarchy in France (1830–48). Most recently, Le Mens examines the visual iconography of "hermaphrodism" across roughly 200 years of art history, culture, and medicine in *Modernité hermaphrodite*. Le Mens's book reproduces many images of intersex genitalia, including of young children, that intersex activists and bioethicists have long argued should no longer be disseminated.

29 The use of the term "gender outlaw" references the complex ways in which the bodies of historical intersex people came into conflict with binary gender. It pays homage to Bornstein's seminal book of 1994, without suggesting that historical figures were working out their gender in the same, ever-changing ways as we are today. In the 2016 update to *Gender Outlaw*, Bornstein recounts using the term some twenty years previously to describe "transexuals – those of us who saw ourselves as men and women in need of a physical transition," whereas today, "trans men and trans women routinely tell me that they are not gender outlaws. And I agree." For Bornstein, "today's transgender men and women live well in accordance with the binary view of gender: they are not gender outlaws" (xvii). Chapter 2 of this book explores the way historical intersex people came into conflict with the French Civil Code, a more literal meaning of "gender outlaw."

30 The subjects in this book share these qualities with many other historical gender-nonconforming people, including those presented by Manion (*Female Husbands*, 14).

31 Justin Benoît (1840, 23–37). Further references in the text.

32 Benoît's case is also summarized in the *Gazette médicale* in 1841, where the doctor's name is recorded as "Jules Benoît."

33 Even doctors who were against allowing "hermaphrodites" to marry often warned their colleagues not to overstep professional bounds. See Delore (1899a, 69). Others ignored doctor-patient privilege entirely and alerted the authorities about their patients. Poitier-Duplessy proudly reports: "We informed the municipal authority of this unusual fact, so that the civil status of A... Ch... can be rectified" (1867, 435). Fortunately, such actions are not representative of the medical profession as a whole. Nevertheless, Poitier-Duplessy's belief that his patient is lying to him about her menstruation, and his evident hostility toward her, liken him to proponents of degeneration theory (see Chapter 4).

34 Dreger, *Hermaphrodites*, 28.

35 Doctors also studied in France, witnessing cases of hermaphrodism. See, for example, Parmly (1886, 931–46).

36 In *Scenes of Seduction*, Matlock shows how critics hostile to Balzac used the term "realism" first in the 1840s in an attack leveled against the author's aesthetic principles. As Samuels points out in *The Spectacular Past*, "to speak of Realism in regard to Balzac and Stendhal, then, is to accept anachronism in exchange for a convenient designation" (10).

Chapter 1

1 Barbin's memoirs were published in Dr. Ambroise Tardieu's *Question médico-légale de l'identité* in 1874; the first volume had earlier appeared in the *Annales d'hygiène publique et de médecine légale* in 1872 (1874, 126). Further references to Barbin's memoirs are in the text, and are my translations of the 1874 edition, unless otherwise indicated. The memoirs were later republished in a dossier compiled by Michel Foucault in 1978, and were translated into English with a preface by Foucault in 1980 (there is no preface to the French edition). Unlike Barbin's memoirs, case histories generally provide only glimpses into a patient's point of view. Like "Marie B." discussed in the Introduction to this book, patients often refused surgeries or failed to show up for them. Féré complains that his patient "escaped in order to avoid investigation" before he could conduct a thorough examination (1893, 602).

2 Foucault, ed., *Herculine Barbin*, trans. McDougall, 69.

3 Barbin's writings inspired the German psychiatrist and writer Oskar Panizza's *Ein skandalöser Fall* (1893). Panizza had lived in France, and Foucault republished Panizza's novella in the 1980 English edition of Barbin's memoirs as *A Scandal in the Convent*, spelling the author's name "Oscar" (Foucault, ed., *Herculine Barbin*, trans. McDougall, 154). Panizza uses the name "Alexina" for his protagonist, and the medical exam described by Barbin, but also diverges considerably from the memoirs. The intertextual tangle has led to confusion about who influenced whom (Albert, "Du mythe," 112). In fact, Caufeynon's novel postdated that of Panizza.

4 In 1903, Caufeynon published *Hermaphrodisme; bi-sexués, féminins, infantiles, viragos, hommes à mamelles*, a popular, sensationalist medical treatise, as well as "L'hermaphrodisme" in the *Bibliothèque populaire des connaissances médicales*. Moore determines that Fauconney had no medical qualifications, since he appears in no official medical listings between 1870 and 1930, although, as she points out, "Fauconney" could itself be a pseudonym belonging to an unknown doctor. See Moore, "Frigidity," 347, n. 2.

5 Holmes shows how Eugenides's problematic view is merely one example of the way intersex bodies have long been sites of projection for someone else's belief about "true sex." Instead, Holmes resists the "production of overdetermined declarations" of Barbin's "true sex" (*Intersex*, 89).

6 Ibid., 89.

7 In John Forrester's preface to *Case Studies and the Dissemination of Knowledge*, ed. Damousi, Lang, and Sutton, he situates the "golden age" of the case study after 1850, linking it to the confluence of multiple new technologies, including "the growing maturity and cultural entrenchment of the novel" and the invention of the detective story (x).

8 Dreger demonstrates that Barbin influenced contemporary biomedical treatment of intersex and was widely referenced. Owing to Barbin's importance, Dreger begins her study in 1868. See Dreger, *Hermaphrodites*, 28–29.

9 Editors of Foucault's lectures at the Collège de France, "Les anormaux," explain that "whether it was really a matter of a book devoted entirely to hermaphrodites or rather, according to the plan given in *The History of Sexuality* (1976), of a part of the volume on the *Perverse*, it is nonetheless the case that Foucault published nothing else on this theme apart from the Herculine Barbin dossier." See Foucault, *Abnormal*, trans. Burchell, 340.

10 See Tardieu (1874, 63, n. 2). Scholars have rendered Barbin's gender in diverse ways. Tardieu uses the masculine pronoun while Foucault, in his preface to the English edition of the memoirs, and Houbre use only the feminine pronoun. See Houbre, "The Bastard Offspring," 61–73. Butler (*Gender Trouble*) and Dreger (*Hermaphrodites*) use both *she* and *he*. Holmes uses the biopotential pronoun *hir* (*Intersex*). One might make a case for an anachronistic use of the nonbinary *they*, especially since Barbin's fictional avatar, Camille, was undoubtedly chosen for its gender-neutral nature in French. Chapter 3 of this book investigates other literary forerunners. Because gender identity is a highly personal choice, I mirror Barbin's own shifting identification between feminine and masculine.

11 Tardieu announces his selection in a rare, bracketed note in the text: "here ends the really interesting part of young B.'s memoirs" (1874, 159).

12 Foucault (1978) includes a transcription of Alexina/Abel's birth record in his documentation. See Foucault, ed., *Herculine Barbin dite*, 160.

13 Foucault, ed., *Herculine Barbin*, trans. McDougall, xiv. Foucault walks back part of this claim in the dossier, mentioning that "medical literature of the end of the nineteenth century and the beginning of the twentieth century refers to Alexina rather often. I have left out what were simply quotations borrowed from the text that was published by Tardieu" (ibid., 120).

14 Neugebauer's magnum opus, *Hermaphroditismus beim Menschen*, contained summaries of hundreds of case studies of hermaphrodism. He references "Alexina" in numerous publications. See Neugebauer (1900*a*, 457) and (1900*b*, 146). For a selection of the articles discussing Barbin's case, see Poppesco (1874, 12); Legrand Du Saule (1874, 28–30) and (1860, 510–11); Lutaud (1886, 8); Gérin-Roze (1884, 372); Dandois (1886, 52); Pozzi (1890, 354, n. 2); Blanc (1893, 195–6); Bacaloglu and Fossard (1899, 331–3); and Delore (1899*b*, 193–205; 230). Most works on the medico-legal implications of hermaphrodism also discuss Barbin. See, for example, Debierre (1886, 323); Lacassagne (1887, 85); and Vincentelli (1884, 81).

15 Neugebauer claims that, in spite of "immense progress," "cases of erroneous sex determination, either in children or adults, are still rather frequent," and "ignorant" doctors "are not even aware of the great responsibility that could hinder them as a result of an erroneous determination, which has already caused so many unfortunate events, suicides, such as that poor Parisian railroad worker [. . .] Mademoiselle B... (Alexina) and another person in Kiev" (1899, 195).

16 See, for example, Alibert (1906, 84–85); Le Contellec (1910, 49). In general, early twentieth-century cases resemble their nineteenth-century predecessors

until 1939, when Ombrédanne uses Alexina's story to argue radically that doctors ought to consider the tastes and preferences of their patients rather than evaluating "more doubtful" gonadal evidence:

> The only conclusion that one can draw from such facts is that before pronouncing a verdict on the so-called true sex, the doctor will have the moral obligation to weigh not only the primary somatic characteristics, which are sometimes unreliable, but also the secondary characteristics and even the subject's expressed desire, especially if this logical desire is in harmony with possible genital functionality. (1939, 89)

17 Dr. Tapie postulates that "The moving story of an unfortunate young man . . . Alexina . . . is ultimately restored to his true sex, and this discovery disturbs his mind to such a point, that he ends his life in suicide" (1888, 306). Brouardel attributes the suicide to depression caused by the body itself: "Tardieu cites the cases of a wayward individual with hypospadias. Once this poor boy learned his condition, he fell into a profound despair; and, after having written his memoirs in the most melancholic style, committed suicide" (1887, 57). Eugène Azam had already argued that unless a patient was threatening suicide, risky surgical operations should be avoided. Azam had refused to operate on his patient because "the only advantage would be to facilitate sterile pleasures for the patient," which was "not worth the risk" (1857, 542). Whether he means the risk to the patient or the perceived risk to morality is left inexplicit. Thézet references another patient who warned of suicide if an operation that he believed would enable marriage was denied to him (1876).

18 Tardieu (1874, 63).

19 Foucault explains that Neugebauer had mistakenly indicated that Alexina was pictured by an engraving in the text. See Foucault, ed., *Herculine*, trans. McDougall, xiv, n. 1. On Nadar's series, see Linton, "The Dangers of Looking," as well as Aubenas, "Beyond the Portrait," and Le Mens, *L'hermaphrodite.*

20 Plates xvi and xvii in Goujon (1869, 599–616).

21 See Houel (1881). The former Musée Dupuytren has lost these specimens, but has retained wax molds of intersex genitalia with labels reading "Adèle Henri," "Louis Pierre Fortier 1894, 17 ans," "Eugénie Laru, absence de vagin, 1883," and "Henriette." Patients were also displayed before medical societies, and surgeries were sometimes performed with an audience. See, for example, Charon (1893). Marc prescribes caution during sex determinations: "one should, whenever possible, without injuring or causing intense pain, probe the present orifices in order to learn their depth and direction" (1821–28). Orfila's medico-legal lessons duplicate this language (1823, 160). Painful operations were sometimes avoided: an 1828 article titled "Hermaphrodite" in the *London Medical Gazette*, rejects surgery on the grounds that it would provide little benefit for the patient and perhaps provoke "exquisite torture," even though it might have advanced scientific knowledge (190). Bouillaud cites one patient who "refused the examination that we wanted to perform on

his genital parts with unyielding stubbornness," but when said patient had the misfortune of dying in the hospital, his body was nevertheless subjected to autopsy (1833, 484).

22 Butler, *Gender Trouble*, 134.

23 Foucault calls the novel "medico-libertine." Foucault, ed., *Herculine Barbin dite* (1978), 132. In his 1980 preface, Foucault adds that "A. Dubarry, a versatile writer of adventure stories and medico-pornographic novels of the kind that were so popular at the time, obviously borrowed several elements for his *Hermaphrodite* from the story of Herculine Barbin," without elaborating on which elements (Foucault, ed., *Herculine*, trans. McDougall, xiv). Dubarry's multiplication of incredible peripeteia and bizarre travels differentiate his story from Alexina's tale, except that Dubarry's protagonist, Brigitte Lambert, commits suicide like Barbin using carbon monoxide poisoning. Apparently because he remained unaware of Caufeynon's novel, Foucault alleged that Panizza's novel was the only fictional rendition of the memoirs. In fact, Caufeynon borrows more heavily from Barbin's autobiography. On Dubarry's "medical grafting" of case studies onto fictional stories, see Verhoeven, "The Lunatics of Love."

24 Caufeynon, *L'hermaphrodite au couvent*, 15. Further references in the text.

25 See Caufeynon's description of breast and hip development (ibid., 47–48).

26 For example, he adds Paule's nocturnal ejaculations, which Barbin had confided to doctors, but omitted from the memoirs: "and in the morning she woke up surprised to feel herself wet or to find her nightgown stained and stiff as if starched" (ibid., 33). Chesnet's case history had noted: "More than once, in the night, her dreams were accompanied by indefinable feelings, she felt herself wet, and found, in the morning, on her linens, greyish stains, stiff as if starched" (1860, 207).

27 Caufeynon, *L'hermaphrodite au couvent*, 17–18. Tardieu makes the same argument:

> The struggles and agitations to which this unfortunate being fell victim are described in such pages that no novelistic fiction could surpass them in interest. It is difficult to read a more heartbreaking story, told with truer emphasis, and even though his story does not constitute in and of itself a striking truth, we have, with the authentic and official documents that I will include, the proof that the story is one of the utmost exactitude. (1874, 81)

28 Swept up by their patient Badré's narrative, both Drs. Legros and Dany record his preposterous exploits as veritable. Legros cites lascivious details, all in the name of science, of course:

> One Sunday, like any other, he was invited by five girls and had to pay his fee in *a particular way*. He satisfied them all, not successively, but at the same time, that is to say, he *passed between* [*a traversé*] these women, and only one was inseminated; for Badré makes, he says, a few moments after orgasm, a thick and abundant seed [. . .]. I should have to excuse myself for entering into such details, if they were to be read with sentiments other than those in which they

were written; I submitted them for a medico-philosophical purpose; these are materials for the history of physiology. (1835, 273)

Dany also reports believing Badré's account, but Badré's autopsy later reveals that he was not able to ejaculate. Rather than this detail casting doubt on Badré's entire narrative, this lie is merely interpreted by the medical men as a way to save face. See Legros (1835, 276) and Dany (1835, 462).

29 Tardieu promises: "One understands, without it being necessary to dwell on it, the cause of these pains. Far from announcing the arrival of the menstrual flow, they were produced by the strangulation of the seminal gland [. . .]. The doctor's visit, which will be recounted later, can leave no doubt in the matter" (1874, 109).

30 Another medical popularizer, Garnier adapted his writings to different audiences. See *La médecine populaire* (1881). Bouillaud's much earlier case study of a man named Valmont (echoing the womanizer of *Les liaisons dangereuses*) includes similarly hysterical questions once he learns that Valmont was a widower. Bouillaud cannot help but wonder *how* his patient had sex:

> Thus, an individual who was endowed with the essential organs of the female sex, although he possessed, obviously, only the so-called accessory organs of the male sex, did not fear to contract an alliance in which he was to play the role of the husband! How did he behave in the act of coitus? What feelings of joy could he have with a woman [. . .]? Since he had a womb, had Valmont menstruated (forgive me this sort of hermaphrodism of language)? . . . If Valmont's wife had been alive, she would have had, without doubt, precious and curious revelations to tell us. It does not seem that she had children during the course of this monstrous union! Assuming that the opposite had taken place, certainly it would not be upon Valmont that the honors of paternity would have been bestowed. (1833, 476–77)

31 On what constitutes erotic and pornographic literature, see Cryle, *Geometry in the Boudoir*. On the "medico-libertine" or "medico-erotic" *roman des moeurs*, see his "Foretelling Pathology," as well as Finn's "Female Sterilization" and *Hysteria, Hypnotism, the Spirits*.

32 See Brouardel (1887, 59), who is later quoted by Laurent (1894, 176). Similarly, "Dr. Laupts" evokes another patient dubbed "Henry, the fair-haired boy" (Henri le blondin) by his admirers (1896, 182–83).

33 Laupts (1896, 360–61). Channeling his best Baudelaire, Laupts had also blamed the "malaise," "ennui," and "spleen" "weighing so heavily" on society on "perverted" sexuality (ibid., 361).

34 On the "hermeneutic code," see Chapter 3 of this book.

35 Guermonprez (1892a, 337). Further references in the text. Guermonprez also published the case under the same title in the *Annales d'hygiène publique et de médecine légale* (1892b).

36 Holmes, *Intersex*, 90–92.

37 See Chesnet: "There is a vagina, rather shallow in truth, rather narrow, but then what is it if it isn't a vagina?" (1860, 209).

38 At least, this is one popular claim of contemporary doctors: "It remains evident that Alexina is a displaced being, unfit for reproduction and relegated to eternal celibacy" (Legrand du Saulle, 1874, 30). Poppesco disagrees, suggesting that Barbin was not necessarily sterile (1874, 39). For laws concerning marriage, see Chapter 2 of this book.

39 Foucault, ed., *Herculine*, trans. McDougall, viii.

40 Ibid., viii–ix.

41 Much of what Foucault wrote in 1980 remains unchanged: "The idea that one must indeed finally have a true sex is far from being completely dispelled. Whatever the opinion of biologists on this point, the idea that there exist complex, obscure, and essential relationships between sex and truth is to be found – at least in a diffused state – not only in psychiatry, psychoanalysis, and psychology, but also in current opinion" (ibid., x).

42 According to Foucault, from the Middle Ages through the sixteenth century, hermaphrodites were destroyed as demonic incarnations or harbingers of evil, but in the seventeenth century, hermaphrodites were no longer condemned for their anatomy, but rather, for their morals. Brisson suggests that Foucault falsely draws this conclusion based on limited source material. In contrast to the rupture posited by Foucault, he suggests continuity between representations of hermaphrodism from medieval times to the eighteenth century (*Le sexe incertain*, 106).

43 Laqueur writes: "During much of the seventeenth century, to be a man or a woman was to hold a social rank, to assume a cultural role, and not to *be* organically one or the other of two sexes. Sex was still a sociological, not an ontological, category" (*Making Sex*, 143).

44 See Butler, *Gender Trouble*, 126–44.

45 See Houbre, "The Bastard Offspring," and Le Mens, *L'hermaphrodite*.

46 See Mak, *Doubting Sex*, and "Doubting Sex from Within."

47 One potential problem with this method is that Mak relies on case studies written by doctors. Because case studies are not objective pieces of scientific evidence, but, rather, authored documents distributed to the wider scientific community because their author believed the findings were noteworthy, case studies arrive already steeped in the very power dynamic Mak hopes to sidestep. I believe it is possible to consider what doctors thought about "true sex" without taking them at their word, and that, even an incomplete medical record can help tell, even if only partially, previously untold stories of historical precursors to intersex.

48 Mol, *The Body Multiple*.

49 See Mak, "Doubting Sex from Within," 351.

50 Mak points out that Guermonprez does not examine Louise-Julia-Anna's ejaculate to determine the presence of spermatozoa, and he does not conduct a biopsy of her "testicles." Instead, he focuses on her overall appearance, which he deems masculine (*Doubtful Sex*, 143). Dreger suggests that biopsies were not done in living patients until 1910 (*Hermaphrodites*, 149), but in "Conflicting Heterosexualities," Mak cites several starting in 1900. See also Linton, "Mutating Bodies."

51 This confirms the view of Donaldson-Evans, who argues that the literati harbored resentment toward the enduring success of their medical brethren despite their seeming adulation. See Donaldson-Evans, *Medical Examinations.*

52 As Schehr wrote: "The ideological problem posed by realism is the following: to the extent that the ideology is visible in the writing, the literary work is seen as having failed to attain the goal of realist writing founded on logic, continuity, and reason" (*Rendering Realism*, 11–12). Here, Schehr writes about realism, but the crisis he describes may be more acute in scientific writings, since the premise of the genre is that the writer's ideology is supposed to give way to neutral, "objective" parcels of scientific evidence.

53 Guermonprez (1892a, 343).

54 Laqueur, *Making Sex*, 136.

55 Hallopeau (1895, 410–412). Further references in the text. Lagneau (1895) summarizes Hallopeau's case in the *Gazette médicale de Paris*. François Henri Hallopeau (1842–1919) was a decorated professor at the Faculté de médecine, specializing in dermatology.

56 Jablonsky published her case in the *Poitou médical* on December 1, 1897, and she was scheduled to be presented to the Medical School on December 17. A write-up of that meeting was published in the *Gazette des hôpitaux de Toulouse* in 1898. Further references in the text are to the 1898 version.

57 Dreger writes that "true hermaphroditism started to disappear because medical and scientific authorities cooperatively revised the criteria for this condition such that it became almost impossible by the end of the century for any body to satisfy those guidelines" (*Hermaphrodites*, 139).

58 Some doctors used publications on hermaphrodism to secure positions in elite groups. See, for example, Féré's write-up of a case of hermaphrodism presented to the Society of Anatomy of Paris by Jonathan Hutchinson *fils*, who was hoping to join its ranks (1884, 265–66).

59 Samuel Pozzi (1846–1918) became the first Chair of Gynecology at the Faculté de médecine in 1901, which he held until his assassination in 1918. During medical school in Paris, Pozzi studied under the famous Paul Broca, earning the prestigious bronze medal for his 1873 thesis. As an "agrégé de chirurgie," Pozzi secured a teaching position at the Faculté in 1875. Pozzi was an early proponent of Lister's methods in France, as he explains in the meticulous compilation of his own work that he carefully preserved for posterity (*Notice*, 2). In 1880, he took over at the Hôtel-Dieu, while teaching pathology between 1878 and 1898, and also serving as head surgeon at the Asiles publics d'aliénés de la Seine. In 1883, he replaced Verneuil at La Pitié, offering courses in gynecology at the Faculté while teaching at the Broca Hospital. Pozzi became president of the Society of Anthropology in 1888, and of the Society of Obstetrics, Gynecology, and Pediatrics in 1901 (see, Huguet, *Les professeurs*, 180–82). Pozzi published extensively on hermaphrodism, even offering his own classification system in 1912, which he had been refining since 1890. See, for example, his publications from 1884, 1885, 1890, 1896, 1911, and 1912. For more on Pozzi, see Vanderpooten, *Samuel Pozzi*, and Barnes, *The Man in the Red Coat.*

60　See Vanderpooten, *Samuel Pozzi*, 497–99, and De Costa and Miller, *The Diva and Doctor God*, 111. Marcel's brother, Robert, was a physician and Pozzi's assistant for ten years at the Broca Hospital. Proust's letters reveal his deep admiration for Pozzi (ibid., 248–49).

61　Sargent's portrait inspired Barnes's *The Man in the Red Coat*, which brings to life Pozzi's influence during the Belle Époque.

62　De Costa and Miller, *The Diva and Doctor God*, 243–46.

63　Pozzi's opposition to the term "hermaphrodite" was so formidable that colleagues sometimes resorted to paradoxical circumlocutions in his presence. Duhousset publishes a case in 1881 for the Society of Anthropology, based on the same individual Magitot had described in the alleged stand against hermaphrodism by the Society of Surgery. Avoiding the term "hermaphrodite," Duhousset nevertheless characterizes the patient as "The individual whom we might call *neuter*" (1881, 510).

64　In another infraction against the gonadal rule, Guinard defines hermaphrodism more broadly as the "more or less complete coexistence [...] of testicles and ovaries, of male genital tracts and of female genital tracts" (1898, 180). In many case studies, gonads do not decisively determine "true sex" even when identified via microscope. In Rondeau's case, some doctors determined that the patient was a male owing to two testicles, while others, including Rondeau, were unsure, since "nothing of the male revealed itself either in the outward shapes, in movements, in his character, in his voice, or in his deportment" (1881, 410). Rondeau's patient had lived with a male lover for fifteen years, and doctors note the close, loving relationship between them in hospital visits. Perhaps this relationship, coupled with his patient's externally feminine appearance, prevented Rondeau from abiding by the gonadal definition. Or perhaps in Belgium, where it was published, the gonadal definition held less sway.

65　Though hermaphrodism defined by self-impregnation cannot exist in humans, Jouin argues "it does exist if one deduces the masculine sex from the presence of the testicle, and the feminine sex from the existence of the ovary" (1891, 259). Dr. Pajot tenders a more radical definition of hermaphrodism when questioning Dr. Polaillon: "Here is a person who is outwardly a woman, and a man if one examines the internal organs, why do you class him as a pseudo-hermaphrodite? This is a true hermaphrodite or hermaphrodism does not exist" (ibid., 258). Pajot's question is the pretext for Jouin's article.

66　Ibid., 266.

67　These meetings often record heated exchanges. For example, Richard's 1859 case, in which he had boldly claimed that all hermaphrodites were "really males," sparked a lively debate in which his colleague Dr. Giraldès accused Richard of inattention verging on scientific misconduct because his claim passed over "dissections which found either a womb, or ovaries with testicles, or still other organs of which the nature could not be determined, even by microscopic examination" (1859, 157). Giraldès's ire might stem from his colleague's apparent disregard for his earlier publications on the subject.

68 Magitot (1881*a*, 443). Further references in the text. See also his case in *Bulletins de la Société d'Anthropologie* (1881*b*).

69 Hypospadias describes a urethral opening that is not located on the tip of the glans. Cryptorchidism, also often related to uncertain sex in the nineteenth century, describes one or both of the testes undescended into the scrotum.

70 The possibility of menstruating without ovaries is also a subject of fierce debate in nineteenth-century medicine, but a significant body of literature actually shored up Pozzi's seemingly paradoxical assertion. Time and again, doctors published cases of menses unimpeded by dual ovariectomies and even total hysterectomies. Tendered explanations ranged from the presence of ovarian tissue having evaded the scalpel to the body's "monthly habit" of "defying scientific laws." See Boddaert (1874, 102).

71 Tillaux responds: "Regarding Mr. Pozzi's explanation, I cannot rally around it, even though I know well cases of menstruation occurring in women with their ovaries and uterus removed. I myself presented a case at the Academy of Medicine" (Magitot, 1881*a*, 451). Mr. See thinks he remembers a case of "true hermaphrodism," although he is vague on the details: "true hermaphrodism is characterized by the coexistence of the ovary and the testicle. Today we generally contest the phenomenon; however, I remember having read, about three years ago, in a journal whose name I forget, a case of it that was supported by an autopsy" (ibid., 452). Magitot posits an imaginative transformation in which the patient who was first a woman, then later became a man, which Pozzi finds derisory: "it is inadmissible that this subject was successively a woman and a man" (ibid., 452). Pozzi was not entirely right about this. Today, 5-alpha-reductase (5-AR) deficiency, one variety of intersex, can lead to an apparent female-to-male transformation at puberty.

72 According to Faucher and Bourdin, this may be due to the role of arrested development in hermaphrodism:

> S. Pozzi denies its [hermaphrodism's] existence categorically; whereas Hermann, Debierre, E. Laurent, and the majority of other authors along with them accept it. One can perhaps explain these divergences of opinion if one goes back to the earliest phases of embryogenesis; there exists a period in which ovaries or testicles are not yet clearly differentiated, and one has published autopsies of hermaphrodites in which the genital glands remained, at least one of them, at this moment of evolution. (1899, 300)

Many other doctors either explicitly do not define sex gonadally, or make no comment about gonadal sex whatsoever, basing sex determinations on other factors. Meige, for example, defines hermaphrodism broadly in his treatise as "those for whom abnormally developed genital organs can give rise to misunderstandings about the true sex" (1895*b*, 6). See also his article (1895*a*). Lagneau defines hermaphrodism as an individual with male genitalia, but with breasts – a "common condition," in his estimation (1895, 416).

73 Laurent's work compiles numerous cases, and he even cites Pozzi, so he must have noticed that certain authors disputed the existence of hermaphrodism

(1894, 160). For francophone articles with "true hermaphrodism" in the title, see Sand (1923) and Firket (1927).

74 Dechambre, Duval, and Lereboullet allege that internal hermaphrodism is possible since the embryonic origins of these organs are either hermaphroditic or double. The dictionary also claims that "a marriage contracted with a true hermaphrodite is null" (1885, 750). J. W. Ballantyne defines a hermaphrodite as an individual in which sex is doubtful, meaning that there are "many hermaphrodites" (1887, 100). Often, when doctors did contend that "true hermaphrodism" was impossible, their arguments relied more on rhetoric than on scientific evidence. See, for example, Crecchio (1866, 178).

75 Mak's *Doubting Sex* cites predominately German cases. With only thirty-eight French cases cited in the bibliography, and only four before 1850 (Isidore Geoffroy Saint-Hilaire's work is not referenced), Mak's book does not have a broad or deep enough archive from which to draw nuanced conclusions about hermaphrodism in France for the entire period.

76 On hermaphrodism and the *Encyclopédie*, see McGuire, "La représentation du corps hermaphrodite." However, not all eighteenth-century cases make any clear claims about whether or not hermaphrodism is possible. Renauldin, for example, limits his writings to descriptions of his patients, without drawing any larger conclusions about hermaphrodism in general. See Renauldin (1797*a*) and (1797*b*).

77 Richerand was professor at the Paris Faculté de médecine, and head surgeon at the Saint-Louis Hospital, and his popular physiology treatise was already in its seventh edition in 1817.

78 There is some ambiguity about when the "Age of the Gonads" took place. Initially, Dreger argues that "it was decided among biomedical experts by about 1890 to instate what I call a gonadal definition of sex [. . .] I therefore call this period the "Age of the Gonads" (*Hermaphrodites*, 11). Later, however, she argues for a wider time range:

> During this period, 1870–1915, what I call the Age of the Gonads, scientific and medical men, faced with and frustrated by case after case of "doubtful sex," came to an agreement that every body's "true" sex was marked by one thing and one thing only: the anatomical nature of the gonadal tissue as either ovarian or testicular. Not coincidentally, such a definition virtually eliminated "true" hermaphroditism in theory and in practice, even if – probably because – people with challenging bodies kept popping up. (Ibid., 29)

79 Ombrédanne (1939, 29) and Laurent (1894, 155).

80 Béclard (1815, 273–74). He rates other characteristics as "secondary signs, normally in alliance with, it is true, but sometimes in opposition to essential characteristics of sex" (274). These include height, proportions, breast development, menstruation, lactation, and sexual attraction, among other things (274). The anatomist Pierre-Auguste Béclard (1785–1825) was chief surgeon at the Pitié Hospital and was one of the experts commissioned to determine Marie-Madeleine Lefort's sex. His influential anatomy treatises

underwent multiple reprints throughout the century and he and other colleagues at the Faculté de médecine collaborated on the *Nouveau dictionnaire de médecine, chirurgie, pharmacie* [. . .], which offered the verbatim definition of hermaphrodism quoted by Cuisin in his novel (31) (see Chapter 3 of this book). For Béclard's biography, see the "notice" published in the second edition of his anatomy treatise by Charles-Prosper Olivier (1827, 1–24).

81 See Worbe (1815*a*, 371). Worbe describes a different patient, Marie-Marguerite, during the same year (1815*b*). The latter describes Marie-Marguerite's legal sex reassignment punctuated by Worbe's novelistic interjections, including the orator's "O tempora! O mores!": "Will one be able to believe that in the nineteenth century, fifteen leagues from Paris, an individual with an interesting face, intelligent, well raised for a country dweller, did not know his sex for twenty-two years? Oh what times! Oh what customs!" (1815*b*, 488).

82 Hermann echoes this claim in his dictionary entry for hermaphrodism (1889, 613). On the early adoption of microscopic technology in Paris, see La Berge, "Medical Microscopy." I find an increasing emphasis on histology from the 1860s, but that does not necessarily prove that it was not already important by the 1830s. Each decade of the nineteenth century surpasses its predecessor in the number of published cases of hermaphrodism, rendering absolute comparisons less meaningful. Moreover, histology was predominately performed on deceased individuals, so it was not a readily available option in living patients (exploratory abdominal surgery was risky and not frequently performed). See Dodeuil (1865) and Blanche (1867). Blanche's case was rejected by the Society of Surgery because he had not cited microscopic evidence. Crecchio confirms that determining sex during life is "sometimes very difficult, and often even impossible" and he is only able to determine the sex of his patient, Joseph Marzo after he passes (1866, 180). Dr. Jules Rochard suggests that early adopters of the microscope in the Paris School were active from the 1840s and 1850s, with Dr. C. Morel publishing the first French treatise on human histology in 1859 (1875, 293). Ombrédanne cites the widespread "fallibility" of histology in his twentieth-century treatise because of faulty examinations or because of intermediary tissues, and he lists many instances in which histology could not determine a patient's sex or led to erroneous determinations (1939, 31).

83 Geoffroy Saint-Hilaire (1832–37, 2: 31). Volume 2, treating "hermaphrodism," was published in 1836, and a section of volume 3 discusses the medico-legal implications for "doubtful sex." Geoffroy Saint-Hilaire's early interest in a broad definition of hermaphrodism is already apparent in his 1832 article, "Cas singulier," in which the doctor "realized that the sexual organs of this cadaver presented anomalies such that one could not determine with certainty to which of the two sexes it could have belonged, even though, during life, she had passed for being of the feminine sex" (75). Summaries of Geoffroy Saint-Hilaire's early work were also published. See, for example, Dutrochet (1833) and Serres et al. (1833).

84 According to Huet's *Monstrous Imagination*, Geoffroy Saint-Hilaire coined "teratology" in 1830, although she does not specify where he first used it (108). Nye writes that Geoffroy Saint-Hilaire coined the term in 1832 (*Masculinity*, 63). At the very least, Geoffroy Saint-Hilaire assured the use of the term "teratology" after the publication of his influential treatise.

85 In Bouillaud's 1833 stand for the existence of true hermaphrodism, he suggests that the critical consensus up until his watershed publication was that true hermaphrodism was mere myth. He adds that this consensus situates sexual difference in the gonads, with the first order of sexual characteristics including "in man, the testicles along with their associated organs, and in woman, the ovaries along with their annexes" (478, n. 1).

86 Marc's 1837 dictionary entry for hermaphrodism is identical to earlier editions except for the new, effusive section dedicated to Geoffroy Saint-Hilaire's classification system.

87 See, for example, Landouzy (1849), Larrey (1859), and Huette (1856).

88 The class "hermaphrodism without excess" includes four orders: masculine, feminine, neuter, and mixed hermaphrodism. "Hermaphrodism with excess" is subdivided into the three orders: complex masculine hermaphrodism, complex feminine hermaphrodism, and bisexual hermaphrodism (Geoffroy Saint-Hilaire, 1832–37, 2: Table II, 36). Further references in the text. Dreger includes detailed analysis of Geoffroy Saint-Hilaire's taxonomy. See *Hermaphrodites*, esp. 140–42.

89 Ombrédanne contrasts Meckel's classification system to that of Geoffroy Saint-Hilaire (1939, 29).

90 Part of Geoffroy Saint-Hilaire's volume 3 on the implications of doubtful sex and the law was reprinted in an 1837 article (1837, 435).

91 Le Mens, for example, mistakenly claims that only one doctor in the entire nineteenth century thought it possible for a "hermaphrodite" *not* to have a "true sex" (*L'hermaphrodite*, 11). The parallel claim that only one doctor in the entire nineteenth century protested against the need to assign a true sex to hermaphrodites is paradoxically repeated in Le Mens' 2019 monograph, even though multiple treatises and case studies that she cites contradict it. See Le Mens, *Modernité*, 64.

92 Most of Debierre's work credits Geoffroy Saint-Hilaire. See, for example, Debierre (1886, 330). In 1883, Garnier had even amazingly cited Geoffroy Saint-Hilaire's work as evidence for the relative frequency of transverse hermaphrodism (1883, 486). Benoist also evokes Saint-Hilaire's fifty-year-old statistics (1886, 84). In 1899, Faucher and Bourdin cite Geoffroy Saint-Hilaire's definition (299). Follin accepts Geoffroy Saint-Hilaire's definition of neuter hermaphrodism (1851, 24). Garnier incorrectly credits him with sparking nineteenth-century interest in hermaphrodism (1885, 287). Guinard, in 1898, uses Geoffroy Saint-Hilaire's terminology (181), as does Jouin's 1891 article (259); Odin's 1874 publication (217), and Péan's case in 1884 (106). In 1880, Trélat advocates retaining only some of Geoffroy Saint-Hilaire's terms (42).

93 Laqueur's translation of Tardieu's *Question medico-légale* (1874). See Laqueur, *Making Sex*, 136.

94 For examples of cases in which sex could not be determined, see De Mortillet (1885) and Descoust (1886). Descoust used chloroform to sedate his patient while conducting a thorough physical exam and while probing cavities, but was nevertheless unable to locate testicles, a prostate, or a uterus, and microscopic analysis of white secretions revealed no spermatozoids. Despite the fact that "none of the organs (testicles, prostate, uterus) characteristic of the masculine or feminine sex" were discovered, Descoust suggests that his patient is "a poorly developed individual of the masculine sex" (90). This conclusion is fervently challenged by Descoust's colleagues. Dr. Polaillon suggests that the patient is instead a woman, and Dr. Hemey alleges that "In order to determine sex one must find testicles or ovaries. If one cannot find those organs, it is impossible to make a sex determination" (ibid., 90). While both Descoust and Polaillon were ready to declare sex without the gonadal definition (albeit opposite ones), only Hemey insists on a gonadal definition of "true sex," and this means that only he cannot posit any sex at all. In 1887, Sentex sexes his patient as a "a pseudo-hermaphrodite with male appearance" without ever identifying testicles (55).

95 Laqueur, *Making Sex*, 136.

96 In 1939, Ombrédanne reveals that histology was frequently inconclusive: "on multiple occasions, Wirchow refused to make a declaration about the histological nature of a gland with homogeneous appearance … Zacharias, out of thirty-four histological examinations, declared sixteen times that it was impossible to make a determination" (31).

97 This is a widespread phenomenon. See, for example, Boddaert's case (1874).

98 For a discussion of the increasing specialization of gynecology in England and the widening rift between gynecologists/obstetricians and general surgeons fighting to claim the authority to perform lucrative ovariotomies, see Moscucci, *The Science of Woman*. See also Weisz, "The Development of Medical Specialization," and *Medical Mandarins*.

99 Weisz reveals how such rivalries shaped medicine in his excellent *Medical Mandarins*.

Chapter 2

* This chapter grew out of work from an earlier article published in *Representations*. I am grateful to the editor for allowing me to reuse materials from it. See Linton, "Hermaphrodite Outlaws."

1 The article appears on August 18, 1881, on the second page of *The New York Times*. The French case spurred confusion in America, since "the petitioner does not specify whether the bride and groom are both boys or both girls."

2 See the 1881 issues for July 30, December 21, and December 28.

3 *Gazette des tribunaux*, December 21, 1881, 1251. Further references in the text.

4 Brisson discusses hermaphrodite trials in the seventeenth and eighteenth centuries in *Le sexe incertain*, 101–46.

5 See Orfila (1823), Meckel (1825), Burdach (1837), Beck (1838), Briand and Chaudé (1874), Legrand du Saulle (1874), Lacassagne (1887), Péan (1888), and Pozzi (1874 and 1897). Tourdes's dictionary entry for "hermaphrodism" speculates on all of these categories (1889, 643). In an 1827 article, Dugès argues that irrefutable cases of hermaphrodism did exist, and he worries about marriage, conscription, and the regulations for recording civil status. See also Houzé d'Aulnoit (1861). Azam's 1857 case explores the intersections of surgery, physiology, and legal medicine.

6 Vincentelli explains that before the Revolution, legal separation (séparation du corps) was determined by canon law (droit canon), but after the Revolution, in 1792, the law of September 20–25 abolished separation and added divorce. The Napoleonic Code of 1804 reestablished separation along with divorce. Divorce was outlawed with the First Restoration (law of May 8, 1816), and only legal separation remained. Divorce was finally reestablished in 1884. See Vincentelli (1884, 12–14). Even when divorce was illegal, however, couples could file for separation for all of the same reasons as they could file for divorce when it was legal. A third option was marriage annulment. While divorce ended marriage, annulment essentially rendered it void, which meant that the former spouses could remarry (which was not the case with separation). In Orfila's 1823 medico-legal lessons, he explains: "Current legislation no longer authorizes divorce. The first two articles of the Law of May 8, 1816, stipulate: '1. Divorce is abolished; 2. All requests and proceedings for divorce, for specific causes, are converted into requests and proceedings for *legal separation*'" (164–65). For expert treatment of divorce in literature during the long nineteenth century, see White, *French Divorce Fiction*.

7 See, for example, Cruveilhier's article (1843), or that of Thore (1846), in which autopsy reversed previous clinical evaluation. Chalmers's 1882 article proves that British doctors faced the identical problem.

8 Most medico-legal treatises offer guidelines on how to conduct sex determinations. Orfila (the famous doctor sent to confirm the Duchess du Barry's scandalous pregnancy) recommended the following:

> 1. The exterior examination of the reproductive parts cannot be undertaken with too much care and exactitude; as much as possible, and without wounding or causing sharp pain, probe the visible openings in order to learn their depth and their direction. 2. The inspection of the entire surface of the body is no less essential, in order to be able to determine the predominance of constitutional characteristics of either sex. 3. To this effect, one should observe for a long time, multiple times, the tastes and tendencies of the individuals whose sex is to be determined. In applying findings that will result from this observation, one should be especially careful not to confuse those habits resulting from the social position of individuals with their innate penchants, or those that depend on their organic makeup. 4. A very important circumstance in ambiguous cases is to determine whether there is, through any type of opening in the sexual parts, a bloody menstrual excretion, given that this alone is nearly sufficient to prove

that there is a predominance of the female sex. 5. Nothing is more conducive to errors than attempting, in all cases, to determine *shortly after birth* the sex of children, whose genital parts are irregular. When an individual's conformation raises the slightest doubt about the true sex, it is preferable to alert the authorities, and to take, if necessary, years to observe the progressive physical and moral development, rather than to hazard a judgment on sex that subsequent phenomena could reverse sooner or later. (1823, 160–61)

These rules had been around for decades. See also Marc (1811) and Béclard (1815). On the Duchess's pregnancy, see Samuels, *The Betrayal of the Duchess*, 263.

9 Doctors relied on Article 57 of the Civil Code: "The birth certificate will announce the day, the hour and the place of birth, the sex of the child, and the names given to him" (quoted by Brouardel, 1900, 31). See also, Brouardel's article on the "third sex" (1904). In 1878, Dr. Martin published a case of doubtful sex in a stillborn preterm infant. The anxiety surrounding sex at birth was such that Dr. Martin worried how the child would have been sexed if s/he had survived (32).

10 For example, Faguet's case published by Delefosse (1892), in which the patient's sex was only revealed at the age of twenty-four.

11 Quoted by Dailliez (1892, 11).

12 Quoted by Tuffier and Lapointe (1911, 249).

13 Gatcheff claims that "Cases of sexing errors brought about by birth defects, without being very frequent, are less exceptional than generally supposed" (1901, 2).

14 See, for example, Thore (1846) and Polaillon (1891). Polaillon suspected that his patient possessed testicles despite her outwardly feminine body, but he was not able to confirm this until after her death, when histology revealed testicular cells. As we saw in Chapter 1, Pozzi was a fervent proponent of histology, without always practicing what he preached. He argued: "it is only via autopsy and biopsy that one will be able to determine the exact classification to which the present subject belongs" (1911, 274).

15 The illustration is of Marie-Madeleine Lefort's abdomen at autopsy from Dr. Charles Debierre's 1891 treatise on hermaphrodism. Debierre was professor at the Faculté de médecine in Lille, and mentions Mademoiselle de Campos's case in the same work. He published widely on hermaphrodism. See also his articles from 1886, 1894, and his treatise on congenital variations in female genitalia (1892).

16 Dacorogna eventually published Lefort's autopsy, which identified ovarian cells via microscope (1865). See also Cruveilhier (1865).

17 The case was originally reported by Giraud, but is mentioned by Neugebauer (1899, 202) and Houel (1881, 556).

18 Mak, "Doubtful Sex," 197.

19 Loir's 1854 paper was first delivered on September 17 to the Académie, but he reports having read another piece on October 17, 1846, that advocated: "If the sex determination leaves any doubt, one should indicate on the [birth] certificate the necessity of an 'ulterior examination at a more advanced age'" (27).

20 Brouardel mentions Dubois and Béclard's stance in 1887 (57).

21 Marc's dictionary entries (1921–28 and 1837), Orfila's medico-legal lessons from 1823, and Geoffroy Saint-Hilaire's 1832–37 treatise, all note the insufficiency of French law to account for human diversity.

22 Marc, summarizing Everard Home, writes that certain hermaphrodites, "whose number is greater than one would think, often present the appearance of an equal mix of the characteristics of the two sexes" (1811, 182).

23 Doctors themselves often obscured historical precedent by claiming originality. Garnier, for example, alleges he was the first to contest the legitimacy of Article 57, even though the authors he cites in his footnotes had already called for the very same amendment (1885, 285–86).

24 Delore, however, was against Debierre's call for a neuter class of citizens:

> After gathering all possible information, the members of the meeting will announce their decision, perhaps approximative, no doubt arbitrary, but which in any case will be preferable to the incertitude and probably to a classification of *neuter sex*, the new category that Siébold, Orfila, and Debierre aim to create. It is of utmost importance for a young individual to have a sex as soon as possible, because it determines the direction of one's entire life, indicating rights and responsibilities. (1899*b*, 68)

25 In apparent defiance of this rule, Dr. Ricoux records that his 72-year-old patient had been originally listed as "hermaphrodite sex" on the birth certificate (1899, 183). Trouvenin makes the identical claim: "I had the opportunity to see a one-year-old child there who was listed on the civil registry, under the name of Claude-Marie-Joseph, and designated as a hermaphrodite, and who was considered by the mother to be a girl" (1830, 406). In 1846, Guersant's controversial sex determination (he claimed the patient was a boy even though he was unable to locate testicles), incited him to remark that sex assignments should be held off until puberty.

26 Loir (1854) cites Geoffroy Saint-Hilaire's famous observation in part on the first page of his treatise (referencing, in error, volume 2 of Geoffroy Saint-Hilaire's *Histoire générale*). Instead, Loir is quoting from a presentation given by Geoffroy Saint-Hilaire during the February 4, 1833, meeting of the Académie des sciences, that was widely reported on in multiple medical publications. See, for example, Geoffroy Saint-Hilaire (1833, 115). Debierre also echoes Saint-Hilaire's claim that the "current legislation is defective" since nonbinary people exist (1891, 146).

27 Mak, "Doubtful Sex in Civil Law," 197.

28 Bouillaud wrote: "Supposing that one day the civil and political death penalty could be imposed on monsters of Valmont's species, it would be far less severe than the barbarism of the Law of the Twelve Tables, that condemned them to a physical death" (1833, 495). Further references in the text. Bouillaud also published a *Traité de nosographie médicale* (1846), in which he again discusses Valmont in relation to Geoffroy Saint-Hilaire's recent taxonomy.

29 See Lesbre and Fougeot (1902, 75).

30 Incredibly, Dr. Baldetti's 1930s thesis for doctor of veterinary medicine even takes a stand (in favor of Debierre's legislation) (1932, 69). Pancrazi is another supporter of Debierre's proposal (1910, 45). Leblond's 1885 article also argues that "doubtful sex" should be added to the birth certificate of infants whose sex was difficult to determine, and that a formal clause should be added to the Code which would both prevent hermaphrodites from marrying and provide grounds for nullifying a marriage.

31 See, for example, Gatcheff (1901, 83).

32 See also Lacassagne (1887, 94).

33 Iacub, *Le crime*, 102–3. Further references in the text.

34 Siredey (1874, 469). Further references in the text.

35 See Brouardel (1887, 58). Further references in the text.

36 See Bègue's 1963 thesis, *La définition*, 38. "In Germany, the *Law of 18 August, 1835*, banned the marriage of any known sterile individuals (except in the case in which both spouses were sterile), requiring a medical certificate affirming non-sterility before a marriage could take place" (ibid., 39).

37 Brouardel (1887, 58).

38 Ibid., 57. See also Tuffier and Lapointe (1911, 257); Brouardel (1900, 30); and Tourdes (1889, 646–47).

39 Brouardel (1887, 57). For expert analysis of historical tensions between France and Germany affecting debates in sexology from the Second Empire to the twentieth century, see Rosario, *The Erotic Imagination*. In a bizarre work of medical eroticism from 1875, Davenport alleges that according to the Church, hermaphrodites remained able to select their own sex (180).

40 Mak argues that "German proposals show a more interesting perspective in their attempt to support hermaphrodites," but the old French law actually closely resembles the Prussian law ("Doubtful Sex," 198).

41 In Articles 229 through 232. Brouardel explains in his 1887 treatise that Article 231 stipulates that "The spouses can reciprocally demand divorce for 'excesses, cruelty, or abuse of one against the other'" (58). The difference between "excès" and "service" depended largely on degree, with "excès" constituting the more egregious offenses. Beating a pregnant wife was considered an "excès," while general wife beating or "defenestration" (!) is described by Brouardel as merely a "service," because, writes Brouardel "a husband has, up to a certain point, the right to correct his spouse" (ibid.). Some experts wondered whether hermaphrodism could constitute grounds for divorce as a "service."

42 Despite the fact that impotence did not constitute legal grounds for divorce according to the Code, several medico-legal treatises and experts persisted in claiming that an individual's ability to procreate dictated their ability to marry. See, for example, Marc (1837, 260) and his dictionary entry (1821–28, 78). The architects of the Napoleonic Code had abolished impotence as grounds to annul a marriage, and only retained the term for the "disavowal of legitimate parentage, when the impossibility of having sex was accidental and perceptible via external examination" (Iacub, *Le crime*, 103).

43 See Vermeil (1765) and Champeaux (1765). Foucault discusses the Grandjean case (see *Abnormal*, trans. Burchell, 71–75). Though he won the appeal, Grandjean was forced to dress as a woman and was forbidden to see Françoise Lambert or another woman, because Grandjean's attraction to women was seen as "monstrous" (ibid., 73).

44 Articles 147 and 180 invoked "error of the person" as grounds for marriage nullity. Most nineteenth-century authors agreed that this clause was only intended to allow for divorce or separation when the incorrect person had been married in error, and not when one of the newlyweds had some kind of bodily variation. A minority of authors contended that hermaphrodism either was or should be counted as an "error of the person." One such author is Costilhes (1853), who believed that should his patient marry, Article 180 would nullify it. Debierre, as we have seen, was another, although by calling for a revision of this clause in the Civil Code, he implicitly acknowledged that the law was not always interpreted as such (1886, 334). Lutaud also claimed that "Article 180 of the Civil Code allows for the nullity of marriage when an individual had allegedly been deceived about the sex of the person to whom he or she was married" (1886, 7). So too did Orfila:

> Let it be remarked that although the Civil Code does not *expressly* authorize annulment requests as soon as a physical cause opposes the propagation of the species, the most famous jurisconsults are right to believe that marriage is legally annulled as soon as a physical cause prevents propagation of the species, and, as it happens one of these causes is impotence and certain congenital defects of the sexual parts. (1823, 121)

As evidence, Orfila cited the 1808 ruling of the court of appeal of Trèves (121–22).

45 See Lacassagne (1887, 92). Iacub argues that up until the court of Grenoble's 1958 ruling that impotence should be considered as a cause for annulling a marriage, it was never considered as such in the case record (*Le crime*, 101). It *was*, however, considered a cause for annulment in the 1808 appeal in Trèves, in the sense that the ruling declared that "physical causes and defects, which oppose the natural and legal aim of marriage, are impediments which automatically nullify it" (quoted in ibid., 107). Apparently because the husband likens his marriage to a marriage between two individuals of the same sex (owing to his wife's inability to engage in coitus because of her genital variation), Iacub interprets this case as one in which sexual identity eventually resulted in marriage annulment, rather than one in which impotence eventually resulted in marriage annulment. Nineteenth-century doctors, however, often interpret this case as jurisprudence that impotence constituted grounds for rendering a marriage null (see Orfila, 1823).

46 See, for example, "A Curious Medico-Legal Case," *The British Medical Journal*, November 13, 1869, 2: 543 "Action for Nullity in Marriage in France," *The Medical Times and Gazette*, July 26, 1873, 2: 100–1.

47 Courty (1871, 473).

48 See, for example, Legrand du Saulle's 1874 medico-legal treatise (15–21). Legrand du Saulle publishes the full names of both parties, whereas Courty referenced only last names, and Tardieu aims to preserve anonymity by recording them as "M. D…" and "Justine A. J…" (1874, 6). Further references in the text.

49 "Action for Nullity of Marriage in France," *The Medical Times and Gazette*, July 26, 1873, 2: 100–1. Further references in the text.

50 The case record is replete with the low regard in which many doctors held midwives. See, for example, Granier (1894, 331).

51 Jumas's refusal to submit to an examination provoked debate about the legality of requiring such an inspection in a civil trial. See Tourdes (1889, 657).

52 Mak also discusses this case, arguing convincingly that Jumas's refusal to submit to an examination worked against her in the end (*Doubting Sex*, 118–35). She mistakenly claims, however, that Jumas was never examined medically. Dr. L. Carcassonne apparently did so, since he provides a physical description of her external genitalia.

53 As Tardieu records: "The Court reforms the judgment of first instance and declares that, since the evidence offered was neither relevant nor admissible, the first judges wrongly ordered it" (1874, 9). For the full text of the ruling, see ibid., 10.

54 Ibid.

55 Elected to the Academy of Medicine in 1859, Tardieu (1818–1879) was a professor of forensic medicine in Paris from 1861 until his death, and a frequent contributor to the *Annals of Public Hygiene and Legal Medicine*. Rosario explains that it was his acclaimed *Medico-Legal Study on the Assaults on Decency* that gained him the professorship at the Faculté de médecine, which was re-edited six times over a twenty-year span, virtually doubling in length (*The Erotic Imagination*, 72).

56 Courty (1871, 473). Further references in the text.

57 Courty endeavors to explain the "immense" difference between the way the "essential" organs are formed and the way the "accessory organs are formed," a choice intended to validate his method of relying on internal organs to sex Jumas (1871, 478). For example, Petit examined an individual in 1879 who outwardly appeared to be male, but who possessed internal ovaries.

58 Courty avers: "I know of a young man, in this very city, who is obviously a boy, but whose testicles are retained, and who presents, as the result of arrested development, the exact appearance of the external reproductive parts as the outward genital appearance of a veritable woman" (ibid., 479). He also mentions the converse situation: "I know of a man in a neighboring department who was listed […] as a girl, who has not requested the rectification of this erroneous sex determination (this perhaps serves his interests; he no doubt exploits and abuses the situation)" (ibid., 480).

59 Tardieu (1874, 7). Further references in the text.

60 Perhaps influenced by Tardieu's logic, Dechambre, Duval, and Lereboullet's entry for hermaphrodism in the *Dictionnaire usuel des sciences médicales* (1885)

reads: "marriage contracted with a true hermaphrodite is null but congenital defects that render intercourse impossible do not constitute error on the person, and, as a consequence, marriage nullity" (750). The case record does not support the first part of their claim about true hermaphrodism and nullifying a marriage.

61 "This certificate has nevertheless influenced the Court's opinion, even though it neglects fundamental realities by confining itself to appearances" (Tardieu, 1874, 15).

62 Ibid., 25–26.

63 For example, they cite the insufficiencies of Carcassonne's certificate, and Courty's claim that "the art of medicine seems today to possess rather precise means of diagnosis in order to recognize, principally in the abdomen of a thin woman [. . .] ovaries and especially a womb, and if these organs are normally developed within her" (Tardieu, 1874, 26). Further references in the text. Here, Courty was not claiming that no organs had been found in Jumas, only that if she had not refused examination, an even clearer outcome could have been presented. Of course, numerous case studies at the same time were alleging that manual examinations proved nothing about the somatic nature of internal organs, and that only histology was sufficient. The courts, it seems, were unaware of this fact – largely because the forensic consultants charged with making them aware of relevant scientific data failed to do so.

64 For examples of this, see Heppner and Doumie (1872) and Debierre (1892).

65 Brouardel (1879, 2). On Tardieu's external "stigmata" of pederasty, see chapter 3 of Rosario, *The Erotic Imagination*, 69–111.

66 See Brouardel (1900, 17).

67 These issues did not evaporate in the nineteenth century, but rather continued well into the twentieth. See Bègue's thesis from 1963, which posits many of the same questions that were debated throughout the previous century. Bègue wonders:

> since the sex of each spouse is listed on their birth certificate, and since the hermaphrodite is classed a priori in one or the other of the two sexes, s/he legally has the right to marry a person of the opposite sex. If, on the other hand, one allowed for a hermaphrodite to belong to a third sex, could s/he freely get married as either a woman or a man? Here again, no response can be offered. (*La définition*, 30–31)

The Civil Code's enduring silence regarding all matters concerning intersex meant that well into the twentieth century, it was still difficult to articulate the legal rights of intersex persons concerning marriage with any degree of certainty. Even in 1975, Demonsant's thesis still advocates the early nineteenth-century recommendation that if an infant's sex is difficult to determine at birth, "it is more prudent to declare the infant's sex as undetermined" (*L'assignation*, 21).

68 Quoted by Iacub, *Le crime*, 110.

69 Ibid. Further references in the text.

70 The 1958 ruling in Grenoble stated this explicitly: "The notion of error on the person afforded by Article 180 of the Civil Code among the defects of consent should be broadened to give to these cases of marriage annulment the scope of the nature of marriage." See Iacub, *Le crime*, 117, for analysis of the ruling.

71 Quoted in ibid., 121.

72 Garnier had made the identical argument in his 1883 book (498).

73 See Banon (1852, 67).

74 Delacroix describes a medical team tasked with determining the "wife's" sex. Ultimately, they resolve that "there is no need to dissolve the marriage, it is null by the mere fact that there is a union of two people of the same sex" (1870, 59). One doctor remarks, however, that by furnishing her with a "a certificate of virility, one would authorize a new marriage," an idea he bemoans since he believes the patient to be "no more a man than a woman" (58). The article does not clearly state the patient's decision, but it would seem that she refused to petition to have her marriage dissolved since she complained "of the scandal that such a procedure would make" in her village (57).

75 Interestingly, Neugebauer cites Blondel's case as one of his "fifty cases," and the "tender love" between the spouses, without ever evoking Blondel's proposed surgery (1899, 198).

76 See Debout (1890, 40–44).

77 As Ombrédanne warns: "in legal terms, removal of genital organs constitutes the crime of castration, punishable by forced labor in perpetuity if things go well, and by death for the surgeon if the patient dies during the forty days following the operation (Article 316 of the Penal Code)" (1939, 184). Some leeway was apparently allowed as long as the surgeon operated with an intent to cure. See, for example, Dor (1892), who suggests that since internal testicles often become cancerous, they should always be removed. Dr. Paul Philippe, of Canada, removes first one and then, a month later, the second testicle from his patient, who complained they were causing her severe pain (1893). He describes this case as one of "apparent hermaphrodism" under Geoffroy Saint-Hilaire's classification system, and does not suggest that his patient is "really a man" following the gonadal model, or, indeed, if he even revealed that the excised organs were testicles (507). In 1895, Péan published a case of a woman who had no vagina, and for that reason, had been determined to belong to the male sex by a different doctor. When the woman could not find employment as a man, she came to Péan who performed exploratory surgery expecting to find internal testicles. Instead, he found ovaries and a uterus. He then attempted, without success, to create an artificial vagina connecting to the uterus. According to Neugebauer, Péan nevertheless left the wound to allow for "vaginal" intercourse (!): "He did not sew up this wound (thinking that a future husband would make use of it), but he removed the woman's ovaries" (Neugebauer, 1900*a*, 485).

78 Guermonprez's stinging vituperative against Louise-Julia-Anna simply was not legally sound. Guermonprez, you will recall, informed his patient that marriage was expressly forbidden by the law (1892*a*, 371). Ignoring

Guermonprez's threats, Louise-Julia-Anna simply crossed the border into Belgium and convinced a surgeon there to perform the desired surgery. Some doctors do claim that if a hermaphrodite voluntarily deceived his/her spouse about his/her physical conformation, then that spouse would be able to divorce on the grounds of an "injure grave" (abuse). See, for example, Ombrédanne: "The infertility of a hermaphrodite is not a cause for divorce, unless it was known and intentionally hidden from a spouse before marriage (possibility of abuse)" (1939, 181). However, I have not identified any divorce cases involving uncertain sex that actually invoked this clause.

79 Pozzi (1911, 278).

80 See, for example, Gaffé and Lucas-Championnière (1885, 65). Their case is atypical in that they did not examine the individual whose sex was in question, but rather met with his fiancée and her mother, who sought to discourage the marriage. The betrothed, however wanted to marry her sterile cousin precisely for that reason: "No matter what, she wants to marry him. It is obviously not for gain, but, she says, out of inclination, and especially because she heard that, by marrying her cousin she would never have a child, and she does not want children" (ibid.). In the end, Gaffé merely discourages the marriage, leaving the choice up to her.

81 Tuffier and Lapointe write:

> We remember that certain of these homosexual unions were never disturbed, each of the spouses was satisfied with what the other could offer. Do we have the right to inform them about the mistake that they have made, to put an end to the harmony that reigns between them and to create two sad people? The situation is most precarious and we would be tempted to respect their ignorance, especially if it had been going on for a long time. (1911, 262)

82 For Polaillon's patient, marriage was a subject of bitterness: "One day I asked him why he wasn't married, and he answered ill-humoredly: *how could I be married in my condition?*" (1887, 871).

83 Marzo's case became famous. See, for example, Accolas (1889, 143–44), Laugier and Tardieu's dictionary entry (1873, 504, 510), and Dailliez (1892, 30).

84 Laugier and Tardieu opine that Marzo's case revealed both legal and scientific insufficiencies:

> In such an instance, there would only be two possible hypotheses for an expert perfectly aware of the hermaphrodite's life: 1. The individual examined is a cryptorchid man; 2. It is impossible to determine the sex. And, in the two hypotheses, it would be necessary to conclude that the marriage is valid! The error of such a union, if ever it came to be revealed, could only happen after death, via autopsy. (1873, 510)

85 Houbre includes biographical information on Gauthier in the *Livre des courtisanes*, without indicating which archive in the Préfecture de Police contains her file. I located it in BA/881 "Dossier de quelques prostituées." Further references in the text to Gauthier's case are to this archive.

86 In 1856, Dufour examines an "Emilie Gautier," age fourteen, from La Villette (262). The police report from 1873 indicates that the adult Emilie Gauthier was born on January 3, 1842, in La Villette (Seine), which is why I believe the two individuals were likely one and the same (that is, they share the same birthplace and were both age fourteen in 1856). Dufour's case study of Emilie Gautier confines itself to an anatomical description, referring to her throughout as a girl. She has "a rudiment of a penis, with a small glans, without a foreskin. This penis is about 5 centimeters in a state of flaccidity" (1856, 262). The police file describes Gauthier's genital conformation similarly: "in place of a clitoris, she has a penis of 3 centimeters, which, when erect lengthens another 2 centimeters, the glans is exposed [and resembles] that of a twelve-year-old circumcised child" (np). Nowhere does Dufour allege that Gautier is a "hermaphrodite," but instead he describes his case as one of a "congenital defect of the genital organs" (ibid.).

Chapter 3

* Some work on this chapter grew out of an earlier article published in *Romanic Review*. I am grateful to the editor for allowing me to reuse that material. See Linton, "Lusting after the Louvre Hermaphrodite."

1 Cuisin, *Clémentine, orpheline et androgyne*, 146. Further references in the text.

2 Locker, "Merriam Webster Names 'They' as Its Word of the Year for 2019," *Time*, December 10, 2019 (time.com/5746516/merriam-webster-word-of-the-year-2019/).

3 Mesch describes the ways Rachilde and Marc de Montifaud create gender non-conformity in the absence of gender-neutral pronouns, in "The Nonbinary Nineteenth Century," *Los Angeles Review of Books*, December 23, 2019 (blog .lareviewofbooks.org/essays/nonbinary-19th-century/).

4 See Chapter 1 of this book for a description of Valmont in Dr. Bouillaud's 1833 case, in which he wonders "Since he had a womb, had Valmont menstruated? (forgive me this sort of hermaphrodism of language)" (476).

5 The term is used by Théophile Gautier's character d'Albert in his famous novel *Mademoiselle de Maupin*, in reference to multiple layers of meaning created when characters act in Shakespeare's *As You Like It* (1: 431).

6 In *Reading for the Plot*, Brooks writes:

> Narrative as a dominant mode of representation and explanation comes to the fore [...] with the advent of Romanticism and its predominantly historical imagination: the making and the interpretation of narrative plots assumes a centrality and importance in literature, and in life, that they did not have earlier, no doubt because of a large movement of human societies out from under the mantle of sacred myth into the modern world where men and institutions are more and more defined by their shape in time. (xiii)

7 In *La Comédie humaine*, Balzac famously planned a "vast tableau of society" containing between two and three thousand characters ("Avant-propos," 1: 19).

While Balzac's "study of manners" (étude de mœurs) focuses on the Restoration and the July Monarchy (1815–48), Zola's twenty novels comprising *Les Rougon-Macquart* trace the influence of heredity and environment during the Second Empire (1852–70).

8 See Hage, *La quête de l'androgyne*, and Smith, *Romantic Androgyny*. On androgyny in Maupassant, see Hartig, *Struggling under the Destructive Glance*. For readings of androgyny in *Mademoiselle de Maupin*, see Sadoff, *Ambivalence, Ambiguity and Androgyny*, and Barsoum, *Théophile Gautier's Mademoiselle de Maupin*.

9 Barthes defines the hermeneutic code as an enigma which only further reading can resolve: "Let us call the hermeneutic code all of the elements that have the function of articulating, in multiple ways, a question, its answer, and the various accidents that can either prepare the question or delay its answer: or rather, to formulate an enigma and bring about its decipherment" (*S/Z*, 24–25). For Lambert, Barthes's text reifies nineteenth-century sexual stereotypes which the novel itself undermines in a "reconciling androgynous vision" ("S/Z", 170).

10 Albouy sees Gautier's use of androgyny as a rehearsal of idealized myth stretching back to Plato ("Le mythe," 603). For studies of androgyny in English Romanticism, see Long Hoeveler, *Romantic Androgyny*, and Stevenson, *Romanticism and the Androgynous Sublime*.

11 See Delcourt, *Hermaphrodite, mythes*, and "Deux interpretations." Eliade relies on the Jungian archetype to explain hermaphrodism in literature, in *Méphistophélès et l'androgyne*.

12 Busst, "The Image," 4. Further references in the text.

13 In *L'androgyne romantique*, Monneyron traces the transformation from myth to "literary myth" in an attempt to locate the specificity of the nineteenth-century moment.

14 Eliade writes: "Among the decadent writers, the androgyne is understood only as a hermaphrodite in which the two sexes coexist anatomically and physiologically" (*Méphistophélès et l'androgyne*, 123).

15 See Busst, "The Image," 77–85. Frappier-Mazur discusses how Balzac's use of androgyny fits into both Busst's decadent and romantic categories ("Balzac et l'androgyne," 254–61).

16 As Manion explains, "to say someone 'transed' or was 'transing' gender signifies a process or practice without claiming to understand what it meant to that person or asserting any kind of fixed identity on them" (*Female Husbands*, 11).

17 For a history of the theory of "maternal impressions" see Huet, *Monstrous Imagination*.

18 This had already been alleged in the eighteenth century. Brisson quotes treatises claiming that between "the 30th degree of north latitude and the equator, the clitoris and the labia would be 'more pronounced' ['plus épanchés'] than elsewhere" (*Le sexe incertain*, 30). Numerous case studies mention this phenomenon. See, for example, Banon (1852, 69). Masturbation was also posited as an explanation for hypertrophied clitorises.

19 See Rubino, *Androgny and Modernity*, 4.

20 When the doctor's daughter Nathalia (a sometime-sisterly figure and occasional source of sexual tension) mentions the word "fortu*ite*" (fortunate), Clémentine nearly faints: "What awful light Nathalia had just shone upon my painful memories. [. . .] This dear friend did not know that a single syllable had made all my wounds bleed deeply" (Cuisin, *Clémentine*, 1: 73).

21 This definition does not correspond to any version of the Académie française's dictionaries, but it is a near perfect copy of the entry for "hermaphrodisme" in the *Nouveau dictionnaire de médecine, chirurgie, pharmacie, physique, chimie, histoire naturelle, etc.* written by Béclard (who had examined Lefort in 1815) and his colleagues at the Faculté de médecine, but which postdates Cuisin's novel (1821–22, 33). Here, the entry for "hermaphrodite" adds "hermaphrodites are monsters" and are "incapable of reproduction" (33). The Académie's dictionary has been digitized by the University of Chicago; none of the editions contemporary to Cuisin allowed for the possibility of hermaphrodism (artfl-project.uchicago.edu/node/17). The 1694 edition defines a hermaphrodite as "one who has both sexes," adding: "It is said that hermaphrodites are common in certain countries" (1: 561). By the fourth edition (1762), hermaphrodism was deemed impossible: "someone whom one claims [qu'on prétend] has both sexes. Modern physicians claim [prétendent] that there are no perfect Hermaphrodites" (1: 873). The fifth edition (1798) repeats the same definition. The sixth edition (1836) returns to the possibility afforded in the first, only to squelch it with a seemingly contradictory definition: "Is said of a person who has both sexes. *There are no perfect hermaphrodites*" (1: 887). It is not until the seventh edition (1878) that the caveat about perfect hermaphrodism is suppressed entirely, and Geoffroy Saint-Hilaire's broad definition reappears: "It is said of a person who unites certain characteristics of both sexes" (1: 878). The eighth edition (1932–35) repeats the 1878 definition: "being who unites certain characteristics of both sexes." So, while hermaphrodism was temporarily "impossible" according to the Académie when Cuisin was published, it became possible again from 1878 through to World War II.

22 See the case of Dorothée Derier/Charles Durgé, an individual who traveled throughout Europe just before *Clémentine* was published. In 1836, Dr. Mayer describes the case in the *Gazette médicale de Paris*:

> Derier made rounds in all the various universities of Germany, and traveled to France, England, and Holland between 1816 and 1817. He was employed in several anatomy museums. A large number of doctors and scientists had the opportunity to examine him: most of them, and namely Kopp, Kansch, Mursina, Rosenmüller, Osiander, Lawrence, Green, and the Faculté de médecine of Paris, declared themselves for the male sex. Hufeland, [. . .] Gall, and Brooks, spoke in favor of the female sex. Others, among them Drs. Schneider and Lauth, Schmidtmüller and Ritgen, opined that Derier belonged to no sex; different parts of the body were considered as belonging sometimes to the masculine, sometimes to the feminine type. (1836, 609)

The medical record is replete with similar stories. See, also Adeline Lefort described by Jacquemin (1815, 373). Bally presents a patient to the Académie royale de médicine whom M. Martin-Solon claims was also examined at the hospital in Beaujon (1833, 342). The patient's surgical scars cause debate about how he was alerted to his sex variation (ibid., 342). Beck's *Elements of Medical Jurisprudence* (1838) mentions a case quoted by Everard Home, in which a French woman "was shown as a curiosity; and in the course of a few weeks, made 400 pounds" (128).

23 Instead, Cuisin contrives an evil Jewish doctor to embody the worst side of contemporary medicine. He extends the 100,000-franc contract to Clémentine, who, in tears, later shreds the document. Cuisin's anti-Semitism anticipates a theme that Donaldson-Evans situates at the fin de siècle (*Medical Examinations*, 186–94).

24 In *Medical Examinations*, Donaldson-Evan rereads classic works by Flaubert, the Goncourt brothers, Zola, Huysmans, Maupassant, and Alphonse and Léon Daudet, all as efforts (to varying degrees) to "discredit the medical practitioner" (175).

25 Historians have posited numerous explanations, ranging from the refusal of scientists to translate their jargon to the layperson, to the widely publicized scientific debates which did little to instill public confidence. See, Zeldin, *France, 1848–1945: Intellect, Taste and Anxiety.*

26 The historical record, conversely, brims with evidence of unhappily hirsute patients having tried any number of unsuccessful treatments. See, for example, Hills (1873) or Audain (1893).

27 Saint-Elme is also the name of one of the Marquis de Sade's characters from *Juliette* (1801), a novel in which Durand and Volmar are "hermaphroditic." See Brisson, *Le sexe incertain*, 95–96.

28 Counter argues that Cuisin's novel fits into the plot of "a marriage thwarted by impediment," common before 1830 (*The Amorous Restoration*, 38).

29 On *La fille* and androgyny, see Frappier-Mazur, "Balzac et l'androgyne," 256–57, and Delattre, "De *Séraphîta* à *La fille.*"

30 The seventeenth-century swashbuckling opera singer and bisexual, Julie d'Aubigny (1670/1673–1707), known as "La Maupin," was a historical precedent. Gautier borrowed some characteristics from her life, as may well have Cuisin.

31 Clémentine's future husband attempts to alert his love interest to an impending incestuous marriage with Saint-Elme by leaving optical illusions in her hotel room. One scene depicts Phaedra professing love to her stepson (Cuisin, *Clémentine*, 2: 96).

32 Information about Cuisin's life is sparce. The BnF lists his lifespan dubiously as (1777–1845?), describing him as a "polygraphe" (a non-specialized writer of many subjects) and, among other things, as the "Curator of the Dupont Anatomy Collection." It further notes Cuisin's multiple pseudonyms (catalogue.bnf.fr/ark:/12148/cb14584855p). An 1883 review argues that Cuisin's writing "testifies to the prodigious activity, in the absence of talent,

of this author" ("*Clémentine*," 793). Counter notes that although Cuisin was a marginal figure, his books often enjoyed multiple reprints, as did *Clémentine* (*The Amorous Restoration*, 113). Counter is the first critic to treat Cuisin extensively (see ibid., esp. chapter 3, 111–143).

33 See Hale, "Cuisin," 299–301. Hale admits that *Clémentine* is not an erotic novel, but somewhat misleadingly identifies Cuisin as an "essayist and short story writer," although he was also a prolific novelist, and *Clémentine* extends to two volumes (299).

34 "*Clémentine*" (1883), 793.

35 Pigoreau, *Petite bibliographie*, 174. Further references in the text.

36 "*Clémentine*" (1883), 794.

37 Drujon's catalog of censored works between 1814 and 1877 records that Cuisin's novel, *Bonaparte ou l'homme du destin* (1821) was deemed "seditious" and earned the publisher one month of prison (*Catalogue des ouvrages, écrits, et dessins*, 58). *Clémentine* was also "seditious" and was "placed on the index, by order of the police" in 1825. Multiple other works were deemed "immoral" (162). All told, six of Cuisin's works were indexed as seditious in 1825 (287–88). Counter suggests that *Clémentine* was seized by police likely for suggesting lesbianism or bisexuality, since there is nothing "even remotely like a sex scene" in it (*The Amorous Restoration*, 130).

38 Jasinski cites *Le Figaro* (April 12, 1833), and *Le cabinet de lecture* (July 22, 1835) (*Les années romantiques*, 286–88).

39 In 1861, Louis Jourdan published a pirated and sensationalized version of the Chevalier d'Éon's story under the title *Un hermaphrodite*, refueling interest. Another version by a different author was published in 1865. See Kates, *Monsieur d'Eon Is a Woman*.

40 See Bullough, *Sex, Society, and History*, 152.

41 See Fargeaud, notes to the Pléiade edition of Balzac, *La Comédie humaine*, 2: 1479, n. 1. Sand also wrote her own version of the androgyne novel tested out by Latouche, Gautier, and Balzac. Like its predecessors, Sand's play *Gabriel* (1839) relies on the mystery of sex to perpetuate plot. See Prasad, "Deceiving Disclosures."

42 See Ségu, *Un romantique républicain*, 376–436.

43 Balzac's thoughts on *Fragoletta* vacillate between praise and criticism. In addition to citing *Fragoletta* as the inspiration for *Séraphîta*, Balzac alludes to it in *La peau de chagrin* and *La fille aux yeux d'or*. See Crouzet, "Monstres," 25. Nevertheless, he also wrote disparagingly of Latouche and the novel.

44 Many have incorrectly alleged that *Fragoletta* was the first novel to "describe an overtly androgynous character; that is, a character whose sex remains indeterminate" (Smith, "Androgyny," 81). See Crouzet, "Monstres," 25; Pelckmans, "Androgyne," 13; and Monneyron, *L'androgyne romantique*, 56.

45 Robb, *Balzac*, 151.

46 For more on Balzac and Latouche's ambiguous relationship, see ibid., 150–56. In 1829, Balzac reviewed Latouche's *Fragoletta* in *Le Mercure de France au XIXe siècle*. See Balzac, *La Comédie humaine*, 11: 1605.

47 According to Monneyron, who quotes Balzac's conclusion: "As *The Hermaphrodite, Fragoletta* will remain a monument" (*L'androgyne romantique*, 84).

48 Quoted in Robb, *Balzac*, 153.

49 Ségu details the contemporary criticism of *Fragoletta* in 1829. See Ségu, *Un romantique républicain*, 340–42.

50 Crouzet compiles an exhaustive list of authors mentioning *Fragoletta* in "Monstres," 25–26.

51 Ségu, *Un romantique républicain*, 342.

52 Crouzet warns against considering Latouche a little-known genius and *Fragoletta* a forgotten "masterpiece" ("Monstres," 27). Although generally the most laudatory study, Ségu's *Un romantique républicain* laments Latouche's "lack of taste," wishing that Latouche had never written about lesbianism: "Repulsive scenes between Caroline and Lady Hamilton take place or are suggested. I wish that these pages were not written" (342).

53 Balzac's remark appeared in an article published in June 1829 in the *Mercure du XIXe siècle*, cited in its entirety by Ségu (*Un romantique républicain*, 75–79). Smith, "Androgyny," discusses Sainte-Beuve's remark.

54 Planche, "De la haine littéraire," 522.

55 Latouche, *Fragoletta*, 1: vi. Further references in the text.

56 There is room for an entire book on the far-ranging influence of this sculpture. "Earl Lind," the author of an American twin to the French *Roman d'un inverti-né*, entitled *Autobiography of an Androgyne*, includes a photograph of himself posed nude as "a Modern Living Replica of the Ancient Greek Statue of 'Hermaphroditus'," alongside a photo of the Greek statue housed in Florence, for comparison (1918, 5–6). See also the sequel, *The Female-Impersonators*, published by "Ralph Werther" (1922). Both Lind and Werther are pseudonyms for the still-unknown author, who also went by the name "Jenny June."

57 We can identify the sculpture Latouche describes with certainty as the "Louvre hermaphrodite," since he references the cushion Bernini fashioned for it in 1619 (*Fragoletta*, 1: 87). Without providing further detail, Sainte-Beuve reports merely that "a friend" had given Latouche the idea of writing a psychological novel about a hermaphrodite (quoted by Ségu in *Un romantique républicain*, 329).

58 According to Giraud, Gautier "haunted the Greek collection in the Louvre" in order to contemplate the statue ("Winckelmann's Part," 173). His 1852 poem "Contralto" is the most famous of all the Parnassian poems evoking the beauty of form in sculpture. Gautier also alludes to Balzac's *Séraphîta* in the poem "Symphonie en blanc majeur." See Mickel, "An Interpretation," 343.

59 Claims Anatole France: "Did you not know that Louvre Hermaphrodite's marble has been worn down by visitors' caresses, and that the administration of museums had to protect this monstrous and charming figure with a barrier?" (*Balzac, prince du mal*, quoted in Graille, *Les hermaphrodites*, 9).

60 It could also be said that Gautier's *Mademoiselle de Maupin* approaches Nathalia's plotline on a more modest level, when Madeleine beds both

Théodore and, apparently, Rosette, while the sexual cruelty of Latouche's Philippe Adriani in *Fragoletta* echoes it more sinisterly.

61 In another nineteenth-century reaction to the sculpture, Cornay recounts that he once saw a scandalized woman approach the sculpture to spit before it on the Louvre's marble floor (*Cosmogonie*, 53).

62 Monneyron offers a different interpretation: "Camille's embarrassment in front of the marble hermaphrodite is that of a being who sees her own anomaly idealized" (*L'androgyne romantique*, 57). I believe that Camille's discomfort derives from d'Hauteville's derision of a body like hers, rather than her shame that this body could be presented as beautiful.

63 Monneyron determines that Latouche must have read Jaucourt's encyclopedia entry recounting the brutal historical treatment of hermaphrodites (*L'androgyne romantique*, 53). Jaucourt also references hermaphrodites' sterility, which might explain some of Fragoletta's enigmatic utterances: "Myself, I am ashamed to offer the impossible love that I am asking for; for shame! The inanity, the sterile dangers, this is the dowry that I bring and the fate that I offer: defend yourself against me!" (Latouche, *Fragoletta*, 2: 182).

64 Until this transitional moment, I have intentionally referred to Camille using the feminine pronoun "she" because a feminine identity was not yet called into question. After the museum scene, however, Camille will assume a male identity and s/he self-identifies as an individual who is neither exclusively female nor exclusively male. For this reason, I signal Camille/Fragoletta/Philippe's unstable sexual identity through the use of combined masculine and feminine pronouns.

65 Which is precisely how Crouzet reads this scene ("Monstres," 28).

66 The word "monster" comes from the Latin *monstrare* (meaning "to show," but also "to accuse or condemn"). Benveniste argues that *monstrum* and *monstrare* are related to *moneo*, "to warn" (*Le vocabulaire*, 256–57).

67 Barthes, *S/Z*, 24–25. Crouzet also discusses Barthes in reference to the impossibility of interpreting *Fragoletta* ("Monstres," 34). For Crouzet, this impossibility is rooted to androgyny itself, which, he believes, does not exist in the world (ibid.). I agree with Crouzet that Fragoletta's nudity cannot be unveiled, but I believe the sculpture scene illustrates precisely the moment of encounter between a timeless myth of androgyny (embodied by the ancient sculpture) and an intersex character who also feels exiled from his/her own historical moment because contemporary science alleged that his/her anatomy alienated him/her from love.

68 That sexual truth was legible on a naked (woman's) body is a common fantasy of nineteenth-century fiction. In *La fille aux yeux d'or*, Balzac hints that the Marquise slays her lover after finding proof of her infidelity in this way.

69 In what testifies to the ambiguity of Latouche's writing, Pelckmans cites this same quotation in support of his interpretation that no rape in fact took place, taking Philippe at his word ("Androgyne," 25). However, it is my contention that the overall structure of the scene and its vilification of Philippe invite us to doubt him.

70 Monneyron seems to be the only scholar willing to admit that something happened between Eugénie and Adriani, although he euphemistically glosses over the full shock of the scene. Philippe Adriani, he writes, "seduces d'Hauteville's sister, Eugénie, and after having declared their union impossible, dishonors her" (*L'androgyne romantique*, 57). For Monneyron, intersex is not the focus of the novel (ibid., 58).

71 Ségu, *Un romantique républicain*, 331.

72 Pelckmans, "Androgyne," 25.

73 "Du roman historique de *Fragoletta*," quoted by Monneyron in *L'androgyne romantique*, 85. The journalist's differing interpretation may be related to legal definitions of marriage. The *Gazette* author insinuates that the girl's husband was impotent or could not perform sexual intercourse because of some kind of bodily variation (by referring to her as a virginal "demoiselle"). However, as illustrated previously, impotence was rarely grounds for divorce. *Fragoletta* suggests the converse, possibly because the Napoleonic Code was not yet in effect when the action of the novel takes place. Camille claims s/he cannot fulfill the role of wife to d'Hauteville after reading medical treatises, although the rape scene shows that s/he can inflict sexual violence.

74 For the importance of the active/passive distinction in the nineteenth century, see Nye, *Masculinity*, and Rosario, *The Erotic Imagination*. On impotence, see Waller, *The Male Malady*.

75 For Bornet, Balzac applies Emanuel Swedenborg's teachings religiously. See Bornet, "La structure," 250.

76 In the letter, dated November 20, 1833, Balzac describes seeing "the most beautiful masterpiece that exists" in the sculptor Théophile Bra's studio, and records, "There, I conceived of *Séraphîta*" (Balzac, *Lettres à l'étrangère*, 88).

77 Monneyron contrasts *Séraphîta* to *Fragoletta* in the following terms: "Balzac wants to substitute an androgyne detached from historical contingencies, an androgyne free from Matter and from all corporality, for an androgyne who is a prisoner of Matter and of his physiological anomaly" (*L'androgyne romantique*, 85). Like Monneyron, Henri Gauthier describes the novel as a "superb myth" in his preface to the Pléiade edition of *Séraphîta*, emphasizing the idealized, otherworldly nature of the protagonist as "a mythical figure" at the expense of her/his bodily reality (in Balzac, *La Comédie humaine*, 11: 698, 725).

78 See Gauthier, preface, in Balzac, *La Comédie humaine*, 11: 700.

79 In the preface to the Pléiade edition, Gauthier cites Balzac's claim that *Séraphîta* perfectly reflected Swedenborg's teachings, while showing that Balzac perpetuates misconceptions from Daillant de La Touche's reading, among others (ibid., 11: 702–4). Further references in the text.

80 Gauthier argues that Balzac's strategy of revising his novel in order to suppress material references to sex conforms to this traditional, biblical representation of androgyny (ibid., 11: 721).

81 Balzac, *Séraphîta*, in *La Comédie humaine*, 11: 736. Further references in the text.

82 Gauthier makes this point in the Pléiade edition, observing that the hybrid flower is a sign of the androgyny of the central protagonist (II: 1635–36, n. 1 and n. 2).

83 Butler, *Gender Trouble*, 128. Further references in the text.

84 As previously noted, the novel is titled *Séraphîta*, but the first chapter describes Séraphitüs, whereas the second is titled "Séraphîta," and the third suggests nonbinary synthesis with the title "Séraphîta-Séraphitüs."

85 See, for example, Marc's dictionary entry for "Hermaphrodisme" (1837, 263), and Orfila (1823, 161).

86 Gautier, *Mademoiselle de Maupin*, ed. Laubriet, 1: 486.

87 Murat suggests that Maupin's outside status reveals the fragility of binary sex, serving as an avatar of Butler's theory (*La loi*, 86–87). Wing had earlier shown the "performative" nature of gender in *Mademoiselle de Maupin*, using both Butler's terminology and Derrida's writings on Austin (*Between Genders*, 32).

88 See Delcourt, *Hermaphrodite*; Eliade, *Méphistophélès*; and Busst, "The Image." Critics of *Mademoiselle de Maupin* have been more attentive to historical and cultural context. See Albouy, "Le mythe"; Monneyron, *L'androgyne romantique*; and Weil, *Androgyny*, and "Romantic Androgyny."

89 Following a recent shift in historical trans studies, I use the gender-neutral pronouns they/them for Maupin, not because I think Maupin would have identified in that way had those pronouns existed in nineteenth-century France (Maupin is a fictional character), but because, as Manion writes, "'They' is a powerful, gender neutral way to refer to someone whose gender is unknown, irrelevant, or beyond classification" (*Female Husbands*, 14). Maupin is different from the other characters and historical figures examined in this book in that it is Maupin's unknown gender, not unknown sex, that drives the narrative forward.

90 Weil offers an incisive analysis of the "myth of the androgyne" as it relates to Gautier's notion of aesthetics and romanticism. Weil, *Androgyny*, esp. 113–42.

91 Gautier, *Mademoiselle de Maupin*, ed. Laubriet, 1: 382. Further references in the text.

92 Rothfield investigates the relationship between "realist narrative" and "medical narrative" in *Vital Signs*. Here, I examine narrative as it relates to unknown gender rather than theorizing it in relation to a single genre. See Foucault, *La naissance de la clinique*.

93 Critics are divided about how subversive *Mademoiselle de Maupin* really is. Mielly argues that it is very subversive ("Madeleine séductrice"), while Araque seems to suggest that Gautier is more misogynistic than revolutionary (*Gautier*).

94 For an expert analysis of the science of seeing in nineteenth-century France and its relationship to literature of the time, see Goulet, *Optiques*.

95 Brooks, *Realist Vision*, 17.

96 Foucault, ed., *Herculine*, trans. McDougall, viii. As we saw, many case studies predating Isidore Geoffroy Saint-Hilaire's treatise in the 1830s support this claim, but Geoffroy Saint-Hilaire's work marks a shift in medical consensus.

Several medico-legal experts like Lacassagne (1887), for example, called for a modification of the Civil Code to reflect "doubtful sex."

97 Badré was also examined by Dr. Legros, who describes Badré's adolescence novelistically: "Deprived of an education and unfettered, he soon began to make a game out of his conformation, which became the curiosity of his homeland. Soon boys presented themselves in their turn, offering homages, that is to say drinks, and easily obtained favors from *Joséphine* Badré; it was without pleasure and most often with pain for *her*" (1835, 273).

98 See Legros (1835) and Dany (1835).

99 For expert analysis of the relationship between case histories and fiction in Victorian England, see Kennedy, *Revising the Clinic*.

100 Dany (1835, 461–62).

101 For example, the narrator interrupts the letters at the beginning of chapter 6 (1: 332).

102 Gaston d'Hailly's novel *L'hermaphrodite* (1885) references Gautier repeatedly. Camille speaks "in a full contralto voice," alluding to Gautier's poem, and travels with a loyal companion named Sam, like Théodore's Isnabel (59). Camille also harkens back to Balzac's Séraphîta, who appeared both as male and female perfection to Minna and Wilfrid respectively: "Dolorès had dreamed of Camille; she positively adored this woman, who, for her, achieved the ideal beauty of the archangel Saint Michael" (422).

103 D'Albert constantly laments his "monstrous" love (1: 426). See also 1: 361, 362.

104 Weil, "Romantic Androgyny," 355.

105 On transvestism as it relates to gender decidability, see Garber, *Vested Interests*, esp. 73–77. For Roulin, "Deep down, the androgyne does not exist: Théodore Rosalinde only exists as one in chapter XI; in the following chapters, she is a woman in the most carnal sense of the word" ("Confusion," 40). On the contrary, d'Albert is not sure whether Théodore is a woman at all throughout the novel, and in letters, Maupin often explains how they are *not* like a woman, or how dressing as a man makes them feel like a man. Albouy also claims that "Madeleine de Maupin is neither a hermaphrodite nor an androgyne; she is a woman in drag, and a woman whose femininity is considerably more indicated and highlighted than the ambiguity that should have been her chief characteristic" ("Le mythe," 601). But this overlooks Maupin's self-descriptions as a person outside of binary sex. Murat argues that Maupin's outside status reveals the fragility of the binary: "Mademoiselle de Maupin really embodies – and Gautier insists on it – the perfect type of one who is outside of sex" (*La loi*, 85).

106 Of course, Clémentine does suddenly integrate into society at the end of the novel, despite the initial prognosis that such integration was impossible. Apparently, Clémentine's acquisition of wealth and title enables a happy ending. In Cuisin's world, class trumps gender.

107 Gautier, *Mademoiselle de Maupin*, ed. Crouzet, 54.

Chapter 4

1 This case is described in Georges Dailliez's 1892 medical thesis, published in 1893, 35. Further references in the text. Dr. Guermonprez, whose callous treatment of Louise-Julia-Anna was examined in Chapter 1, was Dailliez's mentor, which likely contributed to his pupil's particularly pejorative view of hermaphrodism.

2 As White writes, Des Esseintes is "the last in a long line of consanguineously degenerating aristocrats" in which the men progressively effeminized, likening him to Dailliez's patient (*The Family in Crisis*, 128).

3 Zola announces his project in the preface to the first novel in his series, *La fortune des Rougon*, in *Les Rougon-Macquart*, dir. Lanoux, 1: 4.

4 In the notes to the Pléiade edition, Henri Mitterand explains that *La curée* appeared partially in serial format in *La Cloche* between September and November 1871, until the newspaper received the scandalous "incest" scene, suspending publication of the entire novel (Zola, *Les Rougon-Macquart*, dir. Lanoux, 1: 1578). This edition contains the novel's original preface (1: 1583). Unless otherwise indicated, references from *La curée* are to this edition.

5 Reid characterizes Zola's "social teratology" as a systematic transgression of familial boundaries. Since Zola's "monsters" will require decipherment, his twin project of art and science allows him to become the "guardian of their cultural intelligibility" (*Families in Jeopardy*, 248).

6 See Becker and Lavielle's transcription and facsimile of Zola's *Dossier préparatoire* for *La curée*, in Zola, *La fabrique*, 1: 542, 544. See the folio edition of *La curée*, prefaced by Jean Borie and annotated by Henry Mitterand, for more complete notes than the Pléiade edition (395).

7 Significantly, Zola repeats the same tropes yet a third time in a letter to Louis Ulbach from November 6, 1871. Here, Zola perseverates on the "man-woman" as a product of "exhausted societies" in his study of "social monstrosities" (quoted by Reid, *Families in Jeopardy*, 240).

8 White asserts that "Maxime's ambiguity offers a metonymy of the demise of family life" (*The Family in Crisis*, 116). Borie suggests in his preface to *La curée* that Maxime is a kind of case study: "It is perfectly clear that Maxime from *La curée* is taken from the mythology of degeneration that is perfectly conformed to the model drawn by Morel" (15). Malinas agrees, identifying Maxime as "the symbol of the race's degeneration" (*Zola*, 146). Reid writes: "No doubt about it, Maxime is the *homme-femme* announced by Zola in the preface" (*Families in Jeopardy*, 164). Hamon rightly insists on the importance of ambiguity and androgyny throughout the *Rougon-Macquart* (*Le personnel*, 195–96). Berta argues that Zola labels Maxime "a neuter being [. . .] in order to insist on the fact that Maxime is on the margins of other groups in the society in which he evolves" (*De l'androgynie*, 74). However, the abundance of androgynous characters enumerated by Berta would tend to suggest that Maxime is more representative than exceptional.

9 In his preface to the folio edition of *La curée*, Borie observes:

> Toward the end of the nineteenth century, at the same time as natalist fanaticism was spreading, medical discourse liked to privilege a new symptom, in the abundant semiotic paraphernalia of degeneration: the attenuation or disappearance of the opposition of sexual characters. Two typical characters bear witness to this phenomenon, the effeminate man and the emancipated woman, heralds of the apocalypse. (19)

Borie cites Féré's *L'instinct sexuel* (1899) as one example of this line of thinking. Laupts's *Perversion et perversité sexuelles* (1896) would be another. *La curée* forms part of a first wave of what becomes, according to Pick, "a flood of works in France whose very titles evoked the sense of political impotence and national catastrophe: *La Fin du monde latin, 1871! Les Premières Phases d'une décadence, Des Causes de la décadence française, La Chute de la France, République ou décadence?, La France dégénérée*" (*Faces of Degeneration*, 97).

10 Zola, preface to *Roman d'un inverti-né*, in Laupts (1896), 3. Further references in the text.

11 Zola's preface is actually a letter he sent to Dr. Laupts in 1895. Dr Laupts published Zola's letter alongside the *Roman d'un inverti-né* in his 1896 treatise, *Tares et poisons* [. . .].

12 For example, Pierre Stéphan's medical thesis from 1901 still relies on Geoffroy Saint-Hilaire's 1837 definition of hermaphrodism as "the coexistence in the same individual of both sexes or of some of their characteristics" (35).

13 That Maxime's sex "hesitated," or was prematurely arrested, evokes "male pseudo-hermaphrodites" in the medical language of the times. ("Female pseudo-hermaphrodites" resulted from excess development, according to this hypothesis.) Geoffroy Saint-Hilaire preferred the terms "apparent hermaphrodism" to "pseudo-hermaphrodism," but his theory of arrested or excess development continued to dominate. See, for example, Charles Debierre's contention that hermaphrodism results from "birth defects of the genital organs that have either arrested these organs at one of their embryonic phases in a man, or have excessively developed certain parts of a woman" (1892, 332). Debierre's earlier treatise also cites multiple examples of "true hermaphrodism" (1891, 105–9).

14 Rosario credits Morel with popularizing degeneration in France (*The Erotic Imagination*, 80). Delamotte, following Borie, argues that Lucas's work had already garnered much popularity among doctors in the 1850s, before Morel's treatise (*La médecine*, 299). Both Borie and Cabanès relate Lucas's notion of naturalized, universal heredity to the bourgeois rejection of the hereditary privilege of class. See Cabanès, *Le corps et la maladie* (389), and Borie, *Mythologies de l'hérédité* (12). Zola records over sixty pages of notes on his "dear Lucas" – to use Malinas's term (*Zola*, 40) – in his *Dossier préparatoire*, suggesting his research was less cursory than some critics have claimed. See *La fabrique*, 1: 84–142.

15 Zola's *Dossier* lists Morel's *Traité des dégénérescences* (1857) as a source used by the author (*La fabrique*, 1: 346).

16 Quoted by Armand Lanoux in the preface to the Pléiade edition of Zola, *Les Rougon-Macquart*, 1: ix. Lanoux notes that Zola read an 1864 translation of

Charles Darwin (1: xvi). Darwin's work was beginning to be registered in French psychiatry by the 1870s, but Lamarckism would continue to influence the eugenics projects of the twentieth century. See Pick, *Faces*, 101.

17 Rosario, *The Erotic Imagination*, 77. Delamotte describes how "heredity becomes the scapegoat of all of the great miseries of body and soul," and her thesis renders explicit Zola's many borrowings from Lucas and Morel (*La médecine*, 322).

18 See Pick, *Faces of Degeneration*; Nye, *Crime, Madness and Politics*, and *Masculinity*.

19 "My work must have a few hereditary illnesses, killing two or three of my characters" (Zola, *La fabrique*, 1: 142). Zola notes especially the degenerative effects of alcoholism, which become crucial to his cycle (ibid., 1: 138).

20 Quoted in Pick, *Faces*, 48, n. 33.

21 Zola, *La fabrique*, 1: 124.

22 Nye, *Masculinity*, 77.

23 Ibid., 77–78.

24 Nye cites 1890, 1892, 1895, 1900, 1907, and 1911 as the years before World War I in which deaths outstripped the birthrate (ibid., 78).

25 In the Pléiade edition, Mitterand notes that for Zola, the words "collégien" (schoolboy) and "vicieux" (perverted) "are basically synonymous" (*Les Rougon-Macquart*, 1: 1597). Schor makes the parallel observation: "in Zola's idiolect, 'pensionnaire' ['schoolgirl'] is another way of saying 'lesbien' ['lesbian']" (*Zola's Crowds*, 94).

26 The February 2, 1870, article is reproduced in Zola, *L'Atelier de Zola*, 220–21.

27 "There is a social wound there, and wounds do not get better unless they are cauterized with a red-hot iron" (ibid., 220). He adds, "and if I did not love liberty so well, I would petition for the closure of all convent schools" (222).

28 Zola notes that Renée is tainted by convent school: "daughter of a former merchant, a forthright man of bourgeois honesty, [Renée] was unfortunately brought up in convent school, among young dolls. To better highlight the luxurious and vicious life she will lead, we must give her a sister, ugly, raised in a bourgeois environment . . . Here then the question of the environment, the question of education adding to the temperament" (*La fabrique*, 1: 456).

29 Zola, *L'atelier de Zola*, 22. Foucault traces attempts to curb the sexuality of schoolchildren to the eighteenth century, when it became "a public problem," but the advent of degenerate heredity raises the stakes (*L'histoire de la sexualité*, 1: 40). If the preoccupation with sexuality and boarding school was not a new phenomenon in the nineteenth century, it gains increasing importance following the natality crisis.

30 "At the end of the chapter, the readers must understand the drama [. . .] Maxime will succumb to incest, through a natural, vicious inclination; [Renée] puts some effort [. . .] into resisting it" (Zola, *La fabrique*, 1: 470).

31 As Berta remarks: "We are entering into the world of Phaedra. Zola does not skimp on the number of details that allow us to identify Maxime as Hippolyte, Louise as Aricie, Celeste as Oenone, and Aristide as Theseus" (*De l'androgynie*,

29). For Berta, such allusions are "clichés" by the time *La curée* was written (ibid.). Perhaps another overlooked reason for Zola's return to the Phaedra myth (or further confirmation of the cultural cachet of Berta's cliché) is its importance as a leitmotif in Cuisin's *Clémentine* (1820). As we saw, Cuisin uses the Phaedra myth as a *mise en abyme* to draw attention to potential incest, but unlike Zola, Cuisin's protagonist heeds the warnings and narrowly avoids marriage with a knight who turns out to be her brother. Even if Zola did not intentionally reference Cuisin's long-forgotten novel, metaliterary and metatheatrical themes established themselves early as a hallmark of literary hermaphrodism.

32 Thompson, *Naturalism*, 110.

33 Reid, *Families in Jeopardy*, 267.

34 Zola uses the epithet "les inséparables" to describe Mme la marquise d'Espanet and Mme Haffner, Renée's fellow "pensionnaires." In Herculine Barbin's memoirs, s/he writes that s/he and his/her first lover were known as "les inséparables," although their publication postdated *La curée*. It is possible that the term "inséparable" was already a coded reference to lesbianism in French culture.

35 White, *The Family in Crisis*, 117.

36 Morel discusses *stigmates de l'hérédité* or *stigmata hereditatis* and their legal implications (1866, 29).

37 Bernheimer, *Decadent Subjects*, 140.

38 Rosario, *The Erotic Imagination*, 85.

39 Nye, *Masculinity*, 109.

40 Nye, "The History of Sexuality," 399. Dreger shows that despite "this image of the anatomically 'normal' invert [. . .] many sexologists inside and outside of France still retained nagging suspicions that the bodies of at least some inverts leaned toward the hermaphroditic" (*Hermaphrodites*, 134). Dreger cites Havelock Ellis and Richard von Krafft-Ebing as examples (ibid.).

41 Both Chevalier and Laupts (Georges Saint-Paul) studied under Alexandre Lacassagne, the prominent professor of forensic medicine at Lyon's Faculté de médecine (and, as we saw in Chapter 2, a staunch supporter of Debierre's call to revise the Civil Code). Kiernan also makes Chevalier's point:

> the original bi-sexuality of the ancestors of the race, shown in the rudimentary female organs of the male, could not fail to occasion functional, if not organic, reversions, when mental or physical manifestations were interfered with by disease or congenital defect. It seems certain that a femininely functioning brain can occupy a male body and vice versa. Males may be born with female external genitals and vice versa. The lowest animals are bisexual, and the various types of hermaphroditism are more or less complete reversions to the ancestral type. (Quoted in Laupts 1896, 213)

42 The quote appears in Charcot and Magnan's 1882 article on inversion (54). Nye observes that Charcot and Magnan introduced the term "inversion of the genital sense" in this article (*Masculinity*, 111). Dreger discusses this case and Pozzi's work with Magnan without relating it to the larger context of

hereditary degeneration in France or mentioning that Pozzi labels the patient a "degenerate" (*Hermaphrodites*, 128–30).

43 Nye, *Masculinity*, 64.

44 See Geoffroy Saint-Hilaire (1832–37, 1: 183, n. 1). Further references in the text.

45 Nye, *Masculinity*, 65.

46 Geoffroy Saint-Hilaire, quoted and translated by Nye (ibid., 65).

47 In the Table of Contents for his *Histoire générale*, Geoffroy Saint-Hilaire writes that "some of them [hermaphrodites] truly form a third sex" (1832–37, 4: ix).

48 Foucault famously announced the advent of "the homosexual" in 1870, with Carl Westphal's *conträre Sexualempfindung*. Sedgwick (*Epistemology*) has criticized Foucault's narrative, showing that early sexual categories reappear in later ones in a non-linear fashion. Halperin has argued that the distinction between sexual acts and sexual identities was "falsely attributed to Foucault," and unjustifiably mitigates social constructionism (*How to Do the History*, 8–9). Of course, the medical "construction of homosexuality" occurred in the absence of the term itself, which although introduced in 1869, did not become widely used in French (as homosexualité) until the late 1890s. See Courouve, *Vocabulaire*, 129–33; Nye, *Masculinity*, 108.

49 For more on Pozzi, see Chapter 2 of this book and Dreger, *Hermaphrodites*, 63–64. For Dowbiggin, Valentin Magnan marked the heyday of hereditarianism in French psychiatry, and he identifies him as "the most illustrious representative of French psychiatry at the end of the nineteenth century" (*Inheriting Madness*, 121). Magnan started at Sainte-Anne in 1867, where he promoted the theory of degenerate neuropathology throughout his career, creating the diagnosis of "inversion of the genital sense" with Jean Martin Charcot of the Salpêtrière. Rosario describes Magnan and Charcot as "two of the most prominent neurologists of the Third Republic" (*Erotic*, 70). For more on both doctors, see ibid., 85.

50 See Dreger, *Hermaphrodites*, 128–31. Courouve attributes the condensation of "inversion of the sexual instinct" to "sexual inversion" to Julien Chevalier (*Vocabulaire*, 143). In his three classes of inversion, Chevalier called congenital inverts "moral hermaphrodites" (quoted by Courouve, *Vocabulaire*).

51 Pozzi's joint endeavor with Magnan is not the only time that he publishes about the intersex patient known only as "M. X." Pozzi provides follow up (1911, 276).

52 Dr. Guinard mentions having seen the same patient, later the subject of an article by Jourdanet, twice at meetings of the Society of Anthropology (1898, 180). The anonymity of patients often obfuscates which ones were examined by multiple doctors. Nevertheless, it is likely that Marie/Marius, whom Magnan identified as a "pseudo-hermaphrodite" in his 1887 presentation on the psychological effects of abnormal genital morphology, is the same person on whom Benoist published in 1886, after helping Marie change his civil status to male, becoming Marius. I base this claim on the identical birthplace cited in both cases, and descriptions of a later trip to Martinique. Additionally, Magnan describes Marie's legal sex

revision taking place in 1886 in Saint-Nazaire, which fits with the details of Benoist's case. Magnan's portrait of Marie also bears an uncanny resemblance to an engraving published by Émile Laurent, although Laurent provides no explanation for the origin of the engraving or the patient's biographical information (1894, planche II, 171). Marie's case includes incredible "exotic" adventures, which may have inspired Armand Dubarry's *L'hermaphrodite*.

53 For Magnan, "the study of hereditary degeneracies is, for the last several years, on contemporary to-do lists" (1887, 88). Degenerates present with the stigmata of degeneracy, as Morel had claimed: "just as many disorders that one can look upon as true psychic stigmata of hereditary degenerations, as well as the birth defects which are its physical stigmata" (1857, 89).

54 Magnan defines inversion as near psychological hermaphrodism:

> The subjects with inversion of the genital sense, that is to say, subjects who, with all the attributes, the external conformation of one sex, offer feelings, aptitudes, appetites, and instincts of another sex; a man's brain, for example, in the service of a woman's body and vice versa, which creates this strange anomaly of the man who is exclusively in love with man and indifferent to the woman, and vice versa the woman exclusively demonstrating a penchant for the woman. (1887, 90)

55 Pozzi (1911, 233).

56 Pick describes Magnan's influence:

> Valentin Magnan, the psychiatrist of Zola's *L'Assommoir*, enjoyed a highly successful Parisian career [...]. Magnan's vision of *dégénérescence* had a powerful impact, speaking to the hopes and fears of Parisian culture in the wake of France's military defeat and social turmoil. His teaching at the St.-Anne Hospital was acclaimed and his interventions at the Medico-Psychological Society given great attention. Up until his death in 1916, he was still admired by students and devotees. (*Faces*, 99)

57 Ibid., 100.

58 Rosario points out Laupts's "knack for breaking the action at moments of sexual climax" between installments (*The Erotic Imagination*, 95). Laupts reiterates his detailed instructions for "all observers" in his 1896 treatise (40).

59 For typical early case studies of hermaphrodism, see Mayer (1836), Volpelière (1827), Vrolik (1836), and Trouvenin (1830), or Saunié's even more laconic 1810 case. Occasionally, early case studies do include details about the sexual orientation or psychology of their patients, but the vast majority of those cases do not link psychology and genitals until after the advent of degeneration theory. Itard de Riez's case, for example, mentions the patient's depression and lack of sexual drive, but does not relate these facts to genital configuration (1798–99, 295). Similarly, Renauldin's 1797 case study, "Observations sur deux," mentions the intersex patient's "lively and playful spirit" (1797*b*, 475). One exception is Marc, whose 1811 article does relate intelligence to healthy genital development (183). Marc's claim won't become widespread until after the advent of degeneration theory.

60 Dreger evokes degeneration only briefly, when comparing "inversion" in the French and German models, without explaining that the theory becomes a widespread explanation for hermaphrodism itself in fin-de-siècle France (*Hermaphrodites*, 138).

61 On December 1, 1905, "G. M. . ." arrived at the Saint-Louis Hospital for unrelated treatment (1906, 49–50). At publication, doctors planned to begin "a sperm treatment" (une opothérapie spermatique) with the eventual goal of producing a more masculine appearance in the patient (ibid., 58).

62 Pozzi and Broca examine photographs and X-rays of G. M., agreeing with their findings (1906, 52, 55). Pinard disagreed, thinking the abdomen was that of a woman (ibid., 52).

63 See Guermonprez (1892*a*, 376). Laupts also cautions that celibacy can be a carefully constructed disguise for deviant sexuality (1896, 292).

64 See Pozzi (1911, 319). At other times, multiple instances of hermaphrodism in the same family are simply observed, without being commented upon. See, for example, Mabaret du Basty (1890).

65 As degeneration theory swept through Europe, the addition of family histories became a feature of countless articles. In Neugebauer's compendium of "Forty-Four Sexing Errors" from 1900, he cites several cases in which a hermaphrodite descended from a family of psychopaths or sexual deviants – even though his document only includes a brief description of each case study. When summarizing one British case, Neugebauer adds: "Interesting fact: the 28-year-old sister of this person did not menstruate or have a trace of a womb. The father of these two girls was a psychopath" (1900*a*, 467). See also Perrée's 1906 case, in which he notes a causal relationship between the patient's hermaphrodism and degenerate heredity (187); or Paul Petit's 1891 case, in which the mother is a "neuropath" (130).

66 Faucher and Bourdin admit ignorance of the patient's family history (1899, 293).

67 Dr. Émile Laurent (1861–1904) was the author of *Les bisexués, gynécomastes et hermaphrodites* (1894), which reads at times more like pornographic fiction than medical science. In addition to works on inversion, sadomasochism, degeneracy, and criminal anthropology, he also wrote a treatise entitled *La poésie décadente devant la science psychiatrique*, which might explain his lyric penchant. In spite of his wide-ranging publications on human sexuality, the BnF identifies Laurent as a Belgian botanist who died at sea while returning from a colonial mission to the Congo. That Laurent's treatise was cited by so many doctors as a serious medical tome indicates the complex interplay between low- and high-brow medical publications.

68 Tuffier and Lapointe cannot find an antecedent in their patient's family history, but they nevertheless conclude that the "disease" is related to heredity: "what makes up the abnormal impulse that leads to hermaphrodism? We do not know and must confine ourselves to the obvious influence of heredity" (1911, 222). This is also true of Faucher and Bourdin's case described above.

69 Mak, "Doubting Sex," 337.

70 It is possible that Mak arrives at this conclusion since she includes cases of hermaphrodism outside of France. Dreger has also shown that the British were comparatively less interested in sexual inversion than in France, and often confined their case studies to address anatomy rather than psychology (*Hermaphrodites*, 130). Another explanation for Mak's differing view is that she predominantly analyzes case studies, whereas Dreger has already convincingly illustrated that, in practice, doctors occasionally make medical decisions that defy the one-body-one-sex rule, and often show compassion or at least moral deference to their patients' sexual plights.

71 Earlier doctors appear much more likely to believe patients. See Dany (1835) and Legros (1835).

72 In Champeaux's 1765 case, he alleges that hermaphrodites deceive "[in] order to be seen as marvelous creatures" (11).

73 This phrase is often repeated verbatim in case studies. See Marc's dictionary entry for "Hermaphrodisme" (1837, 263), and Orfila (1823, 161).

74 In his "nouvelle série," Neugebauer cites a similar case from 1899 in which the patient "displays himself publicly as a hermaphrodite, dressed as a man. Moreover, it is easy to understand that a person showing himself as an object of curiosity to the public, for money, must easily add some lies to the truth to increase the interest in his case" (1900*b*, 140). Neugebauer deemed the patient's claim to have given birth to be apocryphal.

75 G. M. states: "It is mostly because of salary that I want to change my civil status. Since a man earns more than a woman, I would be able to better provide for my needs and I would have much less if I remain a woman" (De Beurmann and Roubinovitch, 1906, 56). But his doctors remain unconvinced: "In reality, the sexual instinct that attracts her to women is likely the cause of this androgyne's claims" (ibid., 54). Further references in the text.

76 In fact, the idea had been around for quite some time, but makes a marked resurgence in the context of degeneration theory. Robb's biography of Balzac quotes the author stating: "Nothing is insignificant – the mother's diet, the father's virility, and, most important of all, the 'posture' of the parents at the moment of conception" (*Balzac*, 3). Zola's "scientific" authority on the subject is Lucas. Taking notes on Lucas's treatise, Zola often remarks that the location and emotions of two people making love greatly impacts the health of their child (*La fabrique*, 1: 130; 132). In his *Traité de la médecine légale*, Morel also observes that "a strong emotion felt by the mother [. . .] can have a fatal effect on the conditions of fetal life" (1866, 28).

77 Pozzi's 1896 case is cited by Neugebauer (1900*a*, 470). Dr. Holt reports another case in 1861, in which he blames the child's hermaphrodism on the mother's "terrible fright" during pregnancy, confirming the belief in the theory of maternal impressions beyond France (328).

78 After consulting familial antecedents in vain in one case of hermaphrodism, Pozzi suspects that alcohol might be to blame, since his patient was conceived after a wedding (1911, 316).

79 Taking notes on Lucas in his *Dossier*, Zola records "madness of the mother" (*La fabrique*, 1: 112): "The nervous system seems to me to derive most often from the woman. Mental illnesses most often come from mothers" (ibid., 1: 138).

80 Malinas, *Zola*, 81.

81 Cuisin, *Clémentine*, 1: xiii. Further references in the text.

82 Armand Dubarry (1836–1910) was a journalist and author of novels, poetry, and short stories. The full title of the series is *Les déséquilibrés de l'amour: L'hermaphrodite*. Further references in the text.

83 On the *roman de mœurs*, see Cryle, "The Open Secret."

84 On December 15, 1907, Laupts wrote a piece in the *Archives d'anthropologie criminelle* titled "À la mémoire d'Émile Zola." The same year, he published a four-act play under the pseudonym Georges Espé de Metz, titled *Plus fort que le mal, essai sur le mal innomable*. For more on Laupts/Georges Saint-Paul (1870–1937), see Daniel Grojnowski's introduction to Arthur W., *Confessions d'un inverti-né*, 41–45.

85 See Rosenfeld, *Confessions d'un homosexual à Émile Zola*.

86 Malinas writes: "It's worth recognizing that the documentation is extremely weak and the author was very poorly directed" (*Zola*, 33).

87 Borie and Malinas, among others, observe the mythic quality of degeneration theory. Malinas blames nineteenth-century doctors for Zola's scientific shortcomings (*Zola*, 40). Serres agrees, arguing: "in fact, *Les Rougon-Macquart* roughly reflects the contemporary state of knowledge" (*Feux*, 34). The problem, according to Malinas, is that Zola relies on doctors and psychologists rather than experimental scientists. The first description of what would come to be known as "chromosomes" in 1888 takes place in 1873, but Zola's knowledge of these advances as well as the work of Naudin, Mendel, and De Vries was nonexistent (Malinas, *Zola*, 53).

88 Moreau de Tours (1859, 327–28). Borie's preface to the folio edition of *La curée* associates Zola's family tree in *Le Docteur Pascal* with Moreau de Tours's work (14).

89 See Zola's notes on Dr. Moreau de Tours's *Psychologie morbide*: "Mixed state among adults – often affective troubles – doubtful conformations, neither man, nor woman: Henri III, sort of moral hermaphrodites" (*La fabrique*, 2: fol. 135).

90 See Rosario, *The Erotic Imagination*, 77.

91 Dowbiggin explains that from the 1860s to the 1880s, hereditarianism continued to gain popularity within mental medicine (*Inheriting Madness*, 130).

92 Lombroso, quoted by Bernheimer, *Decadent Subjects*, 150.

93 Zola, "La fin de l'orgie," in *Œuvres complètes*, 3: 502–3.

94 Zola writes:

> When the jaded are bored, they invent some monstrosity to distract themselves. The Empire threw at them so many gallant girls, so many adulterous wives, that a true woman has undoubtedly become for them a meager treat; [...] But

a woman who is a man, a dress [. . .] which contains a big bearded fellow, there is something that piques the spirit's curiosity, that is excellent for shaking up satiated boredom and restoring taste to existence. And what will become of women? They will dress as men, by golly! If they are bored, perhaps our golden youth will come back to them, attracted by the lie of their costume. If they are committed to wearing tight pants, low-cut vests and fake straight collars, the pretty men are likely to go back to loving them madly, forgetting that they are only women. (Ibid., 503)

95 From the outset, Étienne and Catherine's relationship is charged with near homoerotic tension: "These boys' clothes [. . .] on this girl's flesh, excited and unsettled him" (Zola, *Germinal*, 94).

96 Thompson, *Naturalism Redressed*, 101.

97 Reid, *Families in Jeopardy*, 252.

98 Harrow notes Sidonie's quality as an in-between character (*Zola, La Curée*, 60–61). For Harrow, Sidonie represents the old-style procuress, now outmoded and replaced by a new generation of more refined matchmakers. The increased visibility of prostitution during the Second Empire owing to wide, well-lit boulevards renders Sidonie's back-alley dealings a kind of "anachronism" (ibid., 63).

99 Harrow writes that Sidonie's basket full of "plots in the making" "establish[es] a humorous parallel between the broker and the implicit author for both dream up scenarios for others to play out and exercise masterly control over every last plot" (*Zola, La Curée*, 61). I read Sidonie as author as a much more disquieting figure – Zola's dark other half, as it were, gleefully plunging her hands into the muck that Zola hoped to keep at arm's length with normalizing discourse.

100 She also might have brought about both events. During Angèle's illness, Sidonie administers herbal infusions to the patient that do nothing to improve her condition: "in spite of her crushing work, [Sidonie] found a means of coming each evening to make herbal tea, which she claimed was the best cure" (*La curée*, 1: 374). She also "confidently predicts" Renée's miscarriage, which, coming from Sidonie, insinuates some type of sinister control over the event (1: 376).

101 Reid, *Families in Jeopardy*, 252.

102 *Roman d'un inverti-né*, 89. *Autobiography of an Androgyne* (1918) by Earl Lind contains the memoirs of an American "androgyne" who describes having a female soul trapped in a male body, just like his French predecessor, and both memoirs were published with an intended medical audience, in America, by *The New York Medico-Legal Journal*. A note on the verso of the title page of the Beinecke's first edition indicates that the memoir was "sold, only by mail order, to physicians, lawyers, legislators, psychologists, and sociologists."

103

Heredity has its laws, like gravity. By solving the double question of temperaments and environments, I will try to find and to follow the thread that leads mathematically from one man to another. And when I hold all the threads, when I have a whole social group in my hands, I will show this group at work as an actor of a historical epoch, will create it acting in the complexity of its efforts, will analyze both the amount of will of each of its members and the general thrust of the whole. (1: 550)

104 Thompson investigates the tension between Zola's "inability to step outside the binary gender divide," and his use of "the transvestite" as a figure used to flag "epistemological, narrative and, ultimately, representational crisis" (*Naturalism Redressed*, 98).

105 Borie titles one part of *Zola et les mythes* "Les fatalités du corps," although he is the first to admit that determinism cannot account for the full richness of Zola's characters, whom he calls "infinitely ambiguous" and "infinitely complex" (56, 48). Shideler calls Zola "the first modern novelist to treat his human characters *as*, not like, animals" (*Questioning the Father*, 29).

106 Thiher uses this metaphor to describe Zola's concept of heredity (*Fiction Rivals Science*, 144).

107 Beizer calls Zola's hybrid use of myth and science "Zola's hermaphroditic authorship," and she investigates his "hermaphroditic textuality" in *Le Docteur Pascal*, which opposes "male and female paradigms" in the persons of Pascal and his niece, Clotilde (*Ventriloquized Bodies*, 70–74).

108 Thiher, *Fiction Rivals Science*, 138.

109 Ibid.

Epilogue

1 The term comes from Le Fort's 1863 dissertation (205). Le Fort had apparently sent Louise D. to Dr. Debout, later entrusting the surgery to Dr. Hugier, since Le Fort had earlier witnessed Hugier successfully perform a similar operation (ibid.).

2 Further references in the text.

3 The operation on December 10, 1859, is described by Le Fort (1863, 205–6).

4 Le Fort includes a print illustrating Louise D.'s genitals (ibid., 174). Louise D.'s case is also described by Neugebauer (1900*a*, 513).

5 Was it really? Intersex advocates cite sometimes debilitating and life-long side effects from the multiple surgeries endured as children.

6 Halberstam points out a similar situation for precursors to trans identities in the nineteenth century: "Until the middle of the last century, countless transgender men and women fell between the cracks of the classification systems designed to explain their plight and found themselves stranded in unnamable realms of embodiment. Today we have an abundance of names for who we are and some people actively desire that space of the unnamable again," because "having a name for oneself can be as damaging as lacking one" (*Trans**, 4). See also Stryker, *Transgender History*.

7 Preves cites the conservative statistic of intersex births (*Intersex and Identity*, 3). Eric Vilain, who cites the surgical statistic, records seeing six to eight patients in the U.C.L.A. intersex clinic each month (quoted by Lehrman, "Going Beyond," 41–42).

8 See Blackless et al., "How Sexually Dimorphic Are We?", and Fausto-Sterling, *Sexing the Body*.

9 Dreger makes this comparison in *Hermaphrodites*. Preves bases her figure on "an exhaustive review of recent medical literature" (*Intersex and Identity*, 2).

10 Dreger cites the first exploratory laparotomies in 1910 in France and England. Because her timeline excludes cases before 1868, Dreger was not aware that the British were not the only ones performing surgeries like the one on Louise D. cited earlier, or performed by Coste (1835). See Dreger, *Hermaphrodites*, 149.

11 Further references in the text.

12 Meyerowitz's *How Sex Changed* shows how endocrinology and surgery were used by doctors for medical gender confirmation starting in the 1920s in Germany and the 1930s in the United States, and then increasingly after World War II. In *Changing Sex*, Hausman discusses surgeries during the same period. Ombrédanne's 1939 treatise includes multiple pediatric surgeries, in spite of the patience he recommended. See also Ombrédanne (1933).

13 My discussion of the modern medical management of intersex is informed by Fausto-Sterling, *Myths of Gender* and *Sexing the Body*; Davis, *Contesting Intersex*; Dreger, *Hermaphrodites* and *Intersex in the Age of Ethics*; Kessler, *Lessons from the Intersexed* and "The Medical Construction of Gender"; Holmes, *Intersex*, and Holmes, ed., *Critical Intersex*; Preves, *Intersex and Identity*; Karkazis, *Fixing Sex*; Reis, *Bodies in Doubt*; and Viloria, *Born Both*.

14 Fausto-Sterling explains that pediatric urologists define an "adequate penis" as one that is about 2 centimeters at birth, whereas a clitoris exceeding 1 centimeter in length is considered "too large." These parameters have changed over time, reflecting their socially (and culturally) constructed nature (*Sexing the Body*, 59–63).

15 Not all females have an XX genetic or chromosomal pattern, and not all males have an XY chromosomal pattern (see Dreger, *Hermaphrodites*, 4). Dreger explains that a host of other factors like hormones, the body's ability to detect them, environmental agents, and surgery all influence sexual development (ibid., 4). Some people have X, XXY, or even different chromosomal patterns in different parts of their bodies (Preves, *Intersex and Identity*, 3). Furthermore, genes affecting sex are located in other places beside the X and Y chromosomes.

16 Additionally, from a surgical standpoint, it is relatively easier to remove testes and/or to build vulvas and vaginas, than it is to construct a "functional" penis (which is not yet surgically possible). By contrast, genetic (XY) males with "adequate" penis size may have their penises surgically altered to look "normal," and remain male. In addition to being large enough, a "functional penis" must become flaccid and erect, and be able to pass both urine and semen through the urethra at the tip of the glans. On the other hand, all

genetic females (infants without a Y chromosome) are declared girls, and their genitalia are altered accordingly. This is done because of the social value placed on a woman's ability to reproduce, which is preserved whenever possible. Approximately the same protocols are applied to intersex infants possessing both ovarian and testicular cells. See Fausto-Sterling, *Sexing the Body*, 60.

17 Psychological problems include the possibility of "dysphoric" or "unwell or unhappy" states. See Dreger, *Hermaphrodites*, and *Intersex in the Age of Ethics*; Kessler, *Lessons from the Intersexed*; and Preves, *Intersex and Identity*.

18 Rosario shows how psychiatrists used degeneration theory as a means of increasing their professional clout (*The Erotic Imagination*, 69–111).

19 As shown in Chapter 1 of this book, Barbin describes the horrors of genital examination in the memoirs. The only surviving images of Barbin are engravings of the genitals. Even in medical narratives, evidence suggests that genital exams and photographs (or engravings, or wax molds) were sometimes traumatic for patients.

20 Yet, in the 2020 update of *Sexing the Body*, Fausto-Sterling reports that pediatric surgeons have "not moved much on the topic," in spite of a marked shift in both national and international outcry against early surgery on intersex children: "three U.S. Surgeons General, the United Nations' World Health Organization, Physicians for Human Rights, the American Academy of Family Physicians, Human Rights Watch, and Amnesty International now oppose medically unnecessary surgery" on intersex children (322).

21 On the DSD nomenclature, see Viloria, *Born Both*; Holmes, *Intersex*; and Davis, *Contesting Intersex*.

22 Davis, *Contesting Intersex*, 2.

23 Pagonis is a nonbinary person who has reclaimed the term "hermaphrodite" for themself. Pagonis underwent multiple genital surgeries before the age of four, and years of hormone treatment, and was told that their ovaries had been removed because they were cancerous. Only as an adult did Pagonis learn by reading their medical file that the organs removed had been internal testes (pid.ge). See Pagonis, "The Son They Never Had."

Works Cited

Primary Works

Accolas. "Cas de pseudo-hermaphrodisme." *Revue médico-chirurgicale des maladies des femmes* 11 (1889): 140–44.

Alibert. *Anatomie descriptive des organes génitaux [. . .]*. Paris: Librairie de la Nouvelle France, 1906.

Audain, Léon. "Hermaphrodisme: double kyste dermoïde des ovaires [. . .]." *Bulletins de la Société anatomique de Paris* 7 (1893): 501–4.

Auvray. "Fibrome utérin chez une femme pseudo-hermaphrodite aux organes génitaux externes masculins [. . .]." *Bulletin de la Société d'obstétrique et gynécologie de Paris* 1 (1912): 321–28.

Azam, Eugène. "Nouvelle variété d'hypospadias simulant un hermaphrodisme." *Union médicale de la Gironde* 2 (1857): 540–45.

Bacaloglu, and Fossard. "Deux cas de pseudo-hermaphroditisme (gynandroïdes)." *La presse médicale* 2.97 (1899): 331–33.

Baldetti, François. *Contribution à l'étude de l'hermaphrodisme*. Diss. Lyon, 1932.

Ballantine, J. W. "Hermaphroditism." In *A System of Gynaecology*. Ed. Thomas Clifford Allbutt. New York: Macmillan Co., 1887: 100–6.

Bally. "Hermaphrodisme." *Bulletin de l'Académie royale de médecine* 1 (1836–37): 341.

Balzac, Honoré de. *La Comédie humaine*. Dir. Pierre-Georges Castex. 12 vols. Paris: Gallimard (Pléiade), 1976–81.

Lettres à l'étrangère, 1833–1842. Paris: Calmann-Lévy, 1899.

Banon, A. P. "Observations on Hermaphroditism." *Dublin Quarterly Journal of Medical Science* 14 (1852): 66–87.

Barbey d'Aurevilly, Jules Amédée. *Œuvres romanesques complètes*. Ed. Jacques Petit. Vol. 1. Paris: Gallimard (Pléiade), 1964.

Barbin, Herculine. *Herculine Barbin dite Alexina B.* Ed. Michel Foucault. Paris: Gallimard, 1978.

Baudelaire, Charles. *Le spleen de Paris; La fanfarlo*. Paris: Flammarion, 1987.

Beck, Theodric Romeyn. *Elements of Medical Jurisprudence*. 6th ed. Vol. 1. Philadelphia: Thomas, Cowperthwait, 1838.

Béclard, Pierre-Auguste. *Éléments d'anatomie générale [. . .]*. 2nd ed. Paris: Béchet Jeune, 1827.

"Extrait d'un mémoire intitulé: 'Description d'un individu dont le sexe a quelque chose d'équivoque' [...]." *Bulletin de la Faculté de médecine de Paris* 4.11 (1815): 273–88.

Béclard, Pierre-Auguste, et al. *Nouveau dictionnaire de médecine, chirurgie, pharmacie, physique, chimie, histoire naturelle, etc.* Vol. 2. [Paris], 1821–22.

Benoist, Alcide. "Rapport sur un cas d'hermaphrodisme." *Annales d'hygiène publique et de médecine légale* 16 (1886): 84–87.

Benoît, Jules. "Consultation sur un cas d'hermaphrodisme." *Gazette médicale* 12 (1841): 249–50.

Benoît, Justin. "Consultation sur un cas d'hermaphrodisme." *Journal de la Société de Médecine-Pratique de Montpellier* 2 (1840): 23–37.

Blanc, Louis. "Anomalie des organes génitaux externes [...]." In *Les anomalies chez l'homme et les mammifères*. Paris: J.-B. Baillière, 1893.

Blanche. "Consultation sur un cas d'hermaphrodisme." *Bulletins de la Société anatomique de Paris* 12 (1867): 21–23.

Blondel, Raoul. "Observation de pseudo-hermaphrodisme: Un homme marié à un homme." *Journal de médecine de Paris* 11 (1899): 75–77.

Boddaert, Richard. "Étude sur l'hermaphrodisme latéral." *Annales de la Société de médecine de Gand* 52 (1874): 81–139.

Boeckel, E. "Extirpation d'une matrice [...]." *Gazette médicale de Strasbourg* 51 (1892): 87–89.

Bouillaud, Jean. "Exposition raisonnée d'un cas de nouvelle et singulière variété d'hermaphrodisme observée chez l'homme." *Journal universel et hebdomadaire de médecine et de chirurgie pratiques* 10 (1833): 467–500.

——. *Traité de nosographie médicale*. Paris: J.-B. Baillière, 1846.

Briand, Joseph, and Ernest Chaudé. *Manuel complet de médecine légale*. 9th ed. Paris: J.-B. Baillière, 1874.

Brouardel, Paul. "Étude critique sur la valeur des signes attribués à la pédérastie." *Annales d'hygiène publique et de médecine légale* 3 (1879): 1–8.

——. "Hermaphrodisme; impuissance; type infantile." *Gazette des hôpitaux civils et militaires* 60 (1887): 57–59.

——. *Cours de médecine légale de la Faculté de médecine de Paris*, Vol. 8: *Le mariage*. Paris: J.-B. Baillière, 1900.

——. "Malformation des organes génitaux de la femme: Y a-t-il lieu de reconnaître l'existence d'un troisième sexe?" *Annales d'hygiène publique et de médecine légale* 1.3 (1904): 93–204.

Burdach, Karl Friedrich. "Hermaphrodisme." In *Traité de physiologie considérée comme science d'observation*. Trans. A. J. L. Jourdan. 2nd ed. Paris: J.-B. Baillière, 1837.

Caufeynon, Dr. [pseud. Jean Fauconney]. "L'hermaphrodisme." In *Bibliothèque populaire des connaissances médicales*. Vol 10. Paris: Nouvelle librairie médicale, 1902–3.

——. *Hermaphrodisme: Bi-sexués, féminins, infantiles, viragos, hommes à mamelles*. Paris: C. Offenstadt, 1903.

——. *L'hermaphrodite au couvent*. Paris: L. Chaubard, 1905.

Chalmers, J. "Hermaphrodite." *Transactions of the Obstetrical Society of London* 24 (1882): 239.

Champeaux, Claude. *Réflexions sur les hermaphrodites, relativement à Anne Grand-Jean [. . .].* Lyon: Claude Jacquenod, 1765.

Charcot, Jean-Martin, and Valentin Magnan. "Inversion du sens génital." *Archives de neurologie* 3 and 4 (1882): 53–60; 296–322.

Charon. "Atrésie du rectum s'ouvrant au milieu du raphé du scrotum, chez un pseudo-hermaphrodite de trois mois." *La clinique* 7 (1893): 17–22.

Chesnet. "Question d'identité; vice de conformation des organes génitaux externes. – hypospadias. – erreur sur le sexe." *Annales d'hygiène publique et de médecine légale* 14 (1860): 206–9.

Chevalier, Julien. *L'inversion sexuelle: Psycho-physiologie, sociologie, tératologie, aliénation mentale, psychologie morbide, anthropologie, médecine judiciaire.* Lyon: A. Storck, 1893.

Cornay, Joseph-Émile. *Cosmogonie légale: Mémoire sur la genèse animale, la loi d'hermaphrodisme, la loi des sexes et la loi de fécondité.* Paris: J.-B. Baillière, 1866.

Coste, E. "Conformation vicieuse des organes génitaux chez une femme." *Journal des sciences médico-chirurgicales* (1835): 276–77.

Costilhes. "Hypospadias ou hermaphrodisme apparent." *Revue médicale française et étrangère* 2 (1853): 622–27.

Courty, Amédée. "Consultation médico-légale à l'appui d'une demande en nullité de mariage." *Montpellier médical* 28.6 (1871): 473–88.

Crecchio, Luigi de. "Apparences viriles chez une femme." *Annales d'hygiène publique et de médecine légale* 25 (1866): 178–91.

Cruveilhier. "Extrait des procès – verbaux de la Société." *Bulletins de la Société anatomique de Paris* 3(1843): 196–202.

　　"Rapport de M. Cruveilhier sur un cas d'hermaphrodisme, présenté par M. Dacorogna." *Bulletins de la Société d'Anthropologie de Paris* 10 (1865): 468–73.

Cuisin, J.-P.-R. *Clémentine orpheline et androgyne, ou les caprices de la nature et la fortune.* Paris: Davi et Locard, 1820.

"A Curious Medico-Legal Case." *British Medical Journal* 2 (November 13, 1869): 543.

Dacorogna. "Hermaphrodisme apparent chez une personne de sexe féminin." *Bulletins de la Société anatomique de Paris* 39 (1865): 481–88.

Dailliez, Georges. *Les sujets de sexe douteux, leur état psychique, leur condition relativement au mariage.* Diss. Paris, 1892.

Dandois. "Un exemple d'erreur de sexe par suite d'hermaphrodisme apparent." *Revue médicale* 5 (1886): 49–52.

Dany. "Observation pour servir à l'histoire de l'hermaphrodisme." *Gazette médicale de Paris* 3 (1835): 461–63.

Davenport, John. *Curiositates Eroticae Physiologiae, or Tabooed Subjects Freely Treated.* London, 1875.

De Beurmann, and Roubinovitch. "Pseudo-hermaphrodisme masculin." *Annales d'hygiène publique et de médecine légale* 4 (1906): 47–58.

Debierre, Charles. *L'hermaphrodisme: Structure, fonctions, état psychologique et mental, état civil et mariage, dangers et remèdes*. Paris: J.-B. Baillière, 1891.

———. "L'hermaphrodite devant le Code civil: L'hermaphrodisme, sa nature, son origine, ses conséquences sociales." *Archives de l'anthropologie criminelle et des sciences pénales* 1 (1886): 305–42.

———. "Pourquoi dans la nature y a-t-il des mâles et des femelles? La fécondation, l'origine des sexes, l'hérédité." *Semaine médicale* 14 (1894): 454–56.

———. *Les vices de conformation des organes génitaux et urinaires de la femme*. Paris: J.-B. Baillière, 1892.

Debout. "Hermaphrodite." *Bulletins de la Société de médecine de Rouen* 4 (1890): 43–44.

———. "Présentation de malade." *Bulletins et mémoires de la Société de chirurgie de Paris* 10 (1859): 115–19.

Dechambre, A., Mathias Duval, and L. Lereboullet. "L'hermaphrodisme." In *Dictionnaire usuel des sciences médicales*. Paris: G. Masson, 1885: 749–50.

Delacroix. "M. Delacroix présente à la Société médicale des photographies relatives à un cas d'hermaphrodisme très-remarquable." *Bulletin de la Société médicale de Reims* 9 (1870): 53–59.

Delefosse. "'Hypospadias périnéo-scrotale' par M. Faguet [. . .]." *Annales des maladies des organes génito-urinaires* 11 (1892): 227.

Delore, Xavier. "Des étapes de l'hermaphrodisme." *L'écho médicale de Lyon* 7 (1899*b*): 193–207.

———. "De l'hermaphrodisme dans l'histoire ancienne et dans la chirurgie moderne." *Journal des sciences médicales de Lille* 22 (1899*a*): 63–70.

Descoust, Alcide. "Sur un cas d'hermaphrodisme." *Annales d'hygiène publique et de médecine légale* 16 (1886): 87–90.

Dodeuil. "Vice de conformation simulant l'hermaphrodisme." *Société anatomique de Paris* 10 (1865): 473–81.

Dor. "Cryptorchide hypospade atteint de blenorragie et d'épididymite." *Lyon médical* 70 (1892): 266–67.

Dubarry, Armand. *Les déséquilibrés de l'amour: L'hermaphrodite*. 21st ed. Paris: Chamuel, 1898.

Dufour. "Note sur un sujet atteint d'un vice de conformation des organes génitaux externes." *Bulletins de la Société anatomique de Paris* 1 (1856): 262–64.

Dugès. "Mémoire sur l'hermaphrodisme." *Éphémérides médicales de Montpellier* 5 (1827): 1–54.

Duhousset. "Sur l'hermaphrodisme." *Bulletins de la Société d'Anthropologie de Paris* 4 (1881): 510–13.

Dutrochet. "Travaux académiques. Académie des Sciences." *Gazette médicale* 1.18 (1833): 112–18.

Faucher, and Bourdin. "Idiotie congénitale; hypospadias et pseudo-hermaphrodisme externe." *Archives de neurologie* 8 (1899): 291–305.

Féré, Charles. "Contribution à l'étude des équivoques des caractères sexuels accessoires." *Revue de médecine* 13 (1893): 600–13.

———. *La famille névropathique: Théorie tératologique de l'hérédité et de la prédisposition morbides et de la dégénérescence*. 2nd ed. Paris: F. Alcan, 1898.

"L'Hermaphrodisme [. . .]." *Bulletins de la Société anatomique de Paris* 59 (1884): 265–66.

Firket, Jean. "Hermaphrodisme bilatéral vrai et pseudo-hermaphrodisme surrénalien." *Bruxelles médical* 37 (1927): 1148–50.

Flaubert, Gustave. *Bouvard et Pécuchet, Dictionnaire des idées reçues*. Ed. Stéphanie Dord-Crouslé. Paris: Flammarion, 1999.

Follin, E. *Recherches sur un cas remarquable d'hermaphrodisme, avec quelques considérations sur la détermination du sexe*. Paris: Plon Frères, 1851.

Gaffé (de Nantes), and J. Lucas-Championnière. "Un cas d'hermaphrodisme." *Journal de médecine et de chirurgie pratiques* 56 (1885): 65–67.

Garnier, Pierre. *Hygiène de la génération: La stérilité humaine et l'hermaphrodisme*. Paris: Garnier Frères, 1883.

"Physiologie: Hermaphrodisme humain." *La médecine populaire* 23 (February 24, 1881): 356–57.

"Du pseudo-hermaphrodisme comme impédiment medico-légale à la déclaration du sexe dans l'acte de naissance." *Annales d'hygiène publique industrielle et sociale* 14 (1885): 285–93.

Gatcheff, Petre. *Pseudo-hermaphrodisme et erreur de personne*. Diss. Toulouse, 1901.

Gautier, Théophile. *Mademoiselle de Maupin*. Dir. Pierre Laubriet. Vol 1. Paris: Gallimard (Pléiade), 2002.

Mademoiselle de Maupin. Ed. Michel Crouzet. Paris: Gallimard, 1973.

Geoffroy Saint-Hilaire, Isidore. "Académie des sciences, séance du 4 février 1833." *Gazette médicale*, 1.18 (9 fév., 1833): 113–15.

"Cas singulier et paradoxal d'hermaphroditisme." *Gazette médicale de Paris* 3 (1832): 72–76.

"Des rapports de la tératologie avec la médecine légale." *Annales d'hygiène publique et de médecine légale* 17 (1837): 431–43.

Histoire générale et particulière des anomalies de l'organisation chez l'homme et les animaux [. . .] Traité de tératologie. 3 vols. Paris: J.-B. Baillière, 1832–37.

Gérin-Roze. "Un cas d'hermaprodisme faux [. . .]." *Bulletin de la Société médicale des hôpitaux de Paris* 21 (1884): 369–76.

Gillette. "Hermaphrodisme d'apparence mâle." *L'union médicale* 28 (1874): 122.

Goujon, E. "Étude d'un cas d'hermaphrodisme bisexuel imparfait." *Journal de l'anatomie et de la physiologie normales et pathologiques de l'homme et des animaux* 5 (1869): 599–616.

Granier. "Note sur un sujet atteint d'hypospadias pris jusqu'à 20 ans pour une femme." *Nouveau Montpellier médical* 3 (1894): 329–33.

Guermonprez, François Jules Octave. "Une erreur de sexe avec ses conséquences." *Journal des sciences médicales de Lille* 2 (1892a): 337–49; 361–76.

"Une erreur de sexe avec ses conséquences." *Annales d'hygiène publique et de médecine légale* 28.3 (1892b): 242–75; 296–306.

Guersant. "Société de chirurgie de Paris [. . .] Séances des 25 février et 4 Mars 1846." *Gazette des hôpitaux* 8 (1846): 127.

Guinard, L. A. "À propos d'un homme hermaphrodite." *Mémoires et comptes rendus de la Société des sciences médicales de Lyon* 38 (1898): 179–83.

Hailly, Gaston d'. *L'hermaphrodite.* Paris: C. Marpon et E. Flammarion, 1885.

Hallopeau. "Sur un androgyne." *Bulletin de l'Académie nationale de médecine* 33 (1895): 410–12.

Heppner, and Doumie. "Sur l'hermaphrodisme vrai dans l'espèce humaine; par le Docteur C.-L. Heppner (De Saint-Pétersbourg)." *Gazette médicale de Paris* 21.25 (1872): 290–92.

Hérail. *Notice sur l'homme-femme: Connu sous le nom de Mademoiselle Savalette de Lange.* Versailles: Brié, 1859.

Hermann, G. "Hermaphrodisme (tératologie)." *Dictionnaire encyclopédique des sciences médicales. (F–K).* 4th ser. Ed. A. Dechambre and L. Lereboullet. Paris: G. Masson, 1889: 609–35.

"Hermaphrodite." *London Medical Gazette* 1 (1828): 189–90.

Hills, William C. "A Case of Hermaphroditism." *The Lancet* 101.2578 (1873): 129–30.

Houzé de l'Aulnoit. "Réflexions tératologiques et médico-légales au sujet d'un hermaphrodite sans excès de l'ordre des hermaphrodites neutres [...]." *Bulletin médical du nord de la France.* June (1861): 177–83.

Holt, William. "Acephalous Hermaphrodite Monster." *The Lancet* 77.1961 (1861): 328.

Houel. "Pièces d'hermaphrodites conservées au musée Dupuytren; par M. Houel." *Bulletins de la Société d'Anthropologie de Paris* 4 (1881): 554–58.

Huette. "Hermaphrodisme apparent chez le sexe masculin." *Comptes rendus des séances et mémoires de la Société de biologie* 2 (1856): 155–57.

Hugier. "Présidence de M. Marjolin. Séance du 25 Janvier 1860." *Bulletins et mémoires de la Société de chirurgie de Paris* 1 (1860): 45–47.

Huysmans, Joris-Karl. *À rebours.* Ed. Pierre Waldner. Paris: Garnier-Flammarion, 1978.

Itard de Riez. "Observation sur un jeune homme sans testicules." *Mémoires de la Société médicale d'émulation,* 3e année, an. VIII (1798–99): 293–95.

Jablonsky. "Note sur un cas d'hermaphrodisme." *Gazette des hôpitaux de Toulouse* 12.15 (1898): 124–25.

———. "Note sur un cas d'hermaphrodisme." *Le Poitou médical* 12 (1897): 274–76.

Jacquemin. "Description de l'organisation vicieuse de l'appareil génital d'une prétendue hermaphrodite." *Journal général de médecine, de chirurgie et de pharmacie* 53 (1815): 372–75.

Jalabert. "Examen doctrinal de jurisprudence civil par M. Ph. Jalabert, doyen de la Faculté de droit de Nancy." *Revue critique de législation et de jurisprudence* 2 (1872): 129–50.

Jalifier. "Hermaphrodisme masculin." *Lyon médical* 42 (1910): 866–68.

Jarricot, Jean. *Note sur un cas de pseudo-hermaphrodisme, avec autopsie.* Lyon: A. Rey, 1903.

Jouin. "Hermaphrodisme vrai et pseudo-hermaphrodisme." *Gazette de gynécologie* 6 (1891): 257–66.

Jourdan, Louis. *Un hermaphrodite.* Paris: E. Dentu, 1861.

La Vaudère, Jane de. *Les androgynes roman passionnel.* Paris: A. Méricant, 1903.

Les demi-sexes. Paris: P. Ollendorff, 1897.

Lacassagne, Alexandre. *Les actes de l'état civil: Étude médico-légale de la naissance, du mariage, de la mort.* Lyon: A. Storck, 1887.

Lagneau. "A Propos de l'hermaphrodisme." *Gazette médicale de Paris* 66.16 (April 20, 1895): 188–89.

Lagneau, M. G. "Sur deux cas d'hermaphrodisme." *Bulletin de l'Académie de médecine* 33 (1895): 415–18.

Lahaye, Paul. *Réflexion au sujet d'un cas d'hermaphrodisme tubulaire masculin interne.* Diss. Paris, 1920.

Landouzy, H. "Hermaphrodisme." In *Dictionnaire de médecine usuelle.* Ed. J.-P. Beaude. Paris: Académie royale de médecine, 1849: 189–94.

Larrey. "Hermaphrodisme." *Bulletins et mémoires de la Société de chirurgie de Paris* 10 (1859): 122–25.

Latouche, Henri de. *Fragoletta: Naples et Paris en 1799.* 2 vols. Paris: Levavasseur, 1829; Boston: MA, Adamant Media Corporation, 2005.

Laugier, Maurice, and Ambroise Tardieu. "L'Hermaphrodisme." In *Nouveau dictionnaire de médecine et de chirurgie pratiques.* Vol. 17. Paris: J.-B. Baillière, 1873: 488–513.

Laupts, Dr. [pseud. Georges Saint-Paul, and G. Espé de Metz]. *Tares et poisons, perversion et perversité sexuelles, une enquête médicale sur l'inversion, [. . .] Le roman d'un inverti-né.* [. . .], préface par Émile Zola. Paris: Georges Carré, 1896.

Plus fort que le mal, essai sur le mal innomable [sic], pièce en quatre actes. Paris: A. Maloine, 1907.

Laurent, Émile. *Les bisexués, gynécomastes, et hermaphrodites.* Paris: G. Carré, 1894.

La poésie décadente devant la science psychiatrique. Paris: A. Maloine, 1897.

Lautréamont, comte de [pseud. Isidore Ducasse]. *Les Chants de Maldoror; Poésies I et II; Correspondance.* Ed. Jean-Luc Steinmetz: Paris: Flammarion, 1990.

Le Contellec, Louis. *Contribution à l'étude du pseudo-hermaphrodisme.* Diss. Montpellier, 1910.

Le Fort, Léon. *Des vices de conformation de l'utérus et du vagin et des moyens d'y remédier.* Diss. Paris, 1863.

Leblond, Albert. "Du pseudo-hermaphrodisme comme impédiment médico-légal à la déclaration du sexe dans l'acte de naissance." *Annales d'hygiène publique et de médecine légale* 14 (1885): 293–302.

Legrand du Saulle, Henri. "Cas d'erreur sur le sexe." *Gazette des hôpitaux civils et militaires* 27.125 (1860): 510–11.

Traité de médecine légale et de jurisprudence médicale. Paris: Adrien Delahaye, 1874.

Legros, Félix. "Homme hypospade pris pendant 22 ans pour une femme." *Journal des connaissances médico-chirurgicales* 3 (1835): 273–76.

Lesbre and Fougeot. "Étude d'un cas rare d'hermaphrodisme [. . .]." *Publications de la Société Linnéenne de Lyon* 21 (1902): 66–76.

Lind, Earl [pseud.]. *Autobiography of an Androgyne.* New York: Medico-Legal Journal, 1918.

Loir, J. N. *Des sexes en matière d'état civil: Comment prévenir les erreurs résultant de leurs anomalies.* Paris: Cotillon, 1854.

Lucas, Prosper. *Traité philosophique et physiologique de l'hérédité naturelle [. . .].* 2 vols. Paris: J.-B. Baillière, 1847–50.

Lutaud, Auguste [pseud. Dr. Minime]. *L'hermaphrodisme au point de vue médico-légal.* Paris: J.-B. Baillière, 1886.

Mabaret du Basty. "Absence d'une partie des organes génitaux externes chez deux sœurs." *Progrès médical* (1890): 503.

Magitot, G. "Sur un nouveau cas d'hermaphrodisme." *Bulletins de la Société d'Anthropologie de Paris* 4 (1881*b*): 487–96.

"Un nouveau cas d'hermaphrodisme." *Bulletins et mémoires de la Société de chirurgie de Paris* 7 (1881*a*): 443–53.

Magnan, Valentin. "Trois cas de conformation vicieuse des organes génitaux: Atrophie testiculaire, cryptorchidie, pseudo-hermaphrodisme mâle." *Bulletins de la Société d'Anthropologie de Paris* 10 (1887): 88–104.

Magnan, Valentin, and Samuel Pozzi. "Inversion du sens génital chez un pseudo-hermaphrodite féminin [. . .]." *Bulletin de l'Académie nationale de médecine* 65 (1911): 223–59.

Maizeroy, René [pseud. René-Jean Toussaint]. *La fête.* Paris: Ollendorff, 1893.

Marandon de Montyel, E. "Des anomalies des organes génitaux externes chez les aliénés et de leurs rapports avec la dégénérescence et la criminalité." *Archives d'anthropologie criminelle de criminologie et de psychologie normale et patholo-gique* (1894): 497–519.

Marc. "Hermaphrodite." In *Dictionnaire de médecine.* Ed. Adelon Béclard. Paris: Béchet Jeune, 1821–28: 71–82.

"Hermaphrodisme." In *Dictionnaire de médecine.* Paris, 1837: 241–67.

"Sur l'hermaphrodisme: Supplément ajouté par le Docteur Marc [. . .]." *Bulletin des sciences médicales* 8 (1811): 179–89.

Marivaux, Pierre Carlet de Chamblain de. *La vie de Marianne.* Paris: Gallimard, 1997.

Martin, E. "Mémoire sur un cas de persistance des canaux de Müller." *Journal de l'anatomie et de la physiologie normales et pathologiques* 14 (1878): 21–33.

Maupassant, Guy de. *Short Stories of the Tragedy and Comedy of Life.* Vol. 3. Akron, Ohio: St. Dunstan Society, 1903.

Mayer (de Bonn). "Description anatomique d'un hermaphrodite connu tour-à-tour sous les noms de Marie Dorothée Derier et Charles Durgé." *Gazette médicale de Paris* 4 (1836): 609–11.

Meckel, J. F. *Manuel d'anatomie générale, descriptive et pathologique.* Trans. A. J. L. Jourdan. Vol. 3. Paris: J.-B. Baillière, 1825.

Meige, Henri. "Infantilisme chez la femme." *Nouvelle iconographie de la Salpêtrière* 4 (1895a): 218–24.

L'infantilisme, le féminisme et les hermaphrodites antiques. Paris: G. Masson, 1895b.

Moreau, J. L. "Quelques considérations sur l'hermaphrodisme." *Mémoires de la Société médicale d'émulation de Paris* (l'an V de la République; 1796–97): 243–47.

Moreau, Jacques-Joseph (de Tours). *La Psychologie morbide dans ses rapports avec la philosophie de l'histoire* [. . .]. Paris: V. Masson, 1859.

Moreau, Jean Michel. *Garçon et fille hermaphrodites vus et dessinés d'après nature par un des plus célèbres artistes et gravés avec tout le soin possible pour l'utilité des studieux.* Paris, 1773.

Morel, Bénédict-Auguste. *Traité ses dégénérescences physiques, intellectuelles et morales de l'espèce humaine* [. . .]. Paris: J.-B. Baillière, 1857.

  Traité de la médecine légale des aliénés dans ses rapports avec la capacité civile [. . .]. Paris: V. Masson, 1866.

Mortillet, A. de. "Jeune hermaphrodite." *Bulletins et mémoires de la Société d'Anthropologie de Paris* 8 (1885): 650–52.

Neugebauer, Franz Ludwig. "Cinquante cas de mariages conclus entre des personnes du même sexe, avec plusieurs procès de divorce par suite d'erreur de sexe." *Revue de gynécologie et de chirurgie abdominale* 3 (1899): 195–210.

  Hermaphroditismus beim Menschen. Leipzig: W. Klinkhardt, 1908.

  "Quarante-quatre erreurs de sexe révélées par l'opération [. . .]." *Revue de gynécologie et de chirurgie abdominale* 4 (1900*a*): 457–578.

  "Une nouvelle série de 29 observations d'erreur de sexe." *Revue de gynécologie et de chirurgie abdominale* 4 (1900*b*): 133–74.

Odin. "Hermaphrodisme bi-sexuel." *Lyon médical* 16 (1874): 214–18.

Ombrédanne, Louis. *Les hermaphrodites et la chirurgie.* Paris: Masson, 1939.

  Une jeune fille dans une situation difficile: Hermaphrodite gynandroïde parfaite. Paris: Masson, 1933.

Orfila, Mathieu-Joseph-Bonaventure. *Leçons de médecine légale.* Vol. 1. Paris: Béchet jeune, 1823.

Pancrazi, Louis. *Hermaphrodisme et pseudo-hermaphrodisme.* Diss. Paris, 1910.

Panizza, Oskar. *Un scandale au couvent.* Trans. Jean Bréjoux. [Paris]: Éditions de la Différence, 1989.

Parmly, G. D. "Hermaphrodism." *American Journal of Obstetrics* 19 (1886): 931–46.

Péan. "Hermaphrodisme masculin complexe: Arrêt de développement des organes génitaux mâles." *Gazette des hôpitaux civils et militaires* 57 (1884): 105–7.

  Leçons de clinique chirurgicale professées à l'Hôpital Saint-Louis [. . .]. Paris: J.-B. Baillière, 1888.

  "Sur un cas d'hermaphrodisme." *Bulletin de l'Académie nationale de médecine* 33 (1895): 381–38.

Péladan, Joséphin. *De l'androgyne: Théorie plastique.* Paris: E. Sansot et Cie, 1910.

  L'androgyne. Paris: Dentu, 1891.

Perrée. "Spina bifida-extropie de la vessie, hermaphrodisme apparent." *Normandie médicale* 21 (1906): 187–88.

Petit, Paul. "Pseudo-hermaphrodisme périnéoscrotal." *Bulletins et mémoires de la Société obstétricale et gynécologique de Paris* 6 (1891): 130–31.

Philippe, Paul. "Notes sur un cas d'hermaphrodisme apparent." *L'union médicale du Canada* 46 (1893): 505–8.

Pigoreau, Nicolas-Alexandre. *Petite bibliographie biographico-romancière.* Paris: Pigoreau, Libraire, 1821.

Poitier-Duplessy. "Hermaphrodisme masculin." *Recueil de mémoires de médecine et de chirurgie et de pharmacie militaires* 3rd ser. (Nov. 19, 1867): 432–35.

Polaillon. "Séance du 12 mai, 1887." *Journal de médecine de Paris* 12 (1887): 870–72.

"Sur un cas d'hermaphrodisme. " *Bulletin de l'Académie de médecine* 25 (1891): 557–61.

Poppesco, Basile. *De l'hermaphrodisme aux points de vue médico-légale et scientifique.* Paris: Henry Ray, 1874.

Hermaphrodism, from a Medico-Legal Point of View, Paris, 1874. Trans. Dr. Sawyer. Chicago: Keen, Cooke & Co., 1875.

Pozzi, Samuel. *Homme hypospade considéré depuis vingt-huit ans comme femme (pseudo-hermaphrodite)* [. . .]. Paris: H. Lauwereyns, 1884.

"De l'hermaphrodisme." *Gazette hebdomadaire de médecine et de chirurgie* 27.30 (1890): 351–55.

"Neuf cas personnels de pseudo-hermaphrodisme." *Revue de gynécologie et de chirurgie abdominale* 16 (1911): 269–339.

"Note sur deux nouveaux cas de pseudo-hermaphrodisme." *Comptes rendus des séances de la Société de biologie* 2 (1885a): 22–29.

"Note sur deux nouveaux cas de pseudo-hermaphrodisme." *Gazette médicale de Paris* 2 (1885b): 109–12.

Notice sur les travaux scientifiques du Dr. S. Pozzi. Paris: Masson, 1912.

"Présentation d'un pseudo-hermaphrodite mâle par le docteur S. Pozzi." *Séances et mémoires de la Société de biologie* 1 (1884): 42–45.

"Pseudo-hermaphrodite mâle." *Bulletins et mémoires de la Société d'anthropologie de Paris* 12 (1889): 602–8.

"Sur un pseudo-hermaphrodite androgynoïde, prétendue femme ayant de chaque côté un testicule [. . .]." *Bulletin de l'Académie de médecine* 36 (1896): 132–45.

Traité de gynécologie clinique et opératoire. 3rd ed. Paris: Masson, 1897.

Rachilde [pseud. Marguerite Vallette-Eymery]. *La jongleuse.* Paris: Brodard et Taupin, 1982.

Madame Adonis. Paris, 1888.

La Marquise de Sade. Paris: Mercure de France, 1981.

Monsieur Vénus. Ed. Melanie Hawthorne and Liz Constable. New York: Modern Language Association of America, 2004.

Nono. Paris: Mercure de France, 1994.

Renauldin. "Observation sur une conformation particulière." *Mémoires de la Société médicale d'émulation* 1 (1797a): 241–42.

"Observations sur deux conformations vicieuses des organes de la génération de la femme." *Mémoires de la Société médicale d'émulation* 7 (1797b): 470–76.

Richard. "Deux sujets hermaphrodites." *Bulletins et mémoires de la Société de chirurgie de Paris* 10 (1859): 155–59.

Richerand, Balthasar-Anthelme. *Nouveaux éléments de physiologie.* 7th ed. Vol. 2. Paris: Caille et Ravier, 1817.

Ricoux, and Aubry. "Un prétendu androgyne dans un service de femmes." *Le progrès médical* 9–10.37 (1899): 183–84.

Rochard, Jules. *Histoire de la chirurgie française au XIXe siècle* [. . .]. Paris: J.-B. Baillière, 1875.

Rondeau, J. "Anomalie congénitale par arrêt de développement des organes génitaux; hermaphrodisme avec prédominance du sexe masculin." *La presse médicale belge* 33 (1881): 409–12.

Sand, Knud. "Hermaphrodisme (vrai) glandulaire alternant chez un individu de dix ans." *Journal d'urologie médicale et chirurgicale* 3 (1923): 181–94.

Saunié, F. "Description des parties génitales d'un enfant mâle ayant l'apparence d'un hermaphrodite." *Bulletin de la Faculté de médecine de Paris* 2 (1810): 62–64.

Sentex, L. "Pseudo-hermaphrodisme apparent [. . .]." *Journal de médecine de Bordeaux et du sud-ouest* 16 (1887): 54–55.

Serres, Dumérie, and Dutrochet. "Rapport sur le mémoire de M. Isidore Geoffroy Saint-Hilaire, intitulé recherche sur l'hermaphrodisme." *Gazette médicale* 1.30 (1833): 196–98.

Siredey, Fr. "Impuissance." In *Nouveau dictionnaire de médecine*. Ed. Sigismond Jaccoud. Vol. 18. Paris: J.-B. Baillière, 1874: 445–73.

Stéphan, Pierre. *De l'hermaphrodisme chez les vertébrés*. Diss. Marseille, 1901.

Tapie, Jean. "Un cas d'erreur sur le sexe, malformation des organes génitaux externes [. . .]." *Revue médicale de Toulouse* 13 (1888): 301–13.

Tardieu, Ambroise. *Question médico-légale de l'identité dans ses rapports avec les vices de conformation des organes sexuels* [. . .]. 2nd ed. Paris: J.-B. Baillière, 1874.

Thézet. "Un cas singulier d'anomalie des organes génito-urinaires." *L'Union médicale* 22 (1876): 612–17.

Thore. "Observation d'hermaphrodisme féminin." *Gazette médicale de Paris* 1 (1846): 89–90.

Tourdes, G. "Hermaphrodisme (méd. lég.)." In *Dictionnaire encyclopédique des sciences médicales. (F–K)*. 4th ser. Ed. A. Dechambre and L. Lereboullet. Paris: G. Masson, 1889: 635–63.

Trélat. "De l'hermaphrodisme féminin." *Journal des connaissances médicales pratiques et de pharmacologie*. 3rd ser., 2 (1880): 41–42; 58–59.

Trouvenin. "Prétendu hermaphrodisme." *Annales de la médecine psychologique* 17 (1830): 406–7.

Tuffier, Théodore, and André Lapointe. "L'hermaphrodisme – ses variétés et ses conséquences pour la pratique médicale." *Revue de gynécologie et de chirurgie abdominale* 17 (1911): 209–68.

Vanswygenhoven, C. "Note sur un hermaphrodisme incomplet, accompagné d'hypospadias, observé sur un enfant du sexe masculin." *Journal de médecine, de chirurgie et de pharmacologie* 2 (1844): 49–53.

Vermeil, François-Michel. *Mémoire pour Anne Grandjean, connu sous le nom de Jean-Baptiste Grandjean* [. . .]. Paris, 1765.

Vincentelli, Alphonse. *Essai sur l'intervention du médecin légiste dans les cas de séparation de corps et de divorce* [. . .]. Paris: A. Delahaye et E. Lecrosnier, 1884.

Volpelière. "Observation sur un prétendu hermaphrodite." *Journal général de médecine, de chirurgie, et de pharmacie* [. . .] (1827): 338–40.

Vrolik. "Description anatomique d'un fœtus hermaphrodite." *Gazette médicale de Paris* 4 (1836): 761–63.

W., Arthur. *Confessions d'un inverti-né: Confidences et aveux d'un Parisien.* Ed. Daniel Grojnowski. Paris: Corti, 2007.

Werther, Ralph [pseud.]. *The Female-Impersonators.* Ed. Alfred W. Herzog. New York: Medico-Legal Journal, 1922.

Worbe. "Observation sur un hypospadias qui a rendu l'existence civile d'un individu fort ambiguë [sic]." *Bulletin de l'École puis de la Faculté de médecine de Paris* 4.5 (1815*a*): 364–72.

"Observation sur un individu réputé du sexe féminin." *Bulletin de la Faculté de Médecine de Paris* 4 (1815*b*): 479–92.

Zola, Émile. *L'atelier de Zola: Textes de journaux, 1865–1870.* Ed. Martin Kanes. Genève: Droz, 1963.

La curée. Ed. Henri Mitterand and Intro. Jean Borie. Paris: Gallimard, 2002 [c.1981].

La fabrique des Rougon-Macquart: Édition des dossiers préparatoires. Ed. Colette Becker and Véronique Lavielle. 3 vols. Paris: H. Champion, 2003.

Germinal. Ed. Adeline Wrona. Paris: Flammarion, 2000.

Œuvres complètes: La naissance du naturalisme, 1868–1870. Ed. Colette Becker and Jean-Louis Cabanès. Vol. 3. Paris: Nouveau monde, 2003.

Les Rougon-Macquart: Histoire naturelle et sociale d'une famille sous le second Empire. Dir. Armand Lanoux. 5 vols. Paris: Gallimard (Pléiade), 1960–67.

Secondary Works

Albert, Nicole. "Du mythe à la pathologie." *Diogène* 4.208 (2004): 132–44.

Saphisme et décadence dans Paris fin de siècle. Paris: Martinière, 2005.

Albouy, Pierre. "Le mythe de l'androgyne dans *Mademoiselle de Maupin*." *Revue d'histoire littéraire de la France* 72 (1972): 600–8.

Araque, Mercedes Montoro. *Gautier, au carrefour de l'âme romantique et décadente.* New York: Peter Lang, 2018.

Aubenas, Sylvie. "Beyond the Portrait, Beyond the Artist." In *Nadar.* Ed. M. M. Hambourg, F. Heilbrun and P. Néagu. New York: Metropolitan Museum of Art, 1995: 95–106.

Barnes, Julian. *The Man in the Red Coat.* London: Jonathan Cape, 2019.

Barsoum, Marlène. *Théophile Gautier's Mademoiselle de Maupin: Toward a Definition of the "Androgynous Discourse."* New York: Peter Lang, 2001.

Barthes, Roland. *S/Z.* Paris: Seuil, 1970.

Bègue, Josette Buscaglia. *La définition du sexe et la condition juridique de l'hermaphrodite.* Diss. Paris, 1963.

Beizer, Janet. *Ventriloquized Bodies: Narratives of Hysteria in Nineteenth-Century France.* Ithaca, NY: Cornell University Press, 1994.

Benveniste, Émile. *Le vocabulaire des institutions indo-européennes, II. Pouvoir, Droit, Religion.* Paris: Minuit, 1969.

Bernheimer, Charles. *Decadent Subjects: The Idea of Decadence in Art, Literature, Philosophy, and Culture of the Fin de Siècle in Europe.* Baltimore, MD: Johns Hopkins University Press, 2002.

Berta, Michel. *De l'androgynie dans Les Rougon-Macquart et deux autres études sur Zola.* New York: Peter Lang, 1985.

Blackless, Melanie, et al. "How Sexually Dimorphic Are We?" *American Journal of Human Biology* 12.2 (2000): 151–66.

Borie, Jean. *Mythologies de l'hérédité au XIXe siècle.* Paris: Galilée, 1981.

Zola et les mythes: Ou, de la nausée au salut. Paris: Seuil, 1971.

Bornet, Richard. "La structure symbolique de *Séraphîta* et le mythe de l'androgyne." *L'Année balzacienne* (1973): 235–52.

Bornstein, Kate. *Gender Outlaw: On Men, Women, and the Rest of Us.* New York: Vintage Books, 1994 [2016].

Brisson, Luc. *Le sexe incertain: Androgynie et hermaphrodisme dans l'Antiquité gréco-romaine.* Paris: Les Belles Lettres, 1997.

Brooks, Peter. *Reading for the Plot: Design and Intention in Narrative.* Cambridge, MA: Harvard University Press, 1992.

Realist Vision. New Haven, CT: Yale University Press, 2008.

Bullough, Vern L. *Sex, Society, and History.* New York: Science History Publications, 1976.

Busst, A. J. L. "The Image of the Androgyne in the Nineteenth Century." In *Romantic Mythologies.* Ed. Ian Fletcher. London: Routledge, 1967: 1–95.

Butler, Judith. *Gender Trouble.* 2nd ed. London and New York: Routledge, 1990 [2006].

Cabanès, Jean-Louis. *Le corps et la maladie dans les récits réalistes (1850–1893).* 2 vols. Paris: Klincksieck, 1991.

Charon, Rita. *Narrative Medicine: Honoring the Stories of Illness.* New York: Oxford University Press, 2008.

Charon, Rita, and Martha Montello, eds. *Stories Matter: The Role of Narrative in Medical Ethics.* New York: Routledge, 2002.

"*Clémentine, orpheline et androgyne.*" *Le livre: Revue du monde littéraire, bibliographie moderne.* Paris: A. Quintin, 1883: 793–94.

Counter, Andrew J. *The Amorous Restoration: Love, Sex and Politics in Early Nineteenth-Century France.* Oxford: Oxford University Press, 2016.

Inheritance in Nineteenth-Century French Culture: Wealth, Knowledge, and the Family. Oxford: Legenda, 2010.

Courouve, Claude. *Vocabulaire de l'homosexualité masculine.* Paris: Payot, 1985.

Crahay, Géraldine. *"On aurait pensé que la nature s'était trompée en leur donnant leurs sexes": Masculine Malaise, Gender Indeterminacy and Sexual Ambiguity in July Monarchy Narratives.* Diss. Bangor University, 2015.

Crouzet, Michel. "Monstres et merveilles: Poétique de l'androgyne: A propos de *Fragoletta.*" *Romantisme* 14.45 (1984): 25–41.

Cryle, Peter. "Foretelling Pathology: The Poetics of Prognosis." *French Cultural Studies* 17.1 (2006): 107–22.

Geometry in the Boudoir: Configurations of French Erotic Narrative. Ithaca, NY: Cornell University Press, 1994.

"The Open Secret: Hiding and Revealing Sexuality in the *Roman de Mœurs* (1880–1905)." *Romanic Review* 97.2 (2006): 185–200.

Damousi, Joy, Birgit Lang, and Katie Sutton, eds. *Case Studies and the Dissemination of Knowledge.* London and New York: Routledge, 2015.

Davis, Georgiann. *Contesting Intersex: The Dubious Diagnosis.* New York and London: New York University Press, 2015.

De Costa, Caroline, and Francesca Miller. *The Diva and Doctor God: Letters from Sarah Bernhardt to Doctor Samuel Pozzi.* Coppell, TX: Xlibris Corporation, 2010.

Delamotte, Isabelle. *La médecine, le malade et le médecin dans l'œuvre de Zola.* Diss. Université de la Sorbonne Nouvelle, Paris III, 1992.

Delattre, Geneviève. "De *Séraphita* à *La fille aux yeux d'or.*" *L'Année Balzacienne* (1970): 183–226.

Delcourt, Marie. "Deux interprétations romanesques du mythe de l'androgyne: *Mignon* et *Séraphita.*" *Revue des langues vivantes* 38 (1972): 228–40, 340–47.

Hermaphrodite, mythes et rites de la bisexualité dans l'Antiquité classique. Paris: Presses Universitaires de France, 1958.

Demonsant, Odile Janine Jacqueline Pernin. *L'assignation du sexe dans le pseudo-hermaphrodisme masculin.* Diss. Paris, 1975.

Donaldson-Evans, Mary. *Medical Examinations: Dissecting the Doctor in French Narrative Prose, 1857–1894.* Lincoln, NE: University of Nebraska Press, 2000.

Dowbiggin, Ian Robert. *Inheriting Madness: Professionalization and Psychiatric Knowledge in Nineteenth-Century France.* Berkeley: University of California Press, 1991.

Dreger, Alice Domurat. *Hermaphrodites and the Medical Invention of Sex.* Cambridge, MA: Harvard University Press, 1998.

Intersex in the Age of Ethics. Hagerstown, MD: University Publishing Group, 1999.

"Jarring Bodies: Thoughts on the Display of Unusual Anatomies." *Perspectives in Biology and Medicine* 43.2 (2000): 161–72.

Drujon, Fernand. *Catalogue des ouvrages, écrits, et dessins de toute nature poursuivis [. . .].* Paris: Librarie ancienne et moderne, 1879.

Eliade, Mircea. *Méphistophélès et l'androgyne.* Paris: Gallimard, 1962.

Epstein, Julia. "Either/Or – Neither/Both: Sexual Ambiguity and the Ideology of Gender." *Genders* 7 (1990): 99–142.

Eugenides, Jeffrey. *Middlesex.* New York: Picador, 2002.

Fausto-Sterling, Anne. *Myths of Gender: Biological Theories about Women and Men.* New York: Basic Books, 1992.

Sexing the Body: Gender Politics and the Construction of Sexuality. New York: Basic Books, 2000 [2020].

Finn, Michael. "Female Sterilization and Artificial Insemination at the French Fin de Siècle: Facts and Fictions." *Journal of the History of Sexuality* 18.1 (2009): 26–43.

Hysteria, Hypnotism, the Spirits, and Pornography: Fin-de-siècle Cultural Discourses in the Decadent Rachilde. Newark: University of Delaware Press, 2009.

Foucault, Michel. *Abnormal: Lectures at the Collège de France, 1974–1975*. Ed. Valerio Marchetti and Antonella Solomoni. Trans. Graham Burchell. Picador: New York, 2003.

L'histoire de la sexualité. 3 vols. Paris: Gallimard, 1994–97.

La naissance de la clinique: une archéologie du regard médical. Paris: PUF, 1963 [2015].

Foucault, Michel. Ed. *Herculine Barbin: Being the Recently Discovered Memoirs of a Nineteenth-Century French Hermaphrodite*. Trans. Richard McDougall. New York: Pantheon Books, 1980.

Herculine Barbin dite Alexina B. Paris: Gallimard, 1978.

Frappier-Mazur, Lucienne. "Balzac et l'androgyne." *L'Année Balzacienne* (1973): 253–77.

Garber, Marjorie. *Vested Interests: Cross-Dressing and Cultural Anxiety*. New York: Routledge, 1992.

Giraud, Raymond. "Winckelmann's Part in Gautier's Perception of Classical Beauty." *Yale French Studies* 38 (1967): 172–82.

Goulet, Andrea. *Optiques: The Science of the Eye and the Birth of Modern French Fiction*. Philadelphia: University of Pennsylvania Press, 2006.

Graille, Patrick. *Les hermaphrodites aux XVIIe et XVIIIe siècles*. Paris: Les Belles Lettres, 2001.

Grosz, Elizabeth. "Intolerable Ambiguity: Freaks as/at the Limit." In *Freakery: Cultural Spectacles of the Extraordinary Body*. Ed. Rosemarie Thomson. New York: New York University Press, 1996: 55–66.

Hage, Renée Boulos. *La quête de l'androgyne dans le récit fantastique du XIXème siècle*. Paris: Pensée Universelle, 1993.

Halberstam, Jack. *Female Masculinity*. Durham, NC: Duke University Press, 1998 [2018].

Trans: A Quick and Quirky Account of Gender Variability*. Oakland: University of California Press, 2017.

Hale, Terry. "Cuisin, P." In *Encyclopedia of Erotic Literature*. Eds. Gaetan Brulotte and John Phillips. New York: Routledge, 2006: 299–301.

Halperin, David. *How to Do the History of Homosexuality*. Chicago: University of Chicago Press, 2002.

Hamon, Philippe. *Le personnel du roman: Le système des personnages dans Les Rougon-Macquart d'Émile Zola*. 2nd ed. Genève: Librairie Droz, 1998.

Hargreaves, Tracy. *Androgyny in Modern Literature*. London: Palgrave Macmillan, 2005.

Harrow, Susan. *Zola, La Curée*. Glasgow: University of Glasgow French and German Publications, 1998.

Hartig, Rachel M. *Struggling under the Destructive Glance: Androgyny in the Novels of Guy de Maupassant*. New York: Peter Lang, 1991.

Hausman, Bernice Louise. *Changing Sex: Transsexualism, Technology, and the Idea of Gender*. Durham, NC: Duke University Press, 1995.

Hillman, Thea. *Intersex (For Lack of a Better Word)*. San Francisco: Manic D. Press, 2008.

Holmes, Morgan. *Intersex: A Perilous Difference*. Selinsgrove, PA: Susquehanna University Press, 2008.

Holmes, Morgan, ed. *Critical Intersex*. New York: Ashgate, 2009.

Houbre, Gabrielle. "The Bastard Offspring of Hermes and Aphrodite: Sexual 'Anomalies' and Medical Curiosity in France." Trans. Nikki Clavarino. In *Sexuality at the Fin de Siècle*. Ed. Peter Cryle and Christopher Forth. Newark: University of Delaware Press, 2008: 61–73.

Le livre des courtisanes: Archives secrètes de la police des mœurs (1861–1876). France: Tallandier, 2006.

Huguet, Françoise. *Les professeurs de la Faculté de médecine de Paris: Dictionnaire biographique, 1794–1939*. Paris: Institut national de recherche pédagogique, 1991.

Huet, Marie-Hélène. *Monstrous Imagination*. Cambridge, MA: Harvard University Press, 1993.

Iacub, Marcela. *Le crime était presque sexuel et autres essais de casuistique juridique*. Paris: Flammarion, 2009.

Jasinski, René. *Les années romantiques de Théophile Gautier*. Paris: Vuibert, 1929.

Karkazis, Katrina. *Fixing Sex: Intersex, Medical Authority, and Lived Experience*. Durham, NC: Duke University Press, 2008.

Kates, Gary. *Monsieur d'Eon Is a Woman: A Tale of Political Intrigue and Sexual Masquerade*. Baltimore, MD: Johns Hopkins University Press, 2001.

Kennedy, Meegan. *Revising the Clinic: Vision and Representation in Victorian Medical Narrative and the Novel*. Columbus: Ohio State University Press, 2017.

Kessler, Suzanne J. *Lessons from the Intersexed*. New Brunswick, NJ and London: Rutgers University Press, 1998.

"The Medical Construction of Gender: Case Management of Intersexed Infants." *Signs* 16.1 (1990): 3–26.

La Berge, Ann. "Medical Microscopy in Paris, 1830–1855." In *French Medical Culture in the Nineteenth Century*. Ed. Ann La Berge and Mordechai Feingold. Atlanta, GA: Rodopi, 1994: 296–326.

Lambert, Deborah G. "S/Z: Barthes' Castration Camp and the Discourse of Polarity." *Modern Language Studies* 16.3 (1986): 161–71.

Laqueur, Thomas. *Making Sex: Body and Gender from the Greeks to Freud*. Cambridge, MA: Harvard University Press, 1990.

Lee, Peter, et al. "Consensus Statement on Management of Intersex Disorders." *Pediatrics* 118.2 (2006): 488–500.

Le Mens, Magali. *L'hermaphrodite de Nadar*. [Paris]: Creaphis, 2009.

Modernité hermaphrodite: Art, histoire, culture. Paris: Éditions du Félin, 2019.

Lehrman, Sally. "Going Beyond X and Y." *Scientific American* (June 2007): 40–41.

Linton, Anne. E. "The Dangers of Looking for 'True Sex' in Nadar's 'Hermaphrodite' Series." *Yale French Studies* 139 (2021): 153–70.

"Hermaphrodite Outlaws: Ambiguous Sex and the Civil Code in Nineteenth-Century France." *Representations* 138 (Spring 2017): 87–117.

"Lusting after the Louvre Hermaphrodite: Medical Discourse and Androgyny in Théophile Gautier's Mademoiselle de Maupin and Its Popular Predecessors." *Romanic Review* 105.3–4 (2014): 293–317.

"Mutating Bodies: Reproductive Surgeries and Popular Fiction in Early 20th-Century France." *Journal of Contemporary French Studies* 22.5 (2018): 579–86.

Long Hoeveler, Diane. *Romantic Androgyny: The Women Within*. University Park, PA and London: Pennsylvania State University Press, 1990.

Mak, Geertje. "Conflicting Heterosexualities: Hermaphroditism and the Emergence of Surgery around 1900." *Journal of the History of Sexuality* 24.3 (2015): 402–27.

"Doubtful Sex in Civil Law: Nineteenth- and Early Twentieth-Century Proposals for Ruling Hermaphroditism." *Cardozo Journal of Law and Gender* 12.1 (2006): 197–211.

"Doubting Sex from Within: A Praxiographic Approach to a Late Nineteenth-Century Case of Hermaphroditism." *Gender & History* 18.2 (2006): 332–56.

Doubting Sex: Inscriptions, Bodies and Selves in Nineteenth-Century Hermaphrodite Case Histories. Manchester: Manchester University Press, 2012.

Malinas, Yves. *Zola et les hérédités imaginaires*. Paris: Expansion Scientifique Française, 1985.

Manion, Jen. *Female Husbands: A Trans History*. Cambridge: Cambridge University Press, 2020.

Massardier-Kenney, Françoise. *Gender in the Fiction of George Sand*. Amsterdam: Rodopi, 2000.

Matlock, Jann. *Scenes of Seduction: Prostitution, Hysteria, and Reading Difference in Nineteenth-Century France*. New York: Columbia University Press, 1994.

McGuire, James. "La représentation du corps hermaphrodite dans les planches de l'*Encyclopédie*." *Recherches sur Diderot et sur l'Encyclopédie* 11 (1991): 109–29.

Mesch, Rachel. *Before Trans: Three Gender Stories from Nineteenth-Century France*. Stanford, CA: Stanford University Press, 2020.

The Hysteric's Revenge: French Women Writers at the Fin de Siècle. Nashville, TN: Vanderbilt University Press, 2006.

Meyerowitz, Joanne. *How Sex Changed: A History of Transsexuality in the United States*. Cambridge, MA: Harvard University Press, 2002.

Mickel, Emanuel J., Jr. "An Interpretation of Gautier's 'Symphonie en Blanc Majeur'." *Modern Philology* 68.4 (1971): 338–44.

Mielly, Michelle. "Madeleine séductrice/Théodore séducteur: Rupture et réconciliation dans *Mademoiselle de Maupin*." *Nineteenth-Century French Studies* 25.1–2 (2007): 50–59.

Mol, Annemarie. *The Body Multiple: Ontology in Medical Practice*. Durham, NC: Duke University Press, 2002.

Monneyron, Frédéric. *L'androgyne décadent: Mythe, figure, fantasmes*. Grenoble: ELLUG, 1996.

L'androgyne romantique du mythe au mythe littéraire. Grenoble: ELLUG, 1994.

Moore, Alison. "Frigidity, Gender and Power in French Cultural History from Jean Fauconney to Marie Bonaparte." *French Cultural Studies* 20.4 (2009): 331–49.

Moore, Henrietta. *A Passion for Difference: Essays in Anthropology and Gender*. Bloomington: Indiana University Press, 1994.

Moscucci, Ornella. *The Science of Woman: Gynaecology and Gender in England, 1800–1929*. New York: Cambridge University Press, 1990.

Murat, Laure. *La loi du genre: Une histoire culturelle du troisième sexe*. Paris: Fayard, 2006.

Nesci, Catherine. *Le flâneur et les flâneuses: Les femmes et la ville à l'époque romantique*. Grenoble: ELLUG, Université Stendhal, 2007.

Nye, Robert A. *Crime, Madness and Politics in Modern France: The Medical Concept of National Decline*. Princeton, NJ: Princeton Legacy Library, 2016 [1984].

"The History of Sexuality in Context: National Sexological Traditions." *Science in Context* 4 (1991): 387–406.

Masculinity and Male Codes of Honor in Modern France. Berkeley: University of California Press, 1998 (1993).

Pagonis, Pidgeon. "The Son They Never Had." *Narrative Inquiry in Bioethics* 5.2 (2015): 103–6.

Pelckmans, M. Paul. "Androgyne et mythes familiaux une lecture de *Fragoletta* (1829) de Hyacinthe de Latouche." *Orbis Litterarum* 36.1 (1981): 13–27.

Pick, Daniel. *Faces of Degeneration: A European Disorder, c.1848–1918*. New York: Cambridge University Press, 1989.

Planche, Gustave. "De la haine littéraire." *Revue des deux mondes* 4 (1831): 514–23.

Polkinghorne, Donald E. *Narrative Knowing and the Human Sciences*. Albany: State University of New York Press, 1988.

Prasad, Pratima. "Deceiving Disclosures: Androgyny and George Sand's *Gabriel*." *French Forum* 24.3 (1999): 331–51.

Preves, Sharon. *Intersex and Identity: The Contested Self*. New Brunswick, NJ: Rutgers University Press, 2003.

Reid, Roddey. *Families in Jeopardy: Regulating the Social Body in France, 1750–1910*. Stanford, CA: Stanford University Press, 1993.

Reis, Elizabeth. *Bodies in Doubt: An American History of Intersex*. Baltimore, MD: Johns Hopkins University Press, 2009.

Robb, Graham. *Balzac: A Biography*. London: Picador, 1994.

Rosario, Vernon A. *The Erotic Imagination: French Histories of Perversity*. Oxford: Oxford University Press, 1997.

Rosenfeld, Michael. *Confessions d'un homosexuel à Émile Zola*. Paris: Les Nouvelles Éditions, 2017.

Rothfield, Lawrence. *Vital Signs: Medical Realism in Nineteenth-Century Fiction*. Princeton, NJ: Princeton University Press, 1992.

Roulin, Jean-Marie. "Confusion des sexes, mélange des genres et quête du sens dans *Mademoiselle de Maupin*." *Romantisme* 29.103 (1999): 31–40.

Rubino, Nancy. *Androgyny and Modernity in Nineteenth-Century French Literature.* Diss. Columbia University, 1997.

Sadoff, Janet. *Ambivalence, Ambiguity and Androgyny in Théophile Gautier's "Mademoiselle de Maupin."* Cambridge, MA: Harvard University Press, 1990.

Samuels, Maurice. *The Betrayal of the Duchess: The Scandal that Unmade the Bourbon Monarchy and Made France Modern.* New York: Basic Books, 2020.

The Spectacular Past: Popular History and the Novel in Nineteenth-Century France. Ithaca, NY and London: Cornell University Press, 2004.

Schehr, Lawrence R. *Rendering French Realism.* Stanford, CA: Stanford University Press, 1997.

Schor, Naomi. *Zola's Crowds.* Baltimore, MD: Johns Hopkins University Press, 1978.

Sedgwick, Eve Kosofsky. *Epistemology of the Closet.* Berkeley: University of California Press, 2008.

Ségu, Frédéric. *Un romantique républicain, H. de Latouche, 1785–1851.* Paris: Les Belles Lettres, 1931.

Serres, Michel. *Feux et signaux de brume: Zola.* Paris: B. Grasset, 1975.

Shideler, Ross. *Questioning the Father: From Darwin to Zola, Ibsen, Strindberg, and Hardy.* Stanford, CA: Stanford University Press, 1999.

Smith, Nigel Eric. "Androgyny and the Refusal of Classicism: Rereading *Fragoletta.*" *Romance Quarterly* 43.2 (1996): 81–92.

Romantic Androgyny: Sexual/Textual Subversion in Selected Works of Latouche, Balzac, and Gautier. Diss. University of North Carolina, Chapel Hill, 1991.

Stevenson, Warren. *Romanticism and the Androgynous Sublime.* Madison, NJ: Fairleigh Dickinson University Press, 1996.

Stryker, Susan. *Transgender History.* Berkeley, CA: Seal Press, 2008.

Thiher, Allen. *Fiction Rivals Science: The French Novel from Balzac to Proust.* Columbia: University of Missouri Press, 2001.

Thompson, Hannah. *Naturalism Redressed: Identity and Clothing in the Novels of Émile Zola.* Oxford: European Humanities Research Centre, 2003.

Vanderpooten, Claude. *Samuel Pozzi: Chirurgien et ami des femmes.* Ozoir-la-Ferrière: Éditions In Fine, 1992.

Verhoeven, Jana. "The Lunatics of Love: Armand Dubarry's Psychopathological Novels and Their Publics." In *Case Studies and the Dissemination of Knowledge.* Ed. Joy Damousi, Birgit Lang, and Katie Sutton. London and New York: Routledge, 2015: 172–87.

Viloria, Hida. *Born Both: An Intersex Life.* New York: Hachette Books, 2017.

Waller, Margaret. *The Male Malady: Fictions of Impotence in the French Romantic Novel.* New Brunswick, NJ: Rutgers University Press, 1993.

Weil, Kari. *Androgyny and the Denial of Difference.* Charlottesville and London: University of Virginia Press, 1992.

"Romantic Androgyny and Its Discontents: The Case of *Mademoiselle de Maupin.*" *Romanic Review* 78.3 (1987): 348–58.

Weisz, George. "The Development of Medical Specialization in Nineteenth-Century Paris." In *French Medical Culture in the Nineteenth Century.* Ed. Ann La Berge and Mordechai Feingold. Atlanta, GA: Rodopi, 1994: 149–88.

The Medical Mandarins: The French Academy of Medicine in the Nineteenth and Early Twentieth Centuries. Oxford: Oxford University Press, 1995.

White, Nicholas. *The Family in Crisis in Late Nineteenth-Century French Fiction*. Cambridge: Cambridge University Press, 1999.

French Divorce Fiction from the Revolution to the First World War. Oxford: Legenda, 2013.

Wing, Nathaniel. *Between Genders: Narrating Difference in Early French Modernism*. Newark: University of Delaware Press, 2004.

Zeldin, Theodore. *France, 1848–1945*, Vol. 2: *Intellect, Taste and Anxiety*. Oxford: Clarendon Press, 1977.

Index